WITHDRAWN
NDSU

THE MEDIAEVAL ACADEMY OF AMERICA
PUBLICATION NO. 60

THE RUSSIAN PRIMARY CHRONICLE
LAURENTIAN TEXT

The Russian Primary Chronicle

Laurentian Text

Translated and edited by

SAMUEL HAZZARD CROSS

AND

OLGERD P. SHERBOWITZ-WETZOR

THE MEDIAEVAL ACADEMY OF AMERICA
CAMBRIDGE, MASSACHUSETTS

The publication of this book was made possible by a grant from the Reisinger Fund of the Department of Slavic Languages and Literatures of Harvard University.

COPYRIGHT BY

THE MEDIAEVAL ACADEMY OF AMERICA

Third Printing, 1973

LIBRARY OF CONGRESS CATALOG NO: 53–10264

Table of Contents

Preface	vii
Note on Transliteration	ix
Maps	x-xi
Introduction	3
Laurentian Text	51
Appendix I: The Testament of Vladimir Monomakh	206
Appendix II: A. Letter of Vladimir Monomakh to Oleg, Son of Svyastoslav	216
B. Prayer attributed to Vladimir Monomakh	218
Notes to Introduction	220
Notes to the Russian Primary Chronicle	231
Notes to Appendix I	285
Notes to Appendix II	287
Selected Bibliography	288
Table of Princes	297
Genealogy of the Rurikids	following 298
Index of Names	299

Preface

This translation is based on the English version published by the late Professor Samuel Hazzard Cross in Volume XII (1930) of the *Harvard Studies and Notes in Philology and Literature,* which was the first English rendering of this highly important Slavic source. Professor Cross, however, was not entirely satisfied with this first edition of his translation and intended, for a long time, to prepare a new, revised and enlarged, edition of this work, which was to be accompanied with commentaries. But his many activities during World War II did not allow him to prosecute this task with desired speed; and his premature death occurred while he was still working on it.

I have had the honor and the pleasure of being associated with Professor Cross for many years in the domain of our common interest: mediaeval Slavic texts. I regarded it, therefore, as a great privilege when the Mediaeval Academy of America invited me, after his death, to take over his unfinished work and to prepare it for publication. In carrying out this task, the greatest attention has been given to the identification and incorporation into the final text of everything that had been left by Cross, even in scattered notes and remarks, and, even while bringing it here and there up to date, to keeping the organization of the work along the lines envisaged by Cross.

For permission to use the 1930 version as a basis for this revised translation both I and the Mediaeval Academy of America express grateful appreciation to the President and Fellows of Harvard College and to Dr. Thomas J. Wilson, Director of the Harvard University Press.

Georgetown University OLGERD P. SHERBOWITZ-WETZOR
1 April 1953

Note on Transliteration

The system of transcribing Russian names and terms adopted in this volume is intended to reproduce exactly, in Latin letters, their original spelling without, however, having recourse to symbols wholly alien to the English usage. Hence combinations of letters (like *sh, ch, ts,* etc.), rather than single letters, with or without diacritical marks (like *š, č, c,* etc.), are employed to represent various Russian letters and sounds. Nevertheless, a few diacritical marks are still used. The modern Russian orthography is adhered to throughout, except in some quotations from old texts, ancient terms, and titles of works published before 1917.

Only two diacritical marks are used: "ÿ" to represent the letter ы as distinct from the letter and sound represented by "y", and ' to represent ь or "soft sign." In the few cases where the *ancient régime* orthography is used, "ĕ" represents the letter ѣ. On the other hand, ъ or "hard sign" is not transcribed, nor are the rarer letters of the *ancien régime* alphabet like i, v, ѳ. "Y" is used to represent the letter й as well as the first element in the iotated diphthongs я = "ya" and ю = "yu".

Some traditional Western renderings of Russian names have been retained, such, e.g., as "Olga" for "Ol'ga", "Rurik" for "Ryurik", "Volhynia", "Volhynian" for "Volÿn'", "Volÿnian", and, finally, the ending—"sky" for "-skiy" in family names.

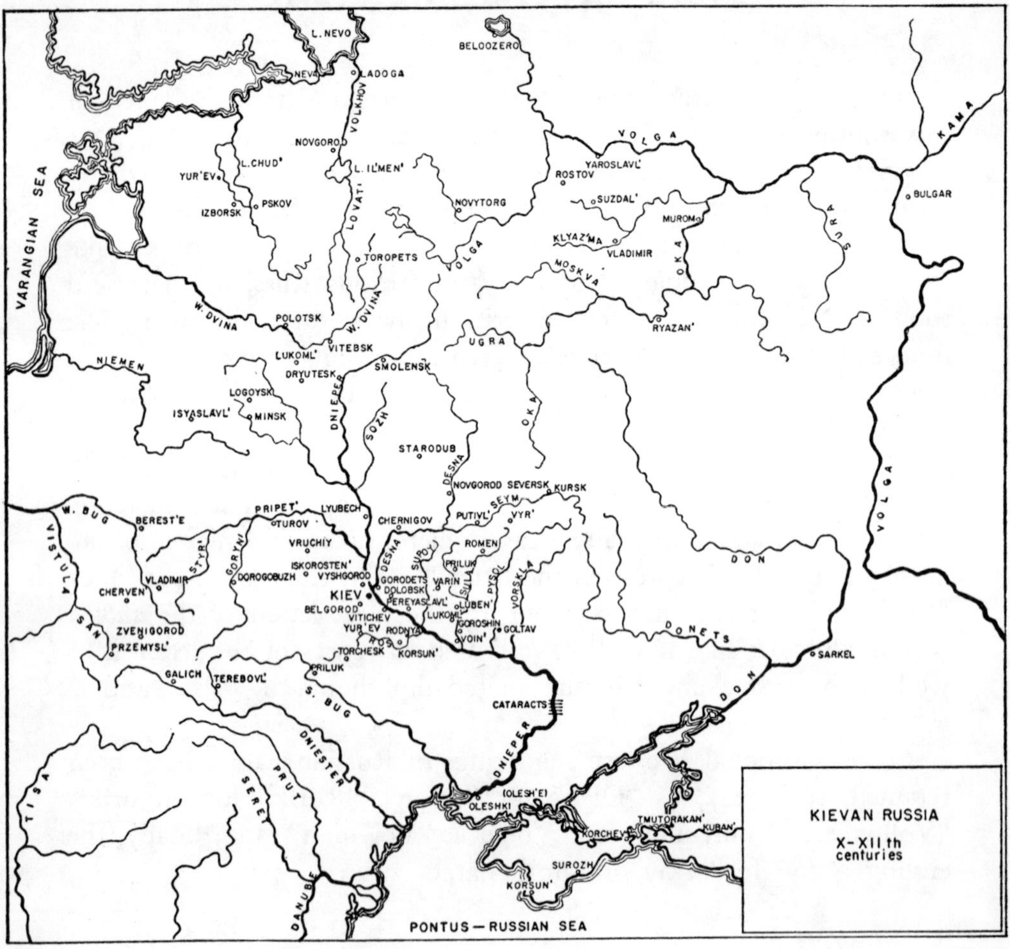
KIEVAN RUSSIA
X-XII th centuries
L. NEVO
NEVA
LADOGA
BELOOZERO
VOLKHOV
NOVGOROD
L. IL'MEN'
L. CHUD'
YUR'EV
PSKOV
IZBORSK
LOVATI
NOVYTORG
TOROPETS
VOLGA
YAROSLAVL'
ROSTOV
SUZDAL'
KLYAZ'MA
VLADIMIR
MUROM
OKA
MOSKVA
RYAZAN'
KAMA
BULGAR
SURA
VARANGIAN SEA
W. DVINA
POLOTSK
VITEBSK
LUKOML'
DRYUTESK
SMOLENSK
UGRA
NIEMEN
LOGOYSK
ISYASLAVL'
MINSK
DNIEPER
SOZH
STARODUB
DESNA
NOVGOROD SEVERSK
KURSK
SEYM
PUTIVL'
VYR'
W. BUG
BEREST'E
PRIPET'
TUROV
LYUBECH
CHERNIGOV
VRUCHIY
ISKOROSTEN'
VYSHGOROD
GORODETS
DOLOBSK
KIEV
BELGOROD
VITICHEV
YUR'EV
RODNYA
TORCHESK
KORSUN'
PEREYASLAVL'
VARIN
PRILUK
ROMEN
SULA
SUPOY
LUKOML'
LUBEN'
GOROSHIN
VOIN'
PYSOL
VORSKLA
GOLTAV
VISTULA
STYR'
GORYN'
VLADIMIR
DOROGOBUZH
CHERVEN'
SAN
ZVENIGOROD
PRZEMYSL'
GALICH
TEREBOVL'
PRILUK
S. BUG
DNIESTER
PRUT
SERET
TISA
DANUBE
DON
DONETS
SARKEL
CATARACTS
OLESHKI
(OLESH'E)
KORCHEV
TMUTORAKAN'
KUBAN'
SUROZH
KORSUN'
PONTUS — RUSSIAN SEA

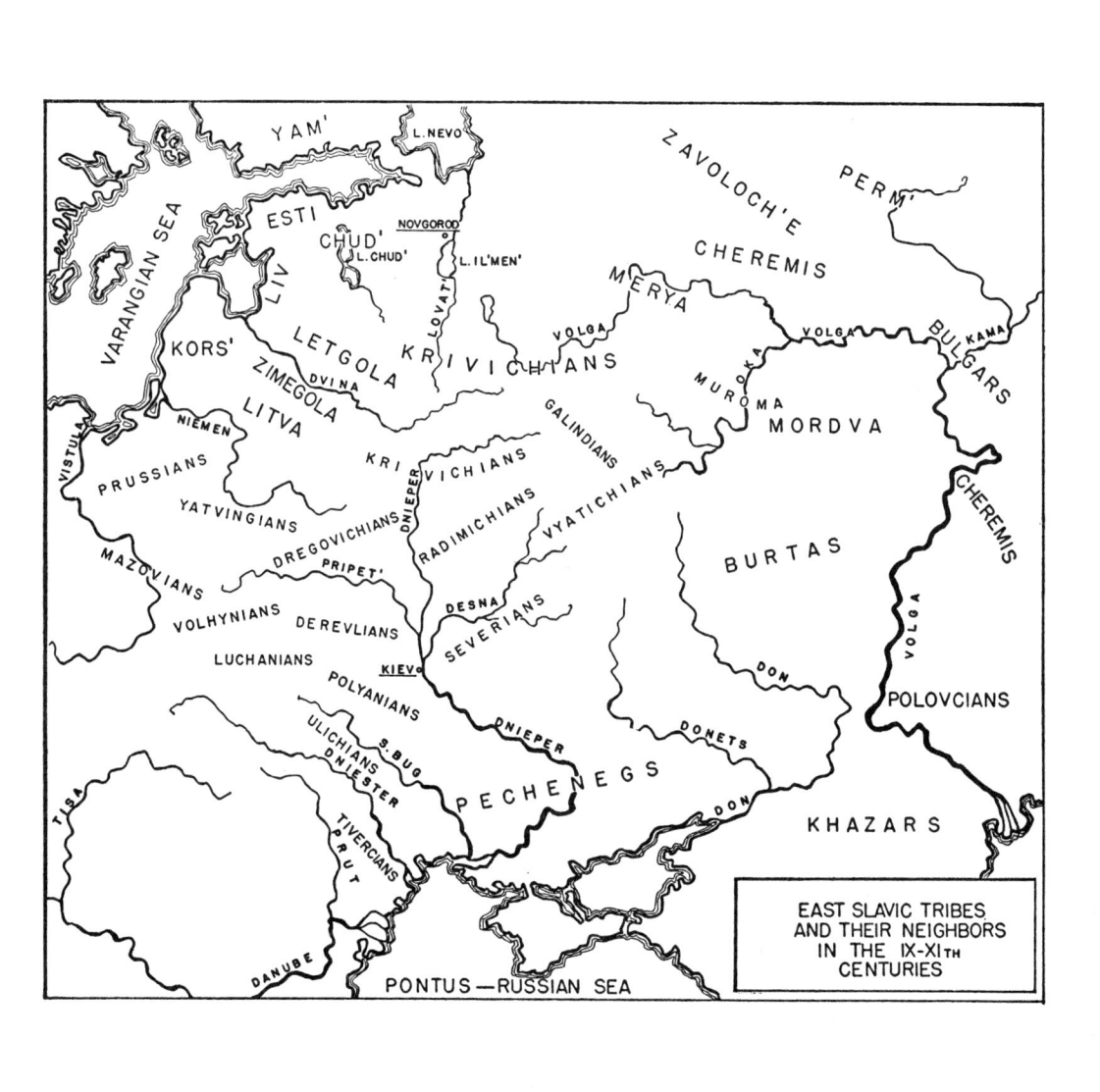

EAST SLAVIC TRIBES AND THEIR NEIGHBORS IN THE IX-XITH CENTURIES

THE RUSSIAN PRIMARY CHRONICLE
LAURENTIAN TEXT

Introduction

Manuscripts and Editions

The earliest native sources for Russian history are the mediaeval annals. Practically all extant Russian chronicle texts include, regardless of their date and nature, a generally uniform account of the period extending from the traditional origins of Rus' to the early twelfth century. This narrative is a literary expression of the civilization and the political system which prevailed while Kiev was the great national and intellectual centre of the Eastern Slavs, and is known as the *Primary Chronicle,* the *Nachal'naya Letopis'*. Until the nineteenth century, it was habitually attributed to the monk Nestor. Modern investigators have not only placed his authorship in doubt, but have also sought to establish by internal evidence that the *Primary Chronicle,* instead of being a homogeneous work, is a compilation from several chronicle texts of greater antiquity.

The complex of Russian annalistic literature thus has its roots in this relatively uniform text. In all surviving annalistic compilations, however, the existence of independent local tradition, and even of local records, is indicated by traces of information originating from other cities besides Kiev. As the domains controlled by scions of the Kievan ruling family became more independent, the practice of keeping annals extended even to the minor principalities. From the early twelfth century, local chronicles thus appear in every Russian centre of any prominence. Some of these, like the Chronicles of Tver, Pskov, and Novgorod, have been preserved, while others, which have disappeared as independent compositions, survive only as excerpted for the construction of later annalistic complexes. With the consolidation of Muscovite authority in the sixteenth century, the importance of local historical literature declined, and the regional chronicles gave way to extensive compilations which cover the totality of Russian historical evolution from the origins to the established supremacy of Moscow.

The Russian *Primary Chronicle,* formerly referred to as the *Chronicle of Nestor* but in modern Slavic critical literature most frequently termed *The Tale of Bygone Years (Povest' Vremennÿkh Let)* from the title occurring at the beginning of the traditional text, thus covers the period which extends from the year 852, the conventional dawn of Russian history, to the second decade of the twelfth century. The *Primary Chronicle* will frequently be referred to in this study as the *Povest'*. The most primitive text is preserved in two outstanding redactions, each of which presents a fairly distinct type of textual tradition. The first of these is the Laurentian redaction, so called because the colophon of the manuscript declares that it was copied between January 14 and March 20, 1377, by the monk Lawrence (Lavrentiy) for Prince Dmitriy Konstantinovich of Suzdal'. The second is the Hypatian redaction, dating from the middle of the fifteenth century and copied probably at Pskov from a South-Russian original. It is named after the Hypatian Monastery at Kostroma, where it was discovered. Of these two manuscripts, the Laurentian belongs to the State Public Library at Leningrad, and the Hypatian to the Russian Academy of Sciences, in the same city.

The text of the *Povest'* in the Laurentian redaction is notable for the fact that the narrative for the year 1110 is followed by this subscription:

"In the hope of God's grace, I Sylvester, Prior of St. Michael's, wrote this Chronicle in the year 6624 (1116), the ninth of the indiction, during the reign of Prince Vladimir in Kiev, while I was presiding over St. Michael's Monastery. May whosoever reads this book remember me in his prayers."

The Hypatian redaction does not contain this colophon, but under the year 1110 supplements at some length the pious reflections contained in the Laurentian text and inspired by the pillar of fire which is alleged to have appeared in that year over the Crypt Monastery. The Laurentian redaction, in distinction to the Hypatian, also includes the *Testament* of Prince Vladimir Monomakh (1035-1126), his letter to Oleg, Prince of Chernigov, and a prayer attributed to Vladimir.[1]

While Peter the Great had directed in 1722 that all chronicle texts should be collected and copied, these documents were not subjected to any critical scrutiny until the nineteenth century. They were, in fact, unknown to western scholars prior to the publication by Gerhard Friedrich Müller, in the first volume of his *Sammlung russischer Geschichte* (Spb., 1732), of excerpts translated from a chronicle text then in possession of the Imperial Academy of Sciences. These selections aroused the curiosity of August Ludwig Schlözer, who arrived in Russia just as the publication of the Königsberg (Radziwiłł) chronicle text was begun (1761). The fruit of Schlözer's preoccupation with the Russian chronicles was his *Probe russischer Annalen* (Bremen and Göttingen, 1768), the first effort at an analysis of the annals and their contents. Though several other chronicles (mostly late texts) were printed before the end of the eighteenth century (the *Sinodal'nÿy* in 1781, the *Nikonovskiy* in 1767-1792, the *Tipografskiy* in 1784, the *Akademicheskiy* in 1786, the *L'vovskiy* in 1792, the *Voskresenskiy* in 1793, and the *Sofiyskiy Vremennik* in 1795), no attempt was made to publish the Laurentian MS. until 1804. This labor was interrupted by the French invasion, in which perished such scanty presswork as was already complete (ten sheets). A second attempt resulted in the publication of thirteen sheets in 1824. A systematic national study of early source material was, however, undertaken only from 1828 forward, when the Imperial Academy of Sciences equipped and sent out an expedition to Northern Russia for the collection and description of literary monuments and documents preserved in local archives and libraries.

For the arrangement and publication of the materials gathered by this expedition, a permanent organ was created in 1834, and designated as the Archaeographical Commission in the Ministry of Public Instruction. A few years later, the Commission, which is a self-perpetuating body existing to the present day, proceeded to the publication of its most important series, the *Full Collection of Russian Chronicles* (*Polnoe Sobranie Russkikh Lětopisey*) of which the initial volume (1846) was the first printed edition of the Laurentian text complete through the year 1305. A reprint of this text through the Sylvestrian colophon but with modified orthography was subsequently edited by Miklosich.[2] The exhaustion of its two reprints from the first edition of the Laurentian text of the *Povest'* led the Commission to sponsor the preparation of a modern diplomatic text imitating the edition of the Hypatian MS. prepared in 1908 by Professor A. A. Shakhmatov for the Commission's collection of annals. The resulting text of the *Povest'*, edited by Professor E. F. Karsky of Leningrad, was thus published in 1926, and it is upon this edition that the present translation is based. The Hypatian MS. was first printed complete in 1843 in the second volume of the *Full Collection*. A reprint of 1871 was superseded first by Shakhmatov's second edition of 1908, and more recently by the third edition of 1923 (to the year 1146), prepared by the same scholar, who was until his death in 1920 the greatest modern student of Russian annalistic literature.[2a]

A reprint of the Hypatian text, with a Polish translation, is contained in *Monumenta Poloniae Historica, I* (Lemberg, 1864). The first translation of the *Povest'* into a Western European language is that of Joseph Müller, *Altrussische Geschichte nach Nestor* (Berlin, 1812), followed by the French translation of L. Paris, *La Chronique de Nestor* (Paris, 1834). The latter was superseded by Louis Léger's rendering under the title *La Chronique dite de Nestor* (Paris, 1884). A Czechish translation by K. Erben appeared in 1867 (*Nestorův Letopis přeložil K.E.*, Prague), a revision of which by Professor Miloš Weingart of the University of Bratislava (Czechoslovakia) is now in preparation. A Danish translation by C. W. Smith is also available (*Nestors Russiske Kronike oversåt og forklaret*, Copenhagen, 1869). The present translation is the first English rendering of the *Povest'*.

AUTHORSHIP

Nestor, to whom the *Primary Chronicle* has long been attributed, was actually a monk of the historic Crypt Monastery in Kiev at the close of the eleventh and the beginning of the twelfth century. He is the undisputed author of two biographical works: (1) *The Narrative of the Life, Death, and Miracles of the Holy and Blessed Martyrs Boris and Gleb;* and (2) *The Life of the Venerable Theodosius,* Prior of the Crypt Monastery. One South-Russian chronicle text of the sixteenth century, the so-called *Khlebnikovskiy,* which is probably derived from the same prototype as the Hypatian, mentions Nestor specifically as the author.[3] The Laurentian redaction, however, contains in its title no characterization whatever of the author or of his monastic affiliations. Nestor was similarly mentioned as the author of the *Chronicle* in three lost chronicle texts used by the historian V. N. Tatishchev (1686-1750).[4] Apart from this somewhat questionable testimony, the only direct evidence of Nestor's activity as an annalist is contained in two passages which occur in all versions of the Kiev *Paterikon,* a biographical work on the solitaries of the Crypt Monastery dating from the first half of the thirteenth century.[5] In the second of these passages, it is also asserted that Nestor likewise wrote biographies of four celebrated monks of the Crypt Monastery (Damian, Jeremy, Matthew, and Isaac). If Nestor was the author or the compiler of the *Povest',* which contains extensive material dealing with SS. Boris and Gleb, on the Prior Theodosius, and on various distinguished solitaries of his establishment, a general agreement in subject matter, as well as marked similarity in style, might be expected to characterize the products of the same pen.

The relation between the Nestorian *Life of Boris and Gleb* and the chronicle account of these saints has been variously viewed, though on the whole there is some reason to believe that Nestor's work was one of the sources of the *Povest'* account.[6] An appreciable diversity in detail is evident, however, between the Nestorian *Life* and the *Chronicle*.

In the former, both Boris and Gleb are described as with Vladimir at the time of his fatal illness; in the *Chronicle*, Vladimir sends Boris forth to fight the Pechenegs, and the news of his father's demise meets Boris upon his homeward journey. Similarly, while the *Chronicle* represents Vladimir as assigning to Boris and Gleb the respective domains of Rostov and Murom, the *Life* by Nestor reports that he assigned to Boris the city of Vladimir, but kept Gleb by his side. The *Life* also remarks that upon Vladimir's death Svyatopolk came to Kiev, but according to the *Povest'*, he was present in the capital at the time. According to Nestor, Boris is killed at once by a thrust through the heart; the *Chronicle* shows him laid upon a cart mortally wounded and dragged off to Svyatopolk, who despatches two Varangians to administer the *coup de grâce*. In the Nestorian *Life*, after the murder of Boris, Gleb flees northward, and is pursued by the minions of Svyatopolk but the *Povest'* account reports Gleb as summoned treacherously by Svyatopolk from Murom. On his way south, he is met and warned by messengers from his brother Yaroslav, but too late to escape Svyatopolk's emissaries, who slay him near Smolensk. The *Chronicle* likewise supplies such factual details as geographical data and the names both of the brothers, servants and of their murderers, all of which are absent from the narrative belonging to Nestor. There is, however, little resemblance in style and method between the *Chronicle* narrative and the Nestorian *Life*. The former is a detailed treatment of the circumstances surrounding the assassination of the two princes. The latter is a religious biography in the best manner of early Russian hagiography.

A comparative study of the two accounts presents no stylistic evidence that Nestor was in any way concerned with the composition or compilation of the *Primary Chronicle*, while the contradictions between the two narratives point rather in the opposite direction.

A somewhat more fruitful basis for comparison is provided by Nestor's *Life of Theodosius* and by the double account of the foundation of the Crypt Monastery at Kiev and the death of Theodosius provided by the *Povest'* under the years 1051 and 1074.

According to the *Povest'*, Hilarion and Antonius were the founders of Russian asceticism. Antonius, after accepting and tonsuring twelve new brethren, retired as prior in favor of Barlaam, who arranged for the construction of the first small Church of the Assumption of the Virgin on the surface above the crypt. As the order grew in numbers, requiring additional quarters, Antonius from his retirement, and upon the request of the brotherhood, begged Prince Izyaslav to present the order with the hill above the crypt. Upon the receipt of this property, and while Barlaam was still prior, a new and larger church and a surface structure for the monastery itself were completed. Izyaslav then established a new monastery of his own, which he dedicated to St. Demetrius, and to which he transferred Barlaam as prior. At Barlaam's departure, and again upon request of the brotherhood, Antonius designated Theodosius as the former's successor.

The record by the Nestorian *Life of Theodosius* is radically different. Therein it is asserted that Antonius himself tonsured none of the brethren, who were thus initiated by his colleague Nikon. Antonius retired to solitude when the brethren numbered fifteen, and not twelve, as stated in the *Chronicle*. In the *Povest'*, Antonius designated Barlaam as his successor before entering into retirement, but according to Nestor, he first shut himself up in his cell, named Barlaam as his successor, and only somewhat later removed to another hill, where he dug a new crypt. Likewise, in Nestor's account, Barlaam constructed only the one small surface church before his transfer to St. Demetrius', while the brethren themselves, after unanimously choosing Theodosius as Barlaam's successor, notified Antonius of their action. The new prior, finding the previous quarters too small, selected a location not far from the old crypt, where he built a large church dedicated to the Immaculate Virgin, together with numerous cells. Though the *Povest'* recounts that the rules of the Studion Monastery were obtained by Theodosius from the monk Michael, who had come to Kiev from Greece with the Metropolitan George, the Nestorian *Life* represents Theodosius as sending a special messenger to Ephraim the Castrate at Constantinople to obtain them. Finally, the *Povest'*, mentions briefly in 1073 Theodosius' foundation of a stone church, which was brought to completion by the Prior Stephen in 1075. The *Life* in this instance enters into extensive detail as to the selection of the site for this church by Prince Svyatoslav.[7]

Additional indication of a diversity of authorship between the Chronicle account of the early history of the Crypt Monastery and the Nestorian *Life of Theodosius* may be gleaned from the statements of the writers themselves. The *Chronicle* narrative of 1051 ends thus: "While Theodosius lived in the monastery, following a virtuous life and the monastic rule, and receiving everyone who presented himself, I, a poor and unworthy servant, came to him, and he accepted me in my seventeenth year. Hence I have set down and certified what year the monastery came into being, and why it is named the Crypt Monastery, but to Theodosius' life we shall recur later."

Nestor, on the contrary, writes (Yakovlev, *op. cit.*, p. lxiii):
"I, the sinful Nestor, least of all those in the monastery of our Father Theodosius, wrote down these facts concerning our great and blessed father which I learned by inquiry from fathers older than myself, who lived in his day. And I was received into the monastery by the venerable Prior Stephen, by whom I was also tonsured, invested with the monastic garb, and later advanced to the rank of deacon, though I was unworthy of it, being coarse and ignorant, and filled from my youth by a multitude of sins."

Thus Nestor, by his own statement, did not know Theodosius personally, and was admitted into the Crypt Monastery only after the great prior's death in 1074. Equally striking divergences in fact appear from any comparison of the *Povest'* account of Theodosius' death and the recital of the same events prepared by Nestor.

In the words of the *Povest'*, Theodosius, on the eve of the Lenten fast (Quinquagesima Sunday, March 2, 1074), according to his habit, admonished the brethren in a brief address concerning their observance of Lent, and then retired to his cell, where he remained in solitude and abstinence until the Friday before Palm Sunday (April 11). He then came forth to celebrate Holy Week and Easter, but on the Saturday following (April 26), he fell ill. On the evening of Wednesday (April 30), after five days' sickness, he requested the brethren to carry him out into the courtyard, and upon informing them that during Lent the imminence of his death had been revealed to him, bade them nominate his successor. The monks, however, left the choice to Theodosius, who in turn begged them to name anyone from their ranks except the brothers Nicholas and Ignatius. A second time, they requested Theodosius to make the nomination, which then fell upon the presbyter James. This choice failed to meet the approval of the community, who forthwith recommended the cantor Stephen. After Theodosius had blessed the new prior, he was borne back to his cell. In the course of the following day, Theodosius was visited by Prince Svyatoslav and his son Gleb. On the seventh day (Friday, May 2) he gave his final admonition to Stephen and the brethren, and then died on Saturday, May 3. He was buried the same night.

In the Nestorian *Life of Theodosius,* the narrative of his demise is abruptly introduced by the observation that he foresaw his approaching death. Theodosius thereupon summoned the brotherhood and admonished them as to their Christian duties. He then retired to his cell, beat his breast, and prayed both for his own salvation and for the monastery. The monks did not understand the purport of his admonition, but thought that, like Antonius, he was perhaps about to leave them to carry out his oft-expressed plan to live in retirement, from which he had previously been dissuaded by the Prince and his associates. Theodosius, however, was attacked by a violent fever, and for three days lay speechless in a comatose state, so that some even thought he was already dead. On the fourth day he arose, summoned the brotherhood, and made known that the time of his death had been revealed to him during Lent. He therefore requested the monks to name his successor, whereupon, after consulting together privately, they immediately elected Stephen. The following day, Theodosius once more assembled them, and approved their choice. After admonishing the order, the prior then foretold that his death would occur after sunrise on the following Saturday. On the morning of that day, he gathered the brethren about him to take their final leave, and then withdrew to his cell. One of the monks saw through a crevice how he uttered his last prayer, and then, after laying himself upon his pallet, calmly passed away. Prince Svyatoslav, who happened to be in the vicinity of the monastery, saw a miraculous pillar of fire above it and understood from the sign that Theodosius was dead. The brethren were momentarily prevented by the presence of crowds about the monastery from giving Theodosius the quiet burial he had desired, until a miraculous shower came up and scattered the assemblage.

Apart from the diversity of fact between the *Povest'* narrative and the Nestorian *Life of Theodosius* as indicated by the foregoing summaries, there are discernible certain variations in emphasis which point to divergent views of the respective authors regarding important details in the history of the Crypt Monastery. In the *Povest'*, Antonius is the great initiator; for Nestor, Theodosius is naturally the dominant figure immediately preceding Nestor's own admission to the monastery. Furthermore, Nestor is better informed than the *Chronicle* as to the relations between Theodosius and the Princes Izyaslav and Svyatoslav, as well as regarding the internal political aspects of the succession to the priorate in the years following Theodosius' death. Since these matters are of some importance, it is not easy to explain why Nestor, if the author or the compiler of the *Povest'*, did not make use of them in that work. An attentive study of the original texts of the two productions also amply justifies Bugoslavsky's observation (*loc. cit.*, p. 163) that the style of the *Chronicle* narrative is markedly different from the Nestorian *Life* in conciseness, wealth of factual detail, and simplicity of literary technique. It is devoid of the quotations and comparisons with Biblical episodes, and free from the repetitions with which Nestor's style abounds.

A juxtaposition of Nestor's attested works with the portions of the *Povest'* dealing with similar subjects thus offers little ground for any assumption that Nestor had any connection with its composition.

It remains to be seen whether the other instances in the *Povest'* where the first person is used by author or compiler (apart from the passage of 1051 quoted above) point in any way to Nestorian authorship. The first (1091), dealing with the discovery of the remains of Theodosius, reports that the narrator was instructed by the prior to dig for the relics and was himself eyewitness and participant in all events here recounted in considerable detail. In view of its general stylistic resemblance to the preceding accounts of the monastery and of Theodosius and a consequent departure from Nestor's ornate verbiage, this passage shows far more kinship with the author of the foregoing items concerning the monastery than with any product of Nestor's pen. Next in order of importance is the account of 1097 which relates the blinding of Vasil'ko in which the narrator refers to himself by name as Vasiliy (Basil). The fact that the same events described in this section are covered again briefly under 1098-1100 leads naturally to the supposition that the Vasiliy account represents an interpolated episode. The remaining three are of more restricted interest. The first (1065) has to do with a monster-child fished out of the Setoml' River, which the narrator and his companions "gazed upon till evening." The next (1096) relates to the raid upon Kiev by the Polovcian chief Bonyak, whose nomads surrounded the monastery "while we [the inmates] were resting in our cells after matins." The writer was thus evidently present in the monastery when the raid took place, and his account is followed by a report concerning a personal conversation with Gyurata Rogovich of Novgorod on the subject of certain barbarians of the north. The final item (1106) reports the death of the venerable Yan, from whom, says the chronicler, "I heard . . . many stories which I have set down in this chronicle as I heard them from his lips."

These seven passages in the first person cast but little light upon the authorship of the *Chronicle*. Along with the account of the foundation of the Crypt Monastery, however, they all fall between the years 1051 and 1106, thus within the lifetime of one man. Even if we assume that the author of the narrative dealing with the beginning of the monastery joined that community about 1057, as soon as Theodosius became prior, and, according to his own statement, was seventeen years old at the time, he would thus have been only seventy years old at the date upon which the *Povest'* concludes (1110). If we disregard for a moment the Sylvestrian colophon, it is not intrinsically impossible that the entire *Povest'* was written or compiled by one monk of the Crypt Monastery in the course of the second half of the eleventh century. In any case, the internal evidence of the *Povest'*, along with the lack of coincidence of its contents with Nestor's works wherever the two are related, is distinctly opposed to the tradition of Nestorian authorship.

COMPOSITION

The early belief that Nestor was the author or the compiler of the whole *Povest'* as it stands has thus been generally abandoned by modern investigators, to be replaced by some scholars with the contention that he was author of one of the sources from which the *Povest'*, in its present form, is alleged to be derived. During the nineteenth century, as knowledge of the various chronicle texts and redactions and the study of their interrelation progressed, it was noted that the *Povest'* contains not only certain contradictions with the attested works of Nestor, but also certain internal incoherences.[8] For example, Pereyaslavl' appears among the list of Russian cities already prosperous in the time of Oleg (907), while an account of its foundation by Vladimir is set forth under 993. Under the year 1060, there appears an account of a successful raid by certain Russian princes upon the nomad Torks, who did not wait for the Russian attack but "are fleeing to this day." In 1080, however, it is related that these Torks in turn risked an attack in Russian territory which was avenged by Vladimir Monomakh under instructions from his father Vsevolod. In the brief mention of the passage of the Magyars before Kiev under 898, the comment is made that they were nomads like the Polovcians. It should be noted that the first mention of the Polovcians as a menace occurs in 1055, though under 1061 the *Chronicle* says plainly that the Polovcians in that year made their first raid. In the narrative for 1044, reference is made to the fact that Prince Vseslav was born with a caul, which, at the recommendation of soothsayers present at his birth, he wore suspended from his neck "to this day," as the *Chronicle* puts it. Vseslav, as it happens, died in 1101. It is also apparent that, while the *Povest'*, itself ends in 1110, the initial chronology is carried through to the death of Svyatopolk in 1113. And finally, students of the *Povest'* speedily observed that all accounts of eyewitnesses and significant occurrences of the first person (except the expressions *otsele pochnem i chisla polozhim* and *no mÿ na prezhen'e vozvratimsya . . . i po ryadu polozhim chisla* under 852) appear after 1050.

These observations, combined with analysis of the sections dealing with Theodosius and the Crypt Monastery as well as with the otherwise unknown Vasiliy's narrative of the blinding of Vasil'ko, led to the belief that a portion of the *Povest'* was written early in the second half of the eleventh century, while the remainder was composed toward the close of the same century or early in the twelfth.[9] Thus Kostomarov concluded that while Nestor had some share in the *Primary Chronicle,* it cannot in its entirety be ascribed to him. In view of the Sylvestrian signature, Kostomarov believed that Sylvester compiled a collection or separate narratives and traditions, to which he added the chronology, and in which he embodied a chronicle prepared in the Crypt Monastery at Kiev, of a portion of which Nestor was the author.[10] Sreznevsky (*op. cit.*, p. 114) in the main accepted the view that Sylvester is the compiler, remarking that the prior of an outstanding monastery and an ecclesiastic of sufficient importance to be elevated in 1118 to the episcopate of Pereyaslavl' would hardly be likely to indulge in the mere copying of an alien work. From the notion that the *Povest'* as we have it is a compilation from earlier productions, it was but a step to efforts toward resolving the *Povest'* into its components and determining their character. It is thus in this channel that study of the *Povest'* has moved during the last fifty years.

The culmination of this analytic process is found in the studies of two Russian scholars, the late Professor A. A. Shakhmatov (1865-1920), and Professor V. M. Istrin. The former, one of the most brilliant philologists that Russia has produced, besides editing several important texts, devoted some forty articles to various phases of chronicle study, and embodied many of the results of his investigations in two works: *Razÿskaniya o Drevněyshikh Russkikh Lětopisnÿkh Svodakh* (*Investigations of the Oldest Russian Annalistic Compilations,* Spb, 1908), and the Introduction to his text of the *Povest'* (*Pověst' Vremennÿkh Lět.* 1, *Vvodnaya chast', Tekst, Priměchaniya,* Spb, 1916). In the latter work, Shakhmatov indicated that the second volume, concerned with a study of the sources of the *Povest'* and a definition of the editorial functions of its compilers, was practically complete in manuscript. It is therefore to be hoped that the Academy of Sciences of the U.S.S.R. will supplement its extremely useful work upon the chronicles by a publication of this manuscript.

A clear distinction must, however, be drawn between the methods of Shakhmatov and those of his precursors. The first period in the study of the chronicles, exemplified by Tatishchev and Schlözer, was characterized by efforts to restore a "pure" text of what was contemporaneously viewed as a homogeneous work. The features of existing texts which, to the modern student, usually indicate the compilatory character of the chronicle, were first viewed as textual corruptions. As the study of the origin and the nature of the chronicle texts progressed, this early notion gave way to the conception of the *Povest'* as the mechanical combination of diversified material on a chronological framework. This idea is well exemplified by the views of Kostomarov, Sreznevsky, and Bestuzhev-Ryumin.[11] Shakhmatov, however, proceeded to the comparative examination of all existing chronicle texts, in order to determine their interrelation and origin, and to reconstruct, if possible, the prototypes from which the various texts are derived, at the same time defining the process of evolution by which the extant texts have reached their present form. As Shakhmatov himself expressed it, a study of the most recent compilations leads up to a definition and a restoration of the more ancient redactions, and the analysis of the latter points to still earlier compilations as their sources.

As Shakhmatov's studies form at present the starting point for any critical examination of the Russian chronicles in general, some detailed synopsis of his conclusions appears a necessity. The *Povest'* itself is a compilation appearing at the beginning of the majority of all annalistic compilations dating from the fourteenth through the seventeenth century. The oldest compilations exhibit a fairly complete and homogeneous text, which is abbreviated or otherwise modified in later versions, while the older annals of Novgorod supplement data originating in Kiev with material related to the ancient history of the northern area. Sylvester's signature constitutes absolute proof that the *Povest'* was compiled in the second decade of the twelfth century to cover the course of events as far as 1111. On the other hand, the fact that the *Povest'* as preserved deals very extensively with events relating exclusively to the Crypt Monastery is for Shakhmatov abundant proof that the Sylvestrian redaction is not the most primitive.

The Laurentian redaction, it will be recalled, contains under 1110 an account of a pillar of fire which appeared over the Crypt Monastery, followed by a short paragraph of pious comment upon its significance.

Introduction

The Hypatian redaction, however, includes not only this passage, but also the remainder of the pious commentary omitted by the Laurentian. Shakhmatov maintains that the mention of the portent, together with the comment thereon, was not found in the original Sylvestrian redaction of the *Povest'* but was added to it from the prototype of the text represented by the extant Hypatian redaction. The commentary on the portent in texts of the Hypatian group serves as introduction to the account of a successful raid upon the Polovcians executed by the Russian princes in March, 1111. It is thus clear, in Shakhmatov's view, that the *Povest'* was continued beyond its original compass during the second decade of the twelfth century. It so happens that the Hypatian redaction, from 1076 on, includes certain material relating to Vladimir Monomakh which does not figure in the Laurentian. Shakhmatov thus deduces from this evidence that, along with the Sylvestrian text, there also existed an additional primitive version of the *Povest'*, differing from the former in certain features prior 1111, and in the fact that it contained a continuation discussing contemporary events somewhat beyond that date. From other internal evidence, combined with the manifest change in tone in the Hypatian narrative from 1118 forward, Shakhmatov concludes that this new redaction, from which the Hypatian and kindred texts derive, was composed in that year. His opinion, therefore, is that the original *Povest'* was compiled in 1111, the year after its close; that Sylvester, according to his colophon, prepared a somewhat modified redaction of it in 1116; and that in 1118 there was prepared in the Crypt Monastery still a third redaction, the prototype of the Hypatian group of texts.

It would appear something of a *tour de force* to explain this appearance of three versions of the same monument within seven years. Shakhmatov assumes that the basic (1111) redaction of the *Povest'* was unduly friendly in tone to Svyatopolk, a prince whose rough, impulsive, and violent character presented a marked contrast to the temperament of Vladimir Monomakh, his pious, judicious, and intelligent successor. The Vydobichi Monastery, over the destinies of which Sylvester presided, had been founded by Vladimir's father Vsevolod. Shakhmatov thus suggests that, in order to place the events of the last principate in their proper light, Vladimir Monomakh in 1116 instructed Sylvester to prepare a new redaction of the *Povest'*, upon completion of which the basic text of 1111 disappeared from circulation. The transfer of official annalistic activity from the Crypt to another and a younger monastery, Shakhmatov thinks, must have been a severe blow to the pride of the older institution, in which a party may well have arisen favoring a policy of friendly understanding with Vladimir. One member of this party thus determined to prepare a new chronicle to replace the redaction eliminated by Sylvester's text, and this third redaction is the hypothetical text of 1118 previously mentioned.

It is significant that while modern scholars generally tend to minimize Nestor's connection with the *Povest'*, Shakhmatov restores his standing by the assumption that he was the compiler of the basic text of 1111, which was suppressed in favor of Sylvester's redaction of 1116. Shakhmatov believes that the title of the *Povest'* originally contained the ascription to "Nestor, a monk of the Theodosian Crypt Monastery", which was omitted in the Sylvestrian redaction. While the second reviser (1118 text) succeeded in restoring the ascription to "a monk of the Theodosian Crypt Monastery", the name of Nestor was banned, and the tradition of his quality as an annalist was retained only in the *Paterikon* (*supra*, Authorship), and in the *Khlebnikovskiy* chronicle text, which might, in Shakhmatov's view, go back to a prototype in the preparation of which the old basic *Povest'* of 1111 was employed. The obvious contradictions between the *Povest'* and Nestor's *Life of Theodosius* Shakhmatov minimizes by the contention that Nestor wrote the *Life* in the eighties of the eleventh century and the *Povest'* in 1111, and further, that he used an earlier hypothetical text, the oldest chronicle of the Crypt Monastery, which he hesitated to modify, just as Sylvester refrained from removing any discrepancies from the text of the *Povest'* as he edited it.

Certain chronicle texts originating in Novgorod (the so-called *First Novgorod Chronicle*, younger series, and related texts) are based in the main, according to Shakhmatov, upon a compilation prepared at Novgorod about 1432. The latter compilation is derived, in Shakhmatov's opinion, from a Novgorod ecclesiastical chronicle beginning only in the twelfth century, and therefore supplemented by a text of southern origin which he considers to have antedated the *Povest'*. Shakhmatov's reasons for believing that this southern chronicle is more primitive than the *Povest'* lie in the absence of quotations from extraneous sources, e.g., Georgius Hamartolus, Nicephorus, the Russo-Greek treaties, the legends of SS. Cyril and Methodius and of St. Andrew, and various items of traditional material. One of the characteristics of this northern family of texts is an extensive introduction which does not appear in either the Laurentian or the Hypatian redactions.[12] The Preface indicates the compiler's intention to cover the period from Michael III to Alexius Comnenus (therefore 842-1081). It also contains sharp criticism of the reigning prince and his retainers, who are charged with injustice and avarice. Shakhmatov has no hesitation in attributing these remarks to John, Prior of the Crypt Monastery, writing in the nineties of the eleventh century, at the moment when the relations between Prince Svyatopolk and the monastery are known to have been strained. He thus concludes that this primary or primitive annalistic compilation originating in the Crypt Monastery was composed about 1095, and extended only as far as the pious reflections concerning two defeats inflicted upon the Russian princes by the Polovcians at Trepol' and on the Zhelan' in May and July, 1093. At this point, Shakhmatov considers that the original contribution of Nestor to the preparation of the *Povest'* begins. The primitive monastery compilation of 1095 was, according to Shakhmatov, Nestor's basic source which he revamped and supplemented with much diversified extraneous material. It is also possible, Shakhmatov thinks, that Nestor contributed some individual touches to the body of the *Chronicle* prior to 1093, especially in the account of the discovery of the relics of Theodosius in 1091. He is, in fact, inclined to the opinion that Nestor was the author of the whole passage, and was entrusted with the search for the relics on account of his authorship of the *Life of Theodosius*.

The functions of Sylvester in the preparation of his text under orders from Vladimir Monomakh, Shakhmatov believes to have been relatively restricted, and mainly confined to editorial corrections. He thus eliminated from the text whatever was unfriendly to Vladimir, and inserted many items of a partisan nature. Shakhmatov thus attributes to Sylvester the continuation of the opening chronological table to the death of Svyatopolk (1113). It will be remembered that Svyatopolk's participation in the conspiracy against Vasil'ko constitutes the gravest blot upon his character. Shakhmatov supposes that Nestor, being well disposed toward Svyatopolk, made an effort to minimize the latter's culpability by transferring most of the blame to David Igorevich. Sylvester, on the other hand, according to Shakhmatov's suggestion, had recourse to the narrative of Vasiliy, apparently the intimate and the confessor of Prince Vasil'ko himself, in order to reestablish the facts.

To the editor of the 1118 text, whom Shakhmatov supposes to have been a monk of the Crypt Monastery intimate with Vladimir Monomakh's son Mstislav, Prince of Novgorod, he attributes the insertion of the testament of Vladimir. It should be noted here that while the hypothetical 1118 redaction is classed by Shakhmatov as the prototype of the Hypatian and related texts, it is not in the texts of this redaction that the *Testament* is preserved, but in the Laurentian redaction, which obviously derives from the Sylvestrian tradition. Shakhmatov is thus obliged to take the position that the *Testament* was interpolated into the Laurentian from a text descended from the 1118 redaction.

Shakhmatov, in his Introduction to the *Povest'*[13] which is summarized in the foregoing paragraphs, thus carries the textual history of the *Povest'* back to a hypothetical compilation dating from 1095. This work does not, however, embody Shakhmatov's conclusions as to the evolution of chronicle literature prior to this date, which he had already developed at length in his *Investigations*[14] The latter work sets forth his views on the beginnings of annalistic activities in Kiev and elsewhere. Shakhmatov believes that the establishment of the Kiev metropolitanate in 1039 inspired the composition, about the same date, of a chronicle text which he designates as the "most ancient Kiev compilation" (*drevněyshiy Kievskiy svod*). For the period prior to the principate of Vladimir I, the compiler, in Shakhmatov's opinion, used for his sources local traditions preserved in folk-songs and *bÿlinÿ*, together with a few written narratives which dealt with Russian saints and events of ecclesiastical interest. From the reign of Yaroslav, the narrative is believed by Shakhmatov to rest on personal recollections of recent events, and from this point, Shakhmatov views the 1039 text as a thoroughly reliable source. The production of this work did not, he thinks, lead to any systematic annalistic activity at Kiev, but in 1073, according to Shakhmatov's conclusions, a continuation of the 1039 text was prepared in the Crypt Monastery. This second text Shakhmatov designates as the "first compilation of the Crypt Monastery" (*pervÿy Kievopecherskiy svod*). He considers its earlier portion to have been mainly a copy of the 1039 text, to which was perhaps added the account of Vladimir Yaroslavich's expedition against Byzantium (1043). The later section, beginning with the account of the death of Yaroslav (1054), represents, according to Shakhmatov, an independent production of the compiler based on personal recollection and contemporary data. In view of the respectable amount of material dealing with the distant colony of Tmutorakan' and with Rostislav, its prince, Shakhmatov attributes the preparation of the 1073 text to Nikon, a member of the Crypt community, who is known from another source[15] to have spent some time in that area, where he founded a monastery, returning to Kiev about 1067. Shakhmatov thus attributes to Nikon the authorship of the article on the foundation of the Crypt Monastery appearing in the present Laurentian text under 1051. He considers, however, that in the text of 1073 this article appeared under 1062, the year in which the monastery was actually founded, though in later redactions the item was shifted back to 1051 to connect it with the death of the metropolitan Hilarion, and in deference to the tradition elsewhere set forth that the monastery was founded, not under Izyaslav but somewhat earlier, in the principate of Yaroslav the Wise. The redaction of 1073 was later supplemented by the familiar account of the death of Theodosius and by annalistic accretions which carry its content to 1093. Then, about 1095, was prepared Shakhmatov's so-called "primary compilation" (*nachal'nÿy svod*), the immediate basis for the various redactions of the *Povest'* as he classes them. Shakhmatov considers this compilation of 1095 to have been the first chronicle text of general Russian content, since he endeavors to show that it embodied not only previous compilations originating in Kiev, but also elements from the annals which he believes were kept at Novgorod during the eleventh century, and was likewise influenced by early Russian native and translated literature of the period.

A thorough critical treatment of Shakhmatov's views would seriously exceed the practicable compass of the present introduction. They rest upon a remarkable knowledge of all published texts and of numerous MSS which a foreign student can scarcely hope to equal. On the other hand, it is apparent that they are at best a tissue of highly tempting hypotheses based upon a subjective and sometimes temperamental interpretation, not only of extant redactions, but also of the events they record. Shakhmatov's method, reduced to its lowest terms, consists in working back through a series of hypothetical intermediates to an equally hypothetical archetype. In the presence of a consistent tradition as to the form of the *Povest'* attested by two MSS of fair age, which give a fully adequate basis for the assumption that we are dealing here with a single homogeneous work, somewhat contracted or expanded according to local preferences wherever it was recopied as an introduction to local annals, Shakhmatov's efforts to establish the existence of a complicated family of earlier texts fails to carry entire conviction. As Professor Brückner remarked,[16] practically no Old-Russian text of any importance is lost; it is thus extraordinary that all annalistic texts prior to 1116, if they really existed, should have disappeared save for the remnants restored by the ingenious and arbitrary mutilation of those that are preserved.

Professor V. M. Istrin's method of dealing with the *Povest'* problem is intimately related to that of Professor Shakhmatov, though his conclusions differ radically from those of his predecessor.[17] Istrin has devoted a large amount of investigation to the Slavic translations of Byzantine historical works (particularly Malalas and Georgius Hamartolus), and his views are naturally tinged by this specialization. He rejects entirely Shakhmatov's hypothetical primitive text of 1039. While Shakhmatov had presupposed a Bulgarian model for this text,[18] Istrin enlarges upon the reaction of foreign influence on the origins of the Russian annals. According to Istrin, a considerable body of Greek clergy must have accompanied the Greek metropolitan to Kiev about 1037. They brought with them, he believes, numerous Greek works, and, as noted in the *Povest'* itself, the second half of Yaroslav's principate (1037-1054) was characterized by increased literary activity, concentrated principally upon translation. Among the works thus translated, in Istrin's view, was the *Chronicle* of Georgius Hamartolus with its continuation to 948. In consequence of its length and the difficulties of certain theological and dogmatic sections of the text, Istrin considers that this work speedily gave place (about 1050) to an abbreviated general history based largely on Hamartolus, and known as the *Chronograph* "according to the long text" (*po velikomu izlozheniyu*). This *Chronograph,* Istrin believes, was speedily supplemented by accounts of purely Russian events. The chronological framework for the latter was thus supplied by the Byzantine originals, which reckoned the dates by years from the Creation, as is the case in the *Povest'*. Istrin holds that the purely Russian material in the *Chronograph* was based partly on tradition and partly on written sources. This Russian material covered the calling of the Varangian princes, the accounts of Oleg's and Igor's raids on Constantinople (the latter being supplemented from Hamartolus and other Greek sources), and the narrative of Vladimir's conversion, which concluded the *Chronograph*. About 1060, after the death of Yaroslav, Istrin maintains that the Russian portions of the narrative were divorced from the items of purely Byzantine reference, and thus arose the first redaction of the *Povest'*, which Istrin considers to have embodied a supplementary account of the principates of Vladimir I and Yaroslav the Wise, along with an introduction designating 852 as the starting point of Russian history, while the chronological table showed the death of Yaroslav as the concluding point of the narrative. The omission of Byzantine items not vitally connected with Russian history resulted, in Istrin's opinion, in the appearance of the so-called "empty years", which occur with tolerable frequency in the first half of the *Povest'* as it stands. Such, in Istrin's view, was the primitive text of the *Povest'*, closely resembling the extant Laurentian and Hypatian redactions as far as it went, and omitting only the extensive introduction now preceding the items for 852 in both these redactions and the lengthy account, now appearing as of 1051, which covers the foundation of the Crypt Monastery.

During the remainder of the eleventh century, the *Povest'* was further extended, Istrin believes, by the entry of current events not necessarily added at regular intervals. Then, at the beginning of the second decade of the twelfth century, the prototype of the *Povest'*, with its various continuations, was again carried forward to the death of Svyatopolk. Istrin considers that the author of this new and complete text was Nestor, who added the introduction, in the preparation of which he used the full text of Hamartolus. He also had at his disposal certain other literary works, such as the *Revelations* of Pseudo-Methodius and Vasiliy's account of the blinding of Vasil'ko. Sylvester's function, in Istrin's opinion, was limited to the preparation, in 1116, of a word-for-word copy of the Nestorian text. Istrin considers that Nestor's original retained in the Crypt Monastery, subsequently underwent the usual continuations and thus became the Kiev Chronicle now represented by the Hypatian redaction. Istrin assumes that Sylvester's copy eventually lost its last pages, while his signature was written either on a special page or on the binding. This loss of a few pages accounts, in Istrin's view, for the conclusion of the Laurentian redaction in 1110 and for the retention of the fuller text for that year in the Hypatian redaction. According to Istrin, Nestor did not introduce his name into the text of the *Povest'* because he was not its author, but simply its continuator, and for the same reason Sylvester made no mention of Nestor in his own copy. The *Povest'* thus remained anonymous, though the tradition of Nestor's annalistic activities was preserved, and took definite form in the *Paterikon,* being likewise reflected in the appearance of Nestor's name in the *Khlebnikovskiy* text.

In the absence of more substantial countervailing testimony than the hypotheses of Shakhmatov and Istrin, the *Povest'* should for the present be viewed as a homogeneous work, the product of one author, preserved with minor variants in one generally prevalent redaction, and dating from about 1113. The fact that all eyewitness material follows the year 1050 renders it both possible and probable that one author only was occupied in its preparation, which extended over a period of one or more decades. The analogy of the chronological arrangement with and the important excerpts from Greek annalistic literature known to the compiler in translation indicates the likelihood that the imitation of Greek models was one of the principal factors in its production.[19] The constant emphasis laid, in the portion of the *Povest'* from 1051 forward, upon the development of the Crypt Monastery, together with the personal references in the accounts of Theodosius, creates a strong presumption that the author of the text as we have it was a respected member of that community. While the thirteenth-century tradition of Nestorian authorship cannot be wholly disregarded, the divergencies between Nestor's own works and the content of the *Chronicle* preclude its acceptance, and suggest the possibility that the similarity in subject-matter between Nestor's writings and certain sections of the *Povest'* inspired his association with the latter. It is entirely probable that some brief native records of historical events (particularly of ecclesiastical interest) may have been kept in Kiev as early as the last decade of the tenth century after the conversion of Vladimir. The Greek literary influence associated by Istrin in a considerably exaggerated degree with the establishment of the metropolitanate in 1037 may, in connection with the *Povest'*, be admitted to the extent that familiarity with Greek annalistic works may well have inspired a monk of some learning to collect such early records and traditions as he could find, which, combined with supplementary material from Greek sources and—for the last century covered by the *Povest'*—with personal observations and the recollections of contemporaries, compose the *Povest'* in its present form. In fact, if the sources and chronology of the *Povest'* are subjected to close analysis, such definition of its origin is inevitable. The presence in the text of the narrative of the blinding of Vasil'ko and of the *Testament* of Vladimir Monomakh in no wise weakens this conception of its character. We have no means of determining the history of the text from the moment of its compilation to the date of the Laurentian MS. (1377). The presence of extensive variants in the *Povest'* wherever it appears as a component of later annalistic compilations would imply that the chances for modification by successive scribes were extremely broad.

The Laurentian redaction as it stands appears (apart from the *Testament* of Vladimir Monomakh and some curtailment at its close) to reproduce the compilation of an otherwise unknown inmate of the Crypt Monastery who was, for his time, well educated and personally familiar with the course of political events from the later years of Yaroslav the Wise through the first decade of the twelfth century. The function of Sylvester in the evolution of the text is not altogether clear. It is manifestly impossible, however, to identify him with the original compiler of the *Povest'*. All that may be said with any degree of certainty is that the Laurentian redaction appears to derive from a prototype prepared by Sylvester, perhaps for his personal use or for the information of his own monastic community, from the primitive compilation originating in the Crypt Monastery. However interesting more detailed hypotheses on the authorship of the *Povest'* may be, none of those so far presented can be justified either from the *Povest'* itself or from any other contemporary evidence. In the complete absence of direct testimony on this subject, conjectures of this nature constitute but a relatively insignificant contribution to the study of this venerable monument.

SOURCES

Reference has already been made to the presence in the *Povest'* of numerous excerpts or reminiscences of Georgius Hamartolus, which appear in special profusion.[20] This Byzantine chronicle, dating from the ninth century, was carried by its author to 842, but from that point the text is derived from another author, Symeon the Logothete. This continuation extends to 948 so as to end with the death of Romanus Lecapenus on the island of Proti on July 15 of that year.

There is some difference of opinion as to the circumstances under which this work was first translated into Old Slavic. Istrin holds that the original translation was made toward the middle of the eleventh century by a Russian schoolman, though it is more probably a Bulgarian product.[21] The exact birthplace of the Slavic version or versions is of minor importance for the present study, since the fact is clear that such a translation existed before the first decade of the twelfth century and was extensively drawn upon by the compiler of the *Povest'* either directly and verbatim or in modified form through various secondary chronographs.

The sections of the *Povest'* either based wholly upon, or suggesting reminiscences of, Georgius Hamartolus are given below.

Date	Subject	Greek Text (von Muralt), page	Slavic Text (Istrin, I), page
	(1) Apportionment of the earth	39	58
	(2) Tower of Babel	36-39	57-58
	(3) Customs of aliens	26-28	49-50
858	(4) Conversion of Bulgarians	732	508
866	(5) Raid by Ascold and Dir	736-737	511
868	(6) Accession of Basil	752	519

887	(7)	Accessions of Leo and Alexander..	766,794	527,540
902	(8)	Leo incites Magyars against Bulgars	772	529
911	(9)	Comet in west	797	541
912	(10)	Apollonius of Tyana	334-335	305-306
913	(11)	Accession of Constantine son of Leo	799	542
914	(12)	Symeon at Constantinople	802	544
915	(13)	Greeks win Pecheneg allies	804-805	545-546
920	(14)	Accession of Romanus	816	552
929	(15)	Symeon ravages Thrace	824	557
934	(16)	Magyars attack Constantinople	840	566
941	(17)	Igor's Greek expedition	841-842	567
942	(18)	Symeon attacks Croats	830	560
943	(19)	Second Magyar attack	844	568
1064	(20)	Portents	208,281,540, 554,653	200,262,421, 428,479

The Chronicle of Georgius Hamartolus is twice specifically referred to as a source in the *Povest'*; first in the discussion of the various alien races: *glagolet Georgiy v lětopisan'i* ("Georgius says in his Chronicle") and second, under 852: *yako pishetsya v lětopisan'i Grech'stěm* ("as is written in the Greek chronicle").

Among other borrowings from Greek sources is the lengthy Creed taught to Vladimir I. This was first identified by Sukhomlinov,[22] who reprints both the Greek text, dating from the ninth century, and an Old-Russian text deriving from a prototype written in 1073. The Creed is thus obviously one of the earliest Greek works translated into Slavic. Its author was Michael Syncellus, an associate of the metropolitan Thomas of Jerusalem, and friend of St. Theodore of Studion (died in 826).[23]

Two additional items of Greek origin are presented by two reminiscences of the *Revelations* of Pseudo-Methodius of Patara on the Ishmaelites and the unclean peoples inclosed by Alexander the Great in the mountains of the north. These reminiscences constitute, in fact, the earliest references in all Slavic literature to a text of which the influence in western Europe was well-nigh universal.[24]

Apart, however, from the echoes of Georgius Hamartolus, the largest body of obviously extraneous material appearing in the *Povest'* is the account of alien religions, a critique of these faiths, and a synopsis of Biblical history supposedly supplied to Vladimir by the Greek missionary. Complete agreement does not as yet prevail as to the source of this material, which has been connected by most investigators with the so-called *Paleya*. This term is, of course, a slightly modified form of παλαιά after which διαθήκη should be supplied. By the *Paleya*,[25] in Old-Russian literature, is understood a synopsis of Old Testament history supplemented by material from apocryphal books and various interpretative accretions. The *Paleya* shows pronounced hostility to Jews and Mohammedans, and thus belongs to the literature of propaganda. As there was no complete translation of the Bible available in Russia till the fifteenth century, this work based largely on the *Pentateuch, Joshua, Judges, Ruth, Kings,* and *Chronicles,* possessed particular importance. The best extant text is that written at Kolomna in 1406.[26] As Sukhomlinov pointed out in 1856 (*op. cit.,* pp. 60 ff), the major portion of the discussion of foreign religions found in the *Povest'* occurs also in the *Paleya*. The same source is indicated for the synopsis of Biblical history, in which departures from the Old Testament account may, for the most part, be explained from the *Paleya*, though the compiler of the *Povest'* appears also to have had before him certain books of the Bible in their full text.[27] Of the foreign material contained in the narrative of Vladimir's conversion, the critique of alien faiths and the synopsis of Biblical history are thus derived from the *Paleya*, while the source of the Creed has been defined above. There remains for explanation the reference to the oecumenical councils. Discussions of these councils occur elsewhere in Old-Russian literary monuments, and specifically in the *Sbornik* copied in 1073 for Prince Svyatoslav of Kiev (son of Yaroslav the Wise) from a Bulgarian original, where an enumeration of the councils follows immediately upon the Creed of Michael Syncellus and, with few exceptions, mentions the same participants in the councils as are detailed in the *Povest'*. Seven councils are also described in scattered passages of Georgius Hamartolus.[28] A detailed account presenting close analogy with the *Povest'* narrative likewise occurs in an epistle of the Patriarch Photius to Boris, Prince of Bulgaria.[29] It is not possible to attach the *Povest'* account of these councils directly to any one of these originals, but it is obvious that plenty of basis in translations from the Greek was available at the time of its composition.

The compiler of the *Povest'* could hardly consider his work as complete without reference to SS. Cyril (Constantine) and Methodius, the proto-apostles to the Slavs. His account is based upon the so-called Pannonian *Life* of Methodius,[30] with modifications of later Bulgarian origin. It is at variance with the accepted version of the events described in disregarding the implications of Rostislav's application to Michael III for missionaries and in associating with this request his nephew Svatopluk, as well as Kotsel, the contemporary prince of Pannonia. Svatopluk, in fact, was allied at the time with the German element in Moravia, and therefore by no means a consistent friend of the Slavic liturgy. Constantine and Methodius first came into contact with Kotsel on their journey of 867 from Moravia to Rome, where Constantine died on February 14, 869. Kotsel subsequently requested the Pope to name Methodius Bishop of Pannonia. There is thus no basis for the statement in the *Povest'* that Constantine continued his missionary activity in Bulgaria, though the influence of Methodius and his disciples was eventually strong in that state. The *Povest'* also makes no distinction between the first contact of both brothers with Rome and Methodius' later journey thither during the pontificate of John VIII. The tradition supplied by the *Povest'*, on the basis of the *Pannonian Legend,* that Methodius translated the previously unrendered sections of the Bible between March 20 and October 6 of one year is generally regarded as apocryphal. It is, on the other hand, conceded that Constantine, at some early stage of his mission, did invent a Slavic alphabet. This was not the so-called Cyrillic alphabet, a derivative of which is still used by Russians, Ruthenes, Serbs, and Bulgarians, but the more curious and difficult *Glagolitsa,* devised from ninth-century Greek cursive with some supplementary letters from other sources.[31]

The only documentary material included in the *Povest'* consists of the various treaties with the Byzantine Empire, and the *Testament* and the *Letter* of Vladimir Monomakh. The textual and archival history of the treaties of 907, 912, 945, and 971 is completely obscure, and it has never been satisfactorily determined whether the copies preserved in the *Povest'* represent Old-Russian texts of the treaties made when they were negotiated, or whether they are translations afterward prepared from Greek originals which subsequently came to light in Kiev itself. It is not likely that the Russian princes of the tenth century, who were by no means superior to Scandinavian freebooters elsewhere on the Continent, attached any grave significance to these scraps of paper, and the fact that there is but one Greek allusion to them would indicate that to the Byzantine authorities they were more a gesture than a contract. The obscurity, the grammatical uncertainty, and the general disregard of style shown by these treaty-texts lead to the conclusion that they were translated at a moment when they had no further value except as casual relics of the past.[32]

The *Testament* (literally *Pouchenie,* "instruction") of Vladimir Monomakh, contained solely in the Laurentian MS. under the year

1096, is in itself a literary monument of some consequence. While Shakhmatov supposed that the *Testament* was interpolated into one of his hypothetical redactions of the *Povest'* during the second decade of the twelfth century, it would appear intrinsically more probable that it was preserved among Vladimir's descendants in the northern principalities and injected into the text of the *Povest'* at a fairly late date.[33] In fact, the *Testament* seems to have been written toward the close of Vladimir's life, in view of its references to his advanced age and decrepitude, and, if we accept the tempting emendation of $\overline{ig}$ (13; L², 247) to $\overline{ng}$ (53), purports to outline his active career during a period of more than half a century. The most reasonable explanation for its appearance in the Laurentian MS. is provided by Istrin's suggestion that it was preserved, along with Vladimir's *Letter* to Oleg and the *Prayer* attributed to him, among his descendants at Suzdal', where it was found by the scribe Lawrence or one of his precursors, who arbitrarily attached the *Pouchenie* and other documents to the narrative for the year 1096 because it was clear that the *Letter* to Oleg was associated with the events there recounted.[34]

The lengthy account of the blinding of Vasil'ko included in the *Povest'* under the year 1097 occupies a somewhat exceptional position. The author mentions himself by name as Vasiliy, and includes in his narrative events which are briefly recorded in the purely chronological items of the *Povest'* under 1098, 1099, and 1100. The narrative of Vasiliy has apparently exercised some influence on the form of the item for 1100, since both end with the same statement that to David the son of Igor' was assigned the domain of Dorogobuzh, where he died, while the city of Vladimir was given to Svyatopolk's son Yaroslav. Of the personality of Vasiliy so much is clear: he was an intimate of Vasil'ko, possibly his confessor, and was probably a native of Galicia or of Volhynia, in view of his familiarity with the geography of both and particularly of the country around Przemyśl. The motives leading Vasiliy to describe at some length the misfortune of his patron, and the circumstances governing the insertion of his account in the *Povest'*, are matters for conjecture only. His narrative was prepared, in any case, after David's death, which occurred May 25, 1112 (H³, 270). In view of the imputations against Svyatopolk, it is not impossible that Vasiliy may not have written until after that prince's death as well (April 16, 1113; H³, 271). Istrin (*loc. cit.*, p. 243) has suggested that Vasiliy's account became known in Kiev contemporaneously with the accession of Vladimir Monomakh, whom Vasiliy depicts in a favorable light, and that the compiler of the *Povest'*, writing at the beginning of

Vladimir's principate, was able to use this narrative very effectively in his compilation, though he retained his year-by-year narrative for the period 1098-1100. It may also be suggested that the detailed account of Vladimir's reaction to the news of the blinding of Vasil'ko may very well be an interpolation in Vasiliy's account.

Apart from the Greek materials employed and the sections of the *Povest'* which, like the *Testament* of Vladimir Monomakh and the narrative of Vasiliy are deliberate reproductions of extraneous documents, the *Povest'* also stands in close relationship to certain extant native Russian literary works which are preserved independently of the *Chronicles*. Among these is the *Discourse on the Law of Moses and Grace through Christ,* attributed to the Metropolitan Hilarion and thus dating from the middle of the tenth century.[35] This work was apparently inspired by contemporary discussions regarding the canonization of Vladimir I, which revolved principally around the question whether the adoption of Christianity by this prince resulted primarily from Greek influence or from Vladimir's own laudable initiative. The *Slovo* is important for the *Povest'* in view of the fact that the Biblical quotations put in the mouth of the Greek missionary and beginning at "Hosea was thus the first" and extending as far as "Then Vladimir inquired", are not taken directly from the Bible, but borrowed bodily from the *Slovo* (Sreznevsky, pp. 45 ff.). The answer of the missionary to Vladimir's question regarding Christ's crucifixion is also influenced by Hilarion's discourse.

Another early work associated with the *Povest'* is the *Memory and Eulogy of Vladimir (Pamyat' i Pokhvala Vladimiru)*, attributed to the monk James, who mentions himself in the text as its author. It differs from the *Povest'*, however, in the essential point that the baptism of Vladimir is reported as occurring prior to the prince's expedition against Kherson and his marriage to the Princess Anna. This variation from the *Povest'* account would seem to rest upon an earlier tradition, while the later narrative of Vladimir's baptism in Kherson appears to have evolved naturally from the information available regarding his attack upon that city, his negotiations with the Eastern emperors for the hand of their sister, and the arrival of the Princess Anna with a numerous suite, including a goodly array of ecclesiastics. In consequence of the confusion caused by Shakhmatov's theories concerning lost chronicle redactions preceding the *Povest'* in its extant form, the relation of the *Povest'* account to the various early biographies of Vladimir cannot yet be viewed as satisfactorily determined.[36]

A problem of similar complexity is presented by the comparison of the *Povest'* account of SS. Boris and Gleb with the *Life* of these saints by Nestor and the additional work concerning them attributed to the monk James.[37] The source-relationship between these three works has never been determined with entire certainty. Shakhmatov (*Razÿskanya*, p. 34) emphatically rejects the idea that the *Povest'* narrative is based upon the account of the monk James, on the ground that, apart from the facts which it recounts in common with the *Povest'*, the latter contains nothing but rhetorical effusions. He therefore considers it superfluous to search for any other source for the Jacobean *Life* except the *Povest'*. Sukhomlinov (*op. cit.*, p. 84) had however, considered the *Povest'* account to be an abbreviation of the Jacobean *Life*. Shakhmatov's contention that James's work is based upon the *Povest'* can be valid only if we admit his thesis that a chronicle text existed in some form prior to 1100, since the monk James, concerning whom next to nothing is known, is usually believed to have lived during the second half of the eleventh century. On the other hand, in spite of the discrepancies already noted between the Nestorian *Life* and the *Povest'* (*supra*), the general resemblance in content and arrangement between the two leads naturally to the conclusion that the Nestorian *Life*, written in all probability in the eighties of the eleventh century, was known and used by the compiler of the *Povest'*, who supplemented Nestor's information with data derived from other sources. Shakhmatov, however (*op. cit.*, pp. 65, 66), rejects this conclusion in favor of the assumption that both the Nestorian *Life* and the *Povest'* used the same earlier source, which, in harmony with his general theory, he considers to have been a primitive chronicle text of the earlier eleventh century.

Reference should finally be made to the discourse under the year 1068 on the religious significance of barbarian incursions, shown by I. I. Sreznevsky to be derived from the *Zlatostruy*, an anthology of the writings of John Chrysostom prepared by or for Tsar Symeon of Bulgaria from a Greek original.[38]

Apart from these textual reminiscences of Greek and earlier Russian authors, the compiler of the *Povest'*, in combining his scanty material for the first century of his narrative, included a series of early traditions of considerable interest. Prominent among these is the legend of Kiy and his brethren, followed by that of the calling of the Varangians, the occupation of Kiev by Ascold and Dir,[39] and the elimination of the latter by Oleg. This prince is himself surrounded by an aura of legend, as is apparent from the account of his death by the bite of a serpent which issued forth from the skull of his dead charger, against which his soothsayers had warned him.[40] Further legendary material may be discerned in the *Povest'* account of the death of Igor' and Olga's complicated procedure of revenge upon the Derevlians.[41] Popular tradition also plays a distinguishable role in the narratives concerning Svyatoslav I and, in a slighter degree, St. Vladimir and Svyatopolk I.[42] The traditional nature of the introductory account of the migrations of the Slavs and their contacts with Huns and Avars is also apparent. From the accession of Yaroslav, however, the *Povest'* rests largely on the personal reminiscences of contemporaries, and thus has the merits and defects of eyewitness narrative.

CHRONOLOGY

It was early discovered that the chronology of the *Povest'* opens with an error. Michael III did not begin his reign in 852, but on January 21, 842. The origin of this initial error as to Michael's accession has been satisfactorily established by Shakhmatov,[43] who points out that, while the compiler of the *Povest'* could find mention both of the accession of Michael and of the first Russian raid upon Constantinople in Georgius Hamartolus, the only chronographic work available in translation in Russia at the beginning of the twelfth century was the Χρονογραφικὸν Σύντομον of Nichephorus the Patriarch (died in 829). The chronological table included in the *Povest'* is, in fact, derived from this source. The compiler of the *Povest'*, taking Nicephorus' erroneous figure of 318 for the interval separating the Nativity from the accession of Constantine the Great (actually A.D. 313), added to it, first, 530—the elapsed time given by Nicephorus between Constantine the Great and Theophilus—and then 12—the number of years of Theophilus' reign. He thus secured a total of 860, which would accordingly be the year of the Christian era in which on the basis of this computation, Michael came to the throne. Adding to this figure the number 5500 which Nicephorus, following the Alexandrian era, gives as the number of years from Creation to Nativity, the compiler thus arrived at the year 6360 from Creation. If this be properly reduced to the reckoning of the Christian era by subtracting 5508, the result is the erroneous year 852.[44]

Shakhmatov also devoted another highly ingenious study to the chronology of the *Povest'* through 945, which, though written on the basis of his earlier hypotheses as to the primitive versions of the *Povest'*, still possesses marked value.[45] As Shakhmatov points out,[46] the only variations in the chronology among the various extant texts of the

Povest' occur prior to 945. In the present study, the position has been taken that the *Povest'* as we have it is a homogeneous work, the compilation of which occupied a period of several years toward the close of the eleventh and the opening of the twelfth century. Even a cursory examination of the text shows, moreover, that the last long series of "empty years" occurs just prior to the narrative of Svyatoslav's campaigns beginning with 964. In fact, the material contained in the *Povest'* between 945 and this date, relating to Igor's campaign against the Derevlians and the picturesque revenge of Olga, is largely legendary in nature. It is thus during the first century of his narrative that the compiler had the greatest difficulty in composing a connected account with the limited material at his disposal, so that he was obliged to depend almost entirely upon Byzantine sources for the framework upon which to hang the scanty data preserved by native Russian tradition. This observation is clearly corroborated by the fact that the dates in the *Povest'* prior to 945 fall into two classes: (a) those which could be derived from Greek sources or computed from data contained in the latter; and (b) those relating to Russian events, which are conventionally inserted among the Greek data at points which appeared logical to the compiler.

In view of the extensive excerpts from the expanded text of Georgius Hamartolus occurring in the *Povest'*, but exclusively from its beginning to 943, it may be safely assumed that this work was the compiler's basic source for this period, particularly since the *Chronograph* of Nicephorus was utilizable only to its conclusion at the accession of Michael III. The compiler could thus derive from Hamartolus the date upon which Romanus Lecapenus crowned his wife Theodora, viz., January 6, 6428, and therefore A.D. 920. He could also conclude from the passage immediately preceding that Romanus was named Caesar in the same year, viz., on September 24, 6428, or A.D. 920.[47] With the latter date as a starting point, it was a simple matter for the compiler of the *Povest'* to compute the dates for the accessions of Leo the Wise and of Basil the Macedonian. Hamartolus (von Muralt, p. 799) states that the youthful Constantine VII Porphyrogenitus, after the death of Leo the Wise, ruled seven years with his guardians and his mother, after being associated one year as a co-Emperor with Leo's brother Alexander (*ibid.*, p. 795). The death of Leo the Wise is thus correctly dated as of 912. Hamartolus records (*ibid.*, p. 766) that Leo's reign lasted twenty-five years and eight months. By using twenty-six years as a computing basis, the compiler thus obtained 886-887 (6394-6395) as the date of Leo's accession, and reading (von Muralt, p. 752) that Basil the Macedonian ruled for nineteen years, he thus deduced that Basil came to the throne in 867-868 (6375-6376). Curiously enough, if the compiler had continued with this method, he would probably have obtained the correct date (842) for the accession of Michael III, but he appears to have contented himself with the original erroneous figure derived from Nicephorus. Beginning thus with the initial date of 852, the compiler found in Hamartolus (*ibid.*, p. 732, l. 15, variant), the attribution of Michael's expedition against the Bulgarians to the fourth year of his reign, and therefore made mention of this event as of 853-858 (6361-6366). The attack upon Constantinople by Ascold and Dir, of which the historical original took place in 860,[48] is set by the compiler in the fourteenth year of Michael's reign, i.e. 866 (6374). This appears to be a case of purely arbitrary fixation. The compiler may conceivably have had before him a text of Hamartolus dating the Rus' raid in the ninth year of Michael.[49] With Michael's accession fixed in 852, the ninth year of this emperor's reign would have brought the date of the raid to 861, which would have conflicted with the date chosen for the legendary "calling of the princes." The compiler thus seems to have moved the raid sufficiently forward to allow the evolution of the traditional process by which the Scandinavian Russes were supposed to have become established.[50]

The date 869 (6387), to which is assigned the conversion of the Bulgarians, appears to be derived, not from Hamartolus, where the conversion is connected with Michael's expedition (dated in the *Povest'* as of 858), but from some source giving the death of St. Cyril (Constantine) as having occurred in 869, which year the compiler took as the date of the Bulgarian adoption of Christianity.

The date 902 (6410), in which Leo the Wise is reported to have used the Magyars as his allies against the Bulgarians, is explained by reading a paragraph number into the text, since in the Slavic translation of Hamartolus (Istrin, 1, 529), the numeral $\overline{d}$ (4) precedes the paragraph, and was read by the compiler of the *Povest'* as the year of Leon's reign. In the two items of 914-915 (6422-6423) concerning Symeon of Bulgaria, the date is derived from an adjacent item in Hamartolus (von Muralt, p. 805: «Σεπτεμβρίῳ δὲ μηνὶ ἰνδικτιῶνος γ', Παγκρατούκας ὁ Ἀρμένιος τὴν Ἀδριανούπολιν τῷ Συμεὼν παρέδωκε»). The compiler identified the third indiction as 915 (6423), probably because the year of Romanus' succession, his basic date (Sept. 919 or 6428), is referred to in Hamartolus as the eighth indiction. Since the first expedition of Symeon is mentioned in Hamartolus (*ibid.*, p. 802) as having taken place in August the compiler of the *Povest'* simply referred it to the previous year (914). The year 929 (6437), given as the date of a third raid by the Bulgarian prince is manifestly wrong, since Symeon died on May 27, 927. The error is due to the text of Hamartolus (von Muralt, p. 824: «Σεπτεμβρίῳ δὲ μηνὶ ἰνδικτιῶνος β' Συμεὼν ὁ ἄρχων Βουλγαρίας πανστρατὶ κατὰ Κωνσταντινουπόλεως ἐκστρατεύει,» where β' [2] is erroneously written for ιβ' [12], i.e. the second indiction [929-6437] for the twelfth [924-6432]). The Russian compiler quite logically figured that if 6428 (920) was the eighth indiction, the next following second indiction should be 6437 (929). Symeon, as it happens, actually died in the fifteenth indiction (927). Similarly, the date 934 (6442) to which is attributed the Magyar attack upon Constantinople, is figured back from the number of the indiction given by Hamartolus (von Muralt, p. 840: «ἐγένετο δὲ ἐκστρατεία πρώτη τῶν Τούρκων κατὰ 'Ρωμαίων ἰνδ, ζ' 'Απρ. μηνί»). The next seventh indiction after 920 (6428) would thus be 934 (6442). In the same way, the date of Igor's expedition of 941 (6449) is derived from the indiction in Hamartolus (von Muralt, p. 841: «'Ιουνίῳ μηνὶ ια' κατέπλευσαν οἱ 'Ρῶς,» without indiction, but cf. Istrin, 1, 567: *Iounya zhe mtsa ii dn' di* [14] *indik priplou Rous'*). The erroneous date supplied for Symeon' death (6450-942) goes back to the mistake in the text of Hamartolus applying to the *Povest'* date of 929 which, as has just been shown, should be 924. The death of Symeon is correctly referred by Hamartolus to the fifteenth indiction (von Muralt, p. 830: «Μαίῳ δὲ μηνὶ κς' ἰνδικτιῶνος ιε, Συμεὼν ὁ ἄρχων Βουλγαρίας ἐτελεύτησε»). The Russian scribe argued that if the last second indiction was 929 (6437), the next fifteenth indiction would be 942 (6450), though actually the previous fifteenth indiction was the correct one for his purposes 927 (6435). Finally, the date of the second Magyar advance upon Constantinople is also supplied from Hamartolus (von Muralt, p 844: «'Ινδικτιῶνι δὲ α', 'Απριλλίῳ μηνὶ ἐπῆλθον πάλιν οἱ Τοῦρκοι μετὰ πλείστης δυνάμεως»), since the next first indiction was naturally 943 (6451). All dates thus referring to items derived from Greek sources are now accounted for except the treaties of 907, 912, and 945, the dates of which are generally assumed to be derived from the texts of these instruments themselves (though that of 945 has no date).

The actual extent of the subject-matter with which the compiler of the *Povest'* was working as far as 945 must be regarded as relatively limited. The native written sources for this period were obviously nil, and legends apparently very scanty. The early traditions covering this epoch centre upon Rurik, the capture of Kiev by Oleg and his subjugation of the adjacent tribes, his Greek expedition, his mythical death (possibly derived from a Scandinavian source), and Igor's raids upon Constantinople. For the period following 945, there were available by the late eleventh century other literary accounts of Olga and her conversion, highly developed traditions and Greek sources concerning Svyatoslav, and a considerable body of material concerning Vladimir I. Where the compiler's ingenuity was principally required was thus in the course of the first century of his narrative. We may suppose that the names of Rurik and his kin, of Askold and Dir, and of Oleg and Igor' survived in popular legend at Kiev in somewhat the same fashion as the heroes of the later *bÿlinÿ*. The problem for the chronicler was to extract from these fragmentary survivals the semblance of an historical account. While there may be some conceivable doubt whether Rurik and his relatives, and possibly Askold and Dir, were actual personages, Oleg and Igor' are soundly attested, presumably with dates, by the treaties with the Greeks in which they are mentioned by name. The chronicler could thus work back from these treaties and attach the subjects of tradition, wherever possible, to a related item of Greek chronology. Regarding Igor' he had no material apart from the fact that he was Rurik's son and the husband of Olga, that he made a treaty with the Greeks, and that he fought consistently with the Derevlians, in one fatal campaign against whom he met his death. From the treaty of 945, he was known to have been a contemporary of Romanus Lecapenus. If there were no traditions as to his age at marriage and accession, it was a simple matter to associate the latter event conventionally with the accession of Constantine VII (913), and date his marriage just before Oleg's Greek expedition of 907. Oleg himself is personally identified by the accords of both 907 and 911. Apart from these two instruments, the only traditions available concerning Oleg were that he was Rurik's kinsman and heir, that he obtained possession of Kiev by slaying the Varangian chiefs then dominating that centre, exacted tribute from the neighboring Slavic tribes, and finally met a curious death against which the soothsayers had warned him. His campaigns against three distinct tribes are used to account for three successive years after his capture of Kiev, and all these events, which the compiler either assumed or were traditionally reported to have occurred after the death of Rurik, are used to cover a stretch of seven years. Prior to Igor', nothing remains for which an approximate date could be fixed, apart from the "calling of the princes" and the raid upon Constantinople attributed to Askold and Dir. The former tradition and the implications of the Norman theory are discussed in some detail in the following section, while the latter, as recounted in the *Povest'* shows evidence of an attempt to combine a native tradition with a Greek historical account. Such material as survived in legend concerning the early migratory movements of the Slavs on Danube and Vistula could scarcely be reduced to even an elementary chronology.

An analysis of the chronological content of the *Povest'* prior to 945 indicates that the skeleton of dates is entirely derived from Greek sources, and that the content of surviving traditions has been overlaid upon this framework. The fragmentary nature of the extant native information covering the epoch preceding the middle of the tenth century points less to the composition of the primitive text suggested by Shakhmatov for 1039, when some survivors of the younger generation of Svyatoslav's day must still have been alive, than to a conscious literary effort made considerably later to preserve in the *Povest'* what few historical *débris* of the earlier period still remained at hand.

It may be assumed that from the conversion of Vladimir sufficient chronological material was preserved in ecclesiastical records to serve as a satisfactory basis for the compiler's work as far as the point where his own notes and reminiscences provided his chronological outline.

THE TRADITIONAL ORIGIN OF RUS'

Almost at its beginning, the *Povest'* introduces the problem of the original and prehistorical habitat of the Slavs, preserving the tradition that "for many years the Slavs had their abode by the Danube, where the Hungarian and the Bulgarian land now lies." From this locality, the *Povest'* represents them as expanding into the valley of the Bohemian Morava, and after attacks by the Vlakhs, it is likewise asserted that the Slavs moved north into the Vistula basin. Further movement is also reported toward the basin of the Dnieper and the area between the Pripet' and the Dvina, while the founders of Novgorod settled upon the shores of Lake Il'men'.

This narrative supplied for centuries the accepted view of Slavic origins until rivaled by the so-called Sarmatian theory, which linked the Slavs not with the Danube, but with the Don, and therefore placed them in close kinship with the Iranian Scyths and Sarmatians, who inhabited South Russia in classic times, or even with the Vandals and the Germans. It was, in fact, not until the time of Karamzin and Dobrovsky, at the beginning of the nineteenth century, that a more scientific conception arose, expressed fundamentally in the famous letter of Dobrovsky to Kopitar: "Mir beweisst alles dies, dass die Slaven keine Dacier, Geten, Thracier, Illyrier, Pannonier sind . . . Slaven sind Slaven, und haben nächste Verwandtschaft mit den Litauern. Also muss man sie hinter diesen suchen am oder hinter dem Dnieper." (V. Jagić, *Pis'ma Dobrovskogo i Kopitara* [Spb.,1885], p. 119). The evolution of a more accurate understanding of the early relations of the Slavs to other European peoples was subsequently furthered, during the early nineteenth century, by the progress of comparative philology from the publication of Bopp's celebrated *Vergleichende Grammatik* (1833). One hundred years ago, however, the Slavs were generally looked upon, even by many scholars of repute, as an intellectually inferior race of obscure Asiatic origin. As Hegel wrote, in his *Lectures on the Philosophy of History* (Jubiläumsausgabe [Stuttgart, 1928], XI, 447): "Sie [die Slaven] müssen aus unserer Betrachtung bleiben, weil sie ein Mittelwesen zwischen europäischem und asiatischem Geist bilden, und weil ihr Einfluss auf den Stufengang des Geistes nicht tätig und wichtig genug ist." This characteristic disparagement of the Slavs by contemporary scholars ranked among the chief motives which inspired the first fundamental work on Slavic origins, the *Starožitnosti Slovanské* of Josef Šafařik (1837), the starting point for all further investigations in this field. The progress of anthropological research and, more recently, of archaeological study, has since that day made vast contributions to our knowledge of the prehistoric movement and differentiation of the Slavic peoples.[51]

Though the tradition preserved in the *Povest'* very likely represents what such Russians of the early twelfth century as gave any thought to the matter believed concerning their racial antecedents, it is not in accord with other sources antedating the *Povest'* by two centuries or more, which indicate that, at the moment of the earliest recorded mediaeval contacts with peoples identifiable as Slavic, the habitat of the latter was considerably to the north of the Danube and even beyond the Carpathians. In fact, the prevailing modern view now places the original habitat of the Slavs at the beginning of Christian era in the vicinity of the upper Vistula, extending eastward to the middle Dnieper basin, but bounded to the northeast by the Lithuanians along the Niemen and the Dvina, while the Mazurian Lakes and swamps at first shut them off from the Baltic. Thus Pliny (*Hist. nat.*, IV, 97), Tacitus (*Germ.*, XLVI), and Ptolemy (*Geogr.*, III, 5, 7), all mention the Venedi (Οὐενέδαι), who are generally admitted to have been Slavs, as inhabiting the Vistula basin or the area to the east of the Germanic tribes and along the Baltic.

The *Povest'* nowhere refers to the dispersion of the Slavs throughout the Balkan peninsula, but makes fairly detailed mention of the Slavic tribes in what is now Polish and Russian territory. By the sixth and seventh centuries A.D., in fact, it is fairly well established that the Eastern Slavs had spread northward as far as Lake Il'men' and southeastward to the Don and the Sea of Azov. They were thus exposed to the inroads of the Huns, beginning in 375, who were followed a century later by the Bulgarians, and about 550 by the Avars, regarding all of whom dim memories are scantily preserved in the *Povest'*. It is, on the whole, curious that these reminiscences should have survived when, as far as the *Povest'* is concerned, all trace of the vast domains of the Slavic Antes or Antae, which figure prominently in historical accounts from the fourth century forward, should have been wiped out. From their headquarters along the Dniester, their raids of the sixth century across the Danube and into the Balkans constituted a serious menace to the Byzantine Empire.[52] They disappear from Byzantine sources after the first decade of the seventh century. Their sudden disappearance is better explained by the fact that from this period the Danube ceased to be the Byzantine frontier than by the supposition that a race referred to by Procopius as literally measureless (*Bell. got.*, IV, 4) should have been totally exterminated by the Avars, with whom they were in bitter conflict. A remote connection between the Antes and the *Povest'* narrative may be established through the mention in the latter of the Dulebians as oppressed by the Avars. This Slavic tribe, as the *Povest'* relates, had its seat upon the Bug, in Volhynia. Mas'ūdī, an Arabic writer of the tenth century, mentions the tradition that in ancient times the Volhynians dominated the rest of the Slavic tribes.[53] These accounts thus point to the existence of a Slavic federation centering in Volhynia, which disintegrated before the violence of the Avars toward the beginning of the seventh century.

According to the *Povest'*, the Slavic tribes on Russian soil were fairly well localized at an epoch which may be assumed to precede by a considerable interval the conventional opening date of Russian history. The Polyanians inhabited the open country on the west bank of the Dnieper between Teterev and Ros', with the Uluchians and the Tivercians as their southern neighbors toward Bug and Dniester. Across the Dnieper, on its eastern shore, between the Desna and the Sula, were settled the Severians, beyond whom, to the northwest, were found the Vyatichians on the southern course of the Oka. The Radimichians lay along the Sozh', and the Krivichians on the upper Volga and the watershed between the latter and the Dvina. North of the

Polyanians, the Dregovichians occupied the wooded country south of the Pripet', while beyond the Dregovichians to the northward, Lithuanian and Finnish tribes lay between Niemen and Dvina. The settlers about Lake Il'men' were the only ones to employ the characteristic name of Slavs (*Slověne*), which, though of uncertain derivation, was destined ultimately to extend to the whole race.[54]

The *Povest'* represents these tribes as bound by language and sense of common origin, but differentiated in customs, usages, and degree of civilization. "These Slavic tribes preserved their own customs, the law of their forefathers, and their traditions, each observing its own usages." The distinction is clearly drawn between the more advanced Polyanians, who lived in the area of the age-old civilization along the Dnieper trade-route, and the rough and brutal customs observed by the tribes of the periphery. No mention is made of their religious beliefs beyond the assertion that certain of the tribes (Radimichians, Vyatichians, and Severians) burned their dead, and preserved the ashes in urns set upon posts beside the highways. The first mention of the Slavic pantheon occurs, in fact, in connection with the treaty of 907, where we find that Oleg's men "swore by their weapons and by their god Perun, as well as by Volos, the god of cattle, and thus confirmed the treaty." The absence in the *Povest'* of any detailed information on the religious life of the early Slavs is readily explained by the supposition that only the pagan priests and initiates knew the details of such religious usages as prevailed, while the elimination of the pagan priesthood upon the introduction of Christianity prevented any diffusion of the beliefs and superstitions which these initiates possessed. There is also very little evidence that anything like a systematic Slavic pantheon ever existed.[55]

The Polyanians are described as a meek and unwarlike people, harassed by the Derevlians, and before the arrival of the Varangians reduced to tribute by the Khazars, who likewise acquired the domination over the Severians, the Vyatichians, and Radimichians.[56] This peaceful temper of the Slavic tribes made them an easy prey for more energetic interlopers. The *Povest'* preserves the tradition that the Slavic tribes of Northern Russia, in common with their Finnish neighbors, were for some time tributary to the "Varangians from beyond the sea." Stirred to revolt by the exactions of the latter the Slavs eventually rebelled, but were unable, according to the *Povest'* to arrive at any satisfactory inter-tribal understanding. To escape from the resulting confusion, the *Povest'* thus reports that they sent overseas "to the Varangian Russes," saying, "Our land is great and rich, but there is no order in it; come and rule and have dominion over us." This invitation was accepted by Rurik and his brethren, each of whom assumed control over a north-Russian centre, with Rurik himself at Novgorod, Sineus at Beloozero, and Truvor at Izborsk. Such, in its simplest terms, is the narrative of the "calling of the princes," which has inspired a larger volume of controversial literature than any other disputed point in Russian history.

Contentious literature on this problem begins with the early studies of Russian history by German scholars who joined the Russian Imperial Academy of Sciences during the first half of the eighteenth century. The natural tendency of these historians, among whom the pioneers were Gottlieb Bayer and Gerhart Friedrich Müller, was to take the *Povest'* narrative at its face value, and to identify the Varangians and the Russes as Scandinavians. This view was vehemently opposed, partly from patriotic bias and partly because of insufficient education, by the native historian Lomonosov, who in 1749 was thus instrumental in preventing the delivery before the Academy of Müller's oration *De origine gentis et nominis Russorum*. The Scandinavian origin of the Russes was, notwithstanding, accepted by a respectable list of older Slavic scholars of the first rank from Karamzin through Šafařik, and the scientific basis of this view, as held during the first half of the nineteenth century, is effectively summarized in the work of E. Kunik, *Die Berufung der schwedischen Ruodsen durch die Finnen und Slaven* (Spb., 1844). The balance of scholarship has thus generally favored the Scandinavian (or Norman) theory, and there was no really serious answer to the Norman school until the appearance, in 1871, of D. Ilovaysky's work, *O Mnimom Prizvanii Varyagov,* ably seconded, in 1876, by S. Gedeonov's study, *Varyagi i Rus'*. From this revival, the adherents of the Slavic (anti-Norman school) increased in numbers and importance, including such names as Zabelin, Pervolf, Filevich, Hrushevsky, and Golubovsky. A fresh aspect of the question was likewise opened up by new studies of Arabic sources, which indicated that the Russes were known on Russian soil prior to the traditional date set for the beginning of Russian history. The salutary contribution of the Slavic school has lain primarily in keeping the question open and in exposing weaknesses in the Normanist system, particularly in connection with the credibility of the *Primary Chronicle*. The best modern exposition of the Norman theory still remains W. Thomsen's *Origin of the Ancient Rus* (London, 1877). With the exceptions just noted, moreover, the ablest representatives of Russian historiography (Pogodin, Solov'ëv, Klyuchevsky,

Milyukov, Pokrovsky) and of Slavic philology (Miklosich, Sreznevsky, Jagić, Shakhmatov, Brückner) have all been adherents of the Norman school. The present tendency in handling this question is to attach less weight to the traditional account in the *Primary Chronicle* and rather to follow the evidence as to early Scandinavian-Russian relations supplied by Greek and Oriental sources and by the results of sound archaeological research.

In a passage inserted in the context of the cosmography derived from Hamartolus, the *Povest'* remarks that the Varangians live on the shores of the Varangian Sea, and that to the race of Japheth belong, among other nations, the Varangians, the Swedes, the Normans, the Russes, and the Angles. The Varangian Sea is identified as the Baltic in the subsequent passage which describes the trade-route connecting it with the Black Sea via the Neva River, Lake Ladoga, the Volkhov, Lake Il'men', the Lovot', and the Dnieper, and likewise by the statement that the river Dvina flows into the Varangian Sea. The Varangians lived according to the *Primary Chronicle*, not merely on the Baltic, but across it.[57] Varangian is a generic term, of which Rus' is a particular. As the *Povest'* puts it: "They . . . went overseas to the Varangian Russes: these particular Varangians were known as Russes, just as some are called Swedes, and others Normans, English, and Gotlanders. . . ." The names of the three brothers who migrated to Russia are readily reduced to Scandinavian originals as Hroerekr, Signiutr, and Þoraðor (Thomsen, *op. cit.*, p. 71). Further, in the armaments of Oleg, Varangians are distinguished from Finnish and Slavic elements. The name Oleg itself corresponds to the Norse Helgi, as Olga to Helga and Igor' to Ingvarr. In the treaty of 912, the *Povest'* preserves a list of Oleg's retainers, much mutilated in transmission, but of which not one is Slavic, while all of them can be reduced to Scandinavian originals without violence to their present textual aspect. In the portion of the account of Oleg's expedition which is of native Russian origin the Russes and the Slavs are clearly distinguished, but in the treaty text itself the whole expedition is designated as Rus'. In the reign of Igor', the Varangian Russes are again distinguished from Polyanians, Slověne, and Krivichians (*anno* 944), and once more, in the treaty of 945, a list of names is supplied of which the majority are not Slavic, but Norse (Thomsen, *loc. cit.*).

Quite apart from any question of the credibility of the *Povest'* narrative, it thus represents a clear-cut tradition that the leaders summoned to Novgorod came from the other side of the Baltic, and belonged to a subdivision called Rus', of the national element known as Varangians, to which belonged various other Germanic tribes. The names of the immediate descendants and of the followers of these princes are specifically Scandinavian. In the recorded raids upon Constantinople, the Rus' element took the lead, with the result that the Greeks negotiating with Scandinavians only supposed the entire expedition to be Rus', regardless of other elements in it.

Contemporary foreign sources testify abundantly that the Byzantine Greeks, even prior to 852, knew the Russes to be Scandinavians. In the *Annales Bertiniani* (ed. G. Waitz [Hanover, 1883], pp. 19, 20), it is reported that in 839 Theophilus sent an embassy to Louis the Pious, along with whom came certain individuals whom the Greeks called *Rhōs*. They were unable to return to their prince (*chacanus*) by their original route on account of the threatening barbarians, so that Theophilus requested the Emperor to speed them on their way. Louis investigated their nationality, and found them to be Swedes.[58] Further, Luidprand of Cremona, who was in Constantinople in 949, writes of the Byzantine capital that it is situated among dangerous neighbors, for at its north it is menaced by Magyars, Pechenegs, Khazars and *Rusii*, "Whom we call Nordmanni [Normans]." The identification of *Rusii* with Normans is repeated in his subsequent account of Igor's foray of 942.[59]

Direct evidence that the language of the Russes was Scandinavian is provided by Constantine Porphyrogenitus (*regn.* 945-959) in his account of the Rus' trading-expeditions down the Dnieper to the Black Sea and Constantinople.[60] This treatise mentions Novgorod (Νεμογαρδάς), Svyatoslav son of Igor' (Σφενδοσθλάβος ὁ υἱὸς Ἴγγωρ τοῦ ἄρχοντος ʽΡωσίας), Smolensk (Μιλινίσκα), Chernigov (Τζερνιγώγα), Vÿshgorod (Βουσιγραδέ) and the tribes of the Krivichians (Κριβιτιαηνοί), and the Luchanians (Λενζανινοί).[61] It is, however, particularly valuable for its mention of the names of most of the cataracts of the Dnieper (a series of rapids south of its junction with the Samara, around which the Russes were obligated to portage their barks), both ʽΡωσιστί and Σκλαβινιστί, i.e. in Rus' and in Slavic.[62]

For the first fall, only one name is given, viz., Ἐσσουπῆ which is translated both in Rus' and in Slavic as "sleep not." This form corresponds roughly to OSl. *ne s'pi*, having the same meaning. It has also been suggested (Pipping, *op. cit.*, p. 21), that it would also correspond to an ON, *ne sofi*. The second bears the Rus' name Οὐλβορσί and the Slavic Ὀστροβουνὶ πράχ translated into Greek as τὸ νησίον τοῦ φραγμοῦ. Thomsen (*op. cit.*, p. 55) proposes for the ON. form *Hólmfors* ("island fall"). The Slavic name reproduces exactly *ostrov'nÿy prag*, with the same meaning. Constantine even correctly reproduces an audible medial ь, together with the OSl. form *prag* instead of Russian *porog*. The third is named only in Rus' as Γελανδρί, with the remark that it is translated into Slavic as ἦχος φραγμοῦ without specific mention of the Slavic form. The Rus' name appears to represent the ON. part. pres. *gjallandi,* meaning "the roaring [fall]" which has its counterpart in the modern Russian name *zvonets* (cf. Pipping, *loc. cit.,* pp. 15, 16). The Rus' name for the fourth is 'Αειφάρ or 'Αειφόρ (Thomsen, *op. cit.,* p. 143), corresponding to a Slavic Νεασήτ. This fall is actually mentioned on a Runic inscription from Gotland as *Aifur* (Arne, *op. cit.,* p. 11). The name is variously interpreted as "ever-rushing" (ON. *eiforr,* Thomsen, *loc. cit.*), or as impassable (ON.*ei-fǫrr,* Pipping, *loc. cit.,* p. 12). Constantine remarks that it is so named «διότι φωλεύουσιν οἱ πελικάνοι εἰς τὰ λιθάρια τοῦ φραγμοῦ,» which corresponds well enough to the OSl. *neyasÿt'* ("pelican"), though Thomsen (*op. cit.,* pp. 61, 62) rejects any connection of *Aifur* with a cognate of Neth. *ooievaar,* and considers that the term signifies only "insatiable". The fifth bears a Rus' name which is transliterated into Greek as Βαρυφόρος, and is called in Slavic Βουλνηπράχ "because it makes great waves" («διότι μεγάλην δίνην ἀποτελεῖ»; cf. Thomsen, *op. cit.,* p. 64). The ON. form would thus be *barufors* ("wave-fall") and the OSl. *vln'nÿy prag* with the same meaning. The sixth is called in Rus' Λεαντί and in Slavic Βερουτζή, translated by Constantine as βράσμα νεροῦ ("boiling of water"). These names reproduce the ON. *hlaejandi,* "laughing," and OSl. *v'rshtivrushchiy* "twisting". Finally, the seventh is named in Rus' as Στρουβούν and in Slavic as Ναπρεζή, translated μικρὸς φραγμός. Neither name has been as yet satisfactorily restored. For a summary of conjectures, cf. Niederle *Slov. Star.,* I, iv, p. 110; Pipping, *loc. cit., pp.* 4-6. Apart from the difficulties presented by the names of the seventh cataract, it is thus clear that Ῥωσιστί does not signify Slavic, but Scandinavian, as far as language is concerned. Two Byzantine sources of the tenth century, one of which is probably dependent upon the other, also class the Russes as belonging to the same race as the Franks.[63]

Corroborative evidence of intimate Scandinavian relations with Russia at an early period is also supplied by archaeological research and, in a restricted degree, by Scandinavian literary monuments. The oldest Swedish objects discovered on Russian soil date from the eighth century, and were unearthed in Courland, over which the Vikings early established their domination. Evidence has also been found of early Swedish settlements on the southwestern shore of

Lake Ladoga during the first half of the ninth century, and about 900, a Swedish colony appears at Gnezdovo (near Smolensk).[64] Relics of the tenth century show the general prevalence of Swedish influence, which disappears again in the eleventh. The custom of erecting inscribed gravestones or cenotaphs became prevalent in Sweden only in the eleventh century, so that early survivals of Runic inscriptions mentioning Russia are comparatively rare.[65] One of the five such survivals has been mentioned in the previous discussion of the Rus' names of the Dnieper cataracts. Two others (one of the early and one of the late eleventh century) remark the activities of Swedish adventurers in Russia, which is referred to as Garðar, the country of fortified towns. Of the two remaining, one, dating from the late eleventh century, mentions the death in Novgorod of a certain Sigviðr, while the other, of about 1100, is a monument to one Spialboði, who met his death in St. Olaf's Church in Novgorod. In both instances, Novgorod bears the later familiar name of Hólmgarðr.

The literary survivals[66] testifying to a traditional close relationship between Scandinavia and Russia are necessarily of much later date, and originate at a period when the memory of contact with Russia had been considerably obscured. The section of Scandinavia enjoying the closest relations with Russia was obviously Sweden, the culture of which evolved more slowly than was the case in either Norway or Denmark. The Swedes were, moreover, not exposed to the English and Irish influences which are of such moment for Icelandic and Norse intellectual development. The period to which archaeological evidence points for the southward expansion of Swedish communities along the Russian watercourses (ninth and tenth centuries) is precisely that in which, after Harald Harfagri's victory at Hafrsfjord (*ca.* 890. Kendrick p. 111), the migration toward Iceland set in, to continue until 930. Since the historical saga reached its zenith only around 1230, during the lifetime of Snorri Sturluson, while the romantic sagas in general do not appear before the middle of the thirteenth century, and since, at the same time, the relations between Scandinavia and Russia lost their intimate character after the death of Yaroslav in 1054, a sufficient period thus elapsed before the rise of Icelandic prose literature for recollections of Russia, regarding which practically all Icelandic information was based on hearsay, to take on an indistinct and confused aspect. It is therefore not surprising that but a few of the oldest Russian cities are mentioned at all in the sagas. Hólmgarðr (Novgorod), Koenugarðr (Kiev), Aldeigjuborg

(Ladoga), Palteskja (Polotzk), Móramar (Murom), Sursdal or Surdalar (Suzdal'), Raþstofa (Rostov), Smoleskja (Smolensk), and Syrnes (probably Chernigov) practically exhaust the list.[67] Novgorod in the sagas also takes precedence over Kiev, though the latter had held the first rank since late in the ninth century. The principal literary evidences of direct Scandinavian contact with the Russian principate relate to the reigns of Vladimir I (972-1015) and of Yaroslav the Wise (1015-54). The traditions surrounding King Olaf Tryggvason describe the youthful prince as growing up at Vladimir's court at Novgorod. The facts underlying this narrative were, however, so remote that Olga, Vladimir's grandmother (she died, according to the *Povest'*, in 969), is transformed into his consort with the name Allogia. The reign of Yaroslav is treated with interesting and more authentic detail in the *Heimskringla*, the *Fagrskinna*, the *Morkinskinna*, and the *Eymundarpáttr Hringssonar*. These accounts are of special moment for their preoccupation with Ingigerðr, Yaroslav's Swedish wife, and with St. Olaf, his son Magnus, and with Harald Harðraði, subsequently the consort of Yaroslav's daughter Elisabeth.[68]

These reminiscences, however fragmentary, are sufficient to demonstrate that the contacts of even Norwegian princes with the Russian court of the tenth and eleventh century were so intimate as not to allow the original Scandinavian affiliations of the Russian ruling house to lapse entirely into oblivion. Such accounts, however, while deserving further study, do not cast the same light on earlier Scandinavian contacts with Russia which is supplied by the results of archaeological research. The latter have established that an extensive commerce between Northern Russia and the districts south of the Caspian developed via the Volga River as early as the seventh century. Relics of Arabic commerce in Northern Russia are particularly common in the provinces at the headwaters of the Volga, and the most notable discoveries have been made in precisely those districts where the Scandinavian colonists were most active. The eastern limit of discovery for Scandinavian relics in Russia passes, in fact, southward through the provinces of Vyatka, Kazan', Saratov, and Voronezh. This early Arabic commerce with the North was unacquainted with the later route up the Dnieper from the Black Sea, which was not widely used until the decline of the Khazar power opened a direct road to Byzantium, as is clearly demonstrated by the fact that the earliest Byzantine coins found in Scandinavia (on the island of Björkö in Lake Maelar) date only from the ninth century. That Scandinavian commerce through Russia was at first primarily concerned with the trans-Caspian Orient is also indicated by the presence of Scandinavian objects in Northern

Russia from the late eighth century forward, though specifically Russian objects do not appear in Scandinavia before the eleventh century, in spite of the fact that objects of oriental origin are found in Sweden by the end of the ninth.[69]

The archaeological evidence of Scandinavian contact with Arabic traders via the Russian watercourses is corroborated by the Arab and Persian geographers, who also refer to the presence of Scandinavian centres of colonization in northern Russia.

Arabic interest in geographical science developed rapidly from the ninth century forward, and by the eleventh, an extensive body of geographical literature had arisen which embodied considerable material concerning the northern area inhabited not only by the Slavs, but also by the Magyars, the Bulgars, the Khazars, and the various nomads of the steppes. One such account of the northern races with particular bearing on the identity of the Russes originated apparently in the work of Al Jayhānī, *Book of the Routes and Realms* written shortly after 922, and derived jointly from an earlier lost work of Abū Muslim al Garmī (*fl.* 845) and from an extant book of the same name (*Kitāb al masālik wal-mamālik*) by Ibn Khurdādhbih, dating from *ca.* 894.[70] All this material appears with different variations in the works of Ibn Rustah (tenth century), Al Bakrī (eleventh century), and Gurdīzī (eleventh century).[71] Further information on the same subject is contained in Mas'ūdī's *Gold Fields and Jewel Mines,* dating from 943. The testimony of the Arabic geographers is appreciably confused by the fact that very few of them possessed any first-hand information, and because they experienced some difficulty in distinguishing the Slavs from other light-complexioned peoples with whom they came in contact. To many of the Arabic geographers, the term Ṣaqlāb designated anyone of blond complexion, particularly of Northern European origin, and thus was applied at one time or another to the Volga Bulgarians, the Germans and the Saxons, the Hungarians and the Varangians.[72] If this fact be borne in mind, the identification of the Russes with the Slavs in so important an author as Ibn Khurdādhbih is not so surprising.[73]

On the other hand, a respectable body of Arabic information distinguishes the Russes from the Slavs within the confines of Russian territory. Ibn Rustah (Khvolson, *op. cit.,* pp. 34, 35) locates the Rus' centre of population on a marshy island in a northern lake, whence they make forays upon the Slavs, and sell their captives as slaves to the Khazars and the Bulgars. To this account, Gurdīzī adds (Barthold, *op. cit.,* p. 123) that the Russes constantly attack the country of the Slavs in companies of one or two hundred men, and seize by violence their useful property, remarking also that many Slavs have taken service with the Russes as a means of self-protection. The approximate location of the Rus' settlements, viz., at the headwaters of the Volga, is indicated by the statement of Al Bakrī (Kunik-Rosen, *op. cit.*, p. 60) that the river Itil (Volga) flows from among the Russes, and empties into the Khazar (Caspian) Sea. In the Arabic writers, there is no reference whatever to the Russes in any connection with the Slavs of the Dnieper valley. Their trading activities at Bolgar are, however, amply attested by Ibn Rustah, who reports (Khvolson, *op. cit.*, p. 23): "The Khazars carry on trade with the Bulgars; likewise the Russes also bring to them their merchandise." Apart from slaves, the principal articles of Rus' trade at Bolgar were sable, ermine, and squirrel, and other furs. As is indicated by the frequent discoveries of Arabic coins (dating 745-900) in Northern Russia, this commerce was largely on a money basis, and we learn from Gurdizī[74] that the inhabitants of the upper reaches of the Volga accepted nothing but coined money in payment for their wares. That the Russes did not originally speak Slavic is attested by the Jew Ibrāhīm ben Ya'qūb (*ca.* 965), who remarks that though not a Slavic people, they were masters of certain Slavic territory and learned Slavic by virtue of their intimate contacts with the Slavs.[75]

The description of the principal seat of the Russes given by Ibn Rustah (Khvolson, *op. cit.*, p. 34) is of special interest. "They are found," he declares, "on an island surrounded by a lake. The circumference of this island on which they live equals three days' journey. It is covered with woods and morasses. It is so unhealthy and damp that the ground, on account of the water absorbed in it, shakes whenever stamped upon." Gurdizī adds (*op.cit.*, p. 123) that about 100,000 live upon this island. In the passages just cited, Ibn Rustah refers to the chief of the Russes as their Khakan, with which should be compared the reference of the Annales Bertiniani (839) to "rex illorum chacanus uocabulo." This insular colony is readily identifiable with the Norse *Hólmgarðr,* the equivalent of Novgorod, so called, according to W. Thomsen, in consequence of its situation upon an island where the river Volkhov flows out of Lake Il'men' (*op. cit.*, p. 101). The chieftain, according to Gurdizī (*op. cit.*, p. 123), collects a tithe from the merchants under his authority. The Russes practise no agriculture, but live from the products of the farm labor of the subjugated Slavs.

It has generally been conceded that the original source from which was derived the information relayed by Ibn Rustah, Al Bakrī, and Gurdizī, was composed during the second quarter of the ninth century. It thus represents the situation at the headwaters of the Volga just before the Russes began their thrust southward along the Dnieper. The Russes are described as warriors and pirates of Viking character. Masʿūdī, in fact, though confusing the Slavs and the Russes, remarks[76] that the latter are divided into many tribes, but that among them is one race known as Norwegians who are the most numerous, and who voyage with their merchandise to Spain, Italy, Constantinople, and Khazaria. Their Norman kinship is thus clearly recognized.

Combined literary and archaeological evidence not only produces a presumption in favor of the Scandinavian origin of the Russes, but also demonstrates that these Russes were established at the headwaters of the Volga considerably before 859, the date under which the *Povest'* first mentions the Finnish and Slavic tribes of the north as tributaries of the Varangians. At the same time, the Arabic references to the systematic forays executed upon the unresisting Slavs suggest the nature of the process by which Varangian domination extended southward along the Dnieper toward the middle of the ninth century. The raids of the Russes around 850 were, in fact, not confined to the plains of the Dnieper basin, but actually extended across the Pontus into Paphlagonia. A report of such a raid carried out in the second quarter of the ninth century is preserved in the Greek *Life of St. George of Amastris,* written prior to 842 and thus providing the earliest Byzantine record of the Russes.[77]. Their southward movement toward the Crimea is apparently reflected in the Slavic *Life of St. Stephen of Surozh* (Sugdaea) by the account of a Russian raid from Novgorod which traversed the countryside from Kherson to Kerch and captured Sorozh after ten days' siege. The event took place shortly after St. Stephen's death, therefore early in the ninth century.[78]

We are therefore fully justified in rejecting the *Povest'* tradition of the "calling of the princes" in favor of the conviction that the Russes, a Scandinavian people of traders and fighters, had established themselves in Northern Russia before the beginning of the ninth century, and before 850 were already in contact with the Byzantine Empire. At the same time, however, the relations between the terms *Varangian* and *Rus'* require some elucidation.

The origin of the name *Rus'* (Greek ‘Ρῶς, Arabic *ar Rūs*) is a matter of considerable dispute.[79] In general, the hypothesis of E. Kunik and W. Thomsen, which derives this appellation from the Finnish name for Sweden and the Swedes, has met with the widest acceptance. The Finnish appellation for Sweden is thus *Ruotsi,* and for Swedes *Ruotsalaiset.* This terminology is common to all Finnish dialects along the Gulf of Finland, and is commonly held to be derived from *Ro(d)slagen* (Kunik, *op. cit.,* p. 163), the name of the coast of the Swedish province of Upland, just opposite the Gulf of Finland. On the principle that "an intellectually or politically inferior people as a rule names a more powerful and more respected neighboring people after the nearest frontier tribe of the latter," T. E. Karsten still accepts this view,[80] though Thomsen (*op. cit.,* p. 95) has objected to it on the ground that *Roslagen* is of too recent origin. The Danish scholar points out (*ibid.*) that the territory now occupied by the modern Swedish provinces of Upland, Södermanland, and East Gotland was known in ancient times as *Roðer* or *Roðin.* It is precisely in this district that the Scandinavian proper names occurring in the Russo-Greek treaties of 912 and 945 are most prevalent (Thomsen, *op. cit.,* p. 72). Thomsen accordingly suggests that *Roðer* is probably derived from an original *roðsmenn or roðskarlar,* meaning "seafarers," "rowers," so that the Finns took this latter term to indicate nationality, and preserved only the first syllable of it in the forms *Ruotsi* and *Ruotsalaiset.* Thomsen remarks in this connection that when a compound word is adopted into Finnish from another language, it is not unusual to take only the first part of it.

In view of the fact that such Scandinavian raiders as first penetrated the territory occupied by Slavic tribes between Lake Il'men' and the headwaters of the Volga must on their way have traversed an area settled by Finns, it is highly probable that the Slavs borrowed their own name for these interlopers from their Finnish neighbors, exactly as the Romans adopted the name *Germani* for the Teutonic tribes from the Celts with whom they came in contact. The vowel-change from *uo* to *u* occurs similarly in the Russian *Sum',* derived from Finnish *Suomi,*[81] and *Rus'* itself, as a feminine collective with *i*-stem, corresponds with the formation of several other similar Finnish tribal names appearing in old Russian as *Yam', Ves', Chud', Liv',* and *Perm'.* In the last analysis, the etymology of the word *Ruotsi-Rus'* is of comparatively slight importance. As Shakhmatov observes (*Izv. Otd. Russk. Yaz. i Slov.* IX, 340), there is no doubt of the identity of the name *Rus'* given the Scandinavians by the Slavs with the name *Ruotsi* which the Finns used to designate these same Scandinavians. A certain amount of difficulty is unfortunately introduced by the Greek form ‘Ρῶς which is used as an indeclinable masculine plural (οἱ ‘Ρῶς, τῶν ‘Ρῶς) and which contains an ω where ου would reason-

Introduction 49

ably be expected. This word has not been satisfactorily explained. Thomsen (*op. cit.,* p. 99) inclined to the belief that it reached the Greeks through the medium of some Turco-Tatar tribe, and thus probably through the Khazars, in view of the fact that in Byzantine Greek many Turco-Tatar words appear as indeclinables. Some considerable variation among ο, ω, and ου in such names is also apparent (Marquart, *Streifzüge,* p. 354). On the other hand, as Marquart remarks (*ibid.*), no Turkish word can begin with *r* or *l* (cf. Hungarian *Orosz,* "Russian"), so that the mediation of any Turco-Tatar language seems improbable.[82]

The name *Rus',* derived apparently from the Finnish appellation of raiders and colonists from eastern Sweden, thus applies in the *Povest'* to the Scandinavian element which, after establishing itself at a strong point near Lake Il'men', gradually imposed its authority over the scattered Slavic tribes of the whole Dnieper basin. This appellation, particularly after the arrival of Kiev at a position of dominance under Rus' sovereignty, not only designated the ruling class, at first exclusively Scandinavian, but gradually came to include as well the subject Slavs, and thus superseded the old tribal nomenclature.

The interpretation of the original significance of the term *Rus'* is to some extent complicated by its association with the name *Varangian* (*Varyagi, Varyazi,* Βάραγγοι, *Væringjar*). As already intimated, *Varangian* is used in the earlier sections of the *Povest'* as a generic term for the Germanic nations on the coasts of the Baltic, including Swedes, Gotlanders, the English, and the Russes. On the other hand, since the *Povest'* in four passages specifically refers to the Varangians "from beyond the sea" (*za more, za morya*), it may be concluded that those Varangians who migrated to Russia were regarded as exclusively Scandinavian. The Arabic geographer Al Bīrūnī (973-1038) also mentions the Baltic as the Varangian Sea, and specifies the Varangians as a people dwelling on its coasts.[83] The Arabs subsequently identified these Varangians with the Swedes.[84] There is reason to believe that the term *Varangian* was not known in Russia before the last half of the tenth century when it came into use there as applied to the Scandinavian warriors who took service with the Russian princes or with the Byzantine emperors, and distinguished the latter from the old line of Scandinavian colonists who, by 1000, must have been well russified. The time limits within which the term *Varangian* was in common use in Russia may be determined with relative accuracy. In the first place, it does not occur in any of the treaties with Byzantium, showing that as a *terminus technicus* it was certainly unknown as late as 945. Furthermore, its last appearance in the *Povest'* occurs in 1037, and it is therefore clear that the word was not in common use at Kiev after the reign of Yaroslav. The Norse equivalent *Væringjar* is by no means a word of such common occurrence as to indicate that it was in everyday use even in the heyday of Scandinavian relations with the Near East. The earliest Scandinavian to take service in Byzantium was apparently Þrkell Þjóstarsson, who spent some seven years about 950 in travel and adventure and, as he expressed it, was a vassal of the king of Miklagardr ("em handgenginn Garðskonunginum").[85] The first datable use of the word in Norse literature appears to occur in the *Geisli* of the skald Einarr Skularson, delivered in 1153. The institution of the Varangian guard was apparently well established by 1000, since we find an Icelander, Kolskeggr Hámundarson, commanding it about that date.[86] In the Byzantine sources, while mention is made of Russes in the imperial service as early as 1016 (Cedrenus, II, 465), it is not until 1034 that the Βάραγγοι are specifically mentioned, and in that instance only as in garrison in the Thracian theme (*ibid.*, pp. 508, 509). In the main, however, the term *Varangian* seems very clearly to have made its first appearance, not in Scandinavia or in Russia, but in Byzantium itself, where the name was introduced to designate a function. It was therefore not brought to Russia from Scandinavia, but, from the fact that it was applied in Byzantium to Norse adventurers who took service there, was extended in Russia to apply to Scandinavian warriors journeying to and from Constantinople or even in the Russian service. Since the term *Rus'*, by the beginning of the twelfth century, had long since lost all Scandinavian connotation, the designation of these adventurers was very naturally extended to their country of origin, so that *Varangian,* to a Russian of the last half of the eleventh century, meant simply Scandinavian, and the Russes, whose Scandinavian extraction was only a matter of legend, were classed as a subdivision of the Varangians.[87] While the available evidence thus leads to a rejection of the naïve *Povest'* tradition of the "calling of the princes," it indicates with equal emphasis that the dominant class in the formative period of the early Russian state was composed of the Scandinavian warrior-merchants who, early in the ninth century, made their way to the south and east along the Russian watercourses in search of commercial contacts with the Orient and with Byzantium.[88]

The Russian Primary Chronicle

Laurentian Text

Note. The columns of the diplomatic text of the *Povest'* (ed. E. F. Karsky, in *P.S.R.L.*, I, 2nd ed., [Leningrad, 1926], and referred to in the Introduction as L²) are indicated in parentheses in the translation.

These are the narratives of bygone years regarding the origin of the land of Rus', the first princes of Kiev, and from what source the land of Rus' had its beginning.

Let us accordingly begin this narrative. *After the flood, the sons of Noah* (Shem, Ham, and Japheth) *divided the earth among them. To the lot of Shem fell the Orient, and his share extended lengthwise as far as India and breadthwise* (i.e., from east to south) *as far as Rhinocurura, including Persia and Bactria, as well as Syria, Media* (which lies beside the Euphrates River), *Babylon, Cordyna, Assyria, Mesopotamia, Arabia the Ancient, Elymais, India, Arabia the Mighty, Coelesyria, Commagene, and all Phoenicia.*

To the lot of Ham fell the southern region, comprising Egypt, Ethiopia facing toward India, the other (2) *Ethiopia out of which the red Ethiopian river flows to the eastward, the Thebaid, Libya as far as Cyrene, Marmaris, Syrtis, and other Libya, Numidia, Massyris, and Maurentania over against Cadiz. Among the regions of the Orient, Ham also received Cilicia, Pamphylia, Mysia, Lycaonia, Phrygia, Camalia, Lycia, Caria, Lydia, the rest of Moesia, Troas, Aeolia, Bithynia, and ancient Phrygia. He likewise acquired the islands of Sardinia, Crete, and Cyprus, and the river Gihon, called the Nile.*

(3) *To the lot of Japheth fell the northern and the western sections, including Media, Albania, Armenia* (both little and great), *Cappadocia, Paphlagonia, Galatia, Colchis, Bosporus, Maeotis, Dervis, Sarmatia, Tauria, Scythia, Thrace, Macedonia, Dalmatia, Molossia, Thessaly, Locris, Pellene* (which is also called the Peloponnese), *Arcadia, Epirus, Illyria,* the Slavs, *Lychnitis and Adriaca, from which the Adriatic Sea is named. He received also the islands of Britain, Sicily, Euboea, Rhodes, Chios, Lesbos, Cythera, Zacynthus, Cephallenia, Ithaca, and Corcyra, as well as a portion of the land of Asia called Ionia, the*

river *Tigris flowing between the Medes and Babylon*,[1] and the territory to the north extending as far as the Pontus and including the Danube, the Dniester, and the Carpathian Mountains, which are called Hungarian, and thence even to the Dnieper. (4) He likewise acquired dominion over other rivers, among them the Desna, the Pripet', the Dvina, the Volkhov, and the Volga, which flows eastward into the portion of Shem.

In the share of Japheth lies Rus', Chud', and all the gentiles: Merya, Muroma, Ves', Mordva, Chud' beyond the portages, Perm', Pechera, Yam', Ugra, Litva, Zimegola, Kors', Let'gola, and Liv'. The Lyakhs, the Prussians, and Chud' border on the Varangian Sea. The Varangians dwell on the shores of that same sea, and extend to the eastward as far as the portion of Shem. They likewise live to the west beside this sea as far as the land of the English and the French. For the following nations also are a part of the race of Japheth: the Varangians, the Swedes, the Normans, the Gotlanders, the Russes, the English, the Spaniards, the Italians, the Romans, the Germans, the French, the Venetians, the Genoese, and so on. Their homes are situated in the northwest, and adjoin the Hamitic tribes.

(5) Thus Shem, Ham, and Japheth divided the earth among them, and after casting lots, so that none might encroach upon his brother's share, they lived each in his appointed portion. There was but one spoken language, and as mankind multiplied throughout the earth, they planned, in the days of Yoktan and Peleg, to build a tower as high as heaven itself. Thus they gathered together in the plain of Shinar to build the tower and the city of Babylon round about it. But they wrought upon the tower for forty years, and it was unfinished. Then the Lord God descended to look upon the city and the tower, and said, "This race is one, and their tongue is one." So the Lord confused the tongues, and after dividing the people into seventy-two races, he scattered them over the whole world. After the confusion of the tongues, God overthrew the tower with a great wind, and the ruin of it lies between Assur and Babylon. In height and in breadth it is 5400 and 33 cubits, and the ruin was preserved for many years.[2]

After the destruction of the tower and the division of the nations, the sons of Shem occupied the eastern regions, and sons of Ham those of the south, and the sons of Japheth the western and the northern lands. Among these seventy-two nations, the Slavic race is derived from the line of Japheth, since they are the Noricians, who are identical with the Slavs.

Over a long period the Slavs settled beside the Danube, where the

Hungarian and Bulgarian lands now lie. From among these Slavs, (6) parties scattered throughout the country and were known by appropriate names, according to the places where they settled. Thus some came and settled by the river Morava, and were named Moravians, while others were called Czechs. Among these same Slavs are included the White Croats,[3] the Serbs, and the Carinthians. For when the Vlakhs attacked the Danubian Slavs, settled among them, and did them violence, the latter came and made their homes by the Vistula, and were then called Lyakhs.[4] Of these same Lyakhs some were called Polyanians, some Lutichians, some Mazovians, and still others Pomorians. Certain Slavs settled also on the Dnieper, and were likewise called Polyanians. Still others were named Derevlians, because they lived in the forests. Some also lived between the Pripet' and the Dvina, and were known as Dregovichians. Other tribes resided along the Dvina and were called Polotians on account of a small stream called the Polota, which flows into the Dvina. It was from this same stream that they were named Polotians. The Slavs also dwelt about Lake Il'men', and were known there by their characteristic name. They built a city which they called Novgorod. Still others had their homes along the Desna, the Sem', and the Sula, and were called Severians. Thus the Slavic race was divided, and its language was known as Slavic.

(7) When the Polyanians lived by themselves among the hills, a trade-route connected the Varangians with the Greeks. Starting from Greece, this route proceeds along the Dnieper, above which a portage leads to the Lovat'. By following the Lovat', the great lake Il'men' is reached. The river Volkhov flows out of this lake and enters the great lake Nevo. The mouth of this lake opens into the Varangian Sea. Over this sea goes the route to Rome, and on from Rome overseas to Tsar'grad.[5] The Pontus, into which flows the river Dnieper, may be reached from that point. The Dnieper itself rises in the upland forest, and flows southward. The Dvina has its source in this same forest, but flows northward and empties into the Varangian Sea. The Volga rises in this same forest but flows to the east, and discharges through seventy mouths into the Caspian Sea. It is possible by this route to the eastward to reach the Bulgars and the Caspians, and thus attain the region of Shem. Along the Dvina runs the route to the Varangians, whence one may reach Rome, and go from there to the race of Ham. But the Dnieper flows through various mouths into the Pontus. This sea, beside which taught St. Andrew, Peter's brother, is called the Russian Sea.[6]

When Andrew was teaching in Sinope and came to (8) Kherson[7] (as has been recounted elsewhere), he observed that the mouth of the

Dnieper was near by. Conceiving a desire to go to Rome, he thus journeyed to the mouth of the Dnieper. Thence he ascended the river, and by chance he halted beneath the hills upon the shore. Upon arising in the morning, he observed to the disciples who were with him, "See ye these hills? So shall the favor of God shine upon them that on this spot a great city shall arise, and God shall erect many churches therein." He drew near the hills, and having blessed them, he set up a cross. After offering his prayer to God, he descended from the hill on which Kiev was subsequently built, and continued his journey up the Dnieper.

He then reached the Slavs at the point where Novgorod is now situated. He saw these people existing according to their customs, and on observing how they bathed and scrubbed themselves, he wondered at them. He went thence among the Varangians and came to Rome, where he recounted what he had learned and observed. "Wondrous to relate," said he, "I saw the land of the Slavs, and while I was among them, I noticed their wooden bathhouses. They warm them to extreme heat, then undress, and after anointing themselves with an acid liquid, they take young branches and lash their bodies. They actually lash themselves so violently that they barely escape alive. Then they drench themselves with cold water, and thus are revived. They think nothing of doing this (9) every day, and though tormented by none, they actually inflict such voluntary torture upon themselves. Indeed, they make of the act not a mere washing but a veritable torment." When his hearers learned this fact, they marveled. But Andrew, after his stay in Rome, returned to Sinope.

While the Polyanians lived apart and governed their families (for before the time of these brothers there were already Polyanians, and each one lived with his gens on his own lands, ruling over his kinsfolk), there were three brothers, Kiy, Shchek, and Khoriv, and their sister was named Lÿbed'. Kiy lived upon the hill where the Borichev trail now is, and Shchek dwelt upon the hill now named Shchekovitsa, while on the third resided Khoriv, after whom this hill is named Khorevitsa. They built a town and named it Kiev after their oldest brother. Around the town lay a wood and a great pine-forest in which they used to catch wild beasts. These men were wise and prudent; they were called Polyanians, and there are Polyanians descended from them living in Kiev to this day.

Some ignorant persons have claimed that Kiy was a ferryman, for near Kiev there was (10) at that time a ferry from the other side of the river, in consequence of which people used to say, "To Kiy's ferry." Now if Kiy had been a mere ferryman, he would never have gone to

Tsar'grad. He was then the chief of his kin, and it is related what great honor he received from the Emperor in whose reign he visited the imperial court. On his homeward journey, he arrived at the Danube. The place pleased him and he built a small town, wishing to dwell there with his kinsfolk. But those who lived near by would not grant him this privilege. Yet even now the dwellers by the Danube call this town Kievets. When Kiy returned to Kiev, his native city, he ended his life there; and his brothers Shchek and Khoriv, as well as their sister Lÿbed', died there also.

After the deaths of these three brothers, their gens assumed the supremacy among the Polyanians. The Derevlians possessed a principality of their own, as did also the Dregovichians, while the Slavs had their own authority in Novgorod, and another principality existed on the Polota, where the Polotians dwell. Beyond them reside the Krivichians, who live at the head waters of the Volga, the Dvina, and the Dnieper, and whose city is Smolensk. It is there that the Krivichians dwell, and from them are the Severians sprung. At Beloozero are situated the Ves', and on the lake of Rostov, the Merya, (11) and on Lake Kleshchino the Merya also. Along the river Oka (which flows into the Volga), the Muroma, the Cheremisians, and the Mordva preserve their native languages. For the Slavic race in Rus' includes only the Polyanians, the Derevlians, the people of Novgorod, the Polotians, the Dregovichians, the Severians, and the Buzhians, who live along the river Bug and were later called Volhynians. The following are other tribes which pay tribute to Rus': Chud', Merya, Ves', Muroma, Cheremis', Mordva, Perm', Pechera, Yam,' Litva, Zimegola, Kors', Narva, and Liv'. These tribes have their own languages and belong to the race of Japheth, which inhabits the lands of the north.

Now while the Slavs dwelt along the Danube, as we have said, there came from among the Scythians, that is, from the Khazars, a people called Bulgars who settled on the Danube and oppressed the Slavs. Afterward came the White Ugrians, who inherited the Slavic country. These Ugrians appeared under the Emperor Heraclius, warring on Chosroes, King of Persia. The Avars, who attacked Heraclius the Emperor, nearly capturing him, also lived at this time.[8] They made war upon the Slavs, (12) and harassed the Dulebians, who were themselves Slavs.[9] They even did violence to the Dulebian women. When an Avar made a journey, he did not cause either a horse or a steer to be harnessed, but gave command instead that three of four or five women should be yoked to his cart and be made to draw him. Even thus they harassed the Dulebians. The Avars were large of stature and proud of spirit, and God destroyed them. They all perished, and not one Avar survived. There is to this day a proverb in Rus' which runs, "They perished like the Avars." Neither race nor heir of them remains. The Pechenegs came after them, and the Magyars passed by Kiev later during the time of Oleg.[10]

Thus the Polyanians, who belonged to the Slavic race, lived apart, as we have said, and called themselves Polyanians. The Derevlians, who are likewise Slavs, lived by themselves and adopted this tribal name. But the Radimichians and the Vyatichians sprang from the Lyakhs. There were in fact among the Lyakhs two brothers, one named Radim and other Vyatko. Radim settled on the Sozh', where the people are known as Radimichians, and Vyatko with his family settled on the Oka. The people there were named Vyatichians after him. Thus the Polyanians, the Derevlians, the Severians, the Radimichians, and the Croats lived at peace. (13) The Dulebians dwelt along the Bug, where the Volhynians now are found, but the Ulichians and the Tivercians lived by the Dniester, and extended as far as the Danube. There was a multitude of them, for they inhabited the banks of the Dniester almost down to the east, and to this day there are cities in that locality which still belong to them. Hence they are called Great Scythia by the Greeks.[11]

These Slavic tribes preserved their own customs, the law of their forefathers, and their traditions, each observing its own usages. For the Polyanians retained the mild and peaceful customs of their ancestors, and showed respect for their daughters-in-law and their sisters, as well as for their mothers and fathers. For their mothers-in-law and their brothers-in-law they also entertained great reverence. They observed a fixed custom, under which the groom's brother did not fetch the bride, but she was brought to the bridegroom in the evening, and on the next morning her dowry was turned over.

The Derevlians, on the other hand, existed in bestial fashion, and lived like cattle. They killed one another, ate every impure thing, and there was no marriage among them, but instead they seized upon maidens by capture.[12] The Radimichians, the Vyatichians, and the Severians had the same customs. They lived in the forest like any wild beast, and ate every unclean thing. They spoke obscenely (14) before their fathers and their daughters-in-law. There were no marriages among them, but simply festivals among the villages. When the people gathered together for games, for dancing, and for all other devilish amusements, the men on these occasions carried off wives for themselves, and each took any woman with whom he had arrived at an understanding. In fact, they even had two or three wives apiece. Whenever a death occurred, a feast was held over the corpse, and then a great pyre was constructed, on which the deceased was laid and burned. After the bones were collected, they were placed in a small urn and set upon a post by the roadside, even as the Vyatichians do to this day. Such customs were observed by the Krivichians and the other pagans, since they did not know the law of God, but made a law unto themselves.[13]

Georgius says in his *Chronicle:*

"Among all the nations, there are some that possess a written law, while others simply observe certain fixed customs, for, among those devoid of law, their ancestral usage is accepted in its stead. To this class belong the Seres, who live at the end of the world, and apply as law the customs of their ancestors, which forbid them to commit adultery or incest, to steal, to bear false witness, to kill, or do any wrong whatsoever.

"The law of the Bactrians, called (15) Brahmans or Islanders, which is derived from the forefatherly prescription, prohibits them for reasons of piety from eating meat, drinking wine, committing adultery, or doing any sort of wrong, solely in consequence of religious scruple. But among the Indians, who dwell beside them, are found murderers, criminals and doers of violence beyond all nature. In the most remote portion of their country, they practice cannibalism and kill travelers and, what is worse still, they devour them like dogs.

"The Chaldeans and the Babylonians have a different code, which allows them to marry their mothers, to commit carnal sin with their nieces, and to commit murder. They regard every shameless deed as a virtue when they commit it, even when they are far from their own country.

"The Gelaeans maintain other customs: among them, the women plough, build houses, and perform men's work. But they indulge in vice to the extent of their desire, for they are by no means restrained by their husbands, nor do the latter at all concern themselves about the matter. There are among them bold women who are capable of capturing wild beasts by virtue of their strength. The women have control over their husbands, and rule them.

"In Britain, many men sleep with one woman, (16) and likewise many women have intercourse with one man. The people carry on without jealousy or restraint the vicious customs of their ancestors.

"The Amazons have no husbands, but like brute beasts they are filled with desire once each year in the springtime, and come together with the neighboring men. This season seems to them, as it were, a time of celebration and great festival. When they give birth to children and a male is born, they kill it, but if the child is of the female sex, then they nurse it and bring it up carefully."[14]

Just so, even in our own day, the Polovcians maintain the customs of their ancestors in the shedding of blood and in glorifying themselves for such deeds, as well as in eating every dead or unclean thing, even hamsters and marmots. They marry their mothers-in-law and their sisters-in-law, and observe other usages of their ancestors. But in all countries we Christians who believe in the Holy Trinity, in one baptism, and in one faith, have but one law, as many of us have been baptized into Christ Lord and have put on Christ.

After this time, and subsequent to the death of the three brothers in Kiev, the Polyanians were oppressed by the Derevlians and other neighbors (17) of theirs. Then the Khazars came upon them as they lived in the hills and forests, and demanded tribute from them. After consulting among themselves, the Polyanians paid as tribute one sword per hearth, which the Khazars bore to their prince and their elders, and said to them, "Behold, we have found new tribute." When asked whence it was derived, they replied, "From the forest on the hills by the river Dnieper." The elders inquired what tribute had been paid, whereupon the swords were exhibited. The Khazar elders then protested, "Evil is this tribute, prince. We have won it with a one-edged weapon called a sabre, but the weapon of these men is sharp on both edges and is called a sword. These men shall impose tribute upon us and upon other lands." All this has come to pass, for they spoke thus not of their own will, but by God's commandment. The outcome was the same in the time of Pharaoh, King of Egypt, when Moses was led before him, and the elders of Pharaoh foretold that he should subjugate Egypt. For the Egyptians perished at the hand of Moses, though the Jews were previously their slaves. Just as the Egyptians ruled supreme, but were themselves subsequently ruled over, so it has also come to pass that the Russes rule over the Khazars even to this day.[15]

In the year 6360 (852), the fifteenth of the indiction,[16] at the accession of the Emperor Michael, the land of Rus' was first named. We have determined this date from the fact that in the reign of this Emperor Russes attacked Tsar'grad, as is written in the Greek Chronicle.[17] Hence we shall begin at this point (18) and record the dates. Thus from Adam to the Flood, 2242 years elapsed; from the Flood to Abraham, 1082 years; from Abraham to the Mosaic Exodus, 430 years; from the Mosaic Exodus to David, 601 years; from David and the beginning of the reign of Solomon to the captivity of Jerusalem, 448 years; from the captivity to Alexander, 318 years; from Alexander to the birth of Christ, 333 years; from the birth of Christ to Constantine, 318 years; and from Constantine to Michael, 542 years. Twenty-nine years passed between the first year of Michael's reign and the accession of Oleg, Prince of Rus'. From the accession of Oleg, when he took up his residence in Kiev, to the first year of Igor's principate, thirty-one years elapsed. Thirty-three years passed between Igor's accession and that of Svyatoslav. From the accession of Svyatoslav to that of Yaropolk, twenty-eight years passed. Yaropolk ruled eight years, Vladimir thirty-seven years, and Yaroslav forty years. Thus from the death of Svyatoslav to the death of Yaroslav eighty-five years elapsed, while sixty years separate the death of Yaroslav from that of Svyatopolk. But we shall now return to the subject, recounting what occurred during this period (for we set our beginning at the first year of Michael's reign) and we shall record the dates in order.

6361-6366 (853-858). (19) Michael the Emperor went forth with an army by land and sea against the Bulgarians. The latter, on catching sight of his armament, offered no resistance, and asked leave to be baptized and to submit themselves to the Greeks. The Emperor baptized their prince with all his warriors, and made peace with the Bulgarians.[18]

6367 (859). The Varangians from beyond the sea imposed tribute upon the Chuds, the Slavs, the Merians, the Ves', and the Krivichians.[19] But the Khazars imposed it upon the Polyanians, the Severians, and the Vyatichians, and collected a white squirrel-skin from each hearth.

6368-6370 (860-862). The tributaries of the Varangians drove them back beyond the sea and, refusing them further tribute, set out to govern themselves. There was no law among them, but tribe rose against tribe. Discord thus ensued among them, and they began to war one against another. They said to themselves, "Let us seek a prince who may rule over us and judge us according to the Law." They accordingly went overseas to the Varangian Russes: these particular Varangians were known as Russes, just as some are called Swedes, and others Normans, English, and Gotlanders, for they were thus named. The Chuds, the Slavs, (20) the Krivichians, and the Ves' then said to the people of Rus', "Our land is great and rich, but there is no order in it. Come to rule and reign over us." They thus selected three brothers, with their kinsfolk, who took with them all the Russes and migrated. The oldest, Rurik, located himself in Novgorod; the second, Sineus, at Beloozero; and the third, Truvor, in Izborsk.[20] On account of these Varangians, the district of Novgorod became known as the land of

Rus'. The present inhabitants of Novgorod are descended from the Varangian race, but aforetime they were Slavs.

After two years, Sineus and his brother Truvor died, and Rurik assumed the sole authority. He assigned cities to his followers, Polotsk to one, Rostov to another, and to another Beloozero. In these cities there are thus Varangian colonists, but the first settlers were, in Novgorod, Slavs; in Polotsk, Krivichians; at Beloozero, Ves', in Rostov, Merians; and in Murom, Muromians. Rurik had dominion over all these districts.

With Rurik there were two men who did not belong to his kin, but were boyars. They obtained permission to go to Tsar'grad with their families. They thus sailed down the Dnieper, and in the course of their journey they saw a small city on a hill. Upon their inquiry as to whose town it was, they were informed that (21) three brothers, Kiy, Shchek, and Khoriv, had once built the city, but that since their deaths, their descendants were living there as tributaries of the Khazars. Askold and Dir remained in the city, and after gathering together many Varangians, they established their dominion over the country of the Polyanians at the same time that Rurik was ruling at Novgorod.

6371-6374 (863-866). Askold and Dir attacked the Greeks during the fourteenth year of the reign of the Emperor Michael.[21] When the Emperor had set forth against the infidels and had arrived at the Black River, the eparch sent him word that the Russes were approaching Tsar'grad, and the Emperor turned back. Upon arriving inside the strait, the Russes made a great massacre of the Christians, and attacked Tsar'grad in two hundred boats. The Emperor succeeded with difficulty in entering the city. He straightway hastened with the Patriarch Photius to the Church of Our Lady of the Blachernae, where they prayed all night. They also sang hymns and carried the sacred vestment of the Virgin to dip it in the sea. The weather was still, and the sea was calm, but a storm of wind came up, and when great waves straightway rose, confusing the boats of the godless Russes, it threw them upon the shore (22) and broke them up, so that few escaped such destruction and returned to their native land.

6375-6376 (867-868). Basil began his reign.

6377 (869). The entire nation of the Bulgarians accepted baptism.

6378-6387 (870-879). On his deathbed, Rurik bequeathed his realm to Oleg, who belonged to his kin, and entrusted to Oleg's hands his son Igor', for he was very young.[22]

6388-6390 (880-882). Oleg set forth, taking with him many warriors from among the Varangians, the Chuds, the Slavs, the Merians and all the (23) Krivichians. He thus arrived with his Krivichians before Smolensk, captured the city, and set up a garrison there. Thence he went on and captured Lyubech, where he also set up a garrison. He then came to the hills of Kiev, and saw how Askold and Dir reigned there. He hid his warriors in the boats, left some others behind, and went forward himself bearing the child Igor'. He thus came to the foot of the Hungarian hill,[23] and after concealing his troops, he sent messengers to Askold and Dir, representing himself as a stranger on his way to Greece on an errand for Oleg and for Igor', the prince's son, and requesting that they should come forth to greet them as members of their race. Askold and Dir straightway came forth. Then all the soldiery jumped out of the boats, and Oleg said to Askold and Dir, "You are not princes nor even of princely stock, but I am of princely birth." Igor' was then brought forward, and Oleg announced that he was the son of Rurik. They killed Askold and Dir, and after carrying them to the hill, they buried them there, on the hill now known as Hungarian, where the castle of Ol'ma now stands. Over that tomb Ol'ma built a church dedicated to St. Nicholas, but Dir's tomb is behind St. Irene's.[24] Oleg set himself up as prince in Kiev, and declared that it should be the mother of Russian cities. The Varangians, Slavs, and others who accompanied him, were called Russes. Oleg began to build stockaded towns, and (24) imposed tribute on the Slavs, the Krivichians, and the Merians. He commanded that Novgorod should pay the Varangians tribute to the amount of 300 *grivnÿ* a year for the preservation of peace.[25] This tribute was paid to the Varangians until the death of Yaroslav.

6391 (883). Oleg began military operations against the Derevlians, and after conquering them he imposed upon them the tribute of a black marten-skin apiece.

6392 (884). Oleg attacked the Severians, and conquered them. He imposed a light tribute upon them and forbade their further payment of tribute to the Khazars, on the ground that there was no reason for them to pay it as long as the Khazars were his enemies.

6393 (885). Oleg sent messengers to the Radimichians to inquire to whom they paid tribute. Upon their reply that they paid tribute to the Khazars, he directed them to render it to himself instead, and they accordingly paid him a shilling[26] apiece, the same amount that they had paid the Khazars. Thus Oleg established his authority over the Polyanians, the Derevlians, the Severians, and the Radimichians, but he waged war with the Ulichians and the Tivercians.

6394-6395 (886-887). Leo, Basil's son (called Lev by us), became Emperor. He called to the throne his brother Alexander, and they ruled together twenty-six years.[27]

(25) 6396-6406 (888-898). The Magyars passed by Kiev over the hill now called Hungarian, and on arriving at the Dnieper, they pitched camp.[28] They were nomads like the Polovcians. Coming out of the east, they struggled across the great mountains, and began to fight against the neighboring Vlakhs and Slavs. For the Slavs had settled there first, but the Vlakhs had seized the territory of the Slavs. The Magyars subsequently expelled the Vlakhs, took their land, and settled among the Slavs, whom they reduced to submission.[29] From that time this territory was called Hungarian. The Magyars made war upon the Greeks, and seized the Thracian and Macedonian territory as far as Salonika. They also attacked the Moravians and the Czechs.

There was at the time but one Slavic race including the Slavs who settled along the Danube and were subjugated by the Magyars, as well as the Moravians, the Czechs, the Lyakhs, and the Polyanians, (26) the last of whom are now called Russes. It was for these Moravians that Slavic books were first written, and this writing prevails also in Rus' and among the Danubian Bulgarians. When the Moravian Slavs and their princes were living in baptism, the Princes Rostislav, Svyatopolk, and Kotsel sent messengers to the Emperor Michael, saying, "Our nation is baptized, and yet we have no teacher to direct and instruct us and interpret the sacred scriptures. We understand neither Greek nor Latin. Some teach us one thing and some another. Furthermore, we do not understand written characters nor their meaning. Therefore send us teachers who can make known to us the words of the scriptures and their sense." The Emperor Michael, upon hearing their request, called together all the scholars, and reported to them the message of the Slavic princes. The scholars suggested that there was a man in Salonika, by name Leo, who had two sons familiar with the Slavic tongue, being learned men as well. When the Emperor was thus informed, he immediately summoned the sons of Leo from Salonika, directing him to send to court forthwith his sons Methodius and Constantine. Upon receipt of this message, Leo quickly sent forth his sons. When they came before the Emperor, he made known to them that the Slavs had communicated to him their desire for teachers who could interpret the holy scriptures to them. The Emperor prevailed (27) upon them to undertake the mission, and sent them into the Slavic country to Rostislav, Svyatopolk, and Kotsel. When they arrived, they undertook to compose a Slavic alphabet, and translated the *Acts* and the

Gospel. The Slavs rejoiced to hear the greatness of God extolled in their native tongue. The apostles afterward translated the Psalter, the *Oktoechos,* and other books.

Now some zealots began to condemn the Slavic books, contending that it was not right for any other nation to have its own alphabet apart from the Hebrews, the Greeks, and the Latins, according to Pilate's superscription, which he composed for the Lord's Cross. When the Pope at Rome heard of this situation, he rebuked those who murmured against the Slavic books, saying, "Let the word of the Scripture be fulfilled that 'all nations shall praise God' (*Ps.* lxxi, 17), and likewise that 'all nations shall declare the majesty of God according as the Holy Spirit shall grant them to speak' (cf. *Acts,* ii, 4). Whosoever condemns the Slavic writing shall be excluded from the Church until he mend his ways. For such men are not sheep but wolves; by their fruits ye shall know them and guard against them. Children of God, hearken unto his teachings, and depart not from the ecclesiastical rule which Methodius your teacher has appointed unto you." Constantine then returned again, and went to instruct the people of Bulgaria; (28) but Methodius remained in Moravia.[30]

Prince Kotsel appointed Methodius Bishop of Pannonia in the see of St. Andronicus, one of the Seventy, a disciple of the holy Apostle Paul. Methodius chose two priests who were very rapid writers, and translated the whole Scriptures in full from Greek into Slavic in six months between March and the twenty-sixth day of October. After completing the task, he appropriately rendered praise and honor to God, who had bestowed such a blessing upon Bishop Methodius, the successor of Andronicus. Now Andronicus is the apostle of the Slavic race. He traveled among the Moravians, and the Apostle Paul taught there likewise. For in that region is Illyricum, whither Paul first repaired and where the Slavs originally lived. Since Paul is the teacher of the Slavic race, from which we Russians too are sprung, even so the Apostle Paul is the teacher of us Russians, for he preached to the Slavic nation, and appointed Andronicus as Bishop and successor to himself among them. But the Slavs and the Russes are one people, for it is because of the Varangians that the latter became known as Rus', though originally they were Slavs. While some Slavs were termed Polyanians, their speech was still Slavic, for they were known as Polyanians (29) because they lived in the fields. But they had the same Slavic language.

6407-6410 (899-902). The Emperor Leo incited the Magyars against the Bulgarians, so that they attacked and subjugated the whole Bulgarian country. When Symeon heard this news, he turned upon the

Magyars who attacked him and conquered the Bulgarians so that Symeon took refuge in Silistria.[31]

6411 (903). As Igor' grew up, he followed after Oleg, and obeyed his instructions. A wife, Olga by name, was brought to him from Pskov.[32]

6412-6415 (904-907). Leaving Igor' in Kiev, Oleg attacked the Greeks.[33] He took with him a multitude of Varangians, Slavs, Chuds, Krivichians, Merians, Polyanians, Severians, Derevlians, Radimichians, Croats, Dulebians, and Tivercians, who are pagans. All these tribes are known as Great Scythia by the Greeks. With this entire force, Oleg sallied forth by horse and by ship, and the number of his vessels was two thousand. (30) He arrived before Tsar'grad, but the Greeks fortified the strait and closed up the city. Oleg disembarked upon the shore, and ordered his soldiery to beach the ships. They waged war around the city, and accomplished much slaughter of the Greeks. They also destroyed many palaces and burned the churches. Of the prisoners they captured, some they beheaded, some they tortured, some they shot, and still others they cast into the sea. The Russes inflicted many other woes upon the Greeks after the usual manner of soldiers. Oleg commanded his warriors to make wheels which they attached to the ships, and when the wind was favorable, they spread the sails and bore down upon the city from the open country. When the Greeks beheld this, they were afraid, and sending messengers to Oleg, they implored him not to destroy the city and offered to submit to such tribute as he should desire. Thus Oleg halted his troops. The Greeks then brought out to him food and wine, but he would not accept it, for it was mixed with poison. Then the Greeks were terrified, and exclaimed, "This is not Oleg, but St. Demetrius, whom God has sent upon us." So Oleg demanded that they pay tribute for his two thousand ships at the rate of twelve *grivnÿ* per man, with forty men reckoned to a ship.

The Greeks assented to these terms and prayed for peace lest Oleg should conquer the land of Greece. Retiring thus a short distance from the city, Oleg concluded a peace with the Greek Emperors Leo and Alexander, and sent into the city to them (31) Karl, Farulf, Vermund, Hrollaf, and Steinvith, with instructions to receive the tribute. The Greeks promised to satisfy their requirements. Oleg demanded that they should give to the troops on the two thousand ships twelve *grivnÿ* per bench, and pay in addition the sums required for the various Russian cities: first Kiev, then Chernigov, Pereyaslavl', Polotsk, Rostov, Lyubech, and the other towns. In these cities lived great princes subject to Oleg.

[*The Russes proposed the following terms:*] "The Russes who come hither shall receive as much grain as they require. Whosoever come as merchants shall receive supplies for six months, including bread, wine, meat, fish, and fruit. Baths shall be prepared for them in any volume they require. When the Russes return homeward, they shall receive from your Emperor food, anchors, cordage, and sails and whatever else is needed for the journey."

The Greeks accepted these stipulations, and the Emperors and all the courtiers declared:

"If Russes come hither without merchandise, they shall receive no provisions. Your prince shall personally lay injunction upon such Russes as journey hither that they shall do no violence in the towns and throughout our territory. Such Russes as arrive here shall dwell in the St. Mamas quarter.[34] Our government will send officers to record their names, and they shall then receive their monthly allowance, first the natives of Kiev, then those from Chernigov, Pereyaslavl', and the other cities. They shall not enter the city save through one gate, unarmed and fifty at a time, escorted by an agent of the Emperor. They may conduct business according to their requirements without payment of taxes."

(32) Thus the Emperors Leo and Alexander made peace with Oleg, and after agreeing upon the tribute and mutually binding themselves by oath, they kissed the cross, and invited Oleg and his men to swear an oath likewise. According to the religion of the Russes, the latter swore by their weapons and by their god Perun, as well as by Volos, the god of cattle, and thus confirmed the treaty.[35]

Oleg gave orders that sails of brocade should be made for the Russes and silken ones for the Slavs, and his demand was satisfied.[36] The Russes hung their shields upon the gates as a sign of victory, and Oleg then departed from Tsar'grad. The Russes unfurled their sails of brocade and the Slavs their sails of silk, but the wind tore them. Then the Slavs said, "Let us keep our canvas ones; silken sails are not made for the Slavs." So Oleg came to Kiev, bearing palls, gold, fruit, and wine, along with every sort of adornment. The people called Oleg "the Sage," for they were but pagans, and therefore ignorant.

6416-6419 (908-911). A great star appeared in the west in the form of a spear.[37]

6420 (912). Oleg despatched his vassals to make peace and to draw up a treaty between the Greeks and the Russes. His envoys thus made declaration:

"This is the copy of the treaty concluded under the Emperors Leo and Alexander. We of the (33) Rus' nation: Karl, Ingjald, Farulf, Vermund, Hrollaf, Gunnar, Harold, Karni, Frithleif, Hroarr, Angantyr, Throand, Leithulf, Fast, and Steinvith,[38] are sent by Oleg, Great Prince of Rus', and by all the serene and great princes and the great boyars under his sway, unto you, Leo and Alexander and Constantine, great Autocrats in God, Emperors of the Greeks, for the maintenance and proclamation of the long-standing amity which joins Greeks and Russes, in accordance with the desires of our Great Princes and at their command, and in behalf of all those Russes who are subject to the hand of our Prince.

"Our serenity, above all desirous, through God's help, of maintaining and proclaiming such amicable relations as now exist between Christians and Russians, has often deemed it proper to publish and confirm this amity not merely in words but also in writing and under a firm oath sworn upon our weapons according to our religion and our law. As we previously agreed in the name of God's peace and amity, the articles of this convention are as follows:

"First, that we shall conclude a peace with you Greeks, and love each other with all our heart and will, and as far as lies in our power, prevent any subject of our serene Princes from committing any crime or misdemeanor. Rather shall we exert ourselves as far as possible to maintain as irrevocable and immutable henceforth and forever the amity thus proclaimed by our agreement with you Greeks and ratified by signature and oath. May you Greeks on your part maintain as irrevocable and (34) immutable henceforth and forever this same amity toward our serene Prince of Rus' and toward all the subjects of our serene Prince.

"In the matter of stipulations concerning damage, we subscribe to the following provisions:

"If clear proofs of tort exist, there shall be a true declaration of such proofs. But if this declaration is contested, the dissenting party shall take oath to this effect, and after he shall have taken oath according to his faith, a penalty shall be assessed in proportion to the apparent trespass committed.

"Whatsoever Russ kills a Christian, or whatsoever Christian kills a Russ, shall die, since he has committed murder. If any man flee after committing a murder, in the case that he is well-to-do, the nearest relatives of the victim shall receive a legal portion of the culprit's property, while the wife of the murderer shall receive a like amount, which is legally due her. But if the defendant is poor and has escaped, he shall be under distress until he returns, when he shall be executed.

"If any man strike another with a sword or assault him with any other sort of weapon, he shall, according to Russian law, pay five pounds of silver for such blow or assault. If the defendant is poor, he shall pay as much as he is able, and be deprived even of the very clothes he wears, and he shall also declare upon oath that he has no one to aid him. Thereafter the case against him shall be discontinued.

"If any Russ commit a theft against a Christian, (35) or *vice versa*, and should the transgressor be caught in the act by the victim of the loss, and be killed while resisting arrest, no penalty shall be exacted for his death by either Greeks or Russes. The victim of the loss shall recover the stolen property. If the thief surrenders, he shall be taken and bound by the one upon whom the theft was committed, and the culprit shall return whatever he has dared to appropriate, making at the same time threefold restitution for it.

"If any person, whether Greek or Russ, employs abusive treatment or violence against another and appropriates by force some articles of his property, he shall repay three times its value.

"If a ship is detained by high winds upon a foreign shore, and one of us Russes is near by, the ship with its cargo shall be revictualed and sent on to Christian territory. We will pilot it through every dangerous passage until it arrives at a place of safety. But if any such ship thus detained by storm or by some terrestrial obstacle cannot possibly reach its destination, we Russes will extend aid to the crew of this ship, and conduct them with their merchandise in all security, in case such an event takes place near Greek territory. But if such an accident befalls near the Russian shore, the ship's cargo shall be disposed of, and we Russes will remove whatever can be disposed of for the account of the owners. Then, when we proceed to Greece with merchandise or upon an embassy to your Emperor, we shall render up honorably the price of the sold (36) cargo of the ship. But if anyone on that ship is killed or maltreated by us Russes, or if any object is stolen, then those who have committed such acts shall be subject to the previously provided penalty.

"From this time forth, if a prisoner of either nation is in durance either of the Russes or of the Greeks, and then sold into another country, any Russ or Greek who happens to be in that locality shall purchase the prisoner and return the person thus purchased to his own native country. The purchaser shall be indemnified for the amount thus expended, or else the value of the prisoner's daily labor shall be reckoned toward the purchase money. If any Russ be taken prisoner by the Greeks, he shall likewise be sent back to his native land, and his purchase price shall be repaid, as has been stipulated, according to his value.

"Whenever you find it necessary to declare war, or when you are conducting a campaign, providing any Russes desirous of honoring your Emperor come at any time and wish to remain in his service, they shall be permitted in this respect to act according to their desire.

"If a Russian prisoner from any region is sold among the Christians, or if any Christian prisoner is sold among the Russes, he shall be ransomed for twenty bezants and returned to his native land.

"In case a Russian slave is stolen or escapes or is sold under compulsion, and if a Russ institutes a claim to this effect which is substantiated, the slave shall be returned to Rus'. If a merchant loses a slave and institutes a complaint, he shall search for this slave until he is found, but if any person refuses to allow him to make this search, the local officer shall forfeit his right of perquisition.

"With respect to the Russes professionally engaged in Greece under the orders of (37) the Christian Emperor, if any one of them dies without setting his property in order and has no kinsfolk there, his estate shall be returned to his distant relatives in Rus'. But if he makes some disposition of his goods, the person whom he has designated in writing as his heir shall receive the property of which he thus disposed. Such shall be the due process of inheritance in the cases of Russes engaging in trade, of casual travelers in Greece, and of those having debts outstanding there.

"If a criminal takes refuge in Greece, the Russes shall make complaint to the Christian Empire, and such criminal shall be arrested and returned to Rus' regardless of his protests. The Russes shall perform the same service for the Greeks whenever the occasion arises.

"As a convention and an inviolable pledge binding equally upon you Greeks and upon us Russes, we have caused the present treaty to be transcribed in vermillion script upon parchment in duplicate. In the name of the Holy Cross and the Holy and Indivisible Trinity of your one true God, your Emperor has confirmed it by his signature and handed it to our envoys. According to our own faith and the custom of our nation, we have sworn to your Emperor, who rules over you by the grace of God, that we will neither violate ourselves, nor allow any of our subjects to violate the peace and amity assured by the articles thus concluded between us. We have transmitted this document for the ratification of your Majesty in order to confirm and promulgate the treaty thus concluded between us this second of September, in the year of Creation 6420 (911), fifteenth of the indiction."[39]

The Emperor Leo honored the Russian envoys with gifts (38) of gold, palls, and robes, and placed his vassals at their disposition to show them the beauties of the churches, the golden palace, and the riches contained therein. They thus showed the Russes much gold and many palls and jewels, together with the relics of our Lord's Passion: the crown, the nails, and the purple robe, as well as the bones of the Saints. They also instructed the Russes in their faith, and expounded to them the true belief. Thus the Emperor dismissed them to their native land with great honor. The envoys sent by Oleg returned to Kiev, and reported to him all the utterances of both Emperors. They recounted how they had made peace and established a covenant between Greece and Rus', confirmed by oaths inviolable for the subjects of both countries.

Thus Oleg ruled in Kiev, and dwelt at peace with all nations.

Now autumn came, and Oleg bethought him of his horse that he had caused to be well fed, yet had never mounted. For on one occasion he had made inquiry of the wonder-working magicians as to the ultimate cause of his death. One magician replied, "Oh Prince, it is from the steed which you love and on which you ride that you shall meet your death." Oleg then reflected and determined never to mount this horse or even to look upon it again. So he gave command that the horse should be properly fed, but never led into his presence. He thus let several years pass until he had attacked the Greeks. After he returned to Kiev, four years elapsed, but in the fifth he thought of the horse through which the magicians had foretold that he should meet his death. He thus summoned his senior squire and inquired as to the whereabouts of the horse which he had ordered to be fed and well cared for. (39) The squire answered that he was dead. Oleg laughed and mocked the magician, exclaiming, "Soothsayers tell untruths, and their words are naught but falsehood. This horse is dead, but I am still alive."

Then he commanded that a horse should be saddled. "Let me see his bones," said he. He rode to the place where the bare bones and skull lay. Dismounting from his horse, he laughed and remarked, "So I was supposed to receive my death from this skull?" And he stamped upon the skull with his foot. But a serpent crawled forth from it and bit him in the foot, so that in consequence he sickened and died. All the people mourned for him in great grief. They bore him away and buried him upon the hill which is called Shchekovitsa. His tomb stands there to this day, and it is called the Tomb of Oleg.[40] Now all the years of his reign were thirty-three.

It is remarkable what may be accomplished through witchcraft and enchantment. During the reign of Domitian, there lived a certain soothsayer named Apollonius of Tyana. *He attained celebrity, and journeyed about performing infernal marvels throughout the cities and towns. From Rome he came to Byzantium, and on being besought of the inhabitants to accomplish this wonder, he drove out a multitude of serpents and scorpions from the city, so that no man should be wounded by them. He also tamed horses of violent temper before the assembled nobles.*

He came likewise to Antioch, and on being besought by the inhabitants (since Antioch was tormented with scorpions (40) and gnats), he made a brass scorpion and buried it in the earth. After setting a small marble post over it, he bade the inhabitants hold reeds in their hands and walk through the city shaking the reeds and crying, "May this city be rid of gnats!" Thus the gnats and scorpions vanished from the city. When he was questioned regarding the earthquakes that threatened the city, he sighed, and wrote on a tablet these words, "Alas for thee, unhappy city! Thou shalt be much shaken by an earthquake and fall a prey to flame, and this river Orontes shall bewail thee by its shores."

Of this magician, the great Anastasius of the City of God remarked, "Even to this day the enchantments of Apollonius remain effective, some for the elimination of four-footed beasts or of birds capable of harming mankind, and others for the control of beds of rivers flowing in unfixed channels, while still others are eminently effective against disease and injury to man." Not only during his life did the demons at his command bring such wonders to pass, but even after his death they hover about his tomb and perform miracles in his name to deceive unhappy men, who are much inclined to such errors through the influence of the devil.

What shall we say of those who perform works of magic? For a certain man was so skilled in magical deception that he ridiculed Apollonius the Sage on the ground that he did not cultivate true (41) philosophical knowledge. "He ought," he asserted, "like me to accomplish his desires by means of a single word, and should not execute his devices by material means." All these things exist through the sufferance of God and the agency of the devil, that by such means our orthodox faith may be tested as to whether it is firm and secure, cleaving to the Lord and not to be seduced by the Enemy through false miracles and satanic acts performed by the servants and slaves of his wickedness. Some have even prophesied in the name of the Lord, like Balaam and Saul and Caiaphas, and have driven out the devil like Jude and the sons of Sceva (Acts, xix, 14-15). For the Lord often gives grace to the unworthy that it may benefit others. Thus Balaam was far from both life and faith, yet in him the Lord gave evidence of grace that others might see. Such was Pharaoh, but to him the Lord showed the future. There was Nebuchadnezzar also, who sinned against the law. To him the Lord revealed what was to occur after many generations, thus showing that many who have a hostile heart perform miracles according to the example of Christ, yet by other means, to deceive men who do not understand good works. Such were Simon the Magician and (42) *Menander. Of such men it has truly been said, "Be not deceived by miracles."*[41]

6421 (913). Igor' succeeded Oleg and began his reign. At the same time began the reign of Constantine, son of Leo and son-in-law of Romanus.[42] The Derevlians offered resistance to Igor' after Oleg's death.

6422 (914) Igor' attacked the Derevlians, and after conquering them, he imposed upon them a tribute larger than Oleg's. In the same year, Symeon of Bulgaria attacked Tsar'grad, and when peace was made, he returned to his own country.

6423 (915). The Pechenegs entered the land of Rus' for the first time, but when they made peace with Igor', they went their way to the Danube. At this time, Symeon subjugated Thrace, and the Greeks summoned the Pechenegs to aid them. When the Pechenegs arrived and wished to attack Symeon, the Greek generals quarreled. The Pechenegs, on seeing how they were quarreling among themselves, returned homeward, but the Bulgarians came to blows with the Greeks, and the Greeks were cut to pieces. Symeon took Adrianople,[43] which was first called the city of Orestes, son of Agamemnon, who in ancient times was cured of a disease by bathing in three rivers, and then named the city after himself on this account. Subsequently the Emperor Hadrian restored (43) it, and named it Adrianople for himself, but we call it Adriangrad.

6424-6428 (916-920). Romanus was set up as Emperor in Greece.[44] Igor' waged war against the Pechenegs.

6429-6437 (921-929). Symeon attacked Tsar'grad, ravaged Thrace and Macedonia, and presumptuously appeared with a large force before Tsar'grad. He then made peace with the Emperor Romanus, and returned into his own country.[45]

6438-6442 (930-934). The Magyars attacked Tsar'grad for the first time, and ravaged the whole of Thrace. Romanus made peace with them.[46]

(44) 6443-6449 (935-941). Igor' attacked the Greeks, and the Bul-

garians sent word to the Emperor that the Russes were advancing upon Tsar'grad with ten thousand vessels.[47] The Russes set out across the sea, and began to ravage Bithynia. They waged war along the Pontus as far as Heraclea and Paphlagonia, and laid waste the entire region of Nicomedia, burning everything along the gulf. Of the people they captured, some they butchered, others they set up as targets and shot at, some they seized upon, and after binding their hands behind their backs, they drove iron nails through their heads. Many sacred churches they gave to the flames, while they burned many monasteries and villages, and took no little booty on both sides of the sea. Then, when the army came out of the east, Pantherius the Domestic with forty thousand men, Phocas the Patrician with the Macedonians, and Theodore the General with the Thracians, supported by other illustrious nobles, surrounded the Russes. After taking counsel, the latter threw themselves upon the Greeks, and as the conflict between them was desperate, the Greeks experienced difficulty in winning the upper hand. The Russes returned at evening to their companions, embarked at night upon their vessels, and fled away. Theophanes pursued them in boats with Greek fire, and dropped it through pipes upon the Russian ships, so that a strange miracle was offered to view.

Upon seeing the flames, the Russians cast themselves into the seawater, being anxious to escape, (45), but the survivors returned home. When they came once more to their native land, where each one recounted to his kinsfolk the course of events and described the fire launched from the ships, they related that the Greeks had in their possession the lightning from heaven, and had set them on fire by pouring it forth, so that the Russes could not conquer them. Upon his return, Igor' began to collect a great army, and sent many messengers after the Varangians beyond the sea, inviting them to attack the Greeks, for he desired to make war upon them.

6450 (942). Symeon attacked the Croats and was beaten by them. He then died, leaving Peter, his son, as Prince of the Bulgarians.[48]

6451 (943). When the Magyars had attacked Tsar'grad, they returned homeward after they had made peace with Romanus.[49]

6452 (944). After collecting many warriors among the Varangians, the Russes, the Polyanians, the Slavs, the Krivichians, the Tivercians, and the Pechenegs, and receiving hostages from them, Igor' advanced upon the Greeks by ship and by horse, thirsting for revenge.[50] The Khersonians, upon hearing of this expedition, reported to Romanus that the Russes were advancing with innumerable ships and covered the sea with their vessels. Likewise the Bulgarians sent tidings to the effect that the Russes were on the way, and that they had won the Pechenegs for their allies. When the Emperor heard this news, he sent to Igor' his best boyars to entreat him to come no nearer, but rather to accept the tribute which Oleg had received, and to the amount of which something should even be added. He likewise sent palls and much gold to the Pechenegs.

Now Igor', when he came to the Danube, called together his retinue, and after some reflection communicated to them the Emperor's offer. (46) Igor's retinue then replied, "If the Emperor speaks thus, what do we desire beyond receiving gold, silver, and palls without having to fight for them? Who knows who will be victorious, we or he? Who has the sea for his ally? For we are not marching by land, but through the depths of the sea. Death lies in wait for us all." Igor' heeded them, and bade the Pechenegs ravage Bulgaria. He himself, after receiving from the Greeks gold and palls sufficient for his whole army, returned again and came to Kiev in his native land.

6453 (945). Romanus, Constantine, and Stephen sent envoys to Igor' to renew the previous treaty, and Igor' discussed the matter with them. Igor' sent his own envoys to Romanus, and the Emperor called together his boyars and his dignitaries. The Russian envoys were introduced and bidden to speak, and it was commanded that the remarks of both parties should be inscribed upon parchment. A copy of the agreement concluded under the most Christian princes Romanus, Constantine, and Stephen follows:

"We are the envoys from the Russian nation: Ivar, envoy of Igor', Great Prince of Rus', and the general envoys as follows: Vefast representing Svyatoslav, son of Igor'; Isgaut for the Princess Olga; Slothi for Igor', nephew of Igor'; Oleif for Vladislav; Kanitzar for Predslava; Sigbjorn for Svanhild, wife of Oleif; Freystein for Thorth; Leif for Arfast; Grim for Sverki; Freystein for Haakon, nephew of Igor'; Kari for Stoething; Karlsefni for Thorth; Hegri for Efling; Voist for Voik; Eistr for Amund; (47) Freystein for Bjorn; Yatving for Gunnar; Sigfrid for Halfdan; Kill for Klakki; Steggi for Jotun; Sverki; Hallvarth for Guthi; Frothi for Throand; Munthor for Ut; the merchants Authun, Authulf, Ingivald, Oleif, Frutan, Gamal, Kussi, Heming, Thorfrid, Thorstein, Bruni, Hroald, Gunnfast, Freystein, Ingjald, Thorbjorn, Manni, Hroald, Svein, Styr, Halfdan, Tirr, Askbrand, Visleif, Sveinki Borich: sent by Igor', Great Prince of Rus', and from each prince and all the people of the land of Rus', by whom is ordained the renewal of the former peace to the confusion of the devil, who hates peace and loves discord, and to the establishment of concord between Greeks and Russes for many years to come.[51]

"Our Great Prince Igor', and his princes and his boyars, and the whole people of Rus have sent us to Romanus, Constantine, and Stephen the mighty Emperors of Greece, to establish a bond of friendship with the Emperors themselves, as well as with all their boyars and the entire Greek nation henceforth and forever, as long as the sun shines and the world stands fixed. If any inhabitant of the land of Rus' thinks to violate this amity, may such of these transgressors as have adopted the Christian faith incur condign punishment from Almighty God in the shape of damnation and destruction forevermore. If any of these transgressors be not baptized, may they receive help neither from God nor from Perun: (48) may they not be protected by their own shields, but may they rather be slain by their own swords, laid low by their own arrows or by any of their own weapons, and may they be in bondage forever."

[*The Greeks stipulated:*] "The Great Prince of Rus' and his boyars shall send to Greece to the great Greek Emperors as many ships as they desire with their agents and merchants, according to the prevailing usage. The agents hitherto carried gold seals, and the merchants silver ones. But your Prince has now made known that he will forward a certificate to our government, and any agents or merchants thus sent by the Russians shall be provided with such a certificate to the effect that a given number of ships has been dispatched. By this means we shall be assured that they come with peaceful intent.

"But if such persons come uncertified and are surrendered to us, we shall detain and hold them until we notify your Prince. If they do not surrender, but offer resistance, they shall be killed, and indemnity for their death shall not be exacted by your Prince. If, however, they flee to Rus', we shall so inform your Prince, and he shall deal with them as he sees fit.

"If Russes come without merchandise, they shall not be entitled to receive monthly allowance. Your Prince shall moreover prohibit his agents and such other Russes as come hither from the commission of violence in our villages and territory. Such Russes as come hither shall dwell by St. Mamas's Church. Our authorities shall note their names, and they shall then receive their monthly allowance, (49) the agents the amount proper to their position, and the merchants the usual amount; first, those from Kiev, then those from Chernigov and Pereyaslavl'. They shall enter the city through one gate in groups of fifty without weapons, and shall dispose of their merchandise as they require, after which they shall depart. An officer of our government shall guard them, in order that, if any Russ or Greek does wrong, he may redress it.

"When the Russes enter the city, they shall not have the right to buy silk above the value of fifty bezants. Whoever purchases such silks shall exhibit them to the imperial officer, who will stamp and return them. When the Russes depart hence, they shall receive from us as many provisions as they require for the journey, and what they need for their ships (as has been previously determined), and they shall return home in safety. They shall not have the privilege of wintering in the St. Mamas quarter.

"If any slave runs away from the Russes and while they are within the territory of our Empire, or from the St. Mamas quarter, he shall be apprehended if found in Greek territory. If he is not found, the Christian Russes shall so swear according to their faith, and the non-Christians after their custom, and they shall then receive from us their due, two pieces of silk per slave, according to previous stipulations. If, among the people of our Empire, whether from our city or elsewhere, any slave of ours escapes (50) among you and takes anything with him, the Russes shall send him back again. If what he has appropriated is intact, the finders shall receive two bezants from its value.

"If any Russ attempts to commit theft upon the subjects of our Empire, he who so acts shall be severely punished, and he shall pay double the value of what he has stolen. If a Greek so transgress against a Russ, he shall receive the same punishment that the latter would suffer for a like offence. If a Russ commits a theft upon a Greek, or a Greek upon a Russ, he must return not only the stolen article, but also its value. If the stolen article is found to have been sold, he shall return double the price, and also shall be punished both by Greek law and statute and by the law of the Russes.

"If the Russes bring in young men or grown girls who have been taken prisoners from our dominions, the Greeks shall pay a ransom of ten bezants each and recover the captives. If the latter are of middle age, the Greeks shall recover them on payment of eight bezants each. But in the case that the captives are old persons or young children, the ransom shall be five bezants. If any Russes are found laboring as slaves in Greece, providing they are prisoners of war, the Russes shall ransom them for ten bezants each. But if a Greek has actually purchased any such prisoner, and so declares under oath, he shall receive in return the full purchase price paid for the prisoner.

"In the matter of the country of Kherson and all the cities in that region, the Prince of Rus' shall not have the right (51) to harass these localities, nor shall that district be subject to you. If the Prince of Rus' calls on us for soldiers wherewith to wage war, we agree to supply him with any number required.

"In case the Russes find a Greek ship cast ashore, they shall not harm it, and if any person remove any object therefrom or enslave a member of the crew, or kill him, he shall be amenable to both Russian and Greek law. If Russian subjects meet with Khersonian fishermen at the mouth of Dnieper, they shall not harm them in any wise. The Russes shall, moreover, not have the right to winter at the mouth of Dnieper, either at Belobereg or by St. Eleutherius, but when autumn comes, they shall return home to Rus.' Regarding the Black Bulgarians, who come and ravage the Kherson district, we enjoin the Prince of Rus' not to allow them to injure that region.

"If any crime is committed by a Greek subject to our Empire, the Russes shall not have the right to punish him, but according to the legislation of our Empire, he shall suffer in proportion to his misdeed.

"If a Christian kill a Russ, or a Russ a Christian, he who has committed the murder shall be held by the relatives of the deceased that they may kill him. If he who has committed murder runs away and escapes, the relatives of the murdered man shall receive the murderer's property in the case that he is wealthy. But if the escaped culprit is poor, he shall be pursued (52) till found, and when he is found, he shall be executed.

"If a Russ assault a Greek, or a Greek a Russ, with sword, spear, or any other weapon, he who has committed this crime shall pay five pounds of silver according to the Russian law, but if he is poor, all his available property shall be sold, even to the garments he walks in, and these too shall be taken from him. Finally he shall swear upon his faith that he has no possessions, and then he shall be released.

"If our government shall desire of you military assistance for use against our adversaries, they shall communicate with your Great Prince, and he shall send us as many soldiers as we require. From this fact, other countries shall learn what amity the Greeks and the Russes entertain toward each other.[52]

"By common consent, we have thus inscribed all this convention upon a double parchment, one portion of which remains in the hands of our government, with a cross and our names subscribed thereon, while your merchants and agents have signed the other. Your representatives shall go forth with the envoys of our government and conduct them before Igor', Great Prince of Rus', and to his subjects. Upon receipt of this document, they shall then bind themselves by oath to observe the truth as agreed upon between us and inscribed upon this parchment, wherein our names are written."

[*The Russes thus bound themselves:*] "Those of us who are baptized have sworn in the Cathedral, by the church of St. Elias, upon the Holy Cross set before us, and upon this parchment, to abide by all that is written herein, and not to violate (53) any of its stipulations. May whosoever of our compatriots, Prince or common, baptized or unbaptized, who does so violate them, have no succor from God, but may he be slave in this life and in the life to come, and may he perish by his own arms.

"The unbaptized Russes shall lay down their shields, their naked swords, their armlets, and their other weapons, and shall swear to all that is inscribed upon this parchment, to be faithfully observed forever by Igor', all his boyars, and all the people from the land of Rus'. If any of the princes or any Russian subject, whether Christian or non-Christian, violates the terms of this instrument, he shall merit death by his own weapons, and be accursed of God and of Perun because he violated his oath. So be it good that the Great Prince Igor' shall rightly maintain these friendly relations that they may never be interrupted, as long as the sun shines and the world endures henceforth and forevermore."

The agents sent by Igor' returned to him with the Greek envoys, and reported all the words of the Emperor Romanus. Then Igor' called the Greek envoys before him, and bade them report what injunction the Emperor had laid upon them. The Emperor's envoys replied, "The Emperor has sent us. He loves peace, and desires to maintain concord and amity with the Prince of Rus'. Your envoys have received the pledge of our Emperors, and they have sent us to receive your oath and that of your followers." Igor' promised to comply with their request.

(54) In the morning, Igor' summoned the envoys, and went to a hill on which there was a statue of Perun. The Russes laid down their weapons, their shields, and their gold ornaments, and Igor' and his people took oath (at least, such as were pagans), while the Christian Russes took oath in the church of St. Elias, which is above the creek, in the vicinity of the Pasÿncha square and the quarter of the Khazars. This was, in fact, a parish church, since many of the Varangians were Christians.[53]

Igor', after confirming the treaty with the Greeks, dismissed their envoys, bestowing upon them furs, slaves, and wax, and sent them away. The envoys then returned to the Emperor, and reported all the words of Igor' and his affection for the Greeks. Thus Igor' began to rule in Kiev, enjoying peaceful relations with all nations. But when autumn came, he thought of the Derevlians, and wished to collect from them a still larger tribute.[54]

6453 (945). In this year, Igor's retinue said to him, "The servants of Sveinald are adorned with weapons and fine raiment, but we are naked. Go forth with us, oh Prince, after tribute, that both you and we may profit thereby." Igor' heeded their words, and he attacked Dereva in search of tribute. He sought to increase the previous tribute and collected it by violence from the people with the assistance of his followers. After thus gathering the tribute, he returned to his city. On his homeward way, he said to his followers, after some reflection, "Go forward with the tribute. I shall turn back, and rejoin you later." He dismissed his retainers on their journey homeward, but being desirous of still greater booty he returned on his tracks with a few of his followers.

The Derevlians heard that he was again approaching, and consulted with Mal, their prince, saying, (55) "If a wolf come among the sheep, he will take away the whole flock one by one, unless he be killed. If we do not thus kill him now, he will destroy us all." They then sent forward to Igor' inquiring why he had returned, since he had collected all the tribute. But Igor' did not heed them, and the Derevlians came forth from the city of Iskorosten' and slew Igor' and his company, for the number of the latter was few. So Igor' was buried, and his tomb is near the city of Iskorosten' in Dereva even to this day.

But Olga was in Kiev with her son, the boy Svyatoslav. His tutor was Asmund, and the troop commander was Sveinald, the father of Mstikha. The Derevlians then said, "See, we have killed the Prince of Rus'. Let us take his wife Olga for our Prince Mal,[55] and then we shall obtain possession of Svyatoslav, and work our will upon him." So they sent their best men, twenty in number, to Olga by boat, and they arrived below Borichev in their boat. At that time, the water flowed below the heights of Kiev, and the inhabitants did not live in the valley, but upon the heights. The city of Kiev was on the present site of the residence of Gordyata and Nicephorus, and the prince's palace was in the city where the residence of Vratislav and Chudin now stands, while the hunting grounds were outside the city. Without the city stood another palace, where the palace of the Cantors is now situated, behind the Church of the Holy Virgin upon the heights. This was a palace with a stone hall.[56]

Olga was informed that the Derevlians had arrived, and summoned them to her presence with a gracious welcome. When the Derevlians had thus announced their arrival, Olga replied with an inquiry as to the reason of their coming. The Derevlians (56) then announced that their tribe had sent them to report that they had slain her husband, because he was like a wolf, crafty and ravening, but that their princes, who had thus preserved the land of Dereva, were good, and that Olga should come and marry their Prince Mal. For the name of the Prince of Dereva was Mal.

Olga made this reply, "Your proposal is pleasing to me; indeed, my husband cannot rise again from the dead. But I desire to honor you tomorrow in the presence of my people. Return now to your boat, and remain there with an aspect of arrogance. I shall send for you on the morrow, and you shall say, 'We will not ride on horses nor go on foot; carry us in our boat.' And you shall be carried in your boat." Thus she dismissed them to their vessel.

Now Olga gave command that a large deep ditch should be dug in the castle with the hall, outside the city. Thus, on the morrow, Olga, as she sat in the hall, sent for the strangers, and her messengers approached them and said, "Olga summons you to great honor." But they replied, "We will not ride on horseback nor in wagons, nor go on foot; carry us in our boats." The people of Kiev then lamented, "Slavery is our lot. Our Prince is killed, and our Princess intends to marry their prince." So they carried the Derevlians in their boat. The latter sat on the cross-benches in great robes, puffed up with pride. They thus were borne into the court before Olga, and when the men had brought the Derevlians in, they dropped them into the trench along with the boat. Olga bent over and inquired whether they found the honor to their taste. They answered that it was worse than the death of Igor'. She then commanded that they should be buried alive, and they were thus buried.

Olga then sent messages to the Derevlians to the effect that, if they really required her presence, they should send after her their distinguished men, so that she might go (57) to their Prince with due honor, for otherwise her people in Kiev would not let her go. When the Derevlians heard this message, they gathered together the best men who governed the land of Dereva, and sent them to her. When the Derevlians arrived, Olga commanded that a bath should be made ready, and invited them to appear before her after they had bathed. The bath-house was then heated, and the Derevlians entered in to bathe. Olga's men closed up the bathhouse behind them, and she gave orders to set it on fire from the doors, so that the Derevlians were all burned to death.

Olga then sent to the Derevlians the following message, "I am now coming to you, so prepare great quantities of mead in the city where you killed my husband, that I may weep over his grave and hold a funeral feast for him." When they heard these words, they gathered great quantities of honey and brewed mead. Taking a small escort, Olga made the journey with ease, and upon her arrival at Igor's tomb, she wept for her husband. She bade her followers pile up a great mound and when they had piled it up, she also gave command that a funeral feast should be held. Thereupon the Derevlians sat down to drink, and Olga bade her followers wait upon them.

The Derevlians inquired of Olga where the retinue was which they had sent to meet her. She replied that they were following with her husband's bodyguard. When the Derevlians were drunk, she bade her followers fall upon them, and went about herself egging on her retinue to the massacre of the Derevlians. So they cut down five thousand of them; but Olga returned to Kiev and prepared an army to attack the survivors.

6454 (946). Olga, together with her son (58) Svyatoslav, gathered a large and valiant army, and proceeded to attack the land of the Derevlians. The latter came out to meet her troops, and when both forces were ready for combat, Svyatoslav cast his spear against the Derevlians. But the spear barely cleared the horse's ears, and struck against his leg, for the prince was but a child. Then Sveinald and Asmund said, "The prince has already begun battle; press on, vassals, after the prince." Thus they conquered the Derevlians, with the result that the latter fled, and shut themselves up in their cities.

Olga hastened with her son to the city of Iskorosten', for it was there that her husband had been slain, and they laid siege to the city. The Derevlians barricaded themselves within the city, and fought valiantly from it, for they realized that they had killed the prince, and to what fate they would in consequence surrender.

Olga remained there a year without being able to take the city, and then she thought out this plan. She sent into the town the following message: "Why do you persist in holding out? All your cities have surrendered to me and submitted to tribute, so that the inhabitants now cultivate their fields and their lands in peace. But you had rather die of hunger, without submitting to tribute." The Derevlians replied that they would be glad to submit to tribute, but that she was still bent on avenging her husband. Olga then answered, "Since I have already avenged the misfortune of my husband twice on the occasions when your messengers came to Kiev, and a third time when I held a funeral feast for him, I do not desire further revenge, but am anxious to receive a small tribute. After I have made peace with you, I shall return home again."

The Derevlians then inquired what she desired of them, and expressed their readiness to pay honey and furs. Olga retorted that at the moment they had neither honey nor furs, (59) but that she had one small request to make. "Give me three pigeons," she said, "and three sparrows from each house. I do not desire to impose a heavy tribute, like my husband, but I require only this small gift from you, for you are impoverished by the siege." The Derevlians rejoiced, and collected from each house three pigeons and three sparrows, which they sent to Olga with their greetings. Olga then instructed them, in view of their submission, to return to their city, promising that on the morrow she would depart and return to her own capital. The Derevlians re-entered their city with gladness, and when they reported to the inhabitants, the people of the town rejoiced.

Now Olga gave to each soldier in her army a pigeon or a sparrow, and ordered them to attach by a thread to each pigeon and sparrow a piece of sulphur bound with small pieces of cloth. When night fell, Olga bade her soldiers release the pigeons and the sparrows. So the birds flew to their nests, the pigeons to the cotes, and the sparrows under the eaves. Thus the dove-cotes, the coops, the porches, and the haymows were set on fire. There was not a house that was not consumed, and it was impossible to extinguish the flames, because all the houses caught fire at once. The people fled from the city, and Olga ordered her soldiers to catch them. Thus she took the city and burned it, and captured the elders of the city. Some of the other captives she killed, while she gave others as slaves to her followers. The remnant she left to pay (60) tribute.[57]

She imposed upon them a heavy tribute, two parts of which went to Kiev, and the third to Olga in Výshgorod; for Výshgorod was Olga's city.[58] She then passed through the land of Dereva, accompanied by her son and her retinue, establishing laws and tribute. Her trading posts and hunting-preserves are there still. Then she returned with her son to Kiev, her city, where she remained one year.

6455 (947). Olga went to Novgorod, and along the Msta she established trading-posts and collected tribute. She also collected imposts and tribute along the Luga.[59] Her hunting-grounds, boundary posts, towns, and trading-posts still exist throughout the whole region, while her sleighs stand in Pskov to this day. Her fowling preserves still remain on the Dnieper and the Desna, while her village of Ol'zhichi[60] is in existence even now. After making these dispositions, she returned to her city of Kiev, and dwelt at peace with it.

6456-6463 (948-955). Olga went to Greece, and arrived at Tsar'grad. The reigning Emperor was named Constantine, son of Leo.[61] Olga came before him, and when he saw that she was very fair of countenance and wise as well, the Emperor wondered at her intellect. He conversed with her and remarked that she was worthy to reign with him in his city. (61) When Olga heard his words, she replied that she was still a pagan, and that if he desired to baptize her, he should perform this function himself; otherwise, she was unwilling to accept baptism. The Emperor, with the assistance of the Patriarch, accordingly baptized her.

When Olga was enlightened, she rejoiced in soul and body. The Patriarch, who instructed her in the faith, said to her, "Blessed art thou among the women of Rus', for thou hast loved the light, and quit the darkness. The sons of Rus' shall bless thee to the last generation of thy descendants." He taught her the doctrine of the Church, and instructed her in prayer and fasting, in almsgiving, and in the maintenance of chastity. She bowed her head, and like a sponge absorbing water, she eagerly drank in his teachings. The Princess bowed before the Patriarch, saying, "Through thy prayers, Holy Father, may I be preserved from the crafts and assaults of the devil!" At her baptism she was christened Helena, after the ancient Empress, mother of Constantine the Great. The Patriarch then blessed her and dismissed her.[62]

After her baptism, the Emperor summoned Olga and made known to her that he wished her to become his wife. But she replied, "How can you marry me, after yourself baptizing me and calling me your daughter? For among Christians that is unlawful, as you yourself must know." Then the Emperor said, "Olga, you have outwitted me." He gave her many gifts of gold, silver, silks, and various vases, and dismissed her, still calling her his daughter.

Since Olga was anxious to return home, she went to the Patriarch to request his benediction for the homeward journey, and said to him, "My people and my son are heathen. May God protect me from all evil!" The Patriarch replied, "Child of the faith, thou hast been baptized into Christ and hast put on Christ. Christ (62) shall therefore save thee. Even as he saved Abraham from Abimelech, Lot from the Sodomites, Moses from Pharaoh, David from Saul, the Three Children from the fiery furnace, and Daniel from the wild beasts, he will preserve thee likewise from the devil and his snares." So the Patriarch blessed her, and she returned in peace to her own country, and arrived in Kiev.

Thus it was when the Queen of Ethiopia came to Solomon, wishing to hear his words of wisdom, and beheld much wisdom and many wonders. Even so, the sainted Olga sought the blessed wisdom of God. But the Queen sought human wisdom, while Olga sought divine wisdom. For those who seek for wisdom shall find it. "Wisdom is celebrated in places of concourse, she lifteth up her voice in the streets; she crieth at the entrance to the walls, at the gates of cities she uttereth speech. For as many years as the just cleave to wisdom, they shall not be ashamed." (*Prov.*, i, 20-22).

From her youth up, the sainted Olga always sought wisdom in this world, and she found a pearl of great price, which is Christ. For Solomon has said, "The accomplished desire of the faithful is sweet to the soul" (*Prov.*, xiii, 19); and, "Incline thine heart to wisdom; I love them that love me, and those that seek me shall find me" (*ibid.*, xi, 2). And the Lord saith, "He who cometh to me I will not cast out" (*John*, vi, 38).

Thus Olga arrived in Kiev, and the Greek Emperor sent a message to her, saying, "Inasmuch as I bestowed many gifts upon you, you promised me that on your return to Rus' you would send me many presents of slaves, wax, and furs, (63) and despatch soldiery to aid me." Olga made answer to the envoys that if the Emperor would spend as long a time with her in the Pochayna[63] as she had remained on the Bosporus, she would grant his request. With these words, she dismissed the envoys.[64]

Now Olga dwelt with her son Svyatoslav, and she urged him to be baptized, but he would not listen to her suggestion, though when any man wished to be baptized, he was not hindered, but only mocked. For to the infidels, the Christian faith is foolishness. They do not comprehend it, because they walk in darkness and do not see the glory of God. Their hearts are hardened, and they can neither hear with their ears nor see with their eyes. For Solomon has said, "The deeds of the unrighteous are far from wisdom. Inasmuch as I have called you, and ye heard me not, I sharpened my words, and ye understood not. But ye have set at nought all my counsel, and would have none of my reproach. For they have hated knowledge, and the fear of Jehovah they have not chosen. They would none of my counsel, but despised all my reproof" (*Prov.*, i, 24-31).

Olga remarked oftentimes, "My son, I have learned to know God, and am glad for it. If you know him, you too will rejoice." But he did not heed her exhortation, answering, "How shall I alone accept another faith? My followers will laugh at that." But his mother replied, "If you are converted, all your subjects will perforce follow your example." Svyatoslav did not heed his mother, but followed heathen usages, for he did not know that whoever does not obey his mother shall come to distress. For it is written, "Whosoever heedeth not his father or his mother (64) shall suffer death (*Exod.,* xxi, 17). But he was incensed at his mother for this reason. As Solomon has said, "He that correcteth the unrighteous getteth to himself reviling, and he that reproveth a wicked man getteth himself a blot. Rebuke not the evil, lest he hate thee" (*Prov.,* ix, 7-8). For rebuke addressed to evildoers provokes offence.

But notwithstanding, Olga loved her son Svyatoslav, and said, "So be the will of God. If God wishes to have pity upon my kin and upon the land of Rus', let him lead my son's heart to return to God, even as God has granted me to do." Thus saying, she prayed night and day for her son and for the people, while she brought him up to manhood and adult age.

6464-6472 (956-964). When Prince Svyatoslav had grown up and matured, he began to collect a numerous and valiant army. Stepping light as a leopard, he undertook many campaigns. Upon his expeditions he carried with him neither wagons nor kettles, and boiled no meat, but cut off small strips of horseflesh, game, or beef, and ate it after roasting it on the coals. Nor did he have a tent, but he spread out a horse-blanket under him, and set his saddle under his head; (65) and all his retinue did likewise. He sent messengers to the other lands announcing his intention to attack them. He went to the Oka and the Volga, and on coming in contact with the Vyatichians, he inquired of them to whom they paid tribute. They made answer that they paid a silver-piece per ploughshare to the Khazars.

6473 (965). Svyatoslav sallied forth against the Khazars.[65] When they heard of his approach, they went out to meet him with their Prince, the Kagan, and the armies came to blows. When the battle thus took place, Svyatoslav defeated the Khazars and took their city of Bela Vezha. He also conquered the Yasians and the Kasogians.[66]

6474 (966). Svyatoslav conquered the Vyatichians and made them his tributaries.[67]

6475 (967). Svyatoslav marched to the Danube to attack the Bulgarians. When they fought together, Svyatoslav overcame the Bulgarians, and captured eighty towns along the Danube. He took up his residence there, and ruled in Pereyaslavets, receiving tribute from the Greeks.[68]

6476 (968). While Svyatoslav was at Pereyaslavets, the Pechenegs invaded Rus' for the first time. So Olga shut herself up in the city of Kiev with her grandsons, Yaropolk, Oleg, and Vladimir.[69] The nomads besieged the city with a great force. They surrounded it with an innumerable multitude, so that it was impossible to escape or send messages from the city, and the inhabitants were weak from hunger and thirst. Those who had gathered on the other side of the Dnieper in their boats remained on that side, and not one of them could enter Kiev, while no one could cross over to them from the city itself.

(66) The inhabitants of the city were afflicted, and lamented, "Is there no one that can reach the opposite shore and report to the other party that if we are not relieved on the morrow, we must perforce surrender to the Pechenegs?" Then one youth volunteered to make the attempt, and the people begged him to try it. So he went out of the city with a bridle in his hand, and ran among the Pechenegs shouting out a question whether anyone had seen a horse. For he knew their language, and they thought he was one of themselves. When he approached the river, he threw off his clothes, jumped into the Dnieper, and swam out. As soon as the Pechenegs perceived his action, they hurried in pursuit, shooting at him the while, but they did not succeed in doing any harm. The party on the other shore caught sight of him, and rowed out in a boat to meet him. They then took him into their boat, and brought him to their company. He thus reported to them that if they could not relieve the city on the next day, the inhabitants would surrender to the Pechenegs.

Then their general, Pretich by name, announced, "Tomorrow we shall approach by boat, and after rescuing the Princess and the young Princes, we shall fetch them over to this side. If we do not bring this to pass, Svyatoslav will put us to death." When it was morning, they embarked before dawn in their boats, and blew loudly on their trumpets. The people within the city raised a shout, so that the Pechenegs thought the Prince himself had returned, and accordingly fled from the city in various directions. Thus Olga went forth with her grandsons and her followers to the boats. When the Prince of the Pechenegs perceived their escape, he came alone to Pretich, the general, and inquired who had just arrived. Pretich replied that it was a boat from the opposite bank. The Prince of the Pechenegs inquired whether Pretich was the Prince himself. The general then replied that he was the Prince's vassal, and that he had come as a vanguard, (67) but that a countless force was on the way under the Prince's command. He made this statement simply to frighten the Pechenegs. So the Prince of the Pechenegs invited Pretich to become his friend, to which request Pretich assented. The two shook hands on it, and the Prince of the Pechenegs gave Pretich his spear, sabre, and arrows, while the latter gave his own breastplate, shield, and sword. The Pechenegs raised the siege, and for a time the inhabitants could no longer water their horses at the Lybed' on account of the retreating enemy.

But the people of Kiev sent to Svyatoslav, saying, "Oh Prince, you visit and frequent foreign lands. But while you neglect your own country, the Pechenegs have all but taken us captive, along with your mother and your children as well. Unless you return to protect us, they will attack us again, if you have no pity on your native land, on your mother in her old age, and on your children." When Svyatoslav heard these words, he quickly bestrode his charger, and returned to Kiev with his retinue. He kissed his mother and his children, and regretted what they had suffered at the hands of the Pechenegs. He therefore collected an army, and drove the Pechenegs out into the steppes. Thus there was peace.

6477 (969). Svyatoslav announced to his mother and his boyars, "I do not care to remain in Kiev, but should prefer to live in Pereyaslavets on the Danube, since that is the centre of my realm, where all riches are concentrated; gold, silks, wine, and various fruits from Greece, silver and horses from Hungary and Bohemia, and from Rus' furs, wax, honey, and slaves." But Olga made reply, "You behold me in my weakness. Why do you desire to depart from me?" For she was already in precarious health. (68) She thus remonstrated with him and begged him first to bury her and then to go wheresoever he would. Three days later Olga died.[70] Her son wept for her with great mourning, as did likewise her grandsons and all the people. They thus carried her out, and buried her in her tomb. Olga had given command not to hold a funeral feast for her, for she had a priest who performed the last rites over the sainted Princess.

Olga was the precursor of the Christian land, even as the day-spring precedes the sun and as the dawn precedes the day. For she shone like the moon by night, and she was radiant among the infidels like a pearl in the mire, since the people were soiled, and not yet purified of their sin by holy baptism. But she herself was cleansed by this sacred purification. She put off the sinful garments of the old Adam, and was clad in the new Adam, which is Christ. Thus we say to her, "Rejoice in the

Russes' knowledge of God," for we were the first fruits of their reconciliation with Him.

She was the first from Rus' to enter the kingdom of God, and the sons of Rus' thus praise her as their leader, for since her death she has interceded with God in their behalf. The souls of the righteous do not perish. As Solomon has said, "The nations rejoice in the praise of the righteous, for his memory is eternal, since it is acknowledged by God and men" (*Prov.*, xxix, 2; *Wis.*, iii, 4). For all men glorify her, as they behold her lying there in the body for many years. As the prophet has said, "I will glorify them that glorify me." (*I Sam.*, ii, 30) Of such persons David also said, "The righteous shall be had in everlasting remembrance, he shall not be afraid of evil tidings. His heart is fixed, trusting in Jehovah, his heart is fixed, and (69) will not be moved" (*Ps.*, cxii, 7-8). And Solomon said, "The righteous live forever, and they have reward from God and grace from the Most High. Therefore shall they receive the kingdom of beauty, and the crown of goodness from the hand of the Lord. With his right hand will he cover them, and with his arm will he protect them." (*Wis.*, v, 16-17) For he protected the sainted Olga from the devil, our adversary and our foe.

6478 (970). Svyatoslav set up Yaropolk in Kiev and Oleg in Dereva. At this time came the people of Novgorod asking for themselves a prince. "If you will not come to us," said they, "then we will choose a prince of our own." Svyatoslav replied that they had need of a prince, but Yaropolk and Oleg both refused, so that Dobrÿnya suggested that the post should be offered to Vladimir. For Vladimir was son of Malusha, stewardess of Olga and sister of Dobrÿnya. Their father was Malk of Lyubech, and Dobrÿnya was thus Vladimir's uncle. The citizens of Novgorod thus requested Svyatoslav to designate Vladimir to be their prince, and he went forth to Novgorod with Dobrÿnya, his uncle.[71] But Svyatoslav departed thence to Pereyaslavets.

6479 (971). Svyatoslav arrived before Pereyaslavets, and the Bulgarians fortified themselves in the city. They made one sally against Svyatoslav; there was great carnage, and the Bulgarians came off victors. But Svyatoslav cried to his soldiery, "Here is where we fall! Let us fight bravely, brothers and companions!" Toward evening, Svyatoslav finally gained the upper hand, and took the city by storm. He then sent messages to the Greeks, announcing his intention to march against them and capture their city, as he had taken Pereyaslavets.[72] The Greeks replied that they were in no position to offer resistance, and therefore begged him to accept tribute (70) instead for himself and his soldiery, requesting him to notify them how many Russes there were, so that they might pay so much per head. The Greeks made this proposition to deceive the Russes, for the Greeks are crafty even to the present day. Svyatoslav replied that his force numbered twenty thousand, adding ten thousand to the actual number, for there were really but ten thousand Russes. So the Greeks armed one hundred thousand men to attack Svyatoslav, and paid no tribute.

Svyatoslav advanced against the Greeks, who came out to meet the Russes. When the Russes perceived their approach, they were terrified at the multitude of the Greek soldiery, and Svyatoslav remarked, "Now we have no place whither we may flee. Whether we will or no, we must give battle. Let us not disgrace Rus', but rather sacrifice our lives, lest we be dishonored. For if we flee, we shall be disgraced. We must not take to flight, but we will resist boldly, and I will march before you. If my head falls, then look to yourselves." Then his warriors replied, "Wherever your head falls, there we too will lay down our own." So the Russes went into battle, and the carnage was great. Svyatoslav came out victor, but the Greeks fled. Then Svyatoslav advanced toward the capital fighting as he went, and destroying towns that stand deserted even to the present time.

The Emperor summoned his boyars to the palace, and inquired what they should do, for they could not withstand Svyatoslav's onslaught. The boyars advised that he should be tempted with gifts, to discover whether Svyatoslav liked gold and silks. So they sent to Svyatoslav gold and silks, carried by a clever envoy. To the latter they gave command to look well upon his eyes, his face, and his spirit. The envoy took the gifts, and went out to Svyatoslav. It was reported to the Prince that Greeks had come bringing greetings, and he ordered that they should be introduced. They then came near and (71) greeted him, laying before him the gold and the silks. Svyatoslav, without noticing the presents, bade his servants keep them. So the envoys returned before the Emperor; and the Emperor summoned his boyars. Then the envoys reported that when they had come before Svyatoslav and offered their gifts, he had taken no notice of them, but had ordered them to be retained. Then another courtier said, "Try him a second time; send him arms."

This suggestion was adopted, and they sent to Svyatoslav a sword and other accoutrements which were duly brought before him. The Prince accepted these gifts, which he praised and admired, and returned his greetings to the Emperor. The envoys went back to the Emperor and reported what had occurred. Then the boyars remarked, "This man must be fierce, since he pays no heed to riches, but accepts arms. Submit to tribute." The Emperor accordingly requested Svyatoslav to approach no nearer, but to accept tribute instead. For Svyatoslav had indeed almost reached Tsar'grad. So the Greeks paid him tribute, and he took also the share of those Russes who had been slain, promising that their families should receive it. He acccpted many gifts besides, and returned to Pereyaslavets with great acclaim.

Upon observing the small number of his troops, Svyatoslav reflected that if haply the Greeks attacked him by surprise, they would kill his retinue and himself. For many warriors had perished on the expedition. So he resolved to return to Rus' for reinforcements. He then sent envoys to the Emperor in Silistria (for the Emperor was then at that place) indicating his intention to maintain peaceful and friendly relations. When the Emperor heard this message, he rejoiced, and sent to Svyatoslav gifts even more valuable than the former ones. Svyatoslav accepted these gifts, and on taking counsel with his retinue declared, "If we do not make peace with the Emperor, and he discovers how few of us there are, the Greeks will come and besiege us in our city. Rus' is far away, and the Pechenegs are hostile to us. So who will give us aid? Let us rather make peace with (72) the Emperor, for the Greeks have offered tribute; let that suffice. But if the Emperor stops paying tribute, we shall once more collect troops in Rus' in still greater numbers, and march again on Tsar'grad." His speech pleased his followers, and they sent their chief men to the Emperor. The envoys arrived in Silistria, and reported to the Emperor. He summoned them before him on the following day, and gave them permission to state their errand. They then replied, "Thus says our Prince: 'I desire to maintain true amity with the Greek Emperor henceforth and forever.'" The Emperor rejoiced, and commanded his scribe to set down on parchment the words of Svyatoslav. One envoy recited all his words, and the scribe wrote them down. He spoke as follows:

"This is a copy of the treaty concluded by Svyatoslav, Prince of Rus' and by Sveinald, with Johannes surnamed Tzimiskes, written down by Theophilus the secretary in Silistria during the month of July, in the year 6479 (971), the fourteenth of the indiction. I, Svyatoslav, Prince of Rus', even as I previously swore, now confirm by oath upon this covenant that I desire to preserve peace and perfect amity with each of the great Emperors, and particularly with Basil and Constantine, and with their successors inspired of God, and with all their subjects. In this resolve concur all Russes under my sway, (73) both boyars, and commons, forever. I will therefore contemplate no attack upon your territory, nor will I collect an army or foreign mercenaries for this purpose, nor will I incite any other foe against your realm or against any territory pertaining thereto, and particularly the district of Kherson, or the cities adjacent, or against Bulgaria. But if any foe plans to attack your realm, I will resist him and wage war upon him. And even as I have given oath to the Greek Emperors in company with my boyars and all my subjects, so may we preserve this treaty inviolate. But if we fail in the observance of any of the aforesaid stipulations, either I or my companions, or my subjects, may we be accursed of the god in whom we believe, namely, of Perun and Volos, the god of flocks, and we become yellow as gold, and be slain with our own weapons. Regard as truth what we have now covenanted with you, even as it is inscribed upon this parchment and sealed with our seals."

After making peace with the Greeks, Svyatoslav journeyed by boat to the cataracts of the Dnieper, and the general, Sveinald, advised him to ride the falls on horseback, for the Pechenegs were encamped in the vicinity. The Prince did not heed him, but went on by boat. The people of Pereyaslavets informed the Pechenegs that Svyatoslav was returning to Rus' after seizing from the Greeks great riches and immense booty, but that his troop was small. When the Pechenegs heard this news, they ambuscaded the cataracts, so that when Svyatoslav arrived it was impossible to pass them. So the Prince decided to winter in Belobereg,[73] but the Russes had no rations, so that there was a severe famine, and (74) they paid as much as half a *grivna* for a horse's head. But Svyatoslav wintered there nevertheless.

When spring came, in 6480 (972), Svyatoslav approached the cataracts, where Kurya, Prince of the Pechenegs, attacked him; and Svyatoslav was killed. The nomads took his head, and made a cup out of his skull, overlaying it with gold, and they drank from it. But Sveinald returned to Yaropolk in Kiev. Now all the years of Svyatoslav's reign were twenty-eight.

6481 (973). The reign of Yaropolk began.

6482-6483 (974-975). The son of Sveinald, Lyut by name, was devoted to hunting, and went out of Kiev to chase wild beasts in the forest. Oleg once saw him, and inquired who he was. He was informed that it was the son of Sveinald; then he rode up and killed him, for Oleg was hunting too. Therefore there sprung up a feud between Yaropolk and Oleg, and Sveinald was continually egging Yaropolk on to attack his brother and seize his property, because he wished to avenge his son.

6484-6485 (976-977). Yaropolk marched against his brother Oleg into the district of Dereva. Oleg sallied out to meet him, and they came to blows. When the companies fought, Yaropolk overcame Oleg. Where Oleg fled with his warriors into the town called Vruchiy, there was a bridge across a moat to the city gates, and as the soldiery pressed hard on each other's heels, they fell into the moat. Oleg also was pushed from the bridge into the ditch; many men fell in, and the horses crushed the soldiers.

When Yaropolk entered (75) his brother's city, he seized the latter's property, and sent in search of him. Upon looking for Oleg, Yaropolk's men were unable to find him, until one native of Dereva reported that he had seen Oleg pushed off the bridge the night before. So Yaropolk sent men to look for his brother. They dragged bodies from the moat from morning till noon, and found Oleg also under the other corpses. They carried him away and laid him upon a rug. Then Yaropolk came and wept over him, and remarked to Sveinald, "See the fulfillment of your wish." So they buried Oleg in the city of Vruchiy, and his tomb is there to this day. Yaropolk seized his property. Now Yaropolk had a Greek wife who had been a nun. For Svyatoslav, his father, had brought her home, and married her to Yaropolk on account of the beauty of her countenance. When Vladimir in Novgorod heard that Yaropolk had killed Oleg, he was afraid, and fled abroad. Then Yaropolk sent his lieutenants to Novgorod, and was thus the sole ruler in Rus'.

6486-6488 (978-980). Vladimir returned to Novgorod with Varangian allies,[74] and instructed the lieutenants of Yaropolk to return to the latter and inform him that Vladimir was advancing against him prepared to fight. He remained in Novgorod, and sent word to Rogvolod in Polotsk that he desired his daughter to wife. Rogvolod inquired of his daughter whether she wished to marry Vladimir. "I will not," she replied, (76) "draw off the boots of a slave's son, but I want Yaropolk instead." Now Rogvolod had come from overseas, and exercised the authority in Polotsk just as Turÿ, from whom the Turovians get their name, had done in Turov. The servants of Vladimir returned and reported to him all the words of Rogned, the daughter of Rogvolod, Prince of Polotsk. Vladimir then collected a large army, consisting of Varangians, Slavs, Chuds, and Krivichians, and marched against Rogvolod. At this time, the intention was that Rogned should marry Yaropolk. But Vladimir attacked Polotsk, killed Rogvolod and his two sons, and after marrying the prince's daughter, he proceeded against Yaropolk.[75]

Vladimir came to Kiev with a large force. Yaropolk could not resist him, but shut himself up in Kiev with his people and with Blud.

Vladimir came to a halt at Dorogozhich, and entrenched himself between there and Kapich[76]; his earthwork is there to this day. Vladimir then sent treacherous proposals to Blud, Yaropolk's general, saying, "Be my friend; if I kill my brother, I will regard you as my father, and you shall have much honor from me. It was not I who began to fight with my brother, but he, and I was for that reason overcome by fear, and therefore have come out against him." Blud replied to the messengers of Vladimir that he would join with him in sincere friendship.

Alas, the evil treachery of men! As David says, "He who did eat of my bread hath lifted up his heel against me" (*Ps.*, xli, 9). For this man plotted treacherously against his prince. And it is further written, "Their tongues have spoken falsely. Hold them guilty, oh God, let them fall by their own counsels; (77) thrust them out in the multitude of their transgressions, for they have angered thee, oh Lord" (*Ps.*, v, 10-11). David has likewise said, "Bloodthirsty and deceitful men shall not live out half their days" (*Ps.*, lv, 23). This is evil counsel upon which they enter for the shedding of blood. Those men are mad who, after receiving honor and gifts from their prince or their lord, think on the life of their prince to destroy it; they are worse than devils. It was thus that Blud betrayed his prince after receiving many honors from him. He became guilty of his blood.

Blud shut himself up with Yaropolk with the intention of betraying him, and he sent frequent messages to Vladimir, urging him to storm the city while he himself planned how he might kill Yaropolk. But on account of the citizens, it was not possible to kill him. So Blud, not being able to destroy him thus, contrived it by means of a ruse, while he urged the prince not to go forth from the city to fight. Thus he craftily suggested to Yaropolk that the people of Kiev were sending messages to invite Vladimir to attack the town so that they might betray Yaropolk into his hands, and advised him to flee from the city. Yaropolk heeded his suggestion, and he fled from Vladimir. He then shut himself up in the city of Rodnya[77] at the mouth of the Ros', while Vladimir entered the city of Kiev, and then laid siege to Yaropolk at Rodnya. There was a great famine there, and we have to this day a proverb which speaks of famine as in Rodnya.

Blud then said to Yaropolk, "Do you see what a large force your brother has? We cannot overcome them. Make peace with your brother." He spoke thus as he plotted treachery against him. But Yaropolk assented. Blud then sent world to Vladimir (78) that he would bring Yaropolk before him, in accordance with his wishes. Vladimir, upon hearing these tidings, went to his father's castle with the hall, of which we previously made mention, and settled there with his retinue. Blud next induced Yaropolk to appear before his brother and express his readiness to accept any terms he might offer. Yaropolk thus went in person to Vladimir, though he had been previously warned by Varyazhko not to go. "My Prince," said he, "they will kill you. Flee rather to the Pechenegs and collect an army." But the prince heeded him not. Yaropolk came accordingly before Vladimir, and when he entered the door, two Varangians stabbed him in the breast with their swords, while Blud shut the doors and would not allow his men to follow him. Thus Yaropolk was slain. When Varayazhko saw that Yaropolk was murdered, he fled from the castle to the Pechenegs, in whose company he fought long against Vladimir till the latter won him over only with difficulty by means of a sworn pledge.

Now Vladimir had intercourse with his brother's wife, a Greek woman, and she became pregnant, and from her was born Svyatopolk.[78] From a sinful root evil fruit is produced, inasmuch as his mother had been a nun, and besides Vladimir had intercourse with her without having married her. Svyatopolk was therefore born in adultery, and for this reason his father did not love him; for he had two fathers, Yaropolk and Vladimir.

At this time, the Varangians said to Vladimir, "This city belongs to us, and we took it; hence we desire tribute from it at the rate of two *grivnÿ* per man." Vladimir requested them to wait until the marten skins should be collected (79) a month thence. They waited a month and he gave them nothing, so that the Varangians protested that he had deceived them, and requested that they should be dismissed to Greece. The Prince urged them to go their way. He then selected from their number the good, the wise, and the brave men, to whom he assigned cities, while the rest departed for Tsar'grad in Greece.[79] But in advance of them Vladimir sent couriers bearing this message: "Varangians are on their way to your country. Do not keep many of them in your city, or else they will cause you such harm as they have done here. Scatter them therefore in various localities, and do not let a single one return this way."

Vladimir then began to reign alone in Kiev, and he set up idols on the hills outside the castle with the hall: one of Perun, made of wood with a head of silver and a mustache of gold, and others of Khors, Dazh'bog, Stribog, Simar'gl, and Mokosh'.[80] The people sacrificed to them, calling them gods, and brought their sons and their daughters to sacrifice them to these devils. They desecrated the earth with their offerings, and the land of Rus' and this hill were defiled with blood.

But our gracious God desires not the death of sinners, and upon this hill now stands a church dedicated to St. Basil, as we shall later narrate.[81]

But let us return to our subject.

Vladimir had appointed his uncle Dobrÿnya to rule over Novgorod. When Dobrÿnya came to Novgorod, he set up an idol beside the river Volkhov, and the people of Novgorod offered sacrifice to it as if to God himself. Now Vladimir was overcome by lust for women. His lawful wife was Rogned, whom he settled on the (80) Lÿbed', where the village of Predslavino now stands.[82] By her he had four sons: Izyaslav, Mstislav, Yaroslav, and Vsevolod, and two daughters. The Greek woman bore him Svyatopolk; by one Czech he had a son Vÿsheslav; by another, Svyatoslav and Mstislav; and by a Bulgarian woman, Boris and Gleb. He had three hundred concubines at Vÿshgorod, three hundred at Belgorod, and two hundred at Berestovo in a village still called Berestovoe.[83] He was insatiable in vice. He even seduced married women and violated young girls, for he was a libertine like Solomon. For it is said that Solomon had seven hundred wives and three hundred concubines. He was wise, yet in the end he came to ruin. But Vladimir, though at first deluded, eventually found salvation. Great is the Lord, and great is his power, and of his wisdom there is no end.

The charm of woman is an evil thing. As Solomon in his repentance said of woman: "Listen not to an evil woman. Honey flows from the lips of a licentious woman, and for a time it delights thy palate. But in the end it will become bitterer than wormwood. They who cleave to her shall die in hell; for she walks not in the path of life, but unstable and foolish are her ways" (*Prov.*, v, 3-6). Thus spoke Solomon of adulteresses, but of a good woman he said, "More precious is she than jewels. Her husband rejoices in her, for she brings him blessedness (81) all the days of her life. She seeks wool and flax, she makes useful things with her hands. She is like a merchant ship that goes out for trade and collects great riches. She rises also while it is yet night, she gives food to the household and tasks to the servants. She considered a field and has bought it, with the fruit of her hands she has planted a vineyard. She has girded up her loins with strength, and has made firm her arm for labor. She has proved how good it is to labor, and her candle goes not out by night. She sets her hands to useful things, and her fingers work with the spindle. She stretches out her hand to the poor, and has given her wealth to the beggar. Her husband is not concerned with the household; wherever she may be, her family is clothed. Double garments she makes for her husband, scarlet and purple are her robes. Her husband is distinguished within the gates when he sits in council with the elders and the inhabitants of the land. She has made garments and sold them. She has opened her lips with wisdom, she speaks fittingly with her tongue. She is clothed in strength and grace. Her almsgivings have raised and enriched her children, and her husband has commended her. For a wise woman is blessed; let her praise the fear of God. Give her the fruit of her lips, that they may praise her husband within the gates" (*Prov.*, xxxi, 10 ff.).

6489 (981). Vladimir marched upon the Lyakhs and took their cities: Peremÿshl', Cherven, and other towns, all of which are subject to Rus' even to this day.[84] In the same year, he conquered the Vyatichians, and imposed (82) upon them tribute according to the number of their ploughs, just as his father had done.[85]

6490 (982). The Vyatichians went to war, but Vladimir attacked them and conquered them a second time.

6491 (983). Vladimir marched on the Yatvingians, conquered them, and seized their territory.[86] He returned to Kiev, and together with his people made sacrifice to the idols. The elders and the boyars then proposed that they should cast lots for a youth and a maiden, and sacrifice to the gods whomsoever the lot should fall upon.

Now there was a certain Varangian whose house was situated by the spot where now stands the Church of the Holy Virgin which Vladimir built. This Varangian had immigrated from Greece. He adhered to the Christian faith, and he had a son, fair in face and in heart, on whom, through the devil's hatred, the lot fell. For the devil, though he had dominion over all the rest, could not suffer this youth. He was like a thorn in the devil's heart, and the accursed one was eager to destroy him, and even aroused the people thereto. Messengers thus came and said to the father, "Since the lot has fallen upon your son, the gods have claimed him as their own. Let us therefore make sacrifice to the gods." But the Varangian replied, "These are not gods, but only idols of wood. Today it is, and tomorrow it will rot away. These gods do not eat, or drink, or speak; they are fashioned by hand out of wood. But the God whom the Greeks serve and worship is one; it is he who has made heaven and earth, the stars, the moon, the sun, and mankind, and has granted him life upon earth. But what have these gods created? They are themselves manufactured. (83) I will not give up my son to devils." So the messengers went back and reported to the people. The latter took up arms, marched against the Varangian and his son, and on breaking down the stockade about his house, found him standing with his son upon the porch. They then called upon him to surrender his son that they might offer him to the gods. But he replied, "If they be gods, they will send one of their number to take my son. What need have you of him?" They straightway raised a shout, and broke up the structure under them. Thus the people killed them, and no one knows where they are buried.[87]

For at this time the Russes were ignorant pagans. The devil rejoiced thereat, for he did not know that his ruin was approaching. He was so eager to destroy the Christian people, yet he was expelled by the true cross even from these very lands. The accursed one thought to himself, "This is my habitation, a land where the apostles have not taught nor the prophets prophesied." He knew not that the Prophet had said, "I will call those my people who are not my people" (*Hosea*, ii, 23). Likewise it is written of the Apostles, "Their message has gone out into all the earth and their words to the end of the world" (*Ps.*, xix, 5). Though the Apostles have not been there in person, their teachings resound like trumpets in the churches throughout the world. Through their instruction we overcome the hostile adversary, and trample him under our feet. For likewise did the Holy Fathers trample upon him, and they have received the heavenly crown in company with the holy martyrs and the just.

6492 (984). Vladimir attacked the Radimichians. His general was named Wolf's Tail, and Vladimir sent him on ahead. He met the Radimichians by the river Pishchan', and overcame (84) them.[88] Therefore the Russes ridiculed the Radimichians, saying that the men on the Pishchan' fled in the presence of a wolf's tail. Now the Radimichians belong to the race of the Lyakhs. They had come and settled in these regions, and pay tribute to the Russes, an obligation which they maintain to the present day.

6493 (985). Accompanied by his uncle Dobrÿnya, Vladimir set out by boat to attack the Bulgars.[89] He also brought Torks[90] overland on horseback, and conquered the Bulgars. Dobrÿnya remarked to Vladimir, "I have seen the prisoners, who all wear boots. They will not pay us tribute. Let us rather look for foes with bast shoes." So Vladimir made peace with the Bulgars, and they confirmed it by oath. The Bulgars declared, "May peace prevail between us till stone floats and straw sinks." Then Vladimir returned to Kiev.

6494 (986). Vladimir was visited by Bulgars of Mohammedan faith,[91] who said, "Though you are a wise and prudent prince, you have no religion. Adopt our faith, and revere Mahomet." Vladimir inquired what was the nature of their religion. They replied that they believed in God, and that Mahomet instructed them to practice circumcision, to eat no pork, to drink no wine, and, after death, promised them complete fulfillment of their carnal desires. "Mahomet," they asserted, "will give each man seventy fair women. He may choose one fair one, and upon that woman will Mahomet confer the charms of them all, and she shall be his wife. Mahomet promises that one may then satisfy every desire, but whoever is poor in this world (85) will be no different in the next." They also spoke other false things which out of modesty may not be written down. Vladimir listened to them, for he was fond of women and indulgence, regarding which he heard with pleasure. But circumcision and abstinence from pork and wine were disagreeable to him. "Drinking," said he, "is the joy of the Russes. We cannot exist without that pleasure."

Then came the Germans, asserting that they were come as emissaries of the Pope.[92] They added, "Thus says the Pope: 'Your country is like our country, but your faith is not as ours. For our faith is the light. We worship God, who has made heaven and earth, the stars, the moon, and every creature, while your gods are only wood.'" Vladimir inquired what their teaching was. They replied, "Fasting according to one's strength. But whatever one eats or drinks is all to the glory of God, as our teacher Paul has said." Then Vladimir answered, "Depart hence; our fathers accepted no such principle."

The Jewish Khazars heard of these missions, and came themselves saying, "We have learned that Bulgars and Christians came hither to instruct you in their faiths. The Christians believe in him whom we crucified, but we believe in the one God of Abraham, Isaac, and Jacob." Then Vladimir inquired what their religion was. They replied that its tenets included circumcision, not eating pork or hare, and observing the Sabbath. The Prince then asked where their native land was, and they replied that it was in Jerusalem. When Vladimir inquired where that was, they made answer, "God was angry (86) at our forefathers, and scattered us among the gentiles on account of our sins. Our land was then given to the Christians." The Prince then demanded, "How can you hope to teach others while you yourselves are cast out and scattered abroad by the hand of God? If God loved you and your faith, you would not be thus dispersed in foreign lands. Do you expect us to accept that fate also?"

Then the Greeks sent to Vladimir a scholar,[93] who spoke thus: "We have heard that the Bulgarians came and urged you to adopt their faith, which pollutes heaven and earth. They are accursed above all men, like Sodom and Gomorrah, upon which the Lord let fall burning stones, and which he buried and submerged. The day of destruction likewise awaits these men, on which the Lord will come to judge the earth, and to destroy all those who do evil and abomination. For they moisten their excrement, and pour the water into their mouths, and anoint their beards with it, remembering Mahomet. The women also perform this same abomination, and even worse ones." Vladimir, upon hearing their statements, spat upon the earth, saying, "This is a vile thing."

Then the scholar said, "We have likewise heard how men came from Rome to convert you to their faith. It differs but little from ours, for they commune with wafers, called *oplatki,* which God did not give them, for he ordained that we should commune with bread. For when he had taken bread, the Lord gave it to his disciples, saying, 'This is my body broken (87) for you.' Likewise he took the cup, and said, 'This is my blood of the New Testament.' They do not so act, for they have modified the faith." Then Vladimir remarked that the Jews had come into his presence and had stated that the Germans and the Greeks believed in him whom they crucified. To this the scholar replied, "Of a truth we believe in him. For some of the prophets foretold that God should be incarnate, and others that he should be crucified and buried, but arise on the third day and ascend into heaven. "For the Jews killed the prophets, and still others they persecuted. When their prophecy was fulfilled, our Lord came down to earth, was crucified, arose again, and ascended into heaven. He awaited their repentance for forty-six years, but they did not repent, so that the Lord let loose the Romans upon them. Their cities were destroyed, and they were scattered among the gentiles, under whom they are now in servitude."

Vladimir then inquired why God should have descended to earth and should have endured such pain. The scholar then answered and said, "If you are desirous of hearing the story, I shall tell you from the beginning why God descended to earth." Vladimir replied, "Gladly would I hear it." Whereupon the scholar thus began his narrative:

"In the beginning, God created heaven and earth on the first day. Upon the second, he created the land which is in the midst of the water. Upon this same day, the waters were divided. A part of them was elevated above the land, and a part placed below it. On the third day, he created the sea, the rivers, the springs, and the seeds. On the fourth, God made the sun, the moon, and the stars, and thus adorned the heavens. When the foremost of the angels, the chief of the angelic host, beheld these works, he reflected and said, 'I shall descend to the earth and seize upon it. (88) I shall then be like to God, and shall establish my throne upon the northern clouds.' But God cast him straightway out of heaven, and in his train fell the tenth order of the angels, who had been subject to him. The name of this adversary was Sathanael, in whose place God set Michael as chief, while Satan, after sinning in his devices and falling from the former glory, is now called the adversary of God.

"Subsequently, upon the fifth day, God created whales, fishes, reptiles, and feathered fowl. On the sixth, God created beasts, cattle, and terrestrial reptiles. He also created man. Upon the seventh day, which is the Sabbath, God rested from his labors. He set up Paradise at the east in Eden. There he placed man, whom he had created, and bade him eat of every tree save one, namely, the tree of the understanding of good and evil. Thus Adam was in Paradise beholding God, and glorified him when the angels glorified him.

"Now God cast a drowsiness upon Adam, and he slept. Then God took from him one rib, and made him a wife, whom he brought to Adam in Paradise. Then Adam said 'This is bone of my bone and flesh of my flesh,' and she was called woman. Adam gave names to the cattle and the birds, the beasts and the reptiles; to man and to woman an angel gave names. God subjected the beasts and the cattle to Adam's rule; he ruled over them and they obeyed his word.

"When the devil saw how God honored man, he hated him. Changing himself into a serpent, he approached Eve and inquired of her, 'Why do you not eat of the tree that stands in the middle of Paradise?' The woman made answer to the serpent, 'God has said: "Ye must not eat of it, or ye shall die the death." Then the serpent said, 'You shall not die the death. God knew (89) that upon the day when you eat of it, your eyes be opened, and you shall be as God understanding good and evil.' Now the woman saw that the tree was good to eat, so she ate of it, and gave of it to her husband. They ate, and their eyes were opened, so that they realized that they were naked, and plaited for themselves girdles of fig-leaves.

"Then God said, 'The earth is accursed of your deeds, and ye shall live in sorrow all the days of your life. If ye stretch out your hand and pluck the fruit of the tree of life, ye will live forever.' So the Lord God drove Adam out of Paradise. He sat opposite the gate of Paradise weeping and tilling the soil, and Satan rejoiced that the earth was accursed. This was the first fall of man, and his bitter punishment, in that he lost the angelic life.

"Adam begot Cain and Abel. Cain was a plowman, and Abel a

shepherd. Now Cain offered God of the fruit of the earth, but God did not accept his gifts. But Abel brought him of his firstling lamb, and God accepted the offerings of Abel. Then Satan entered into Cain, and incited him to kill Abel. So Cain said to Abel, 'Let us go into the field.' When they had gone forth, Cain rose up and wished to kill his brother, but he did not know how to compass the deed. But Satan said, 'Take up a stone and smite him.' So Cain took a stone and killed him. Then God said to Cain. 'Where is thy brother?' and Cain replied, 'Am I my brother's keeper?' So God said, 'The blood of thy brother cries aloud to me; thou shalt groan and tremble unto thy life's end.'

"Adam and Eve wept, but the devil rejoiced, saying, (90) 'Behold, him whom God held in honor I have made to depart from God, and now sorrow has come upon him.' So they mourned Abel for thirty years. His body did not decompose, but they did not know how to bury him. Then, by God's command, two birds flew down, and one of them died. The other dug a trench, and placed the dead bird therein, and buried it. When Adam and Eve beheld this, they dug a trench, and placed Abel in it, and buried him thus with sorrow.

"When Adam was two hundred and thirty years old, he begot Seth and two daughters. Cain married one and Seth the other, and from them the race of men multiplied and increased throughout the earth. But they knew not their Creator, and were filled with every vice and uncleanness, with lust and with hatred, and they lived like cattle. Noah was the only just man in the whole race, and he begot three sons, Shem, Ham, and Japheth. God said, 'My spirit shall not abide among men; I will destroy what I have created, both man and beast.' Then the Lord God said to Noah, 'Build an ark three hundred cubits long and fifty cubits broad, and thirty cubits high (for a *sazhen'* was called a cubit).' The ark was one hundred years building, but Noah foretold that there was to be a flood, and the people mocked him. When the ark was finished, the Lord said to Noah, 'Enter into it thyself and thy wife, and thy sons, and thy daughters-in-law. Take with thee two each of all beasts, birds, and reptiles.' So Noah led them into the ark as the Lord had enjoined him.

"Then God brought a flood upon the earth, and drowned all flesh, but the ark floated upon the water. When the waters had subsided, Noah and (91) his sons and his wife went forth, and by them the earth was peopled. There were many men with but one language, and they said one to another, 'Let us build a tower as high as heaven.' They even began to build it with Nimrod as their chief. But God said, 'Men have multiplied, and their devices are vain.' Then God descended, and divided the nations into seventy-two peoples. But the tongue of Adam was not taken away from Eber, for he alone had not joined in their vanity, saying, 'If God had bidden men to build a tower as high as heaven, he would have ordained it with a word, even as he created the heavens, the earth, the sea, and all things visible and invisible.' Therefore Eber's language was unaltered, and from him are descended the Hebrews.

"The human race was thus divided into seventy-two nations and scattered throughout the world, each one having its own customs. Following the devil's instruction, they sacrificed to trees, springs, and rivers, and did not know God. Between Adam and the Flood, two thousand and forty years passed, and between the Flood and the division of the nations, five hundred and twenty-nine years. Subsequently, the devil cast mankind into yet greater error, so that they undertook to build idols, some of wood, some of brass, others of marble, and still others of gold and silver. They not only worshipped them, but even brought their sons and daughters and killed them before these images, so that all the earth was defiled.

"The author of idolatry was Serug, for he made idols in the name of dead men, kings, heroes, magicians, and evil women. Serug begot (92) Terah, and Terah begot three sons, Abraham, Nahor, and Haran. Terah built idols, having learned the art from his father. But Abraham, having come to reason, looked up to heaven, and upon observing the stars and the sky, said, 'In truth, that is God, and those that my brother makes only deceive men.' Then Abraham announced, 'I will test the gods of my father,' and he inquired, 'Father, why do you deceive men by making idols of wood? It is God who has made heaven and earth.' Abraham then set fire to the idols in the temple. When Haran, Abraham's brother, saw this act, in his zeal for the idols he endeavored to save them, and was himself consumed, so that he died before his father. For prior to that time, no son had passed away before his father, but the father had always died before his son; from this time forth, sons began to perish before their fathers.

"God loved Abraham, and said to him, 'Go forth out of the house of thy father into the land to which I shall guide thee. I shall make of thee a nation, and the generations of the earth shall bless thee.' And Abraham did as the Lord ordained. So Abraham took his nephew Lot (for Lot was both his brother-in-law and his nephew, since Abraham had married his brother's daughter Sarai); and he came to a high oak in the land of Canaan. God said to Abraham, 'To thy seed will

I give this land.' Then Abraham worshipped God. Now Abraham was seventy-five years old when he went out of Haran. But Sarai was barren, and since she was afflicted with her sterility, Sarai said to Abraham, 'Have intercourse with (93) my maid-servant.' So Sarai took Hagar and gave her to Abraham, who had intercourse with her. She conceived and bore a son, and Abraham called him Ishmael. Abraham was eighty-six years old when Ishmael was born. Afterward, Sarai conceived and bore a son, and called his name Isaac. Then God directed Abraham to circumcise the child, and he duly circumcised him on the eighth day. God loved Abraham and his race. He called them his people, and distinguished them from the Gentiles by calling them his own.

"When Isaac was grown up, Abraham, having lived one hundred and seventy years, died and was buried. When Isaac was sixty, he begot two sons, Esau and Jacob. Esau was crafty and Jacob truthful. Jacob served his uncle seven years for his younger daughter, but Laban did not give her to him, saying, 'Take the elder instead.' He thus gave him Leah, the elder, but for the younger demanded of him seven years' further service. So Jacob served seven more years for Rachel and married the two sisters. By them he begot eight sons: Reuben, Simeon, Levi, Judah, Issachar, Zabulon and Asser. From these brothers the Jews are sprung.

"Jacob went to Egypt when he was one hundred and thirty years old, accompanied by his kin to the number of sixty-five souls. He lived in Egypt seventeen years before his death, and his race was in captivity four hundred years. During these years, the Jewish people increased and multiplied, (94) but the Egyptians crushed them with toil. At this time, Moses was born among the Jews, and the Egyptians informed the King a child was born among the Jews who should destroy Egypt. Then the King gave orders to cast the growing children of the Jews into the river. But Moses' mother, fearing his destruction, took the infant and laid him in a basket, and set him in the water.

"At this moment, Thermuthi, the daughter of Pharaoh, went down to bathe, and on seeing the child floating there, she rescued him and named him Moses, and brought him up. The child was fair, and was four years old when the daughter of Pharaoh brought him before her father. When Pharaoh saw Moses, he fancied the child. Moses seized him around the neck, knocked the crown from the King's head, and stamped upon it. A magician who beheld this act protested to the King, 'Oh King, destroy this child, for if you do not destroy him he will ruin all Egypt.' The King heeded him not, but gave command that no more of the Jewish children be killed.

"When Moses grew to manhood, he was great in the house of Pharaoh. But when another King came to the throne, the nobles hated him. Then Moses, since he had killed an Egyptian who was persecuting a Jew, fled from Egypt, and came to the land of Midian. As he was making his way across the desert, he learned from the angel Gabriel about the nature of the whole world, of the first man, what happened after him, about the flood, the confusion of the tongues, the age of each man, the movement and the number of the stars, the dimensions of the earth, (95) and all wisdom. Thereafter God appeared to him in the burning bush, and said to him, 'I have seen the oppression of my people in Egypt, and have descended to take them from the hands of the Egyptians, and lead them forth from the land. Go therefore to Pharaoh, king of Egypt, and say unto him, "Set Israel free, that they may perform sacrifice to God for three days." If the King of Egypt heed thee not, I will smite him with all my wonders.'

"When Moses came before Pharaoh, the King did not heed him. Then God sent ten plagues upon him: rivers of blood, frogs, gnats, dogflies, cattle-plague, burning vesicles, hail, locusts, three days' darkness, and pestilence among the population. Ten plagues were thus visited upon Egyptians, because they drowned the children of the Jews for ten months. But when there was pestilence in Egypt, Pharaoh said to Moses and his brother Aaron, 'Depart hence quickly.' So Moses after gathering the Jews together, departed out of the land of Egypt.

"The Lord led them over the road through the desert to the Red Sea, preceding them by night as a fiery pillar, and by day as a cloud. When Pharaoh heard how the people were escaping, he pursued them, and overtook them by the seaside. When the Jews beheld this, they cried out against Moses, saying, 'Why have you led us out to certain death?' Then Moses called upon God, and the Lord said, 'Why callest thou upon me? Smite the sea with thy staff.' Moses did thus, and the water parted in twain, so that the children of Israel went down into the sea. When Pharaoh beheld this, (96) he pursued them, for the children of Israel were traveling on dry land. But when they reached the shore, the sea closed over Pharaoh and his warriors.

"God loved Israel, and they traveled three days from the sea, and arrived at Marah. There the water was bitter. The people murmured against God, but the Lord showed them a tree, and when Moses placed it in the water, the water was sweetened. Then they still murmured against Moses and Aaron, saying, "It was better for us in Egypt, where we ate meat, onions, and bread till we were filled.' The Lord then said to Moses, 'I have heard the complaint of the children of Israel,' and he gave them manna to eat. Afterward, the Lord revealed the law to them upon Mt. Sinai. But while Moses was with God upon the mountain, the people moulded a calf's head and bowed down before it as if before God himself, and Moses killed three thousand of them.

"Yet again they murmured against Moses and Aaron because there was no water, and the Lord said to Moses, 'Smite the rock with thy rod.' But Moses replied, 'How can water issue from it?' Then the Lord was angry at Moses because he did not glorify him, and for this reason, on account of these murmurings, he did not enter the Promised Land. But Moses died there on the mountain.

"Then Joshua, son of Nun, assumed the leadership. He entered the Promised Land, destroyed the Canaanites, and settled the children of Israel there in their stead. Then, when Joshua died, Judah was judge in his place. There were fourteen other judges. But in their time the people forgot (97) God, who had led them out of Egypt, and they began to serve devils. Then God was wroth, and delivered them over to the violence of the Gentiles. But when they repented, he had mercy upon them. When he had freed them, they returned nevertheless to the worship of devils.

"Next, Eli the priest was judge, and after him, Samuel the prophet. The people said to Samuel, 'Give us a King.' Then the Lord was angered against Israel, and set Saul over them as King. But Saul would not walk in the law of the Lord, so the Lord chose David, and appointed him King over Israel. Now David found favor with God, and to him God swore that a God should be born of his lineage. Thus David began to prophecy concerning the incarnation of God, saying, 'I bore thee from my loins before the morning star' (*Ps.*, xc, 3). He prophesied for forty years, and then died. After him, his son Solomon uttered prophecy. It was he who built a temple to God, and called it the Holy of Holies. He was a wise man, but in the end he fell from grace. He too reigned forty years and then died. After him reigned his son Rehoboam, and in his day the kingdom was divided into two parts, since the Jews lived partly in Jerusalem, and the other portion in Samaria.

"In Samaria reigned Rehoboam, son of Solomon, who made two golden calves, one of which he set up in Bethel on the hill, and the other in Dan, saying, 'These are your gods, oh Israel.' So the people worshiped them and forgot God. Likewise in Jerusalem they forgot

God, and began to worship Baal, called the god of war, who is Ares, and they forgot the God of their fathers. Then God began to send (98) them prophets, and the prophets rebuked them for their iniquities, but when they were rebuked by the prophets, they killed them. Then God was wroth against Israel, and said, 'I shall cast you from me, I shall call other peoples to serve. If they sin, I will not remember their iniquities.'

"So the Lord sent his prophets, saying to them, 'Prophecy of the rejection of the Jews and the calling of the Gentiles.' Hosea was thus the first to prophesy, saying, 'I will cause the kingdom of the house of Israel to cease, I will break the bow of Israel, and I will no more have compassion on the house of Israel. But I will cast them off and reject them, saith the Lord, and they shall be wanderers among the nations' (*Hos.*, i, 4-6; ix, 17). And Jeremiah said, 'If Samuel and Moses arise, I will not have mercy on them' (*Jer.*, xv, i). Further, Jeremiah said, 'Thus saith the Lord: "I have sworn by my great name that my name shall no more be mentioned henceforth by the lips of the Jews"' (*Jer.*, xiv, 26). Likewise Ezekiel said, 'Thus saith the Lord Jehovah: "I will scatter thee and the whole remnant of thee to all the winds, for that thou hast defiled my sanctuaries with thine abominations; I will reject thee and have no more mercy upon thee"' (*Ezek.*, v, 10-11).

"Malachi said, 'I have no pleasure in you, saith Jehovah. From the east to the west my name shall be glorified among the Gentiles. In every place incense shall be offered unto my name, and a pure offering, for great is my name among the Gentiles. Wherefore I will deliver you into exile and to the scorn of all nations' (*Mal.*, i, 10-11; ii, 9). The great Isaiah said, 'Thus saith the Lord: "I will stretch out my hand against (99) thee, I will destroy thee and scatter thee, and restore thee no more"' (*Is.*, i, 25). And further, 'I have hated your feasts and your new moons; your Sabbaths I will not accept' (*Is.*, i, 13-14). Amos the prophet said, 'Hear the word of the Lord: "I will bring mourning upon you; the house of Israel has fallen and was not quick to arise"' (*Amos*, v, 1-2). Malachi said 'Thus saith the Lord: "I will send upon you a curse, and will curse your blessing; I will destroy it, and it shall not be among you"' (*Mal.*, ii, 2).

"Many prophesied of their rejection, and to such prophets God gave his commandment to foretell the calling of other nations in their stead. Thus Isaiah called upon them, saying, 'Law shall go forth from me, and my judgment is the light of nations. My justice approaches quickly; it shall go forth and in my arm shall the Gentiles hope' (*Is.*, li, 4-6). Jeremiah said, 'Thus saith the Lord: "I will establish a new covenant for the house of Judah. I will give laws for their understanding, and write upon their hearts. I will be their God, and they shall be my people"' (*Jer.*, xxi, 31-34). Isaiah said, 'The old things are passed away, but I declare the new. Before their appearance, it has been revealed unto you. Sing unto the Lord a new song. Those who serve me shall be called by a new name, which shall be blessed throughout all the earth. My house shall be called a house of prayer for all nations' (*Is.*, xlii, 9-10; lvi, 5-7). Likewise Isaiah said, 'The Lord will show his right arm before all nations, and all the ends of the earth shall see salvation from our God' (*Is.*, liii, 10). And David said, 'Praise the Lord, all the nations, praise him, all ye people' (*Ps.*, cxviii, 1).

"Since God so loved his new people, he promised (100) to descend among them himself, and to appear as a man in the flesh, and to suffer for the sin of Adam. Thus men began to prophesy concerning the incarnation of God. First David said, 'The Lord said unto my Lord: "Sit upon my right, until I shall set thine enemies as a footstool for thy feet"' (*Ps.*, xc, 1). And again, 'The Lord said unto me: "Thou art my son, this day have I begotten thee"' (*Ps.*, ii, 7). And Isaiah said, 'No ambassador nor messenger, but God himself shall come to save us' (*Is.*, lxiii, 9). And again, 'A child is born to us in whose arm there is authority, and he shall be called the great counsellor of the angels. Great is his might, and of his peace there is no end' (*Is.*, ix, 6). And again, 'Behold, a maiden shall conceive in the womb, and shall bear a son, and they shall call his name Emmanuel' (*Is.*, vii, 14). Micah said, 'Thou, Bethlehem Ephrathah, art scarcely to be of slight account among the thousands of Jews. For out of thee shall come forth a ruler to be prince in Israel, and his going forth is from everlasting. Therefore he will scatter them till the time when the mother travails, and the rest of his brethren return to the sons of Israel' (*Mic.*, x, 2-3). Jeremiah thus said, 'This is our God, and no other shall be compared with him, He has found all the way of wisdom, he has given it to Jacob his servant. Then he appeared on earth and lived among men' (*Baruch*, iii, 35-38). And again, 'Man exists. But who shall know how God exists or how man dies?' (*Jer.*, xvii, 9). Zachariah said, 'They have not heeded my son, and I will not give ear to them, said the Lord' (*Zach.*, vii, 13). Hosea said, 'Thus saith the Lord: "My flesh is from them"' (*Hos.*, ix, 12).

"Prophesies were likewise uttered also concerning his passion. (101) Thus Isaiah said, 'Woe to their souls! For they have counselled evil counsel, saying, "Let us kill the just man"' (*Is.*, iii, 9-10). Likewise he said, 'Thus saith the Lord: "I will not resist them nor speak against them. I offered my back to wounds and my countenance to blows, and I turned my face not away from shame and from spitting"' (*Is.*, i, 5-6). Jeremiah said, 'Come, let us destroy the tree with the fruit thereof, and cut him off from the land of the living' (*Jer.*, xii, 19). Moses said of his crucifixion, 'Thy life shall hang in doubt before thee' (*Deut.*, xxviii, 66). David said, 'Why are the nations stirred up' (*Ps.*, ii, 1). And Isaiah said, 'He was led like a sheep to the slaughter' (*Is.*, liii, 7). And Esdras said, 'Blessed be the Lord: he stretched out his hands and saved Jerusalem' (?) They spoke also of the resurrection. David said, 'Rise up, oh Lord, judge the lands for thou shalt inherit all the nations' (*Ps.*, lxxxii, 8). And likewise, 'Them the Lord awaked as one out of sleep' (*Ps.*, lxxviii, 65) and also, 'Let God arise, let his enemies be scattered' (*Ps.*, lxviii, 1). Likewise, 'Arise, oh Jehovah; oh God, lift up thy hand' (*Ps.*, x, 12). Isaiah said, 'Ye who walk into the land and the shadow of death, upon you shall shine the light' (*Is.*, ix, 2). And Zachariah said, 'In the blood of thy covenant thou hast freed the captives from the waterless pit' (*Zach.*, ix, 11). Many things were prophesied concerning him, all of which have been fulfilled."

Then Vladimir inquired, "When was this fulfilled? Has it happened or is it yet to occur?" The scholar answered him and said:

"All was accomplished when God was incarnate. (102). For as I said before, when the Jews killed the prophets and their kings transgressed against the law, he gave them over to destruction, and they were led into captivity into Assyria because of their sins. They labored there seventy years. Then they returned to their native land, but had no king. Thus the high priests ruled over them until the time of the foreigner Herod, who reigned over them. During his reign, in the year 5500, the Angel Gabriel was sent to Nazareth to the Virgin Mary, of the tribe of David. He said unto her, 'Rejoice, thou who art happy, the Lord is with thee.' In consequence of this Annunciation, she conceived the Word of God in her womb, and bore a son, and called his name Jesus.

"Now behold, wise men came from the east, saying, 'Where is he who is born king of the Jews? For we have seen his star in the east, and are come to worship him.' When King Herod heard this, he was troubled, and all Jerusalem with him. And having called together the scribes and the elders of the people, he asked of them where the Christ should be born. They made reply, 'In Bethlehem of the Jews.' When Herod heard these words, he gave the command to slay all children under two years of age. So his soldiers went forth and killed the children. But in her fear, Mary hid the Child, and Joseph, together with Mary, took the Child and fled into Egypt, where they remained until the death of Herod. In Egypt, the angel of the Lord appeared to Joseph, saying, 'Arise, take the Child and his mother, and return to the land of Israel.'

(103) "When he thus returned, he settled in Nazareth. After the Child grew up, and had reached the age of thirty years, he began to perform miracles, and to preach the kingdom of God. He chose twelve followers whom he called his disciples, and he began to work great marvels; to raise the dead, to cleanse lepers, to heal the lame, to give sight to the blind, and to perform many miracles, even as the prophets had foretold concerning him, saying, 'He healed our sicknesses and cured our diseases' (*Is.*, liii, 4). He was baptized by John in the Jordan, showing regeneration to mankind. When he was baptized, behold, the heavens were opened, and the Spirit descended upon him in the form of a dove, and a voice said, 'This is my beloved Son, in whom I am well pleased.'

"He sent out his disciples to preach the kingdom of God and repentance for the remission of sins. Desirous of fulfilling the prophecy, he began to preach how the Son of Man should suffer, be crucified, and rise again on the third day. While he was teaching in the Temple, the high priests and the scribes, inspired by hatred, set out to kill him, and after taking him captive, they led him before Pilate, the governor. When Pilate discovered that they had arrested him without charge, he desired to release him, but they said, 'If you release this man, you cannot be a friend of Caesar.' Pilate then commanded that they should crucify him. So they led him to the Place of the Skull and crucified him there. And darkness was over all the earth from the sixth hour until the ninth, and at the ninth hour, Jesus gave up the ghost. The veil of the Temple was rent in twain, and many dead arose, whom (104) he bade depart to Paradise.

"When they took him from the Cross, they laid him in a tomb, and the Jews sealed the tomb with a seal, and stationed guards there, saying, 'Perhaps his disciples will steal him away.' Then, upon the third day, he arose, and having arisen from the dead, he appeared to his disciples, saying to them, 'Go among all the nations, and teach all the peoples baptism in the name of the Father and the Son and the Holy Ghost.' He remained with them forty days, appearing to them after the resurrection. When the forty days had elapsed, he bade them go to the Mount of Olives, and there he appeared to them and blessed them, saying, 'Remain in the city of Jerusalem until I send the promise of my Father.' Having thus spoken, he ascended into heaven. They worshipped him, and returned to Jerusalem, where they gathered together in the Temple. When fifty days were passed, the Holy Spirit descended upon the Apostles. After they had received the promise of the Holy Spirit, they separated throughout the world, teaching and baptizing with water."

Then Vladimir said, "Wherefore was he born of woman, and crucified on the tree, and baptized with water?" The scholar answered:

"Since the human race first sinned through woman, when the devil misled Adam through the agency of Eve so that he was deprived of Paradise, God for this reason avenged himself on the devil. Because of the first woman, victory fell to the devil's lot, for it was through woman that Adam fell from Paradise. God suffered pain upon the tree in order that the devil might be conquered by the tree, and that the righteous might taste of the tree of life. (105) As to the regeneration by water: since in the time of Noah, when sin multiplied among men, God brought the flood upon the earth and drowned mankind with its waters, God said, 'Inasmuch as I destroyed mankind with water because of their sins, I will now wash away the sins of man once more through the regeneration by water.' For the Jewish people were cleansed by the sea from the evil custom of the Egyptians, since water was in the beginning the primary element. For it is said 'The Spirit of God hovered over the face of the waters.' Thus men are now baptized with water and the Spirit.

"The first transfiguration was accomplished by means of water, as Gideon performed it. For when the angel came to him and bade him attack the Midianites, he laid a fleece upon the ground and to test God, Gideon said, 'Let there be dew on the whole earth, but let the fleece remain dry.' And it was so. This miracle signifies that the Gentiles were formerly dry, while the Jews were wet, and how afterward there was dew, that is, among the Gentiles, while dryness prevailed among the Jews. For the prophets had foretold that regeneration should be accomplished by means of water.

"Now that the Apostles have taught men throughout the world to believe in God, we Greeks have inherited their teaching, and the world believes therein. God hath appointed a day, in which he shall come from heaven to judge both the quick and the dead, and to render to each according to his deeds; to the righteous, the kingdom of heaven and ineffable beauty, bliss without end, and eternal life; but to sinners, the torments of hell and a worm that sleeps not, (106) and of their torments there shall be no end. Such shall be the penalties for those who do not believe in our Lord Jesus Christ. The unbaptized shall be tormented with fire."

As he spoke thus, he exhibited to Vladimir a canvas on which was depicted the Judgment Day of the Lord, and showed him, on the right, the righteous going to their bliss in Paradise, and on the left, the sinners on their way to torment. Then Vladimir sighed and said, "Happy are they upon the right, but woe to those upon the left!" The scholar replied, "If you desire to take your place upon the right with the just, then accept baptism! Vladimir took this counsel to heart, saying, "I shall wait yet a little longer," for he wished to inquire about all the faiths. Vladimir then gave the scholar many gifts, and dismissed him with great honor.

6495 (987). Vladimir summoned together his boyars and the city-elders, and said to them, "Behold, the Bulgars came before me urging me to accept their religion. Then came the Germans and praised their own faith; and after them came the Jews. Finally the Greeks appeared, criticizing all other faiths but commending their own, and they spoke at length, telling the history of the whole world from its beginning. Their words were artful, and it was wondrous to listen and pleasant to hear them. They preach the existence of another world. 'Whoever adopts our religion and then dies shall arise and live forever. But whosoever embraces another faith, shall be consumed with fire in the next world.' (107) What is your opinion on this subject, and what do you answer?" The boyars and the elders replied, "You know, oh Prince, that no man condemns his own possessions, but praises them instead. If you desire to make certain, you have servants at your disposal. Send them to inquire about the ritual of each and how he worships God."

Their counsel pleased the prince and all the people, so that they chose good and wise men to the number of ten, and directed them to go first among the Bulgars and inspect their faith. The emissaries went their way, and when they arrived at their destination they beheld the disgraceful actions of the Bulgars and their worship in the mosque; then they returned to their country. Vladimir then instructed them to go likewise among the Germans, and examine their faith, and finally to visit the Greeks. They thus went into Germany, and after viewing the German ceremonial, they proceeded to Tsar'grad, where they appeared before the Emperor. He inquired on what mission they had come, and they reported to him all that had occurred. When the Emperor heard their words, he rejoiced, and did them great honor on that very day.

On the morrow, the Emperor sent a message to the Patriarch to inform him that a Russian delegation had arrived to examine the Greek faith, and directed him to prepare the church and the clergy, and to array himself in his sacerdotal robes, so that the Russes might behold the glory of the God of the Greeks. When the Patriarch received these commands, he bade the clergy assemble, and they performed the customary rites. They burned incense, and the choirs sang hymns. The Emperor accompanied the Russes to the church, and placed them in a wide space, calling their attention to the beauty of the edifice, the chanting, and the pontifical services and the ministry of the deacons, while he explained to them the worship of his God. The Russes were astonished, (108) and in their wonder praised the Greek ceremonial. Then the Emperors Basil and Constantine invited the envoys to their presence, and said, "Go hence to your native country," and dismissed them with valuable presents and great honor.

Thus they returned to their own country, and the Prince called together his boyars and the elders. Vladimir then announced the return of the envoys who had been sent out, and suggested that their report be heard. He thus commanded them to speak out before his retinue. The envoys reported, "When we journeyed among the Bulgars, we beheld how they worship in their temple, called a mosque, while they stand ungirt. The Bulgar bows, sits down, looks hither and thither like one possessed, and there is no happiness among them, but instead only sorrow and a dreadful stench. Their religion is not good. Then we went among the Germans, and saw them performing many ceremonies in their temples; but we beheld no glory there. Then we went to Greece, and the Greeks led us to the edifices where they worship their God, and we knew not whether we were in heaven or on earth. For on earth there is no such splendor or such beauty, and we are at a loss how to describe it. We only know that God dwells there among men, and their service is fairer than the ceremonies of other nations. For we cannot forget that beauty. Every man, after tasting something sweet, is afterward unwilling to accept that which is bitter, and therefore we cannot dwell longer here." Then the boyars spoke and said, "If the Greek faith were evil, it would not have been adopted by your grandmother Olga who was wiser than all other men." Vladimir then inquired where they should all accept baptism, and they replied that the decision rested with him.

(109) After a year had passed, in 6496 (988), Vladimir proceeded with an armed force against Kherson, a Greek city, and the people of Kherson barricaded themselves therein.[94] Vladimir halted at the farther side of the city beside the harbor, a bowshot from the town, and the inhabitants resisted energetically while Vladimir besieged the town. Eventually, however, they became exhausted, and Vladimir warned

them that if they did not surrender, he would remain on the spot for three years. When they failed to heed this threat, Vladimir marshalled his troops and ordered the construction of an earthwork in the direction of the city. While this work was under construction, the inhabitants dug a tunnel under the city-wall, stole the heaped-up earth, and carried it into the city, where they piled it up in the center of the town. But the soldiers kept on building, and Vladimir persisted. Then a man of Kherson, Anastasius by name, shot into the Russ camp an arrow on which he had written, "There are springs behind you to the east, from which water flows in pipes. Dig down and cut them off." When Vladimir received this information, he raised his eyes to heaven and vowed that if this hope was realized, he would be baptized. He gave orders straightway to dig down above the pipes, and the water-supply was thus cut off. The inhabitants were accordingly overcome by thirst, and surrendered.

Vladimir and his retinue entered the city, and he sent messages to the Emperors Basil and Constantine, saying, "Behold, I have captured your glorious city. I have also heard that you have an unwedded sister. Unless you give her to me to wife, (110) I shall deal with your own city as I have with Kherson." When the Emperors heard this message they were troubled, and replied, "It is not meet for Christians to give in marriage to pagans. If you are baptized, you shall have her to wife, inherit the kingdom of God, and be our companion in the faith. Unless you do so, however, we cannot give you our sister in marriage." When Vladimir learned their response, he directed the envoys of the Emperors to report to the latter that he was willing to accept baptism, having already given some study to their religion, and that the Greek faith and ritual, as described by the emissaries sent to examine it, had pleased him well. When the Emperors heard this report, they rejoiced, and persuaded their sister Anna to consent to the match. They then requested Vladimir to submit to baptism before they should send their sister to him, but Vladimir desired that the Princess should herself bring priests to baptize him. The Emperors complied with his request, and sent forth their sister, accompanied by some dignitaries and priests. Anna, however, departed with reluctance. "It is as if I were setting out into captivity," she lamented; "better were it for me to die at home." But her brothers protested, "Through your agency God turns the land of Rus' to repentance, and you will relieve Greece from the danger of grievous war. Do you not see how much harm the Russes have already brought upon the Greeks? If you do not set out, they may bring on us the same misfortunes." It was thus that they overcame her hesitation only with great difficulty. The Princess embarked upon a ship, and after tearfully embracing her kinfolk, (111) she set forth across the sea and arrived at Kherson. The natives came forth to greet her, and conducted her into the ctiy, where they settled her in the palace.

By divine agency, Vladimir was suffering at that moment from a disease of the eyes, and could see nothing, being in great distress. The Princess declared to him that if he desired to be relieved of this disease, he should be baptized with all speed, otherwise it could not be cured. When Vladimir heard her message, he said, "If this proves true, then of a surety is the God of the Christians great," and gave order that he should be baptized. The Bishop of Kherson, together with the Princess's priests, after announcing the tidings, baptized Vladimir, and as the Bishop laid his hand upon him, he straightway received his sight. Upon experiencing this miraculous cure, Vladimir glorified God, saying, "I have now perceived the one true God." When his followers beheld this miracle, many of them were also baptized.

Vladimir was baptized in the Church of St. Basil, which stands at Kherson upon a square in the center of the city, where the Khersonians trade.[95] The palace of Vladimir stands beside this church to this day, and the palace of the Princess is behind the altar. After his baptism, Vladimir took the Princess in marriage. Those who do not know the truth say he was baptized in Kiev, while others assert this event took place in Vasil'ev,[96] while still others mention other places.

After Vladimir was baptized, (112) the priests explained to him the tenets of the Christian faith, urging him to avoid the deceit of heretics by adhering to the following creeds:

I believe in God, the Father Almighty, Maker of Heaven and Earth; and also: I believe in one God the Father, who is unborn, and in the only Son, who is born, and in one Holy Ghost emanating therefrom: three complete and thinking Persons, divisible in number and personality, but not in divinity; for they are separated without distinction and united without confusion. God the Father Everlasting, abides in Fatherhood, unbegotten, without beginning, himself the beginning and the cause of all things. Because he is unbegotten, he is older than the Son and the Spirit. From him the Son was born before all worlds, and from him the Holy Ghost emanates intemporally and incorporeally. He is simultaneously Father, Son and Holy Ghost.

The Son, being like the Father, is distinguished from the Father and the Spirit in that he was born. The Spirit is Holy, like to the Father and the Son, and is everlasting. The Father possesses Fatherhood, and Son Sonship, and the Holy Ghost Emanation. For the Father is not transformed into the Son or the Spirit, nor the Son to the Father and the Spirit, nor the Spirit to the Son and the Father, since their attributes are invariable. Not three Gods, but one God, since there is one divinity in three Persons.

In consequence of the desire of the Father and the Spirit to save his creation, he went out of the bosom of the Father, yet without leaving it, to the (113) pure womb of a Virgin, as the seed of God. Entering into her, he took on animated, vocal, and thinking flesh which had not previously existed, came forth God incarnate, and was ineffably born, while his Mother preserved her virginity immaculate. Suffering neither combination, nor confusion, nor alteration, he remained as he was, became what he was not, and assumed the aspect of a slave in truth, not in semblance, being similar to us in every respect except in sin.

Voluntarily he was born, voluntarily he suffered want, voluntarily he thirsted, voluntarily he endured, voluntarily he feared, voluntarily he died in truth and not in semblance. All these were genuine and unimpeachable human sufferings. He gave himself up to be crucified. Though immortal, he tasted death. He arose in the flesh without knowing corruption; he ascended into Heaven, and sat upon the right hand of the Father. And as he ascended in glory and in the flesh so shall he descend once more.

Moreover, I acknowledge one Baptism of water and the Spirit, I approach the Holy Mysteries, I believe in the True Body and Blood, I accept the traditions of the Church, and I venerate the sacred images. I revere the Holy Tree and every Cross, the sacred relics, and the sacred vessels.[97]

Believe, also, they said, in the seven councils of the Church: the first at Nicaea, comprising three hundred and eighteen Fathers, who cursed Arius and proclaimed the immaculate and orthodox faith; the second at Constantinople, attended by one hundred and fifty Fathers, who anathematized Macedonius (who denied the Holy Spirit), and proclaimed the oneness of the Trinity; (114) the third at Ephesus, comprising two hundred Fathers, against Nestorius, whom they cursed, while they also proclaimed the dignity of the Mother of God; the fourth council of six hundred and thirty Fathers held at Chalcedon, to condemn Eutyches and Dioscorus, whom the Holy Fathers cursed after they had proclaimed the Perfect God and the Perfect Man, our Lord Jesus Christ; the fifth council of one hundred and sixty-five Fathers, held at Constantinople, which was directed against the teachings of Origen and Evagrius, whom the Fathers anathematized; the sixth council of one hundred and seventy Holy Fathers, likewise held at Constantinople, which condemned Sergius and Cyrus, whom the Holy Fathers cursed; and the seventh council, comprising three hundred and fifty Holy Fathers, which was held at Nicaea, and cursed those who do not venerate images.

Do not accept the teachings of the Latins, whose instruction is vicious. For when they enter the church, they do not kneel before the images, but they stand upright before kneeling, and when they have knelt, they trace a cross upon the ground and then kiss it, but they stand upon it when they arise. Thus while prostrate they kiss it, and yet upon arising they trample it underfoot. Such is not the tradition of the Apostles. For the Apostles prescribed the kissing of an upright cross, and also prescribed the use of images. For the Evangelist Luke painted the first image and sent it to Rome. As Basil has said, the honor rendered to the image redounds to its original. Furthermore, they call the earth their mother. If the earth is their mother, then heaven is their father, for in the beginning God made heaven and earth. Yet they say, "Our Father which art in Heaven." If, according to their understanding, the earth is their mother, why do they spit upon (115) their mother, and pollute her whom they caress?

In earlier times, the Romans did not so act, but took part in all the councils, gathering together from Rome and all other Sees. At the first Council in Nicaea, directed against Arius, Silvester sent bishops and priests from Rome, as did Athanasius from Alexandria; and Metrophanes also despatched his bishops from Constantinople. Thus they corrected the faith. At the second council took part Damasus of Rome, Timotheus of Alexandria, Meletius of Antioch, Cyril of Jerusalem, and Gregory the Theologian. In the third council participated Coelestinus of Rome, Cyril of Alexandria, Juvenal of Jerusalem. At the fourth council participated Leo of Rome, Anatolius of Constantinople, and Juvenal of Jerusalem; and at the fifth, Vigilius of Rome, Eutychius of Constantinople, Apollinaris of Alexandria, and Domnus of Antioch. At the sixth council took part Agathon of Rome, Georgius of Constantinople, Theophanes of Antioch, and Peter the Monk of Alexandria; at the seventh, Adrian of Rome, Tarasius of Constantinople, Politian of Alexandria, Theodoret of Antioch, and Elias of Jerusalem. These Fathers with the assistance of the bishops, corrected the faith.

After the seventh council, Peter the Stammerer came with the others to Rome and corrupted the faith, seizing the Holy See. (116) He seceded from the Sees of Jerusalem, Alexandria, Constantinople, and Antioch. His partisans disturbed all Italy, disseminating their teaching in various terms. For some of these priests who conduct services are married to one wife, and others are married to seven. Avoid their doctrine; for they absolve sins against money payments, which is the worst abuse of all. God guard you from this evil, oh Prince![98]

Hereupon Vladimir took the Princess and Anastasius and the priests of Kherson, together with the relics of St. Clement and of Phoebus his disciple, and selected also sacred vessels and images for the service.[99] In Kherson he thus founded a church on the mound which had been heaped up in the midst of the city with the earth removed from his embankment; this church is standing at the present day. Vladimir also found and appropriated two bronze statues and four bronze horses, which now stand behind the Church of the Holy Virgin, and which the ignorant think are made of marble. As a wedding present for the Princess, he gave Kherson over to the Greeks again, and then departed for Kiev.

When the Prince arrived at his capital, he directed that the idols should be overthrown, and that some should be cut to pieces and others burned with fire. He thus ordered that Perun should be bound to a horse's tail and dragged down Borichev to the stream.[100] He appointed twelve men to beat the idol with sticks, not because he thought the wood was sensitive, but to affront the demon who had deceived man in this guise, (117) that he might receive chastisement at the hands of men. Great art thou, oh Lord, and marvelous are thy works! Yesterday he was honored of men, but today held in derision. While the idol was being dragged along the stream to the Dnieper, the unbelievers wept over it, for they had not yet received holy baptism. After they had thus dragged the idol along, they cast it into the Dnieper. But Vladimir had given this injunction "If it halts anywhere, then push it out from the bank, until it goes over the falls. Then let it loose." His command was duly obeyed. When the men let the idol go, and it passed through the rapids, the wind cast it out on the bank, which since that time has been called Perun's sandbank, a name that it bears to this very day.

Thereafter Vladimir sent heralds throughout the whole city to proclaim that if any inhabitants, rich or poor, did not betake himself to the river, he would risk the Prince's displeasure. When the people heard these words, they wept for joy, and exclaimed in their enthusiasm, "If this were not good, the Prince and his boyars would not have accepted it." On the morrow, the Prince went forth to the Dnieper with the priests of the Princess and those from Kherson, and a countless multitude assembled. They all went into the water: some stood up to their necks, others to their breasts, and the younger near the bank, some of them holding children in their arms, while the adults waded farther out. The priests stood by and offered prayers.[101] There was joy (118) in heaven and upon earth to behold so many souls saved. But the devil groaned, lamenting, "Woe is me! how am I driven out hence! For I thought to have my dwelling-place here, since the apostolic teachings do not abide in this land. Nor did this people know God, but I rejoiced in the service they rendered unto me. But now I am vanquished by the ignorant, not by apostles and martyrs, and my reign in these regions is at an end."

When the people were baptized, they returned each to his own abode. Vladimir, rejoicing that he and his subjects now knew God himself, looked up to heaven and said, "Oh God, who has created heaven and earth, look down, I beseech thee, on this thy new people, and grant them, oh Lord, to know thee as the true God, even as the other Christian nations have known thee. Confirm in them the true and inalterable faith, and aid me, oh Lord, against the hostile adversary, so that, hoping in thee and in thy might, I may overcome his malice." Having spoken thus, he ordained that wooden churches should be built and established where pagan idols had previously stood. He thus founded the Church of St. Basil on the hill where the idol of Perun and the other images had been set, and where the Prince and the people had offered their sacrifices.[102] He began to found churches and to assign priests throughout the cities, and to invite the people to accept baptism in all the cities and towns.

He took the children of the best families, and sent them for instruction (119) in book-learning. The mothers of these children wept bitterly over them, for they were not yet strong in faith, but mourned as for the dead. When these children were assigned for study, there was fulfilled in the land of Rus' the prophecy which says, "In those days, the deaf shall hear words of Scripture, and the voice of the stammerers shall be made plain" (*Is.*, xxix, 18). For these persons had not ere this heard words of Scripture, and now heard them only by the act of God, for in his mercy the Lord took pity upon them, even as the Prophet said, "I will be gracious to whom I will be gracious" (*Ex.*, xxxiii, 19).

He had mercy upon us in the baptism of life and the renewal of the spirit, following the will of God and not according to our deeds. Blessed be the Lord Jesus Christ, who loved his new people, the land of Rus', and illumined them with holy baptism. Thus we bend the knee before him saying, "Lord Jesus Christ, what reward shall we return thee for all that thou hast given us, sinners that we are? We can not requite thy gifts, for great art thou, and marvelous are thy works. Of thy majesty there is no end. Generation after generation shall praise thy acts" (*Ps.,* cxlv, 4-5).

Thus I say with David, "Come, let us rejoice in the Lord, let us call upon God and our Savior. Let us come before his presence with thanksgiving, praising him because he is good, for his mercy endureth forever, since he hath saved us from our enemies, even from vain idols" (*Ps.,* xcv, 1-2, cxxxxvi, 1, 24). And let us once more say with David, "Sing unto the Lord a new song, sing unto the Lord, all the earth! Sing unto the Lord, praise his name: tell his salvation from day to day. Declare his glory among the heathen, his wonders among all nations (*Ps.,* xcvi, 1-4). For the Lord is great and greatly praised, (120) and of his majesty there is no end" (*Ps.,* clv, 3). What joy! Not one or two only are saved. For the Lord said, "There is joy in heaven over one sinner that repenteth" (*Math.,* xv, 10). Here not merely one or two, but innumerable multitudes came to God, illumined by holy baptism. As the Prophet said, "I will sprinkle water upon you, and ye shall be purified of your idols and your sins" (*Ezek.,* xxxvi, 25). Another Prophet said likewise, "Who like to God taketh away sins and remitteth transgressions? For he is willingly merciful; he turneth his gaze upon us and sinketh our sins in the abyss" (*Mic.,* vii, 18-19). For Paul says, "Brethren, as many of us as were baptized in Jesus Christ were baptized in his death, and with him, through baptism, we were planted in death, in order that as Christ rose from the dead in the glory of the Father, we also might likewise walk in newness of life" (*Rom.,* vi, 3). And again, "The old things have passed away, and new are made (*II Cor.,* v, 7); now hath approached our salvation, the night hath passed, the day is at hand" (*Rom.,* xiii, 12); "Thus we obtained access through faith into this grace of which we are proud and through which we exist" (*Rom.,* v, 2). "Now, being freed from sin, and having become servants of the Lord, ye have your fruit in holiness" (*Rom.,* vi, 20).

We are therefore bound to serve the Lord, rejoicing in him, for David said, "Serve the Lord with fear and rejoice in him with trembling" (*Ps.,* ii, 11). We call upon the Lord our God, saying "Blessed be the Lord, who gave us not as prey to their teeth. The net was broken, and we were freed from the crafts of the devil. His glory has perished noisily, but the Lord endures forever, glorified by the sons of Rus', and praised in the Trinity." But the demons (121) are accursed of pious men and righteous women, who have received baptism and repentance for the remission of sins, and thus form a new Christian people, the elect of God.

Vladimir was enlightened, and his sons and his country with him. For he had twelve sons: Vÿsheslav, Izyaslav, Yaroslav, Svyatopolk, Vsevolod, Svyatoslav, Mstislav, Boris, Gleb, Stanislav, Pozvizd, and Sudislav. He set Vÿsheslav in Novgorod, Izyaslav in Polotsk, Svyatopolk in Turov, and Yaroslav in Rostov. When Vÿsheslav, the oldest, died in Novgorod, he set Yaroslav over Novgorod, Boris over Rostov, Gleb over Murom, Svyatoslav over Dereva, Vsevolod over Vladimir, and Mstislav over Tmutorakan'.[103] Then Vladimir reflected that it was not good that there were so few towns round about Kiev, so he founded forts on the Desna, the Oster', the Trubezh, the Sula, and the Stugna.[104] He gathered together the best men of the Slavs, and Krivichians, the Chuds, and the Vyatichians, and peopled these forts with them. For he was at war with the Pechenegs, and when he fought with them, he often overcame them.

6497 (989). After these events, Vladimir lived in the Christian faith. With the intention of building a church dedicated to the Holy Virgin, he sent and imported artisans from Greece. After he had begun to build, and the structure was completed, he adorned it with images, and entrusted it to Anastasius of Kherson. He appointed Khersonian priests (122) to serve in it, and bestowed upon this church all the images, vessels, and crosses which he had taken in that city.[105]

6499 (991). Vladimir founded the city of Belgorod,[106] and peopled it from other towns, bringing to it many settlers. For he was extremely fond of this city.

6500 (992). Vladimir attacked the Croats.[107] When he had returned from the Croatian War, the Pechenegs arrived on the opposite side of the Dnieper from the direction of the Sula. Vladimir set forth against them, and encountered them on the banks of the Trubezh, where Pereyaslavl' now stands. Vladimir took up his position on the near side, and the Pechenegs theirs on the other, and the Russes did not venture to the farther shore any more than their foes did to this side of the river. The Prince of the Pechenegs came down to the river bank, and calling to Vladimir, proposed to him, "Send one of your warriors, and I will detail one of mine, that they may do battle together. If your man conquers mine, let us not fight together for three years to come. But if our champion wins, let us fight three years in succession." Then each prince returned to his own force.

Vladimir returned to his camp, and sent heralds through it to inquire whether there was any man who would fight with the champion of the Pechenegs. But none was found anywhere. On the morrow, the Pechenegs arrived, bringing their champion; but on our side there was none. Vladimir now began to be concerned as he sought a champion throughout his whole army. Then there came to the Prince an old man who said to him, "Oh Prince, I have a younger son at home. I came forth with four others, (123) but he abides by the hearth. Since his childhood, there has been no man who could vanquish him. One day when I reprimanded him while he was tanning a hide, he flew into a rage at me and tore the leather to bits in his hands." When the Prince heard these words, he rejoiced, and summoned the youth. So he was brought before the Prince, and the Prince informed him of all that had occurred. Then the youth said, "Oh Prince, I know not whether I be capable of this feat; wherefore let them test me. Is there no large and strong bull hereabouts?" Such a bull was soon found, and he directed them to anger the animal. The men put hot irons on him, and then let him go. The bull ran past the youth, and he seized the beast's flank with his hand. He thus pulled off the skin along with as much flesh as he could grasp. Then Vladimir remarked, "You are well qualified to do combat with the champion."

On the morrow the Pechenegs approached, and began to shout, "Is there no champion present? See, ours is ready." Vladimir had given orders that night to rest upon their arms, and at dawn the two champions went forth. The Pechenegs had sent out their man, who was gigantic and fearsome. Vladimir sent forward his champion, and when the Pecheneg saw him, he laughed, for he was of but moderate size. A space was duly measured off between the two armies, and the warriors were allowed to attack each other. They came to grips, and seized upon each other with violence. But the Russ crushed the Pecheneg to death in his arms, and cast him upon the ground. The Russes raised a cheer, and the Pechenegs took to flight. The Russes pursued them, cut them down, and drove them away. In his joy, Vladimir founded a city on this river bank, (124) and called it Pereyaslavl',[108] because this youth had won glory there. Vladimir made him and his father great men, and then returned to Kiev with victory and renown.

6502-6504 (994-996). Vladimir, upon seeing his church completed, entered it and prayed to God, saying, "Lord God! Look down from heaven, behold and visit thy vineyard, and perfect what thy right hand has begun. Make these new people, whose heart thou hast turned unto wisdom, to know thee as the true God. Look upon this thy church which I, thine unworthy servant, have built in the name of the Ever-Virgin Mother of God who bore thee. Through the intercession of the Immaculate Virgin, hear the supplication of whosoever shall pray in this church." After he had offered this prayer, he added, "I bestow upon this church of the Holy Virgin a tithe of my property and of my cities." Then he wrote out a donation and deposited it in the church, declaring, "If anyone violates this promise, may he be accursed." So he gave the tithe to Anastasius of Kherson, and made a great festival on that day for the boyars and elders of the people, distributing also much largess to the poor.[109]

Then the Pechenegs came to Vasil'evo,[110] and Vladimir went forth against them with a small company. When the troops met, he could not withstand the enemy, so he fled, and took position (125) under a bridge, where he concealed himself with difficulty from the foe. Then the Prince vowed to build a church of the Sacred Transfiguration in Vasil'evo, for it was upon this day of the Lord's transfiguration that this battle took place. After he had thus escaped, Vladimir founded the church,[111] and made ready a great festival, for which he caused to be brewed three hundred kettles of mead. He summoned his boyars, his lieutenants, the elders throughout the cities, and many other people, and distributed to the poor the sum of three hundred *grivnÿ*. When the Prince had thus celebrated for eight days, he returned to Kiev on the feast of the Assumption of the Holy Mother of God. There also he held a great festival, and gathered together a countless multitude of people.

When he saw that the people were Christians, he rejoiced in soul and body, and celebrated likewise every year. For he loved the words of the Scriptures, and on one occasion he had heard read in the Gospel, "Blessed are the merciful, for they shall obtain mercy" (*Matt.*, v, 7); and further, "Lay not up for yourselves treasures upon earth, where moth corrupts and thieves steal; but lay up for yourselves treasures in heaven, where neither moth corrupts nor thieves steal" (*Matt.*, vi, 19). And David said, "Blessed is he that considereth the poor" (*Ps.*, xli, 1). Vladimir listened also to the words of Solomon: "He that giveth unto the poor lendeth unto the Lord" (*Prov.*, xix, 17). When he heard these words, he invited each beggar and poor man to come to the Prince's palace and receive whatever he needed, both food and drink, and marten-skins from the treasury.

With the thought that the weak and the sick could not easily reach his palace, he arranged that (126) wagons should be brought in, and after having them loaded with bread, meat, fish, various fruits, mead in casks, and kvass, he ordered them driven out through the city. The drivers were under instructions to call out, "Where is there a poor man or a beggar who cannot walk?" To such they distributed according to their necessities. Moreover, he caused a feast to be prepared each Sunday in his palace for his subjects, and invited the boyars, the court officers, the centurions, the decurions, and the distinguished citizens, either in the presence of the Prince or in his absence. There was much meat, beef, and game, and an abundance of all victuals. On one occasion, however, after the guests were drunk, they began to grumble against the prince, complaining that they were mistreated because he allowed them to eat with wooden spoons, instead of silver ones. When Vladimir heard of this complaint, he ordered that silver spoons should be moulded for his retinue to eat with, remarking that with silver and gold he could not secure a retinue, but that with a retinue he was in a position to win these treasures, even as his grandfather and his father had sought riches with their followers. For Vladimir was fond of his followers, and consulted them concerning matters of administration, wars, and government. He lived at peace with the neighboring Princes, Boleslav of Poland, Stephen of Hungary, and Udalrich of Bohemia, and there was amity and friendship among them.[112]

While Vladimir was thus dwelling in the fear of God, the number of bandits increased, and the bishops, calling to his attention the multiplication of robbers, (127) inquired why he did not punish them. The Prince answered that he feared the sin entailed. They replied that he was appointed of God for the chastisement of malefaction and for the practice of mercy toward the righteous, so that it was entirely fitting for him to punish a robber condignly, but only after due process of law. Vladimir accordingly abolished *wergild* and set out to punish the brigands. The bishops and the elders then suggested that as wars were frequent, the *wergild* might be properly spent for the purchase of arms and horses, to which Vladimir assented. Thus Vladimir lived according to the prescriptions of his father and his grandfather.

6505 (997). When Vladimir went to Novgorod after upland troops with which to fight the Pechenegs (for there was desperate and constant conflict with them), the latter, on perceiving that for the moment there was no prince at hand, came and beset Belgorod.[113] They allowed no sally from the city, and great famine prevailed. Vladimir could not bring succor, for he had no troops with him, and the number of the Pechenegs was great. The siege was thus prolonged, and the famine grew increasingly severe. The inhabitants thus held a council in the city, and said among themselves, "We are about to die of hunger, and no aid is to be expected from the Prince. Is it not better to die? Let us surrender to the Pechenegs, and let them spare some, though they kill others. We are perishing of famine as it is." Thus they came to a decision. But one old man was not present at the council, and inquired what it was about. The people told him that on the morrow they would surrender to the Pechenegs. Upon hearing this decision, he summoned the city-elders, and remarked that he understood (128) they intended to surrender to the nomads. They replied that the people would not endure famine. Then the ancient said, "Listen to me: do not surrender for three days, and do as I tell you." They gladly promised to obey, and he directed them to collect a measure of oats, wheat, or bran apiece. They gladly went in search of these supplies. Then he bade the women prepare the liquid with which they brew porridge, and ordered them to dig a pit. In this pit he bade them place a tub, and to pour the liquid into the tub. Then he ordered them to dig a second pit, and place a tub in the latter likewise. He next commanded them to bring honey, so they fetched a basket of honey that was stored in the Prince's storeroom. He then bade them dilute it greatly, and to pour it into the tub in the other pit.

Upon the morrow, he directed them to send messengers to the Pechenegs. The citizens went forth to the Pechenegs, and offered them hostages, so that ten of the nomads should come into the city to see what was happening in their town. The Pechenegs rejoiced, thinking that they wished to surrender. They therefore accepted the hostages, and selected the chief men of their own party, whom they sent into the city to look over the town and learn what was occurring. The Pecheneg representatives entered the town, and the inhabitants said to them, "Why do you waste your strength? You cannot overcome us if you besiege us for ten years. We secure our sustenance from the earth. If you do not believe it, behold it with your own eyes." They thus conducted the Pecheneg envoys to the pit (129) where the brew was, then drew some up in a pail and poured it into pots. After they had brewed porridge, they conducted the Pechenegs to the other pit. They hauled up the buckets and after eating from them themselves, offered them to the Pechenegs. The latter were astonished, and exclaimed, "Our princes will not believe this marvel, unless they eat of the food themselves." So they poured out a bowl of brew and buckets of mead from the pits, and gave them to the Pechenegs, who returned to their camp and recounted all that had happened. After brewing the porridge, the Pecheneg princes ate it, and were amazed, and upon recovering their own hostages and returning those given by the city, they raised the siege and returned home.

6506-6508 (998-1000). Malfrid died.[114] In this year died also Rogned, Yaroslav's mother.

6509 (1001). In this year died Izyaslav, son of Vladimir and father of Bryachislav.

6510-6511 (1002-1003). In this year died Vseslav, son of Izyaslav and grandson of Vladimir.

6512-6515 (1004-1007). The saints were brought to the Church of the Holy Virgin.[115]

6516-6519 (1008-1011). The Princess Anna, wife of Vladimir, passed away.

(130) 6520-6522 (1012-1014). When Yaroslav was in Novgorod, he paid two thousand *grivnÿ* a year as tribute to Kiev, and another thousand was given to his garrison in Novgorod. All the lieutenants of Novgorod had always paid like sums, but Yaroslav ceased to render this amount to his father.[116] Then Vladimir exclaimed, "Repair roads and build bridges," for he proposed to attack his son Yaroslav, but he fell ill.

6523 (1015). While Vladimir was desirous of attacking Yaroslav, the latter sent overseas and imported Varangian reinforcements, since he feared his father's advance. But God will not give the devil any satisfaction. For when Vladimir fell ill, Boris was with him at the time. Since the Pechenegs were attacking the Russes, he sent Boris out against them, for he himself was very sick, and of this illness he died on July 15. Now he died at Berestovo, but his death was kept secret, for Svyatopolk was in Kiev. But at night his companions took up the flooring between two rooms, and after wrapping the body in a rug, they let it down to the earth with ropes. After they had placed it upon a sledge, they took it away and laid it in the Church of the Virgin that Vladimir himself had built.

When the people heard of this, they assembled in multitude and mourned him, the boyars as the defender of their country, the poor as their protector and benefactor. They placed him in a marble coffin, and buried the body of the sainted Prince amid their mourning.

He is the new Constantine of mighty Rome, who baptized himself (131) and his subjects; for the Prince of Rus' imitated the acts of Constantine himself. Even if he was formerly given to evil lusts, he afterward consecrated himself to repentance, according to the teaching of the Apostle that "when sin increases, there grace abounds the more" (*Rom.*, v, 20).[117] Even if he had previously committed other crimes in his ignorance, he subsequently distinguished himself in repentance and almsgiving. As it is written, "As I shall find you, so shall I judge you"

(*Wis.*, xi, 17). Thus the Prophet says, "as I the Lord Adonai live, I desire not the death of a sinner, but rather that he shall turn from his way and live; turn in repentance from your wicked way" (*Ezek.*, xxxiii, 11). For many of those who act justly and live in righteousness turn from the virtuous road to death and are destroyed; while others live unrighteously, yet are admonished before their deaths, and atone for their sins through laudable repentance.

Thus the Prophet says, "The righteousness of the righteous shall not save him in the day of his transgression. When I say to the righteous man, 'Thou shalt live,' if he trust to his righteousness and commit iniquity, all his righteousness shall not be remembered, and he shall die in the iniquity that he hath committed. And when I say to the wicked, 'Thou shalt die the death,' if he turn from his sin and perform equity and justice, restore his pledge, and give back what he hath stolen, then all his sins that he hath committed shall not be remembered, because he performed equity and justice, and in them shall he live. I shall judge each of you according to his way, oh house of Israel" (*Ezek.*, xxxiii, 12-16, 20).

Vladimir died in the orthodox faith. He effaced his sins by repentance and by almsgiving, which is better than all things else. For the Lord says, "I desire alms, and not a sacrifice" (*Matt.*, ix, 13). Alms are better and more exalted than all other things, since they lead us into the presence of God, even to heaven itself; as the angel said to Cornelius, "Thy prayers and thy almsgiving are remembered before God" (*Acts*, x, 4).

It is indeed marvelous what benefits Vladimir conferred upon the land of Rus' by its conversion. But we, though Christians, do not render him honor in proportion to this benefaction. For if he had not converted us, we should now be a prey to the crafts of the devil, even as our ancestors perished. If we had been zealous for him, and had offered our prayers to God in his behalf upon the day of his death, then God, beholding our zeal, would have glorified him. It is fitting for us to pray God for his sake, inasmuch as through him we have come to know God. But may God grant thee according to thy heart's desire and fulfill all they requests, giving thee the kingdom of heaven which thou didst desire! May God confer upon thee the crown among the righteous, happiness in paradisiacal sustenance, and association with Abraham and the other patriarchs! As Solomon said, "When a righteous man dieth, his hope is not lost" (*Prov.*, xi, 7). The people of Rus', mindful of their holy baptism, hold this Prince in pious memory, and glorify God in prayers and hymns and psalms, singing to God as his new people, enlightened by his Holy Spirit, maintaining the hope of our great God and of our Savior Jesus Christ, that He will give each one of us joy ineffable according to his labors. And may such be the lot of all Christians.[118]

(132) Upon his father's death, Svyatopolk settled in Kiev,[119] and after calling together all the inhabitants of Kiev, he began to distribute largess among them. They accepted it, but their hearts were not with him, because their brethren were with Boris. When Boris returned with the army, without meeting the Pechenegs, he received the news that his father was dead. He mourned deeply for him, for he was beloved of his father before all the rest.

When he came to the Al'ta,[120] he halted. His father's retainers then urged him to take his place in Kiev on his father's throne, since he had at his disposal the latter's retainers and troops. But Boris protested, "Be it not for me to raise my hand against my elder brother. Now that my father has passed away, let him take the place of my father in my heart." When the soldiery heard these words, they departed from him, and Boris remained with his servants.

But Svyatopolk was filled with lawlessness. Adopting the device of Cain, he sent messages to Boris that he desired to live at peace with him, and would increase the territory he had received from his father. But he plotted against him now how he might kill him. So Svyatopolk came by night to Vÿshgorod. After secretly summoning to his presence Put'sha and the boyars of the town, he inquired of them whether they were whole-heartedly devoted to him. Put'sha and the men of Vÿshgorod replied, "We are ready to lay down our lives for you." He then commanded them to say nothing to any man, but to go and kill his brother Boris. They straightway promised to execute his order. Of such men Solomon has well said, "They make haste to shed blood unjustly. For they (133) promise blood, and gather evil. Their path runneth to evil, for they possess their souls in dishonor" (*Prov.*, i, 16-19).

These emissaries came to the Al'ta, and when they approached, they heard the sainted Boris singing matins. For it was already known to him that they intended to take his life. Then he arose and began to chant, saying, "Oh Lord, how are they increased who come against me! Many are they that rise up against me" (*Ps.*, iii, 1). And also, "Thine arrows have pierced me, for I am ready for wounds and my pain is before me continually" (*Ps.*, xxxviii, 2, 17), and he also uttered this prayer: "Lord, hear my prayer, and enter not into judgment with thy servant, for no living man shall be just before thee. For the enemy hath crushed my soul" (*Ps.*, cxl, 1-3). After ending the six psalms, when he saw how men were sent out to kill him, he began to chant the Psalter, saying, "Strong bulls encompassed me, and the assemblage of the evil beset me. Oh Lord my God, I have hoped in thee; save me and deliver me from the pursuers" (*Ps.*, xxii, 12, 16; vii, 1). Then he began to sing the canon. After finishing matins, he prayed, gazing upon the eikon, the image of the Lord, with these words: "Lord Jesus Christ, who in this image hast appeared on earth for our salvation, and won, having voluntarily suffered thy hands to be nailed to the Cross, didst endure thy passion for our sins, so help me now to endure my passion. For I accept it not from those who are my enemies, but from the hand of my own brother. Hold it not against him as a sin, oh Lord!"

After offering this prayer, he lay down upon his couch. (134) Then they fell upon him like wild beasts about the tent, and pierced him with lances. They stabbed Boris and his servant, who cast himself upon his body. For he was beloved of Boris. He was a servant of Hungarian race, George by name, to whom Boris was greatly attached. The Prince had given him a large gold necklace which he wore while serving him. They also killed many other servants of Boris. But since they could not quickly take the necklace from George's neck, they cut off his head, and thus obtained it. For this reason his body was not recognized later among the corpses.

The desperadoes, after attacking Boris, wrapped him in a canvas, loaded him upon a wagon, and dragged him off, though he was still alive. When the impious Svyatopolk saw that he was still breathing, he sent two Varangians to finish him. When they came and saw that he was still alive, one of them drew his sword and plunged it into his heart. Thus died the blessed Boris, receiving from the hand of Christ our God the crown among the righteous. He shall be numbered with the Prophets and the Apostles, as he joins with the choirs of martyrs, rests in the lap of Abraham, beholds joy ineffable, chants with the angels, and rejoices in company with the choirs of saints. After his body had been carried in secret to Vyshgorod, it was buried beside the Church of St. Basil.[121]

The desperate murderers, (135) godless wretches that they were, returned to Svyatopolk in hope of commendation. The names of these contemners of the law are Put'sha, Talets, Elovit, and Lyashko, and their father was Satan himself. For such servants are devils, since devils are sent to do evil, and angels to do good. An angel does no harm to man, but, instead, thinks constantly of his good. Angels render help to Christians, and protect them against their adversary the devil. But devils always seek after evil, and hate man, since they behold him honored of God. Because they envy him, they are swift in their evil mission. An evil man, eager for crime, is worse than a devil, because devils at least fear God, whereas an evil man neither fears God nor is ashamed before men. Devils fear the Cross of the Lord, but an evil man does not even fear the Holy Cross.

The impious Svyatopolk then reflected, "Behold, I have killed Boris; now how can I kill Gleb?" Adopting once more Cain's device, he craftily sent messages to Gleb to the effect that he should come quickly, because his father was very ill and desired his presence. Gleb quickly mounted his horse, and set out with a small company, for he was obedient to his father. When he came to the Volga, his horse stumbled in a ditch on the plain, and injured his leg slightly. He arrived at Smolensk, and setting out thence at daybreak, embarked in a boat on the Smyadÿn'.[122] At this moment, Yaroslav received from Predslava the tidings of their father's death, and he sent word to Gleb that he should not set out, because his father (136) was dead and his brother had been murdered by Svyatopolk. Upon receiving these tidings, Gleb burst into tears, and mourned for his father, but still more deeply for his brother. He wept and prayed with the lament, "Woe is me, oh Lord! It were better for me to die with my brother than to live on in this world. Oh my brother, had I but seen thy angelic countenance, I should have died with thee. Why am I now left alone? Where are thy words that thou didst say to me, my brother? No longer do I hear thy sweet counsel. If thou hast received encouragement from God, pray for me that I may endure the same passion. For it were better for me to dwell with thee than in this deceitful world."

While he was thus praying amid his tears, there suddenly arrived those sent by Svyatopolk for Gleb's destruction. These emissaries seized Gleb's boat, and drew their weapons. The servants of Gleb were terrified, and the impious messenger, Goryaser, gave orders that they should slay Gleb with despatch. Then Gleb's cook, Torchin by name, seized a knife, and stabbed Gleb. He was offered up as a sacrifice to God like an innocent lamb, a glorious offering amid the perfume of incense, and he received the crown of glory. Entering the heavenly mansions, he beheld his long-desired brother, and rejoiced with him in the joy ineffable which they had attained through their brotherly love.

"How good and fair it is for brethren to live together!" (*Ps.*, cxxxiii, 1). But the impious ones returned again (137) even as David said, "Let the sinners return to hell" (*Ps.*, ix, 17). When they returned to Svyatopolk, they reported that his command had been executed. On hearing these tidings, he was puffed up with pride, since he knew not the words of David, "Why art thou proud of thy evil-doing, oh mighty one? Thy tongue hath considered lawlessness all the day long" (*Ps.*, lii, 1).

After Gleb had been slain, his body was thrown upon the shore between two tree-trunks, but afterward they took him and carried him away, to bury him beside his brother Boris beside the Church of St. Basil.

United thus in body and still more in soul, ye dwell with the Lord and King of all, in eternal joy, ineffable light, bestowing salutary gifts upon the land of Rus'. Ye give healing to pilgrims from other lands who draw near with faith, making the lame to walk, giving sight to the blind, to the sick health, to captives freedom, to prisoners liberty, to the sorrowful consolation, and to the oppressed relief. Ye are the protectors of the land of Rus', shining forever like beacons and praying to the Lord in behalf of your countrymen. Therefore must we worthily magnify these martyrs in Christ, praying fervently to them and saying: "Rejoice, martyrs in Christ from the land of Rus', who give healing in them who draw near to you in faith and love. Rejoice, dwellers in heaven. In the body ye were angels, servants in the same thought, comrades in the same image, of one heart with the saints. To all that suffer (138) ye give relief. Rejoice, Boris and Gleb, wise in God. Like streams ye spring from the founts of life-giving water which flow for the redemption of the righteous. Rejoice, ye who have trampled the serpent of evil beneath your feet. Ye have appeared amid bright rays, enlightening like beacons the whole land of Rus'. Appearing in faith immutable, ye have ever driven away darkness. Rejoice, ye who have won an unslumbering eye, ye blessed ones who have received in your hearts the zeal to fulfill God's holy commandments. Rejoice, brethren united in the realms of golden light, in the heavenly abodes, in glory unfading, which ye through your merits have attained. Rejoice, ye who are brightly irradiate with the luminance of God, and travel throughout the world expelling devils and healing diseases. Like beacons supernal and zealous guardians, ye dwell with God, illumined forever with light divine, and in your courageous martyrdom ye enlighten the souls of the faithful. The light-bringing heavenly love has exalted you, wherefore ye have inherited all fair things in the heavenly life: glory, celestial sustenance, the light of wisdom, and beauteous joys. Rejoice, ye who refresh our hearts, driving out pain and sickness and curing evil passions. Ye glorious ones, with the sacred drops of your blood ye have dyed a robe of purple which ye wear in beauty, and reign forevermore with Christ, interceding with him for his new Christian nation and for your fellows, for our land is hallowed (139) by your blood. By virtue of your relics deposited in the church, ye illumine it with the Holy Spirit, for there in heavenly bliss, as martyrs among the army of martyrs, ye intercede for your nation. Rejoice, bright day-springs, our Christ-loving martyrs and intercessors! Subject the pagans to our Princes, beseeching our Lord God that they may live in concord and in health, freed from intestine war and the crafts of the devil. Help us therefore who sing and recite your sacred praise forever unto our life's end."[123]

Now the impious and evil Svyatopolk killed Svyatoslav in the Hungarian mountains, after causing him to be pursued as he fled into Hungary. Then he began to reflect how he would kill all his brethren, and rule alone in Rus'. He schemed thus in his pride, being ignorant that God attributes of power according to his divine plans. For the Most High God appoints emperor and prince, and confers authority according to his desires. Wherever a nation is justified before God, he there appoints a just emperor or prince, who loves law and righteousness, and sets up a governor and a judge to render judgment. For if the princes are righteous in the land, many sins are remitted. But if they are evil and deceitful, then God visits yet greater evil (140) upon that country, for the prince is its head. Thus Isaiah said, "They have sinned from head to foot" (*Is.*, i, 6), meaning from the king down to the common people. "Woe unto that city in which the prince is young, loving to drink wine amid music and in the company of young councillors. God bestoweth such princes in requital for sin, and taketh away from Jerusalem the strong, the giant, the valiant man, the judge, the prophet, the moderate elder, the able councillor, the cunning artificer, the learned, the wise, and the obedient. I shall appoint a youth to be their prince, and a brawler to be their ruler" (*Is.*, iii, 1-4).

The impious Svyatopolk thus began his reign in Kiev. Assembling the people, he began to distribute mantles to some and furs to others, and thus dissipated a large sum.

While Yaroslav had not yet heard of his father's death, he had many Varangians under his command, and they offered violence to the inhabitants of Novgorod and to their wives. The men of Novgorod then rose and killed the Varangians in their market place.[124] Yaroslav was angry, and departing to Rakom,[125] he took up his abode in the castle. Then he sent messengers to Novgorod with the comment that the death of his retainers was beyond remedy, but at the same time he summoned before him the chief men of the city who had massacred the Varangians, and craftily killed them. The same night news came from Kiev sent by his sister Predslava to the effect that his father was dead, that Svyatopolk had settled in Kiev after killing Boris, and was now endeavoring to compass the death of Gleb, (141) and she warned Yaroslav to be exceedingly on his guard against Svyatopolk. When Yaroslav heard these tidings, he grieved for his father and his retainers.

On the morrow, he collected the remnant of the men of Novgorod and regretfully lamented, "Alas for my beloved retainers, whom I yesterday caused to be killed! You would indeed be useful in the present crisis." He wiped away his tears, and informed his subjects in the assembly that his father was dead, and that Svyatopolk had settled in Kiev after killing his brethren. Then the men of Novgorod said, "We can still fight for you, oh Prince, even though our brethren are slain." So Yaroslav collected one thousand Varangians and forty thousand other soldiers, and marched against Svyatopolk.[126] He called on God as his witness and protested, "It was not I who began to kill our brethren, but Svyatopolk himself. May God be the avenger of the blood of my brothers inasmuch as Svyatopolk, despite their innocence, has shed the just blood of Boris and Gleb. Perhaps he will even visit the same fate upon me. But judge me, oh Lord, according to the right, that the malice of the sinful may end." So he marched against Svyatopolk. When Svyatopolk learned that Yaroslav was on his way, he prepared an innumerable army of Russes and Pechenegs,[127] and marched out toward Lyubech[128] on one side of the Dnieper, while Yaroslav was on the opposite bank.

6524 (1016). The beginning of the principate of Yaroslav at Kiev. Yaroslav arrived and the brothers stood over against each other on both banks on the Dnieper, but neither party dared attack. They remained thus face to face for three months. Then Svyatopolk's general (142) rode out along the shore and scoffed at the men of Novgorod, shouting, "Why did you come hither with this crooked-shanks, you carpenters?[129] We shall put you to work on our houses." When the men of Novgorod heard this taunt, they declared to Yaroslav, "Tomorrow we will cross over to them, and whoever will not go with us we will kill." Now it was already beginning to freeze. Svyatopolk was stationed between two lakes,[130] and caroused with his fellows the whole night through. Yaroslav on the morrow marshaled his troops, and crossed over toward dawn. His forces disembarked on the shore, and pushed the boats out from the bank. The two armies advanced to the attack, and met upon the field. The carnage was terrible. Because of the lake, the Pechenegs could bring no aid, and Yaroslav's troops drove Svyatopolk with his followers toward it. When the latter went out upon the ice, it broke under them, and Yaroslav began to win the upper hand. Svyatopolk then fled among the Lyakhs, while Yaroslav established himself in Kiev upon the throne of his father and his grandfather.[131] Yaroslav had then been in Novgorod twenty-eight years.[132]

6525 (1017). Yaroslav took up his abode in Kiev, and in the same year the churches were burned.[133]

6526 (1018). Boleslav attacked Yaroslav with Svyatopolk and his Lyakhs.[134] (143) After collecting Russes, Varangians, and Slavs, Yaroslav marched forth against Boleslav and Svyatopolk, and upon arriving at Volyn', they camped on either side of the river Bug. Now Yaroslav had with him his guardian and general, Budÿ by name. He scoffed at Boleslav, remarking, "We shall pierce your fat belly with a pike." For Boleslav was big and heavy, so that he could scarcely sit a horse, but he was crafty. So Boleslav said to his retainers, "If you do not avenge this insult, I will perish alone," and leaping upon his horse, he rode into the river and his retainers after him, while Yaroslav had no time to align his troops, so that Boleslav vanquished him.[135]

Then Yaroslav fled with four men to Novgorod, and Boleslav entered Kiev in company with Svyatopolk.[136] Boleslav ordered that his force should be dispersed to forage throughout the cities, and so it was done. When Yaroslav arrived at Novgorod in his flight, he planned to escape overseas, but the lieutenant Constantine, son of Dobrÿnya, together with the men of Novgorod, destroyed his boat, protesting that they wished to fight once more against Boleslav and Svyatopolk. They set out to gather funds at the rate of four *kunÿ* per commoner, ten *grivnÿ* from each elder, and eighteen *grivnÿ* from each boyar.[137]

With these funds they recruited Varangians whom they imported, and thus collected for Yaroslav a large army.[138]

While Boleslav was settled in Kiev, the impious Svyatopolk ordered that any Lyakhs found in the city should be killed, (144) and so the Lyakhs were slain. Then Boleslav fled from Kiev,[139] taking with him the property and the boyars of Yaroslav, as well as the latter's two sisters, and made Anastasius[140] steward of the property, for the latter had won his confidence by his flattery. He took with him a large company, and having appropriated to himself the cities of Cherven,[141] he returned to his native land. Svyatopolk thus reigned alone in Kiev, but Yaroslav attacked him again, and Svyatopolk fled among the Pechenegs.

6527 (1019). Svyatopolk advanced with a large force of Pecheneg supporters, and Yaroslav collected a multitude of soldiery, and went forth against him to the Al'ta River.[142] Yaroslav halted at the site where Boris had been slain and, lifting up his hands to heaven, exclaimed, "The blood of my brother cries aloud to thee, oh Lord. Avenge the blood of this just man. Visit upon this criminal the sorrow and terror that thou didst inflict upon Cain to avenge the blood of Abel." Then he prayed and said, "My brethren, although ye be absent in the body, yet help me with your prayer against this persumptuous assassin." When he had thus spoken, the two armies attacked, and the plain of the Al'ta was covered with the multitudinous soldiery of both forces. It was then Friday. As the sun rose, they met in battle, and the carnage was terrible, such as had never before occurred in Rus'. The soldiers fought hand to hand and slaughtered each other. Three times they clashed, so that the blood flowed in the valley. Toward evening Yaroslav conquered, and Svyatopolk fled.

As he fled (145) a devil came upon him and his bones were softened, so that he could not ride, but was carried in a litter. His retainers bore him to Brest[143] in his flight, but he still cried out, "Fly with me, they are pursuing us!" His servants sent back to see who was pursuing them, and there was actually no one following their trail, but still they fled on with him. He lay in a faint, and when he recovered, he still cried out, "Run, they are pursuing us!" He could not endure to stay in one place, but fled through the land of the Lyakhs, pursued by the wrath of God. Upon reaching the wilderness between Poland and Bohemia, he died a miserable death.[144] When judgment thus rightly fell upon him as a sinner, torments seized this impious prince after his departure from this world. That is clearly proved by the fatal wound which was dealt him and which mercilessly drove him to his end; and since his death he abides in bonds and in torment everlasting. His tomb is in the wilderness even to this day, and an evil odor issues forth from it.

This retribution was exhibited by God as an admonition to the princes of Rus' so that, if they do likewise after hearing of this dread example, they shall incur the same punishment, yet even more severe because they, though familiar with this story, shall commit the same evil crime. For Cain received seven punishments for killing Abel, and Lamech seventy, because Cain did not know the penalty to be exacted by God, while Lamech knew of the chastisement visited upon his ancestor, yet still committed murder notwithstanding. For Lamech said (146) to his wives, "I have killed a man to my harm, and a youth to my destruction. Wherefore," said he, "seventy punishments are upon me, because I acted knowingly" (*Gen.*, iv, 23). Lamech killed two brothers of Enoch, and took their wives. Likewise Svyatopolk was a new Abimelech, who was born in adultery, and who killed his brothers, the sons of Gideon. Thus Yaroslav settled in Kiev, together with his followers, and wiped away the sweat of his labors now that victory was won after a hard struggle.

6528 (1020). A son was born to Yaroslav, and he called his name Vladimir.

6529 (1021). Bryachislav, son of Izyaslav, grandson of Vladimir, came and captured Novgorod, and having taken the people of Novgorod and their property, he returned to Polotsk.[145] When he arrived at the Sudomir' River,[146] Yaroslav came thither from Kiev after a seven days' march. He conquered Bryachislav, and returned the people of Novgorod to their city, while Bryachislav fled to Polotsk.

6530 (1022). Yaroslav went to Brest. At this time Mstislav, who was in Tmutorakan', attacked the Kasogians. When Rededya, Prince of the Kasogians, heard the report, he went forth against him, and as both armies stood face to face, Rededya said to Mstislav, "Why do we destroy our forces by mutual warfare? Let us rather fight (147) in single combat ourselves. If you win, you shall receive my property, my wife, and my children, and my land. But if I win, I shall take all your possessions." Then Mstislav assented to his proposal. Rededya thus suggested that they should wrestle instead of fighting with weapons. They straightway began to struggle violently, and when they had wrestled for some time, Mstislav began to tire, for Rededya was large and strong. Then Mstislav exclaimed, "Oh Virgin Mother of God, help me! If I conquer this man, I will build a church in thy name." Having spoken thus, he threw the Kasogian to the ground, then drew his knife and stabbed Rededya. He then penetrated into his territory, seized all his property, his wife, and his children, and imposed tribute upon the Kasogians. When he returned to Tmutorakan', he then founded a church dedicated to the Holy Virgin and built it, as it stands in Tmutorakan' even to the present day.[147]

6531 (1023). Mstislav marched against Yaroslav with a force of Khazars and Kasogians.[148]

6532 (1024). While Yaroslav was at Novgorod, Mstislav arrived before Kiev from Tmutorakan', but the inhabitants of Kiev would not admit him. He thus departed thence and established himself upon the throne of Chernigov,[149] while Yaroslav was at Novgorod. In this year, magicians appeared in Suzdal',[150] and killed old people by satanic inspiration and devil worship, saying that they would spoil the harvest.[151] There was great confusion and famine throughout all that country. The whole population went along the Volga to the Bulgars[152] from whom they bought grain and thus sustained themselves.

When Yaroslav heard of the magicians, (148) he went to Suzdal'. He there seized upon the magicians and dispersed them, but punished some, saying, "In proportion to its sin, God inflicts upon every land hunger, pest, drought, or some other chastisement, and man has no understanding thereof." Then Yaroslav returned and came again to Novgorod, whence he sent overseas after Varangians. Thus Haakon came over with his Varangian followers. Now this Haakon was blind and he had a robe all woven with gold.[153] He allied himself with Yaroslav, and with his support Yaroslav marched against Mstislav who, hearing the news of their coming, proceeded to meet them at Listven'.[154]

At eventide Mstislav marshalled his troops, placing the Severians in the centre opposite the Varangians, while he himself and his personal retainers took up their position on the flanks. When night fell, there was darkness with lightning, thunder, and rain. Mstislav thus ordered his followers to attack. Mstislav and Yaroslav then attacked each other, and the Severians in the centre met the Varangians, who exhausted themselves in opposing them. Then Mstislav came up with his retainers to attack the Varangians, and the combat was violent. As the lightnings flashed, the weapons gleamed and the thunder roared, and the fight was violent and fearsome. Now when Yaroslav saw that he was overpowered, he fled from the field with Haakon, the Varangian prince, who lost his gold-woven robe in his flight. Yaroslav arrived safely at Novgorod, but Haakon departed beyond the sea. Mstislav, however, when on the morrow at dawn he beheld lying dead his own Severians (149) and the Varangians of Yaroslav whom his men had slain, exclaimed in exultation, "Who does not rejoice at this spectacle? Here lies a Severian, here a Varangian, and my retainers are unharmed." Then Mstislav proposed to Yaroslav that the latter, as the eldest brother, should remain in Kiev, while the Chernigov district should belong to Mstislav. But Yaroslav did not dare to return to Kiev until they were properly reconciled. So Mstislav settled in Chernigov, and Yaroslav in Novgorod, though Kiev was occupied by subjects of Yaroslav. In this year was born to Yaroslav a second son, and he was christened Izyaslav.

6534 (1026). Yaroslav recruited many soldiers and arrived at Kiev, where he made peace with his brother Mstislav near Gorodets.[155] They divided Rus' according to the course of the Dnieper. Yaroslav took the Kiev side, and Mstislav the other. They thus began to live in peace and fraternal amity. Strife and tumult ceased, and there was a great calm in the land.

6535 (1027). A third son was born to Yaroslav, and he named him Svyatoslav.

6536 (1028). A portent visible to the whole country appeared in the heavens.

6537 (1029). Peace prevailed.

6538 (1030). Yaroslav captured Bel'z.[156] To Yaroslav was born his fourth son, and he named him Vsevolod. In this year, Yaroslav attacked the Chuds and conquered them. He thus founded the city of Yur'ev.[157] At this same time, Boleslav the Great died in Poland, and there was a revolt in the Polish country. (150) The people arose and killed the bishops, the priests, and the boyars, and there was rebellion among them.[158]

6539 (1031). Yaroslav and Mstislav collected a large force and marched into Poland. They recaptured the cities of Cherven, and ravaged the Polish countryside. They also captured many Poles and distributed them as colonists in various districts. Yaroslav located his captives along the Ros',[159] where they live to this day.

6540 (1032). Yaroslav began to found towns along the Ros'.

6541 (1033). Eustathius, son of Mstislav, passed away.

6542-6544 (1034-1036). While on a hunting expedition, Mstislav fell sick and died, and was laid in the Church of the Redeemer, which he himself had founded.[160] In his time, it was built to a point higher than a man on horseback could reach with his hand. Mstislav was corpulent and red-faced, with large eyes, bold in battle, merciful, and a great lover of his retainers, begrudging them neither treasure nor food nor drink.

Thereafter Yaroslav assumed the entire sovereignty, and was the sole ruler in the land of Rus'. Yaroslav went to Novgorod, where he set up his son Vladimir as prince,[161] and appointed Zhidyata bishop.[162] At this time, a son was born to Yaroslav, and he named him Vyacheslav. While Yaroslav was still at Novgorod, news came (151) to him that the Pechenegs were besieging Kiev. He then collected a large army of Varangians and Slavs, returned to Kiev, and entered his city. The Pechenegs were innumerable. Yaroslav made a sally from the city and marshalled his forces, placing the Varangians in the centre, the men of Kiev on the right flank, and the men of Novgorod on the left. When they had taken position before the city, the Pechenegs advanced, and they met on the spot where the metropolitan church of St. Sophia now stands. At that time, as a matter of fact, there were fields outside the city.¹⁶³ The combat was fierce, but toward evening Yaroslav with difficulty won the upper hand. The Pechenegs fled in various directions, but as they did not know in what quarter to flee, they were drowned, some in the Setoml',¹⁶⁴ some in other streams, while the remnant of them disappeared from that day to this. In the same year, Yaroslav imprisoned his brother Sudislav in Pskov because he had been slanderously accused.¹⁶⁵.

6545 (1037). Yaroslav built the great citadel at Kiev, near which stands the Golden Gate.¹⁶⁶ He founded also the metropolitan Church of St. Sophia,¹⁶⁷ the Church of the Annunciation over the Golden Gate, and also the Monastery of St. George and the convent of St. Irene.¹⁶⁸ During his reign, the Christian faith was fruitful and multiplied, while the number of monks increased, and new monasteries came into being. Yaroslav loved religious establishments and was devoted to priests, especially to monks. He applied himself to books, and read them continually (152) day and night. He assembled many scribes, and translated from Greek into Slavic. He wrote and collected many books through which true believers are instructed and enjoy religious education. For as one man plows the land, and another sows, and still others reap and eat food in abundance, so did this prince. His father Vladimir plowed and harrowed the soil when he enlightened Rus' through baptism, while this prince sowed the hearts of the faithful with the written word, and we in turn reap the harvest by receiving the teaching of books. For great is the profit from book-learning.

Through the medium of books, we are shown and taught the way of repentance, for we gain wisdom and continence from the written word. Books are like rivers that water the whole earth; they are the springs of wisdom. For books have an immeasurable depth; by them we are consoled in sorrow. They are the bridle of self-restraint. For great is wisdom. As Solomon said in its praise, "I (wisdom) have inculcated counsel; I have summoned reason and prudence. The fear of the Lord is the beginning of wisdom. Mine are counsel, wisdom, constancy, and strength. Through me kings rule, and the mighty decree justice. Through me are princes magnified and the oppressors possess the earth. I love them that love me, and they who seek me shall find grace" (*Prov.*, viii, 12, 13, 14-17). If you seek wisdom attentively in books, you will obtain great profit for your spirit. He who reads books (153) often converses with God or with holy men. If one possesses the words of the prophets, the teachings of the evangelists and the apostles, and the lives of the holy fathers, his soul will derive great profit therefrom. Thus Yaroslav, as we have said, was a lover of books, and as he wrote many, he deposited them in the Church of St. Sophia which he himself had founded. He adorned it with gold and silver and churchly vessels, and in it the usual hymns are raised to God at the customary seasons. He founded other churches in the cities and districts, appointing priests and paying them out of his personal fortune. He bade them teach the people, since that is the duty which God has prescribed them, and to go often into the churches. Priests and Christian laymen thus increased in number. Yaroslav rejoiced to see the multitude of his churches and of his Christian subjects, but the devil was afflicted, since he was now conquered by this new Christian nation.

6546 (1038). Yaroslav attacked the Yatvingians.[169]

6547 (1039). The Church of the Blessed Virgin which had been founded by Vladimir, Yaroslav's father, was consecrated[170] by the Metropolitan Theopemptos.[171]

6548 (1040). Yaroslav attacked Lithuania.[172]

6549 (1041). Yaroslav attacked the Mazovians by boat.[173]

6550 (1042). Vladimir, son of Yaroslav, attacked the people of Yam' and conquered them.[174] The horses of Vladimir's soldiery died; and they tore the skins off the horses while the latter were still breathing, (154) so violent was the plague from which the animals suffered.

6551 (1043). Yaroslav sent his son Vladimir to attack Greece,[175] and entrusted him with a large force. He assigned the command to Vyshata, father of Yan. Vladimir set out by ship, arrived at the Danube, and proceeded toward Tsar'grad. A great storm arose which broke up the ships of the Russes; the wind damaged even the Prince's vessel, and Ivan, son of Tvorimir, Yaroslav's general, took the Prince into his boat. The other soldiers of Vladimir to the number of six thousand were cast on shore, and desired to return to Rus', but none of the Prince's retainers went with them. Then Vyshata announced that he would accompany them, and disembarked from his vessel to join them, exclaiming, "If I survive, it will be with the soldiers, and if I perish, it will be with the Prince's retainers." They thus set out to return to Rus'. It now became known to the Greeks how the Russes had suffered from the storm, and the Emperor, who was called Monomakh, sent fourteen ships to pursue them. When Vladimir and his retainers perceived that the Greeks were pursuing them, he wheeled about, dispersed the Greek ships, and returned to Rus' on his ships. But the Greeks captured Vyshata, in company with those who had been cast on land, and brought them to Tsar'grad, where they blinded many of the captive Russes. After peace had prevailed for three years thereafter, Vyshata was sent back to Yaroslav in Rus'. At that same time

Yaroslav married his sister (155) to Kazimir,[176] and as a wedding gift Kazimir surrendered eight hundred captives whom Boleslav had taken when he overcame Yaroslav.

6552 (1044). The bodies of the two princes Yaropolk and Oleg, sons of Svyatoslav, after their remains were baptized, were laid in the Church of the Holy Virgin.[177]

In the same year died Bryachislav,[178] son of Izyaslav, and father of Vseslav; and Vseslav his son succeeded to his throne. Him his mother bore by enchantment, for when his mother bore him, there was a caul over his head, and the magicians bade his mother bind this caul upon him, that he might carry it with him the rest of his life. Vseslav accordingly bears it to this day, and for this reason he is pitiless in bloodshed.[179]

6553 (1045). Vladimir founded the Church of St. Sophia at Novgorod.[180]

6554-6555 (1046-1047). Yaroslav attacked and conquered the Mazovians, killing their prince Moislav, and subjected them to Kazimir.[181]

6556-6558 (1048-1050). The Princess, wife of Yaroslav, died on February 10.[182]

6559 (1051). Yaroslav, after assembling the bishops, appointed Hilarion Metropolitan of Rus' in St. Sophia.[183]

Let us now relate why the Monastery of the Crypts bears this name.[184] Prince Yaroslav was fond of Berestovo and the Church of (156) the Holy Apostles there situated. He gathered a large company of priests, among whom was a presbyter named Hilarion, a virtuous man, learned and ascetic. Hilarion used often to walk from Berestovo toward the Dnieper to a certain hill, where the old Crypt Monastery now is, and made his orisons there, for there was a great forest on the spot. He dug a little catacomb two fathoms deep, and often went thither from Berestovo to chant the hours and offer his prayer to God in secret. Then God inspired the Prince to appoint him Metropolitan in St. Sophia; and the crypt remained as it was.

Not many days afterward, there was a certain man, a layman from the city of Lyubech,[185] in whose heart God had inspired the desire to go on pilgrimage. He made his way to Mt. Athos, beheld the monasteries there, and upon examining them and being charmed by the monastic life, he entered one of the local monasteries, and begged the prior to confer upon him the monastic habit. The latter complied with his request and made him a monk, calling him Antonius, and after he had admonished him and instructed him in his monastic obligations, he bade him return to Rus' accompanied by the blessing of the Holy

Mount, that many other monks might spring from his example. The prior blessed him and dismissed him, saying, "Go in peace." Antonius returned to Kiev, and reflected where he should live. He went about the monasteries and liked none of them, since God did not so will, and subsequently wandered about the hills and valleys seeking the place which God should show him. He finally came to the hill where Hilarion had dug the crypt, and liked this site, and rejoiced in it. He then lifted up his voice in prayer to God, saying amid his tears, "Oh Lord, strengthen me in this place, (157) and may there rest upon it the blessing of the Holy Mount and of the prior who tonsured me." Thus he took up his abode there, praying to God, eating dry bread every other day, drinking water moderately, and digging the crypt. He gave himself rest neither day nor night, but endured in his labors, in vigil, and in prayer. Afterward good men noticed his conduct, and supplied him according to his necessities. Thus he acquired distinction as the great Antonius, and those who drew near to him besought his blessing.

When the Great Prince Yaroslav died,[186] Izyaslav his son inherited his domain and settled in Kiev, while Antonius was celebrated throughout Rus'. Izyaslav observed his manner of life, and came with his retainers to request his blessing and prayers. The great Antonius was thus remarked and revered by everyone. Brothers joined him, and he welcomed and tonsured them. Brethren thus gathered about him to the number of twelve. They dug a great crypt and a church, and cells, which exist to this day in the crypt under the old monastery. When the brethren has thus assembled, Antonius said to them, "God has gathered you together, my brethren, and ye are under the blessing of the Holy Mount, through which the prior at the Holy Mount tonsured me and I have tonsured you also. May there be upon you first the blessing of God and second that of the Holy Mount." And he added this injunction: "Live apart by yourselves, and I shall appoint you a prior; for I prefer (158) to go alone to yonder hill, as I formerly was wont when I dwelt in solitude." So he appointed Barlaam as their prior, and he betook himself to the hill, where he dug a grotto, which is under the new monastery, and in which he ended his life, enduring in virtue, and for the space of forty years never issuing forth from the crypt in which his bones lie to the present day.

The brethren thus abode with their prior, and as the number of monks in the crypt increased, they considered the establishment of a monastery outside the original crypt. Thus the prior and the brethren approached Antonius and said to him, "Father, the brethren have increased in numbers, and we can no longer find room in the crypt. If God and thy prayers so direct us, we might build a small church outside the crypt." Antonius then bade them so to do. They did reverence to him, and built a little chapel over the crypt and dedicated it to the Assumption of the Holy Virgin.

God continued to augment the number of the brotherhood through the intercession of the Holy Virgin, and the brethren took counsel with the prior as to constructing a monastery. The friars again visited Antonius, and said, "Father, our brethren increase in numbers, and we are desirous of building a monastery." Antonius rejoiced and replied, "Blessed be God for all things, and may the prayers of the Holy Virgin and of the fathers of the Holy Mount be with you." Having thus spoken, he sent one of the brotherhood to Prince Izyaslav with the message, "My Prince! Behold, God strengthens the brotherhood, but their abode is small; give us therefore the hill which (159) is above the crypt." When Izyaslav heard these words, he rejoiced, and sent his servant, and gave to them the hill. The prior and the brethren founded there a great church, and fenced in the monastery with a palisade. They constructed many cells, completed the church, and adorned it with eikons. Such was the origin of the Crypt Monastery, which was so named because the brethren first lived in the crypt. The Crypt Monastery thus issued from the benediction of the Holy Mount.

Now when the monastery was completed during the priorate of Barlaam, Izyaslav founded the Monastery of St. Demetrius,[187] and appointed Barlaam prior therein, since he intended, by virtue of his material wealth, to make it superior to the ancient monastery. Many monasteries have indeed been founded by emperors and nobles and magnates, but they are not such as those founded by tears, fasting, prayer, and vigil. Antonius had neither silver nor gold, but accomplished his purpose through tears and fasting, as I have recounted.

When Barlaam had departed to St. Demetrius', the brethren held a council, and then once more visited the ancient Antonius with the request that he should designate them a new prior. He inquired whom they desired. They replied that they desired only the one designated by God and by his own selection. Then he inquired of them, "Who among you is more obedient, more modest, and more mild than Theodosius? Let him be your prior." The brethren rejoiced, and made their reverence before the old man. Being twenty in number, they thus appointed Theodosius to be their prior.[188] When Theodosius took over the monastery, he began to practise abstinence, fasting, and tearful prayer. (160) He undertook to assemble many monks, and thus gathered together brethren to the number of one hundred.

He also interested himself in searching out the monastic rules. There was in Kiev at the time a monk from the Studion Monastery named Michael, who had come from Greece with the Metropolitan George,[189] and Theodosius inquired of him concerning the practices of the Studion monks. He obtained their rule from him, copied it out, and established it in his monastery to govern the singing of monastic hymns, the making of reverences, the reading of the lessons, behaviour in church, the whole ritual, conduct at table, proper food for special days, and to regulate all else according to prescription. After obtaining all this information, Theodosius thus transmitted it to his monastery, and from the latter all others adopted the same institutions. Therefore the Crypt Monastery is honored as the oldest of all.

While Theodosius lived in the monastery, following a virtuous life and the monastic rule, and receiving everyone who presented himself, I, a poor and unworthy servant, came to him, and he accepted me in my seventeenth year. Hence I have set down and certified what year the monastery came into being, and why it is named the Crypt Monastery, but to Theodosius' life we shall recur later.[190]

6560 (1052). Vladimir, Yaroslav's eldest son, died at Novgorod, and was buried in the Church of St. Sophia, which he himself had founded.[191]

6561 (1053). A son was born to Vsevolod by the Greek Princess, and he named him Vladimir.[192]

(161) 6562 (1054). Yaroslav, Great Prince of Rus', passed away. While he was yet alive, he admonished his sons[193] with these words: "My sons, I am about to quit this world. Love one another, since ye are brothers by one father and mother. If ye abide in amity with one another, God will dwell among you, and will subject your enemies to you, and ye will live at peace. But if ye dwell in envy and dissension, quarreling with one another, then ye will perish yourselves and bring to ruin the land of your ancestors, which they won at the price of great effort. Wherefore remain rather at peace, brother heeding brother. The throne of Kiev I bequeath to my eldest son, your brother Izyaslav. Heed him as ye have heeded me, that he may take my place among you. To Svyatoslav I give Chernigov, to Vsevolod Pereyaslavl', to Igor' the city of Vladimir,[194] and to Vyacheslav Smolensk." Thus he divided the cities among them, commanding them not to violate one another's boundaries, not to despoil one another. He laid upon Izyaslav the in-

junction to aid the party wronged, in case one brother should attack another. Thus he admonished his sons to dwell in amity.[195]

Being unwell, he came to Vyshgorod, and there fell seriously ill. Izyaslav at the moment was in Novgorod, Svyatoslav at Vladimir, and Vsevolod with his father, for he was beloved of his father before all his brethren, and Yaroslav kept him constantly (162) by his side. The end of Yaroslav's life drew near, and he gave up the ghost on the first Saturday after the feast of St. Theodore [February 19]. Vsevolod bore his father's body away, and laying it upon a sled, he brought it to Kiev, while priests sang the customary hymns, and the people mourned for him. When they had transported the body, they laid it in a marble sarcophagus in the Church of St. Sophia, and Vsevolod and all his subjects mourned him. All the years of his age were seventy-six.

Izyaslav then took up his abode in Kiev, with Svyatoslav in Chernigov, Vsevolod at Pereyaslavl', Igor' in Vladimir, and Vyacheslav at Smolensk. In this year, Vsevolod attacked the Torks during the winter near Voin' and conquered them.[196] In the same year, Bolush advanced with his Polovcians, but Vsevolod made peace with them, and they returned whence they had come.[197]

6564-6565 (1056-1057). Vyacheslav, son of Yaroslav, died at Smolensk, and Igor' took up his abode in Smolensk, moving over from Vladimir.

6566 (1058). Izyaslav conquered the Galindians.[198]

6567 (1059). Izyaslav, Svyatoslav, and Vsevolod liberated their uncle Sudislav from the prison where he had been confined for twenty-four years, and after they had obtained his oath of fealty, he took the monastic habit.[199]

6568 (1060). Igor', son of Yaroslav, passed away. (163) In the same year, after collecting a numberless army, Izyaslav, Svyatoslav, and Vsevolod made an expedition by horse and ship against the Torks. When the Torks heard of their coming, they were afraid, and are fleeing even to this day. In their flight they perished, pursued by the hand of God, some of them from the cold, some by famine, and others by pestilence and God's judgment upon them. Thus God once more saved the Christians from the pagans.

6569 (1061). The Polovcians invaded Rus' to make war for the first time. On February 2, Vsevolod went forth against them. When they met in battle, the Polovcians defeated Vsevolod, but after the combat they retired. This was the first evil done by these pagan and godless foes. Their prince was Iskal.

6570-6571 (1062-1063). Sudislav, brother of Yaroslav, passed away, and was buried in the Church of St. George.[200] In this same year, the Volkhov at Novgorod flowed backward for five days. This was not a favorable portent, since Vseslav[201] burned the city four years later.

6572 (1064). Rostislav, son of Vladimir and grandson of Yaroslav, fled to Tmutorakan', and with him fled Porey and Vyshata, son of Ostromir, the general of Novgorod. Upon his arrival, he expelled Gleb from Tmutorakan' and occupied his principate himself.

In 6573 (1065) Svyatoslav then marched against Rostislav in Tmutorakan', so that the latter withdrew from the city, not because he feared Svyatoslav, but because he was reluctant to take up arms against his uncle. Svyatoslav, upon his entry (164) into Tmutorakan', reestablished his son Gleb upon the throne, and returned home. Rostislav returned, however, and expelled Gleb, who rejoined his father, while Rostislav remained in Tmutorakan'.[202]

In this year, Vseslav began hostilities. At the time, there was a portent in the west in the form of an exceedingly large star with bloody rays, which rose out of the west after sunset. It was visible for a week and appeared with no good presage. Much internal strife occurred thereafter, as well as many barbarian incursions into the land of Rus', for this star appeared as if it were made of blood, and therfore portended bloodshed.

At this time, a child was cast into the Setoml'. Some fishermen pulled it up in their net. We then gazed upon it till evening, when they cast it back into the water because it was malformed; indeed, it had its privates upon its face, and for reasons of modesty no further account need be given regarding it.[203]

Somewhat before this moment, the sun also suffered alteration, and instead of being bright, became rather like the moon.

Such signs portend no good, for we understand how, in ancient times at Jerusalem, in the reign of Antiochus, it suddenly occurred that during a period of forty days armed men appeared throughout the whole city clad in golden raiment and riding on horseback through the air. Squadrons of them even appeared brandishing their weapons. This apparition presaged the attack of Antiochus (165) upon Jerusalem. Later, during the reign of the Emperor Nero, a star like a spear in its shape shone over the same city of Jerusalem. This sign portended the attack of an army sent by the Romans. Again it happened likewise in the reign of the Emperor Justinian that a star emitting rays appeared in the west. Men called it the brilliant star, and it shone forth for twenty days. Subsequently a shower of stars fell from evening till dawn, so that all thought that the stars of heaven were falling, and again the sun shone without light. This portent presaged rebellions and pestilences, and was fatal to mankind. The following portents similarly occurred during the reign of the Emperor Mauricius: a woman bore a child without eyes and without hands, and a fish-tail grew to his back; a six-legged dog was born; and in Thrace there were born two children, one with four legs, and the other with two heads. Later, during the reign of Constantine the Iconoclast, son of Leo, there was a shower of stars in the sky, and they were cast down upon the earth, so that eyewitnesses thought it was the end of the world. At the same time, the air also was violently perturbed. In Syria, a violent earthquake took place, and the earth split for a distance of three stadia. Strange to relate, a mule issued forth from the earth, speaking with a human voice and prophesying the incursion of the pagans, which actually took place, for the Saracens attacked Palestine. Thus portents in the sky, or in the stars, or in the sun, or such as are made known by birds or from some other source, are not favorable import. Such signs are, on the contrary, of evil significance, presaging the appearance of war, famine, or death.[204]

(166) 6574 (1066). When Rostislav was at Tmutorakan', receiving tribute from the Kasogians and from other regions, the Greeks became afraid of him and sent to him an officer with treacherous intent. When he came before Rostislav and won his confidence, the Prince did him great honor. Then on one occasion while Rostislav was drinking with his retinue, the envoy said, "Oh Prince, I would drink to your health," and Rostislav accepted the compliment. The Greek drank half the goblet, and then offered the other half to the Prince to drink after dipping his finger in the cup, for he had a deadly poison under his fingernail. He thus passed the drink to the Prince, having determined his death for the seventh day thereafter. When the Prince had drunk the draught, the envoy departed to Kherson, where he reported that upon that day Rostislav would die, as did in fact occur. The people of Kherson then slew this officer by stoning him. Rostislav was a man bold in war, fair of stature, and handsome of feature, and he was generous to the poor. His death occurred on February 3, and he was buried there in the Church of the Holy Virgin.[205]

6575 (1067). Vseslav, the son of Bryachislav of Polotsk, undertook a campaign and captured Novgorod. Izyaslav, Svyatoslav, and Vsevolod, the three sons of Yaroslav, though it was the dead of winter, collected a force and set forth against him. They arrived before Minsk, but the citizens barricaded themselves in the city. Then the brethren captured it, put the men to the sword, sold the women and children into slavery, and proceeded to Nemiza.[206] Vseslav came forward to meet them. The two forces thus collided at the Nemiza on March 3, (167) with heavy snow on the ground. They thus attacked, and the carnage was severe. The casualties were numerous, but Izyaslav, Svyatoslav, and Vsevolod won the day, while Vseslav sought safety in flight. On July 10 following, Izyaslav, Svyatoslav, and Vsevolod took oath as to their peaceful intentions and offered Vseslav safe-conduct if he would join them. He put his confidence in their sworn oath, and crossed the Dnieper by boat. Izyaslav preceded Vseslav into their tent, and contrary to their oath, the brethren thus took Vseslav captive on the Orsha,[207] near Smolensk. Izyaslav then brought Vseslav to Kiev and there threw him and his two sons into prison.

6576 (1068). A multitude of those nomads known as the Polovcians attacked the land of Rus', and Izyaslav, Svyatoslav and Vsevolod went forth against them as far as the Al'ta.[208] They joined battle in the dead of night, but since God had let loose the pagans upon us because of our transgressions, the Russian princes fled and the Polovcians were victorious.

God in his wrath causes foreigners to attack a nation, and then, when its inhabitants are thus crushed by the invaders, they remember God. Intestine strife is incited by the craft of the devil. For God wishes men not evil but good; while the devil takes his delight in cruel murder and bloodshed, and therefore incites quarrels, envy, domestic strife, and slander. When any nation has sinned, God punishes them by death or famine (168) or barbarian incursion, by drought or a plague of caterpillars or by other chastisements, until we repent of our sins and live according to God's commandment. For he says unto us through the mouth of his Prophet, "Turn unto me with all your hearts in fasting and lamentation" (*Joel*, ii, 12). If we thus act, we shall all be forgiven our sins. But we return to evil, and persist in wallowing like swine in the mire of iniquity. "I knew that thou art obdurate and thy neck is an iron sinew" (*Is.*, xlviii, 4). "Therefore I have withholden the rain from you. I caused it to rain upon one city, and caused it not to rain upon another city, and it has withered. I have smitten you with heat and various chastisements, but even so ye have not returned unto me. Therefore I have smitten your vineyards, your olive-groves, your fields, and your forests, saith the Lord, but I could not drive out your iniquities. I sent upon you divers diseases and painful deaths, and brought plague upon your cattle, but even so ye have not repented, but said, 'Let us be manful' " (*Amos*, iv, 7-10). "When will ye be sated with your iniquities? For ye have turned aside from my way, saith the Lord, and have committed many transgressions. Therefore I will be a swift witness against my adversaries, against the adulterer and against those who swear falsely by my name, against those that deprive the hireling of his wages, who offer violence to the orphan and widow, and who incline justice to wrong. Why have ye not restrained yourself in your sins, but violated my laws and not (169) kept them? Turn unto me and I will return unto you, said the Lord. I will open upon you the sluices of heaven, and turn away from you my wrath, until all shall be yours in abundance, and your vineyards and your fields shall not fail. But ye have blasphemed against me, saying 'Vain is he who works for God!'" (*Mal.*, iii, 5-14). "They honor me with their lips, but their heart is far from me" (*Is.*, xxix, 13).

For this reason we do not receive what we ask, since the Lord has said, "It shall come to pass that when ye call upon me I shall not hear you, ye evil ones shall seek me and not find me" (*Prov.*, i, 29). Ye have not desired to walk in my path; therefore heaven is closed, or else opens only for a fell purpose, sending down hail instead of rain, or destroying the harvest with frost and tormenting the earth with drought because of our iniquities. But if we repent us of our sins, then he will grant to us as his children all our requests, and will water us with rain early and late, and our granaries shall be full of wheat. "Your vineyards and olive-groves shall abound, and I will restore to you the years which the locusts, the worms, and the caterpillars consumed, the great army that I sent among you," said the Lord Almighty (*Joel*, ii, 23-25). Having heard these words, let us apply ourselves to good, seek justice, and free the oppressed. Let us do penance, not returning evil for evil nor slander for slander, but let us rather bind ourselves with love to the Lord our God. (170) Let us wash away all our transgressions with fasting, with lamentation, and with tears, nor call ourselves Christians as long as we live like pagans.

Do we not live like pagans as long as we attach superstitious significance to meetings? For he turns back who meets a monk, a boar or a swine. Is that not pagan? It is part and parcel of the devil's teaching to retain such delusions. Other people attach special significance to sneezing, which is healthy for the head. By these and other similar customs the devil deceives us, and he alienated us from God by all manner of craft, through trumpets and clowns, through harps and pagan festivals. For we behold the playgrounds worn bare by the footsteps of a great multitude, who jostle each other while they make a spectacle of a thing invented by the devil.

The churches still stand; but when the hour of prayer is come, few worshippers are found in the church, for this reason we shall suffer at the hand of God all sorts of chastisement and then incursion of our foes, and at the command of God we shall endure punishment for our sins.[209].

Let us return now to our subject. When Izyaslav, accompanied by Vsevolod, had fled to Kiev, while Svyatoslav had taken refuge in Chernigov, the men of Kiev who had escaped to their native city held an assembly on the market place and sent the following communication to the Prince:[210] "The Polovcians have spread over the country. Oh Prince, give us arms and horses, that we may offer them combat once more." (171) Izyaslav, however, paid no heed to this request. Then the people began to murmur against his general Constantine.[211] From the place of assembly, they mounted the hill, but when they arrived before the house of Constantine, they could not find him. They then halted before the house of Bryachislav and proposed that they should go and liberate their friends from prison. They then separated into two parties: half of them went to the prison, and half over the bridge.[212] The latter contingent arrived before the Prince's palace, and as Izyaslav was sitting with his retinue in his hall, the crowd standing below began to threaten him. As the prince and his retainers were watching the crowd from a small window, Tukÿ, the brother of Chudin, called to Izyaslav's attention that the people were aroused, and suggested that he should send men to guard Vseslav. While he was thus speaking, the other half of the crowd approached from the prison, which they had thrown open. The retainers, remarking that the situation had become serious, urged the Prince to send pursuers after Vseslav who should entice him to a window by a ruse and then slay him with a sword. Izyaslav, however, did not heed their advice. The mob then gave a shout and went off to Vseslav's prison. When Izyaslav beheld their action, he fled with Vsevolod from the palace. But on September 15, the people thus haled Vseslav from his dungeon, and set him up in the midst of the prince's palace. They then pillaged the palace, seizing a huge amount of gold and silver, furs, and martenskins. Izyaslav made his escape to Poland.[213]

While the Polovcians were ravaging throughout the land of Rus', Svyatoslav was meanwhile at Chernigov. (172) As soon as the pagans raided around Chernigov itself, Svyatoslav collected a small force and sallied out against them to Snovsk.[214] The Polovcians remarked the approaching troop and marshalled their forces for resistance. When Svyatoslav observed their numbers, he said to his followers, "Let us attack, for it is too late for us to seek succor elsewhere." They spurred up their horses, and though the Polovcians had twelve thousand men, Svyatoslav won the day with his force of only three thousand. Some of the pagans were killed outright, while others were drowned in the Snov', and their prince was captured on November 1. Svyatoslav thus returned victorious to his city. Vseslav was meanwhile ruling in Kiev.

God thus revealed the power of the Cross, since Izyaslav violated his oath upon it when he took Vseslav prisoner. It was for that reason that God inspired the incursion of the pagans, and from this calamity the true Cross obviously delivered us. For, on the day of the Exaltation [September 14], Vseslav sighed, and uttered this prayer: "Oh true Cross, inasmuch as I have believed in thee, free me from this abyss!" God demonstrated the power of the Cross as an admonition to the land of Rus' that its people should not violate the true Cross after sealing their oaths by kissing it. If anyone sins against the Cross, he shall suffer not only punishment in this world but also everlasting chastisement in the next. For great is the power of the Cross. By the Cross are vanquished the powers of the 'devil. The Cross helps our princes in combat, and the faithful who are protected by the Cross conquer in battle the foes who oppose them. For the Cross speedily frees from danger those who invoke it with faith, (173) for devils fear nothing as much as the Cross. If a man be importuned by devils, a sign of the Cross on the face drives them away. Now Vseslav remained in Kiev for the space of seven months.[215]

6577 (1069). Reinforced by Boleslav, Izyaslav marched to attack Vseslav, who went forth to meet them, and arrived at Belgorod.[216] But during the night, he hid himself from the men of Kiev, and fled from Belgorod to Polotsk. When the men of Kiev saw on the morrow that their prince had fled, they returned to Kiev, and after calling an assembly, they sent messages to Svyatoslav and Vsevolod saying, "We did wrong in expelling our Prince, and now he leads the Poles against us. Return to your father's city. If you refuse to return, then we have no alternative but to burn our city and depart to Greece."[217] Svyatoslav replied, "We shall communicate with our brother. If he marches upon you with the Poles to destroy you, we shall fight against him, and not allow him to destroy our father's city. If his intentions are peaceful, then he shall approach with a small troop." Then the people of Kiev were pacified.

Svyatoslav and Vsevolod then sent messengers to Izyaslav, announcing that Vseslav had fled, and requesting him accordingly not to lead the Poles in attack upon Kiev, because no one was really opposing him. They also let it be understood that if he intended to nurse his wrath and destroy the city, they would be properly concerned for the ancestral capital. When Izyaslav received these tidings, he left the Poles and came forward, accompanied only by Boleslav himself and a small Polish escort. He sent his son Mstislav ahead of him into Kiev, and upon the latter's arrival, he slew those who (174) had freed Vseslav, to the number of seventy, blinded others, and executed without any investigation others who were entirely innocent.[218] When Izyaslav arrived at the city, the inhabitants went forth to welcome him, and the men of Kiev received him as their Prince. Izyaslav thus resumed his throne on May 2. He scattered the Poles to forage, and then had them secretly killed. Boleslav then returned to his native country.[219] Izyaslav transferred the market place to the hill,[220] and drove Vseslav out of Polotsk, where he set up his own son Mstislav. But the latter soon died, and Izyaslav enthroned in his stead his brother Svyatopolk, since Vseslav had fled.[221]

6578 (1070). A son was born to Vsevolod, and he named him Rostislav. In this year was founded the Church of St. Michael in Vsevolod's monastery.[222]

6579 (1071). The Polovcians raided about Rastovets and Neyatin.[223] In this year, Vseslav expelled Svyatopolk from Polotsk. In the same year, Yaropolk defeated Vseslav near Golotichesk.[224]

At this time, a magician appeared inspired by the devil. He came to Kiev and informed the inhabitants that after the lapse of five years the Dnieper would flow backward, and that the various countries would change their locations, so that Greece would be where Rus' was, and Rus' where Greece was, and that other lands would be similarly dislocated. The ignorant believed him, but the faithful ridiculed him and told him that the devil was only deluding him to his ruin. This was (175) actually the case, for in the course of one night, he disappeared altogether. For the devils, after once encouraging a man, lead him to an evil fate, then laugh him to scorn, and cast him into the fatal abyss after they have inspired his words. In this connection we may discuss infernal incitation and its effects.

While there was famine on one occasion in the district of Rostov, two magicians appeared from Yaroslavl' and said they knew who interfered with the food supply. Then they went along the Volga, and where they came to a trading-post, they designated the handsomest women, saying that one affected the grain, another the honey, another the fish, and another the furs. The inhabitants brought into their presence their sisters, their mothers, and their wives, and the magicians in their delusion stabbed them in the back and drew out from their bodies grain or fish. They thus killed many women and appropriated their property. Then they arrived at Beloozero, and about three hundred men accompanied them. At that moment it happened that Yan, son of Vyshata,[225] arrived in that neighborhood to collect tribute in behalf of Svyatoslav. The people of Beloozero recounted to him how two magicians had caused the death of many women along the Volga and the Sheksna and had now arrived in their district. Yan inquired whose subjects they were, and upon learning that they belonged to his Prince, he directed their followers to surender the magicians to him, since they were subjects of his own Prince. When they refused to obey his command, Yan wanted to go unarmed in search of the magicians, but his companions (176) warned him against such action, urging that the magicians might attack him. Yan thus bade his followers to arm themselves; there were twelve of them with him, and they took their way through the forest in pursuit of the magicians. The latter arranged their forces to offer resistance, and when Yan advanced with his battle-axe, three of their number approached Yan and said to him, "You advance to certain death; go no further." But Yan gave the order to strike them down, and then moved upon the rest. They gathered together to attack Yan, and one of them struck at him with his axe, but Yan turned the axe and struck him with the butt. Then he bade his followers cut them down, but the enemy fled into the forest after killing Yan's priest. Yan returned to the town and the people of Beloozero, and announced to them that if they did not surrender those magicians to him, he would remain among them for a year.

The people of Beloozero then went forth and captured the magicians, whom they brought into Yan's presence. He asked them why they had caused the death of so many persons. They replied, "Because they prevent plenty, and if we remove them, abundance will return. If you so desire, we shall extract from their bodies grain or fish or any other object in your presence." Yan declared, "Verily that is a lie. God made man out of earth; he is composed of bones and has veins for his blood. There is nothing else in him. He knows nothing, and it is God alone who possesses knowledge." The magicians then asserted that they knew how man was made. When Yan asked them how, they replied, "God washed himself in the bath, and after perspiring, (177) dried himself with straw and threw it out of heaven upon the earth. Then Satan quarreled with God as to which of them should create man out of it. But the devil made man, and God set a soul in him. As a result, whenever a man dies, his body goes to the earth and his soul to God." Yan then made answer, 'It is indeed the devil who has put you to this mischief. In what god do you believe?" They answered, "In Antichrist." He then inquired of them where their god had his abode and they replied that he dwelt in the abyss.

Then Yan asked, "What sort of god is that which dwells in the abyss? That is a devil. God dwells in heaven, sitting upon his throne, glorified by the angels who stand before him in fear and dare not look upon him. He whom you call Antichrist was cast out from the number of these angels and expelled from heaven for his presumption. He dwells indeed in the abyss, as you say, and there abides until God shall come from heaven to seize this Antichrist, and bind him with bonds, and cast him out, when he shall have taken him captive with his minions and those who believe in him. As for you, you shall endure torment both at my hands here and now, and also in the life after death." The magicians retorted that their gods made known to them that Yan could do them no harm, but Yan answered that their gods were liars. They then asserted their right to stand before Svyatoslav, and that Yan had no jurisdiction over them. Yan, however, ordered that they should be beaten and have their beards torn out. When they had been thus beaten, and after their beards had been pulled out with pincers, Yan inquired of them what their gods were saying at the moment. They made answer, "That we should stand before (178) Svyatoslav." Yan then directed that they should be gagged and bound to the thwart. Thereupon he sent them on before him by boat, and himself followed after. The party halted at the mouth of the Sheksna, and Yan said to the magicians, "What do your gods now make known to you?" They replied, "Our gods tell us that we shall not escape you alive." Yan remarked that the information supplied by their gods was entirely correct. They then urged that if he released them, it would bring him much advantage, but that if he destroyed them, he should suffer much trouble and evil. Yan retorted that if he let them go he would be more likely to be punished by God.

Then Yan said to the boatmen, "Has any relative of any one of you been killed by these men?" One of them answered that his mother had thus been killed, while another mentioned his sister and another his relatives. So Yan ordered them to avenge their kinsfolk. They then seized and killed the magicians, whom they hanged upon an oak tree. They thus deservedly suffered punishment at God's hand. After Yan had departed homeward, a bear came up the next night, gnawed them and ate them up. Thus they perished through the instigation of the devil, prophesying to other people, but ignorant of their own destruction. For if they had really known the future, they would not have come to that place where they were destined to be taken captive. After being thus captured, why did they declare that they would not die, even while Yan contemplated killing them? But of such nature is the instigation of devils; for devils do not perceive man's thought, though they often inspire thought in man without knowing his secrets. (179) God alone knows the mind of man, but devils know nothing, for they are weak and evil to look upon.

We shall now proceed to discuss their appearance and their magic. At about the same time, it happened that a certain man from Novgorod went among the Chuds, and approached a magician, desiring to have his fortune told. The latter, according to his custom, began to call devils into his abode. The man from Novgorod sat upon the threshold of that same house, while the magician lay there in a trance, and the devil took possession of him. The magician then arose, and said to the man from Novgorod, "The gods dare not approach, since you wear a symbol of which they are afraid." The Novgorodian then bethought him of the cross he wore, and went and laid it outside the house. The magician then resumed his calling of the devils, and they shook him, and made known why the stranger had come. Then the Novgorodian inquired of the magician why the devils were afraid of the cross they wore. The magician made answer, "That is the token of God in heaven, of whom our gods are afraid." Then the man of Novgorod asked who his gods were and where they dwelt. The magician replied, "In the abysses; they are black of visage, winged and tailed, and they mount up under heaven obedient to your gods. For your angels dwell in heaven, and if any of your people die, they are carried up to heaven. But if any of ours pass away, they are carried down into the abyss to our gods." And so it is; for sinners abide in hell in the expectation of eternal torment, (180) while the righteous associate with the angels in the heavenly abode.

Such is the power and the beauty and the weakness of demons! In this way they lead men astray, commanding them to recount visions, appearing to those who are imperfect in faith, and exhibiting themselves to some in sleep and to others in dreams. Thus magic is performed through infernal instigation. Particularly through the agency of woman are infernal enchantments brought to pass, for in the beginning the devil deceived woman, and she in turn deceived man. Thus even down to the present day women perform magic by black arts, poison, and other devilish deceits. Unbelievers are likewise led astray by demons.

Thus in ancient days, in the time of the Apostles, there lived Simon

Magus, who through his magic caused dogs to speak like man, and changed his own aspect, appearing sometimes old, sometimes young, and sometimes he even changed one man to the semblance of another, accomplishing this transfiguration by his magic art. Jannes and Jambres wrought marvels against Moses through enchantment, but eventually they had no power against him. Kunop also practiced devilish arts, such as walking upon the water; and he performed other prodigies, being misled by the devil to his own and others' destruction.[226]

A magician likewise appeared at Novgorod in the principate of Gleb. He harangued the people, and by representing himself as a god he deceived many of them; in fact, he humbugged almost the entire city. For he claimed to know all things, and he blasphemed against the Christian faith, announcing that he would walk across (181) the Volkhov River in the presence of the public. There was finally an uprising in the city, and all believed in him so implicitly that they went so far as to desire to murder their bishop. But the Bishop took his cross, and clad himself in his vestments, and stood forth saying, "Whosoever has faith in the magician, let him follow him, but whoever is a loyal Christian, let him come to the Cross." So the people were divided into two factions, for Gleb and his retainers took their stand beside the bishop, while the common people all followed the magician. Thus there was a great strife between them.

Then Gleb hid an axe under his garments, approached the magician, and inquired of him whether he know what was to happen on the morrow or might even occur before evening. The magician replied that he was omniscient. Then Gleb inquired whether he even knew what was about to occur that very day. The magician answered that he himself should perform great miracles. But Gleb drew forth the axe and smote him, so that he fell dead, and the people dispersed. Thus the man who had sold himself to the devil perished body and soul.

6580 (1072). The relics of the holy martyrs Boris and Gleb were transported to their final resting place.[227] Izyaslav, Svyatoslav, and Vsevolod, the sons of Yaroslav, gathered together, and with them the Metropolitan George, Bishop Peter of Pereyaslavl', Bishop Michael of Yur'ev, Theodosius the Prior of the Crypt Monastery, Sophronius the Prior of St. Michael's, Germanus the Prior of St. Saviour's, Nicholas the Prior of Pereyaslavl', and all the other priors. They instituted a festival and celebrated it with splendor, and they laid the relics in the new church founded by Izyaslav, which is still standing. First of all, Izyaslav, Svyatoslav, and Vsevolod took the relics of Boris in a wooden casket and carried it upon their shoulders, (182) while monks preceded them holding candles in their hands. After them came deacons with censers, and then priests, and following the latter the Bishops accompanied by the Metropolitan. Last came the bearers of the casket. They transported it into the new church, and when they opened the casket, the church was filled with sweetness and fragrance. When they perceived this miracle, they glorified God. Fear overcame the Metropolitan, for he had been uncertain in his faith concerning the relics; he therefore prostrated himself and begged for forgiveness. After kissing the relics of Boris, they placed them in a stone coffin. Then they took Gleb in a stone coffin and laid it upon a sled, which they pulled along by means of ropes attached to it. When they arrived at the church-door, the coffin stopped, and would not move further. Then they bade the people cry, "Kyrie eleison," and thus moved it through. The relics were thus laid away on May 2.[228] When the liturgy had been sung, the brethren dined together, each with his boyars and in great affection. At this time Chudin governed Výshgorod, and Lazarus was in charge of the church. The brethren then departed to their several districts.

6581 (1073). The devil stirred up strife among these brothers, the sons of Yaroslav. When disagreement thus ensued among them, Svyatoslav and Vsevolod united against Izyaslav. The latter left Kiev, but Svyatoslav and Vsevolod arrived there upon March 22 and established themselves on the throne at Berestovo, though they thus transgressed against their father's injunction. Svyatoslav was the instigator of his brother's expulsion, for he desired more power. He misled Vsevolod by asserting that Izyaslav was entering into an alliance with Vseslav for the purpose of attacking them saying, "If we do not forestall him, he will expel us." By this means he irritated Vsevolod against Izyaslav.[229] Now Izyaslav took considerable treasure with him on his flight into Poland with the intention of recruiting supporters there. But the Poles robbed him of all his property, and expelled him from their boundaries.[230] Svyatoslav thus ruled in Kiev after the expulsion of his brother, and thus broke the injunction of his father and of God. For it is a great sin to break the commandment of one's father. It was the sons of Ham who first attacked the land of Seth, but suffered the chastisement of God four hundred years later. From the race of Seth are sprung the Hebrews, who overcame the nation of the Canaanites, and seized the ancestral portion and the territory of the latter. Then Esau broke his father's command and suffered death; for it is not good to encroach upon another's possessions.[231]

In this year the Church of the Crypts was founded by the Prior Theodosius and Bishop Michael, while George the Metropolitan was absent in Greece and Svyatoslav was reigning in Kiev.[232]

6582 (1074). Theodosius, the Prior of the Crypt Monastery, passed away. We shall therefore supply a brief account of his dormition. When the Lenten season approached, upon the eve of Quinquagesima Sunday, Theodosius was accustomed, after he had embraced the brethren according to his practice, to instruct them how to pass the Lenten period in prayer by night and by day, and how to guard against evil thoughts and the temptations of the devil. "For," said he, "demons incite in monks evil thoughts and desires, (184) and inflame their fancy so that their prayers are impaired. One must combat such thoughts when they come by using the sign of the Cross and by saying, "Lord Jesus Christ our God, have mercy on us, Amen!" With this end in view, we must practise abstinence from many foods, for evil desires develop out of excessive eating and immoderate drinking, and by the growth of such thoughts sin is caused. "By this means," said he, "oppose yourselves to the influence of the demons and their malice, guard against laziness and too much sleep, be zealous in churchly song, in the traditions of the fathers, and in the reading of the Scriptures. For it befits monks above all things to have upon their lips the Psalter of David, and thereby to expel the weaknesses caused by the devil. It befits all young persons to show toward their elders love, obedience, and attention, and it behooves all older persons to offer the younger brethren their love and admonition, and to be an example by their continence and vigil, their self-restraint and humility, to counsel and console the youthful, and to spend Lent in such pursuits."

"For," he added, "God has given us these forty days in which to purify our souls. This is a tithe given to God by the body. For the days of the year are three hundred and sixty-five, and giving to God each tenth day as a tithe makes a fast of forty days, during which the soul is cleansed and happily celebrates the Resurrection of the Lord as it rejoices in God. For the Lenten season purifies the heart (185) of man. In the beginning, fasting was first imposed upon Adam, so that he should not taste of one tree. Moses fasted forty days to prepare himself to receive the law upon Mt. Sinai, and then he beheld the glory of God. During a fast, Samuel's mother bore him. Through their fasting, the Ninevites averted the wrath of God. By his fasting, Daniel prepared himself for great visions. After his fast, Elijah was taken up to heaven to receive celestial sustenance. Through their fasting, the Three Children quenched the violence of the fire. And our Lord, by fasting forty days, made known to us the Lenten season. By means of their fasting, the Apostles rooted out the teaching of the devil. By virtue of their fasts, our fathers appeared to the world as beacons that continue to shine after their decease. They exhibited great labors, and continence; for example, the great Antonius, Euthymius, Sabbas, and the other fathers. Let us imitate them, my brethren."

After thus instructing the brotherhood, he kissed them, calling each by name, and then left the monastery, taking with him but a few loaves of bread. He entered a crypt, closed the door behind him, and covered himself with dust. He spoke to no one, unless some object was needful to him, and in any case he conversed only on Saturday and on Sunday through a small window. Upon other days, he remained in fasting and in prayer, maintaining strict abstinence. He returned to the monastery on Friday on the eve of St. Lazarus' day. For on this day ends the forty days' fast, which opens on the first Monday after the week of St. Theodore and concludes on Friday, before the feast of St. Lazarus. Holy Week (186) is then observed as a fast on account of our Lord's passion.[233] Theodosius thus returned according to his custom, embraced the brethren, and with them celebrated Palm Sunday.

When Easter Day came, he celebrated it brilliantly as usual, and then fell ill. When he was taken ill, and had been sick for five days, he bade them carry him in the evening down into the courtyard. The brethren laid him upon a sled and set him before the church.[234] He then desired that the whole brotherhood should be summoned, so the brethren struck upon the bell, and all assembled together. Theodosius then said to them, "My brethren, my fathers, and my children! I now depart from you, for God made known to me, while I was in the crypt during the Lenten season, that I must now quit this world. Whom do you desire for your prior, that I may confer my blessing upon him?" They made answer, "You have been a father to us all. Whomsoever you yourself select shall be our father and our prior, and we shall obey him even as we obey you." Then our father Theodosius said, "Go apart from me and designate him whom you desire, except the two brothers Nicholas and Ignatius:[235] but choose from the rest whomever you prefer, from the eldest down to the youngest."

They obeyed his behest, and upon withdrawing a short distance in the direction of the church, they took counsel together, and then sent two of the brethren back to Theodosius to beg him to designate the one chosen by God and his own holy prayer, and who should be agreeable to Theodosius himself. Theodosius then made answer. "If you desire to receive your prior from me, then I will appoint him not so much from my own choice as by divine disposition," and he designated the presbyter James. (187) This nomination did not meet with the approval of the brotherhood, who objected that James had not taken orders in the monastery, since he had come thither from Letets[236] with his brother Paul. They demanded rather Stephen the Cantor, who was then a pupil of Theodosius, and therefore said, "He has grown up under your hand and has served with you; appoint him as our prior."

Then Theodosius said, "By the commandment of God, I designated James, but you prefer that the appointment should coincide with your own wishes." He gave way to their desire, however, and appointed Stephen to be their prior, and blessed him, saying, "My son! I give over to you this monastery. Guard it with care, and maintain what I have ordained in its observances. Change not the traditions and the instructions of the monastery, but follow in all things the law and our monastic rule."

The brethren then raised him up, carried him to his cell, and laid him upon his bed. At the beginning of the sixth day, while he was seriously ill, Prince Svyatoslav came to visit him with his son Gleb. While the Prince was sitting beside him, Theodosius said, "I depart from this world and entrust this monastery to your guardianship in the event that some disorder arises in it. I confer the priorate upon Stephen; let him not be offended."[237] The Prince embraced him, and after promising to care for the monastery, departed from him. When the seventh day was come, while Theodosius was steadily growing weaker, he summoned Stephen and the brotherhood, and spoke to them these words: "Upon my departure from this world, if I have found favor with God and he has accepted me, then this monastery, after my decease, will grow and prosper through his help. In that event, know that God has accepted me. But if, after my death, the monastery begins to lose in membership (188) and income, be assured that I shall not have found favor in the sight of God." When he had spoken thus, the brethren wept, saying, "Father, intercede with God for us, for we know that he will not scorn your labors." They thus sat out the night with him, and at the begining of the eighth day, being the second Saturday after Easter, in the second hour of the day, he commended his soul into the hands of God, upon May 3, in the eleventh year of the indiction. The brethren thus mourned for him.

Theodosius had given command that he should be buried in the crypt where he had performed many good works. He had also directed that his body should be buried by night, and they followed his injunction in this respect. When evening was come, the brethren took up his body and laid it in the crypt, after conducting it thither in all honor with hymns and candles to the glory of our God Jesus Christ.

While Stephen governed the monastery and the pious flock that Theodosius had gathered, these monks shone out like bright beacons throughout the land of Rus'. Some of them were constant in fasting, some in vigil, some in genuflexion, some in fasting every other day or every third day, others in living on bread and water only, still others in subsisting solely on boiled vegetables, and others only on raw food. They dwelt in love, while the young brethren obeyed the elder, not venturing to speak in their presence, but always comporting themselves obediently and with great consideration. Likewise the elder also gave proof of their love for their younger associates, admonished them, and consoled them like beloved sons. If any brother fell into some sinful way, they consoled him, and three or four of them shared the penance of one brother out of their great affection for him. Such was the brotherly love and such the continence in this monastery. If any brother quit the monastery, all the rest were deeply afflicted on his account, (189) sent in search of him, and recalled him to the monastery. All the brethren then appeared before the prior, and kneeling at his feet, they besought him in their brother's behalf, and received him again into the community with joy. Such was their charity, their continence, and their austerity. I shall mention a few eminent figures from their number.

The first is Damian the presbyter. He was so austere and temperate that he lived only on bread and water till his death. If anyone brought to the monastery a child that was ill and suffering from any disease, or if an adult beset by an illness came to the monastery in search of the great Theodosius, the prior commanded this Damian to offer prayer in behalf of the patient. When he had then prayed and applied an ointment, those who had thus come to him were healed. When he himself fell sick and lay in his weakness at the point of death, an angel came to him in the semblance of Theodosius, and promised him the kingdom of heaven as a reward for his labors. A little later Theodosius himself came with the brethren and when he sat down beside the sick man, Damian in his weakness looked up at the prior and said, "Forget not, father prior, what you have promised me." The great Theodosius understood forthwith that he had seen a vision, and said to him, "Brother Damian, that which I have promised shall be fulfilled." Damian then closed his eyes and commended his soul into the hands of God. The prior and his brethren then buried his body.

There was likewise another brother named Jeremy, who remembered the conversion of Rus'. (190) God had conferred upon him the gift of prophecy, and if he beheld any brother lost in reflection, he reproved him in secret and adjured him to guard against the devil. If any brother was contemplating desertion from the monastery and Jeremy perceived his intent, he sought him out, reproved his thought, and consoled that brother. If he made any prophecy, whether good or evil, the ancient's word was fulfilled.

There was another ancient named Matthew, who also had the gift of second sight. When he was once standing in his place in the church, he lifted up his eyes, and on glancing at the brethren who stood singing on either side of him, he beheld a devil in the guise of a Pole, who carried in a fold of his garment certain flowers called *lepki*. As this devil circulated among the brethren, he took a flower from his bosom and threw it at one of them, and if the flower attached itself to any one of the brethren who were singing, that brother, after standing awhile and weakening in endurance, sought some pretext and left the church. He then went to his cell and fell asleep, and did not return to the church before the close of the service. If the demon cast the flower at some other brother and it did not attach itself to him, he stood firm during the singing until the matins were over, and then went forth to his cell. When the old man beheld this occurrence, he reported it to his brethren.

Upon another occasion, the ancient observed another curious occurrence. When the old man, according to his custom, had once celebrated matins before dawn, the brethren had all departed to their cells, while he followed them somewhat later out of the church. As he walked along alone, he sat down to rest (191) under the bell, since his cell was rather far from the church. Then he noticed a crowd of people issuing forth from the gate, and as he raised his eyes, he saw one person who rode upon a swine, while others ran after him. Then the old man inquired of them whither they were going. Then the demon who rode upon the swine replied, "After Michael Tol'bekovich." The old man straightway made the sign of the cross and went on to his cell. When day had dawned, the ancient reflected, and bade the porter go and inquire whither Michael was in his cell. The answer was returned that he had just jumped from the palisades after matins. The old man then recounted his vision to the prior and his brethren. During the lifetime of this venerable friar, Theodosius passed away, Stephen became prior, and then Stephen was succeeded by Nikon. Once while he was at matins, he raised his eyes to look upon Nikon the Prior, and saw an ass standing in the prior's place, so that he understood that the prior had not yet arisen. The ancient likewise beheld many other visions, and died in this monastery at a ripe old age.

There was also another monk named Isaac. While still in the world, he was very rich, since in the secular life he was by birth a merchant of Toropets. But he resolved to become a monk, and distributed his fortune to the needy and to the monasteries. He then approached the great Antonius in the crypt, and besought him to receive him into the order. Antonius accepted him, and put upon him the monastic habit, calling him (192) Isaac, for his secular name was Chern'. Isaac adopted an ascetic mode of life. He wrapped himself in a hair-shirt, then caused a goat to be brought, flayed it, and put on the skin over his hair-shirt, so that the flesh hide dried upon him. He shut himself up in a lonely gallery of the crypt in a narrow cell only four ells across, and there lamented and prayed to God. His sustenance was one wafer, and that only once a day, and he drank but moderately of water. The great Antonius carried it to him, and passed it in to him by a little window through which he inserted his arm. Thus Isaac received his food. He subsisted thus for seven years without seeing the light of day or even lying down upon his side, for he snatched what sleep he could in a sitting posture.

Once, when evening had fallen, he had knelt till midnight singing psalms, as was his wont, and when he was wearied, he sat down upon his stool. As he sat there, and had as usual extinguished his candle, a light suddenly blazed forth in the crypt as if it shone from the sun, and strong enough to take away man's vision. Two fair youths then approached him. Their faces were radiant like the sun, and they said to him, "Isaac, we are angels; Christ is drawing near to you. Fall down and worship him." He did not understand their devilish artifice nor remember to cross himself, but knelt before the work of the demons as if to Christ himself. The demons then cried out and said, "Now, Isaac, you belong to us." They led him back into his cell and set him down. They then seated themselves around him, and both the cell (193) and the aisle of the crypt was filled with them. One of the devils, who called himself Christ, bade them take flutes and lyres and lutes and play, so that Isaac could dance before them. So they struck up with flutes, lutes, and lyres, and began to make sport of him. After they had tormented him, they left him half alive, and went away when they had beaten him.

The next day at dawn, when it was time to break bread, Antonius came to the window according to his custom and said, "May the Lord bless you, Father Isaac." But there was no answer. Then Antonius said,

"He has already passed away," so he sent into the monastery in search of Theodosius and the brethren. After digging out the entrance where it had been walled up, they entered and lifted him up, thinking him dead, and carried him out in front of the crypt. They then perceived that he was still alive, and Theodosius the prior said, "This comes from the devil's artifice." They laid him upon a bier, and Antonius cared for him.

About this same time it happened that Izyaslav returned from Poland, and was angry with Antonius on account of Vseslav, so that Svyatoslav caused Antonius to escape by night to Chernigov. When Antonius arrived there, he was attracted by the Boldinÿ hills, and after digging another crypt, he settled there. At that spot in the Boldinÿ hills, there is a monastery dedicated to the Virgin even to this day. When Theodosius learned that Antonius (194) had fled to Chernigov, he came with his brethren, took Isaac, and bore him to his own cell, where he cared for him. For Isaac was so weakened in body that he could not turn from one side to the other, nor rise up, nor sit down, but he lay always upon one side, and relieved himself as he lay, so that numerous worms were caused under his back by his excrement. Theodosius washed and dressed him with his own hands, and for two years cared for him thus. It is wondrous and strange that he lay thus for two years, tasting neither bread nor water nor any other food nor fruit, nor did he speak with his tongue, but lay deaf and dumb for the whole two years.

Theodosius prayed to God in his behalf, and offered supplications over him by day and by night, until in the third year he spoke and heard, rose upon his feet like a babe, and began to walk. He would not go faithfully to church, but the brethren carried him thither by force; they also taught him to go to the refectory, but seated him apart from the rest of the brethren. They set bread before him, but he would not take it unless they placed it in his hand. Theodosius then said, "Leave the bread before him, but do not put it in his hand, so that he can eat of his own volition." For a week he ate nothing, but gradually he became aware (195) of the bread and tasted it. Thus he began to eat, and by this means Theodosius freed him from the craft of the devil.

Isaac then assumed severe abstinence. When Theodosius was dead and Stephen was prior in his stead, Isaac said, "Demon, you deceived me once when I sat in a lonely spot. I must not confine myself in the crypt, but must vanquish you while I frequent the monastery." He then clad himself in a hair-shirt, and put on over this a sackcloth coat, and began to act strangely. He undertook to help the cooks in the preparation of food for the brotherhood. He went to matins earlier than the others, and stood firm and immovable. When winter came with its heavy frosts, he stood in shoes so worn that his feet froze to the pavement, but he would not move his feet till matins were over. After matins, he went to the kitchen, and made ready the fire, the water, and the wood before the other cooks came from the brotherhood.

There was one cook who was also named Isaac, who mocked at Isaac and said, "There sits a black crow; go and catch it." Isaac bowed to the ground before him, then went and caught the crow, and brought it back to him in the presence of all the cooks. They were frightened and reported it to the prior and the brotherhood, who began to respect him. But not being desirous of human glory, he began to act strangely, (196) and to play tricks, now on the prior, now on the brethren, and now on laymen, so that the others dealt him blows. Then he began to wander through the country, acting like an idiot. He settled in the crypt where he had formerly lived, for Antonius was already dead. He gathered young men about him and laid upon them the monastic habit, so that he suffered blows from the Prior Nikon as well as from the parents of these youths. But he suffered these hardships, and willingly endured blows and nakedness and cold by day and by night.

One night he lit the stove in a cabin by the crypt. When the stove was heated, fire began to issue forth from the crevices, for it was old and cracked. Since he had nothing to put over the stove, he braced his bare feet against the flame till the stove burned out, and then left it. Many other stories were told about him, and I myself witnessed some such occurrences.

Thus he won his victory over the demons, holding their terrors and apparitions of as little account as flies. For he said to them, "You did indeed deceive me the first time in the crypt, since I did not perceive your craft and cunning. But now that I have on my side the Lord Jesus Christ and my God and the prayers of my father Theodosius, I hope to vanquish you." Many times the demons harassed him, and said, "You belong to us, for you have worshipped us and our leader." (197) But he replied, "Your chief is Antichrist and you are demons," and signed his countenance with the Cross. At this they disappeared. Sometimes, however, they came upon him again by night, and frightened him in his dreams, appearing like a great company with mattocks and spades, and saying, "We will undermine the crypt, and bury this man within it," while others exclaimed, "Fly, Isaac, they intend to bury you alive." But he made answer, "If you were men, you would have come by day; but you are darkness and come in darkness, and the darkness shall swallow you up." Then he made the sign of the Cross against them, and they vanished.

On other occasions, they endeavored to terrify him in the form of a bear, sometimes as a wild beast and sometimes as a bull. Now snakes beset him, and now toads, mice, and every other reptile. But they could not harm him, and said to him, "Isaac, you have vanquished us!" He replied, "You conquered me in the image of Jesus Christ and his angels, of whose sight you are unworthy. But now you rightly appear in the guise of beasts and cattle or as the snakes and reptiles that you are, repulsive and evil to behold." Thereupon the demons left him, and he suffered no more evil at their hands. As he himself related, his struggle against them lasted for three years. (198) Then he began to live still more strictly, and to practice abstinence, fasting, and vigil.

After thus living out his life, he finally came to his end. He fell sick in his crypt, and was carried in his illness to the monastery, where he died in the Lord upon the eighth day. The Prior John and the brethren clothed his body and buried him.

Such were the monks of the monastery of Theodosius, who shine forth like radiant beacons since their decease, and intercede with God in behalf of the brethren here below, as well as for the lay brotherhood and for those who contribute to the monastery in which to this day the brotherhood abides together in virtuous life amid hymns, prayers, and obedience, to the glory of Almighty God, and protected by the intercession of Theodosius, to whom be glory, Amen.

6583 (1075). The crypt church was continued on its foundation by Stephen the Prior. For Theodosius began its foundation, while Stephen continued it thereon, until it was completed on July 11 of the third year of its construction. Ambassadors from Germany came to Svyatoslav in this year, and in his pride, he showed them his riches. They beheld the innumerable quantity of his gold, silver and silks, but remarked, "This is nothing, for it lies dead. Servants are preferable to this treasure, for vassals (199) can win still greater wealth." Thus Hezekiah, King of the Jews, boasted before the ambassadors of the King of Assyria, and all his treasures were carried away to Babylon. Likewise after Svyatoslav's death all his riches were scattered.[238]

6584 (1076). Vladimir, son of Vsevolod, and Oleg, son of Svyatoslav, went forth to aid the Poles against the Czechs.[239] On December 27 of this year Svyatoslav, son of Yaroslav, died from the cutting of a sore, and was buried in Chernigov by the Church of the Redeemer.[240] On January 1, Vsevolod succeeded to his throne. In this year, a son was born to Vladimir; he was named Mstislav, and was grandson of Vsevolod.

6585 (1077). Izyaslav advanced with Polish support,[241] and Vsevolod went forth against him. Boris settled at Chernigov on May 4; his reign lasted eight days until he fled to join Roman in Tmutorakan'.[242] Vsevolod went to Volÿn' to attack his brother Izyaslav. Peace was concluded, so that Izyaslav came and settled in Kiev on July 15. Oleg, the son of Svyatoslav, was with Vsevolod at Chernigov.

6586 (1078). Oleg, son of Svyatoslav, fled from Vsevolod to Tmutorakan' on April 10.[243] In this year, Gleb, the son of Svyatoslav, was killed in Zavaloch'e.[244] Gleb was kindly toward the poor and hospitable to strangers, zealous toward the church, warm in faith, peaceful, and fair in appearance. He was laid to rest (200) in the Church of the Redeemer at Chernigov on July 23.

While Svyatopolk, the son of Izyaslav, was ruling at Novgorod in his stead, and while Yaropolk[245] was reigning in Vÿshgorod and Vladimir[246] at Smolensk, Oleg and Boris led the pagans to attack Rus', and fell upon Vsevolod with their Polovcian reinforcements. Vsevolod advanced to meet them as far as the Sozhitsa.[247] The Polovcians then vanquished the Russes, and many lost their lives. Ivan, son of Zhiroslav, and Tukÿ, the brother of Chudin, along with Porey and many others, met their deaths there on August 28. Oleg and Boris arrived before Chernigov, thinking they had won, and they visited much harm upon the land of Rus'. They shed Christian blood, which God will avenge upon them, and they will have to answer for their destruction of Christian souls.

Vsevolod joined his brother Izyaslav at Kiev, and after embracing each other, they settled there. Vsevolod then reported all that had occurred. Then Izyaslav said to him, "Brother, do not sorrow. Do you not see what misfortune has happened to me? Did they not first expel me and confiscate my possessions? And what was later my second fault, that I was driven out by you, my own brethren? Have I not wandered through foreign lands, and suffered the loss of my estate? I had done no wrong. Let us therefore not give way to sorrow now, my brother. We shall each of us have his share in Rus', and if we lose it, (201) then I am ready to lay down my life for you." With these words he consoled Vsevolod, and ordered that warriors old and young should be gathered together.

Izyaslav set out with Yaropolk his son, and Vsevolod went forth with his son Vladimir. They arrived before Chernigov, but the inhabitants barricaded themselves within the city. Oleg and Boris were not there. Since the citizens of Chernigov would not open the gates, the brethren attacked the city. Vladimir made his attack at the eastern entrance, where he captured the gates from the side of the Strizhen'. They thus opened the outer city and set fire to it, while the inhabitants fled to the inner city. Izyaslav and Vsevolod then learned that Oleg and Boris were on the way to attack them, and hurriedly sallied forth from the city to meet Oleg. Oleg then suggested to Boris that they should not attack, for they could hardly withstand four princes, and he therefore proposed that they should make some proposition to their uncles. Boris replied, "Behold our present strength, I will rather fight them all," boasting exceedingly, because he did not know that God resists the proud, but gives grace to the humble, so that the strong man may not boast of his strength.

They then advanced to the attack. When they were at a place near a village on the meadow of Nezhata,[248] both forces met, and the carnage was awful. Boris, the son of Vyacheslav, who had so proudly boasted, was the first to fall. While Izyaslav was standing among the foot-soldiers, one man suddenly rode up and struck him in the shoulder with his spear. Thus Izyaslav, the son of Yaroslav, met his death. While the battle was still in progress, Oleg himself fled with a small escort, and escaped with difficulty. (202) He took refuge in Tmutorakan'.[249]

Prince Izyaslav was killed on October 3. His body was taken up, and after it was transported by boat, it was laid before Gorodets.[250] The whole city of Kiev went forth to meet it. It was laid upon a sledge, and the priests and the monks escorted it with their chants into the city. But their chanting could not be heard for the lamentation and great mourning, since the whole city of Kiev bewailed him. Yaropolk followed the body, weeping with his retinue. "Father, my father," he lamented, "hast thou lived without sorrow in this world, whilst thou didst suffer many assaults from thy people and thy brethren? He perished not by a brother's hand, but he laid down his life for his brother." His body was brought in and laid in the Church of the Holy Virgin, inclosed in a marble casket.

Izyaslav was a man fair of appearance and imposing in stature, not malicious in temper, but a hater of injustice and a lover of rectitude. In him there was no guile, for he was a simple man who did not render evil for evil. How much hardship the people of Kiev had visited upon him! They had expelled him and plundered his house, yet he did not requite these misdeeds with evil. If any man say, "The executioner has killed such and such a man," it was not Izyaslav who caused this deed, but his son. Then brothers expelled him, and he went wandering through foreign lands. Later, when he was again restored to his throne, and Vsevolod sought refuge at his court, he did not ask Vsevolod how much harm he had endured at Vsevolod's hands. He did not return evil for evil, but consoled his brother, saying, "Brother, you have proved your love for me, and you have restored me to my throne, and (203) you have called me your chief. I will not remember former malice, for you are my brother and I am yours, and I will lay down my life for you," as indeed he did. He did not say to Vsevolod, "How much evil you have done me! Now in your good turn evil has befallen you." He did not say, "All this does not concern me," but instead he took upon himself his brother's sorrow, and proved his great love for him, thus fulfilling the words of the Apostle, "Console the sorrowful" (*I Thess.*, v, 14). If he committed any sin in this world, verily shall it be forgiven him, because he laid down his life for his brother, not because he desired either a greater realm of greater wealth, but in consequence of his brother's wrongs.

The Lord has said of such men, "Let a man lay down his life for his friend" (*John,* xv, 13). Solomon also said, "Brethren, be ready to aid one another in adversity" (*Prov.,* xvii, 17). For love is above all things, even as John said, "God is love. He who dwelleth in love, dwelleth in God, and God dwelleth in him. Love is thus perfected that we may have dignity on the day of judgment, in order that as he is, so we may also be in this world. There is no fear in love, but perfect love casteth out fear, since fear hath torment, and he who is afraid is not perfect in love. If any man say, 'I love God,' and hateth his brother, it is a lie. How can he who hateth his brother whom he seeth love God whom he seeth not? We have this commandment from him, that he who loveth God shall love his brother also" (*I John,* iv, 16-18, 20-21). For all is perfected in love. Through love sins are washed away, out of love the Lord descended to earth and was crucified for us (204) sinners, and after taking away our sins he was nailed to the Cross, thus giving us his Cross for the elimination of the devil's hatred. Out of love this Prince shed his blood for his brother, thus fulfilling the Lord's commandment.[251]

Vsevolod reigned in Kiev on the throne of his father and his brother, after assuming the sovereignty over all Rus'. He set up his son Vladimir at Chernigov and placed Yaropolk at the city of Vladimir [Volÿnsk], to which he added the district of Turov.[252]

6587 (1079). Roman advanced with Polovcian forces as far as Voin',[253] but Vsevolod remained near Pereyaslavl' and made peace with the Polovcians. Roman returned homeward with them, but they killed him on August 2. The bones of Svyatoslav's son and Yaroslav's grandson still lie there even to this day. The Khazars took Oleg prisoner and shipped him overseas to Tsar'grad.[254] Vsevolod appointed Ratibor as his lieutenant in Tmutorakan'.[255]

6588 (1080). The Torks of Pereyaslavl' made an attack upon Rus'. Vsevolod sent forth his son Vladimir, who went out and conquered them.[256]

6589 (1081). David, the son of Igor', and Volodar', the son of Rostislav fled on May 18, and upon their arrival at Tmutorakan', they captured Ratibor and settled there as princes.[257]

(205) 6590 (1082). Osen', Prince of the Polovcians, passed away.

6591 (1083). Oleg returned from Greece to Tmutorakan', and established himself there after he had captured David and Volodar'.[258] He slaughtered the Khazars who had counseled the death of his brother and had plotted against himself, but he released David and Volodar'.

6592 (1084). Yaropolk came to visit Vsevolod upon Easter Day. At this time, the two sons of Rostislav had fled from Yaropolk, and later had returned and expelled him. Vsevolod then despatched his own son Vladimir to drive out the sons of Rostislav.[259] He then set up Yaropolk as prince of the city of Vladimir [Volÿnsk]. In this year, David made captives of the merchants going to Greece at Oleshki, and confiscated their property.[260] Vsevolod sent after him, brought him to Kiev, and presented him with Dorogobuzh.[261]

6593 (1085). Incited by evil advisers, Yaropolk planned an attack upon Vsevolod. When Vsevolod learned of his project, he sent his son Vladimir to oppose him.[262] Yaropolk left his mother and his retainers at Lutsk[263] and fled into Poland. When Vladimir arrived at Lutsk, the inhabitants surrendered. He set up David at the city of Vladimir in the place of Yaropolk, confiscated Yaropolk's property, and brought to Kiev his mother, his wife, and his retainers.

(206) 6594 (1086). Vsevolod founded the Church of St. Andrew[264] during the tenure of the holy Metropolitan John.[265] Beside this church he also built a convent in which his daughter, Yanka by name, became a nun while still a maiden. This same Yanka assembled many nuns, and dwelt among them according to the monastic rule.[266]

Yaropolk returned from Poland and made peace with Vladimir. The latter returned again to Chernigov, while Yaropolk took up his residence at the city of Vladimir [Volÿnsk]. After remaining there a few days, he went to Zvenigorod.[267] Before he had reached that city, he was struck down by the accursed Neradets, who had been incited by the devil and by evil men. As he lay upon his sled, Neradets killed him with his sword on November 22. Yaropolk raised himself up, drew the sword from his body, and cried out in a loud voice, "Ah, enemy, you have caught me!" The thrice accursed Neradets fled to Rurik, in Peremÿshl'. Yaropolk's escort, including Radko, Vÿnkina, and many others, took Yaropolk on their horses before them, and carried him to the city of Vladimir, and thence to Kiev. The pious Prince Vsevolod went out to meet him, accompanied by his sons Vladimir and Rostislav, by all the boyars, and by the blessed Metropolitan John with his monks and presbyters. All the people of Kiev raised great lamentation for him, and brought him with chants and hymns to St. Demetrius.[268]

They then robed his body, and on December 5 laid it honorably in a marble casket in the Church of the Holy Apostle Peter, the construction of which he himself had previously begun. After suffering many misfortunes, expelled (207) by his kinsmen without cause, persecuted, and robbed of his patrimony, he endured in the end a bitter death. But he rendered himself worthy of everlasting life and repose. This blessed prince was calm, mild, moderate, and loving toward his brethren. He gave each year a tithe of his property to the Holy Virgin, and often addressed this prayer to God, saying, "Oh Lord my God! receive my prayer, and grant me a death by an unknown hand like that of my kinsmen Boris and Gleb, so that I may wash away my sin with my blood, and thus escape this vain world and its confusion, as well as the snares of the devil." Our glorious God did not deny his request, and he has attained such blessings "as eye hath not seen nor ear heard, and such as have not entered the heart of man, which God hath prepared for them that love him" (*I Cor.*, ii, 9).

6595-6596 (1087-1088). The Church of St. Michael in Vsevolod's monastery was consecrated by the Metropolitan John, while Lazarus was prior of that monastery. In this same year, Svyatopolk departed from Novgorod to rule in Turov.[269] In this year, Nikon, Prior of the Crypt Monastery, passed away.[270] In this year, the Bulgars captured Murom.[271]

6597 (1089). The Crypt Church of the Holy Virgin in the Theodosian monastery (208) was consecrated by John the Metropolitan; Luke, Bishop of Belgorod; Isaiah, Bishop of Rostov; John, Bishop of Chernigov; and Antonius, prior of St. George's, in the reign of the noble Prince Vsevolod, ruler of the land of Rus', and of his sons Vladimir and Rostislav, while Yan was captain of the Kiev thousand and John was prior.

In this year, John the Metropolitan passed away. John was a man versed in books and study, generous to the poor and to the widows, affable to both rich and poor, calm-tempered and mild, reticent yet eloquent, and able to console the sorrowful with words of Holy Scripture. There never was his like in Rus' before him, nor will there be in later days.

In this year, Yanka, the above-mentioned daughter of Vsevolod, went to Greece. She brought back the Metropolitan John, a eunuch, and when the people saw him, they exclaimed, "A ghost has come." After staying a year in Kiev, he too died. He was not a learned man, but frank and simple in character.[272]

In this year, the Church of St. Michael at Pereyaslavl' was consecrated by Ephraim, the Metropolitan of that church, which he had constructed upon a magnificent scale. For there had previously been a metropolitan church at Pereyaslavl' to which he constructed a large addition, adorning it with all sorts of decorations and churchly vessels. Ephraim was a eunuch (209) of tall stature. At that time, he built many structures: he completed the Church of St. Michael, founded a church over the city gates dedicated to the holy martyr Theodore, as well as another church dedicated to St. Andrew near the church by the gates, and he also constructed a stone bathhouse such as had never heretofore existed in Rus'. He likewise constructed a palisade of stone which started from the Church of the holy martyr Theodore, and embellished the city of Pereyaslavl' with church buildings and other structures.

6599 (1091). The prior and the monks took counsel together, saying, "It is not meet for our father Theodosius to lie outside the monastery and the church, since he founded the church and gathered the monks together." After thus taking counsel, they directed that a place should be prepared in which to lay his bones. Three days before the feast of the Assumption of the Blessed Virgin, the prior ordered that digging should begin at the place where the bones of our father Theodosius lay and at his command, I, sinner that I am, was the first eyewitness of the attendant circumstances. What I here relate I did not learn by hearsay, but I was the initiator of it myself.

When the prior came to me and spoke, I went with him. We went to the crypt of Theodosius. Since no one knew our errand, we looked about where first to dig, and fixed upon a place outside the entrance at which to excavate. The prior then said to me, "Do not make this known to any of the brethren, so that none may learn of it. But choose whom you will (210) to aid you." On that very day I therefore prepared spades with which to dig. On the evening of Tuesday, at twilight, I took with me two brethren, keeping the rest in ignorance of our intent, and went to the crypt. After singing psalms, I began to dig. When I grew weary, I passed the spade to another brother, and so we dug on till midnight. When we were weary and could obtain no results from our digging, I began to be concerned for fear we were digging off at the side. So I took the spade and set myself to digging vigorously, while my companion rested in front of the crypt. He remarked to me that they had just rung the bell, and at that very moment I reached the relics of Theodosius. Even as he made the remark that they had just rung the bell, I made answer, "I have found them." When I had dug down to the relics, fear came over me, and I began to exclaim, "Kyrie eleison." At this same moment, two brethren were sitting in the monastery, looking toward the crypt and waiting till the prior, accompanied by various other monks, should bring out in secret the relics of Theodosius. As the bell rang, they saw three pillars of fire like rainbows which came and stood over the place where Theodosius was laid.

At the same time, Stephen, who had succeeded Theodosius as prior and was now a bishop, saw across country from his monastery a great light shining over the crypt. Thinking that they were transporting Theodosius (for he had been informed of their intentions a day previous), and regretting that Theodosius was being moved in his absence, he leaped upon a horse and quickly set out. He brought with him (211) Clement, whom he later appointed prior as his successor, and as they rode along they beheld a great light. When they drew near, they noticed many lights over the crypt, but when they came to the crypt itself, they saw nothing. They thus descended into the crypt, and found us seated beside the relics.

When I had dug them out, I sent word to the prior that he should join us that we might remove the relics. Thus the prior came with two other brethren. I dug out a large space, and when we stepped into it, we saw the relics lying there. The members were not separated, and the hair of the head still adhered. They laid them in a cloak and carried them out in front of the crypt.

On the next day, the bishops assembled: Ephraim of Pereyaslavl', Stephen of Vladimir, John of Chernigov, Marinus of Yur'ev; and the priors of all the monasteries came with their monks, while all pious citizens gathered. They took up the relics of Theodosius amid incense and candles, and then brought him into his church, where they laid him on the right side of the chapel, on Thursday, August 14, in the fourteenth year of the indiction and at the first hour of the day. They celebrated that day solemnly.[273]

Now I shall briefly relate how a prophecy of Theodosius was fulfilled. While he still exercised the priorship, and directed during his lifetime the flock of monks whom God had entrusted to his charge,[274] he cared for the souls not only of the solitaries themselves, but also of laymen (212) to ensure their salvation; and he was especially zealous in the interest of his spiritual sons, for he consoled and admonished those who sought his aid, and at times even entered their homes and imparted his blessing to them. Sometimes he went thus to the house of Yan to visit him and his wife Maria, for Theodosius loved them, since they lived according to the commandments of the Lord and dwelt in affection with each other. On one occasion while he was visiting them, he instructed them concerning the giving of alms to the poor, the Kingdom of Heaven which the righteous shall inherit, the torments of sinners, and the hour of death. While he was thus discussing with them the laying of the body in the grave, Yan's wife said to him, "Who knows where I shall be laid to rest?" Theodosius made answer to her, "Verily I say unto you, where I lie, there shall you be laid also." His prophecy was actually fulfilled. For after the prior had died, his words were realized eighteen years later. In that year, on August 16, Yan's wife, by name of Maria, passed away. The monks came, and after the customary hymns, they took her up and laid her in the Church of the Holy Virgin, on the left side opposite the tomb of Theodosius.[275] Theodosius had been laid to rest on August 14, and she was buried on August 16.

Thus was fulfilled the prophecy of our blessed father Theodosius, that good shepherd who fed his wise sheep without hypocrisy, in mildness and in prudence, watching over them and protecting them, and abounding in (213) prayer for the flock entrusted to him, for the Christian nations, and for the land of Rus'.

After thy departure from this world, thou prayest for all true believers and for the disciples who, as they gaze upon thy tomb, recall thy instruction and thy abstinence, and glorify God. I thy sinful servant and disciple know not how to praise thy noble life and temperance. But this little I shall say: Rejoice, our father and leader, who has rejected the tumult of the world, who hast loved tranquility, and didst serve God in the peace of the monastic life. Thou hast acquired every divine gift, exalted thyself with fasting, hatred carnal lusts and indulgence, and has cast aside the beauty and the desire of this world to follow in the footsteps of the sublime fathers and to rival them in their tranquility. Thou hast exalted thyself and adorned thyself in thy moderation and hast won happiness through the words of Holy Writ.

Rejoice, thou who wast strengthened in hope, who hast attained eternal bliss. Through thy victory over carnal desire, the source of transgression and confusion, thou hast escaped the crafts of the devil and hast won thy repose among the righteous, where thou receivest requital for thy labors and art become the heir of the patriarchs, since thou hast followed their instructions, their usage, and their continence, and hast maintained their rule. Thou hast further imitated Theodosius the Great in thy character and thy mode of life, since thou didst follow his manner of living and imitate his continence, (214) and by the adoption of his habits thou hast advanced in perfection with thy every action, as thou didst offer the ritual petitions to God, and didst thus lift up the censer of prayer as an offering of sweet-scented incense in the perfume of gratitude. Having conquered earthly lust and the ruler of this world, having trampled underfoot our adversary the devil and his wiles, thou hast stood forth the victor through thy opposition to his hostile darts and proud devices, since thou wast strengthened through God's help in the armor of the Cross and in faith immutable. Pray for me, holy Father, that I may be freed from the snares of the devil, and guard me with thy prayers against the hostile adversary.[276]

In this year, there was a portent in the sun, which seemed about to disappear. At the second hour of the day, on May 21, only part of it remained visible, approximating the size of the moon.[277] In this year, while Vsevolod was hunting wild beasts behind Vyshgorod, and as the men were stretching snares and the beaters were shouting, a huge serpent fell from the sky, and all the people were terrified. At this time the earth uttered a groan audible to many. In this year a magician appeared at Rostov, but perished shortly afterward.

6600 (1092). An extraordinary event occurred at Polotsk. At night there was heard a clatter and a groaning in the streets, and demons ran about like men. If any citizen went forth from his house to look upon them, he was wounded straightway by some invisible (215) demon, and so many perished from such wounds that the people dared no longer leave their houses. The demons later began to appear on horseback during the day. They were not visible themselves, but the hoofs of their horses could be seen. Thus they did injury to the people of Polotsk and the vicinity, so that it was commonly said that ghosts were killing the people of Polotsk. This portent had its beginning in Dryutesk. At this time, a sign appeared in the heavens like a huge circle in the midst of the sky. There was a drought in this year, so that the earth was burned over, and many pine forests and peat-bogs were consumed.[278] There were many portents in various localities, and incursions of the Polovcians were reported from all quarters. They captured three cities, Pesochen, Perevolok, and Priluk,[279] and ravaged many villages on both banks of the Dnieper. In this year the Polovcians attacked the Poles with Vasil'ko son of Rostislav. In this year, Rurik, the son of Rostislav, passed away.[280] At the same time, many died of various diseases, so that the undertakers asserted that in the interval between St. Philip's Day[281] and Lent they had sold seven thousand coffins. This misfortune was occasioned by our sins, because our transgressions and our unrighteousness had increased. God brought this calamity upon us as a summons to repent and to renounce sin, envy, and other evil works of the devil.

6601 (1093), the first year of the indiction. The Great Prince Vsevolod, the son of Yaroslav, (216) and the grandson of Vladimir, died on April 13, and was buried the next day on Thursday of Holy Week. Upon that day he was committed to the tomb in the great Church of St. Sophia.[282] From his childhood, the pious Prince Vsevolod had been a servant of God. He loved justice, aided the poor, rendered due honor to bishops and priests, loved monks exceedingly and ministered to their necessities. He abstained from drunkenness and indulgence, and was therefore beloved of his father, so that the latter said to him, "My son, may God bless you, since I hear of your meekness, and I rejoice that you have rendered my old age peaceful. If God grant that you succeed your brothers upon my throne justly and without the exercise of violence, may you lie beside my tomb where I lie when God takes you from this world, for I love you more than your brethren." This prayer of his father was fulfilled according as he had said, for after the decease of his brethren, Vsevolod inherited the throne of his father as their successor, though while he reigned at Kiev he faced greater obstacles than had beset him when he was Prince in Pereyaslavl'.

While he ruled in Kiev, he suffered distress at the hands of his nephews, who importuned him with their demands for various domains. After he had pacified them, he bestowed various domains upon them. During these troubles, he was afflicted also by sickness, (217) to which old age was added. He then began to take pleasure in the opinions of young men, and consulted with them. They induced him to withdraw his favor from his older retainers. The people no longer had access to the Prince's justice, judges became corrupt and venal, and the Prince in his illness was ignorant of these abuses. When his illness was aggravated, he summoned his son Vladimir from Chernigov, and when Vladimir, upon his arrival, found him critically ill, he wept sorely. Vsevolod thus passed away quietly when his hour came, in the presence of Vladimir and of Rostislav, his younger son, and rejoined his father, after he had ruled for fifteen years in Kiev and a year each in Pereyaslavl' and Chernigov.[283] After he had mourned with his brother Rostislav, Vladimir laid his father's body in the tomb. After the bishops, the priors, the monks, the priests, the boyars, and the common people had assembled together, they took up the corpse with the customary hymns, and laid it in St. Sophia, as we said before.

Vladimir now reflected that if he succeeded immediately to the throne of his father, he would become involved in hostilities with Svyatopolk, because the throne of Kiev had belonged to that Prince's father. After thus taking thought, he summoned Svyatopolk from Turov, while he himself departed to Chernigov and Rostislav to Pereyaslavl'.[284] When Easter was over (218) and the week after Easter had passed, Svyatopolk arrived at Kiev on April 24, the first Sunday after Easter. The inhabitants of Kiev went forth to meet him and offer him homage, and welcome him joyously. He thus occupied the throne of his father and his uncle. At this moment, the Polovcians attacked Rus', but when they learned that Vsevolod was dead, they sent propositions for peace to Svyatopolk. Without consulting with the numerous adherents of his father and his uncle, but taking counsel only with those who had accompanied him to the capital, Svyatopolk seized the Polovcian envoys and cast them into prison. When the Polovcians heard of this outrage, they immediately declared war. A large force of them thus laid siege to the city of Torchesk.[285] Being desirous of peace, Svyatopolk released the Polovcian envoys.

The Polovcians, however, were not anxious for peace, and continued their attacks. Svyatopolk then set out to recruit a force with the intention of attacking them. The wise men advised him not to oppose the nomads, since his force was small. He replied that he had eight hundred of his followers who could easily withstand them. Other rash advisers urged him to pursue his project, but the wiser heads informed him that even if he had a force of eight thousand, it would be none too strong. They reminded him that the country was already impoverished by war and taxes, and suggested that he should ask his cousin Vladimir (219) for aid. Svyatopolk followed their advice, and sent to Vladimir a request for assistance. Vladimir assembled his troops, and requested his brother Rostislav at Pereyaslavl' to give Svyatopolk his support as well. When Vladimir arrived at Kiev, the cousins met at St. Michael's[286] and composed between them their quarrels and disagreements. They were thus reconciled, and kissed the Cross to seal their compact. While the Polovcians were ravaging the countryside, the wise counsellors said to the prince, "Why do you allow discord to part you? Behold, the pagans lay waste the land of Rus'. You may arrive at an understanding at some later time, but for the present go out and meet the pagans either to conclude a peace or to wage war." Vladimir favored a peace, but Svyatopolk was for war.

Svyatopolk, Vladimir, and Rostislav thus proceeded toward Trepol'.[287] They arrived at the Stugna,[288] and before crossing the river, they called their followers into consultation and began to deliberate. Vladimir suggested that in view of the present danger they had better remain on the near side of the river and make peace with the Polovcians. Yan and the other prudent men supported this opinion, but the men of Kiev were not in accord with it, and urged the crossing of the river because they were eager to fight. This counsel found favor, and they crossed the river Stugna, which at the moment was considerably swollen. After marshalling their troops, Svyatopolk, Vladimir, and Rostislav (220) then moved forward. Svyatopolk marched on the right wing, Vladimir on the left, and Rostislav led the centre. When they had passed Trepol' they passed the rampart. Then the Polovcians advanced to the attack with their bowmen in the van. When our men took position between the ramparts they set up their standards, and the bowmen advanced outside the rampart. The Polovcians reached the rampart, raised their standards, and first attacked Svyatopolk, whose troop they broke up. Svyatopolk made a firm stand, but his soldiers fled without resisting the pagan onslaught, and he himself was obliged to flee also. The Polovcians then attacked Vladimir. The battle was fierce, and Vladimir took to flight with Rostislav. In their flight, they arrived at the river Stugna, and dived in. Rostislav straightway began to drown before Vladimir's very eyes. He was anxious to save his brother, and almost perished himself in the attempt. But Rostislav, the son of Vsevolod, thus met his death.

Vladimir swam the river with a small escort, for many of his troops and his boyars had fallen. When he arrived at the other bank of the Dnieper, he bewailed his brother and his followers, and thus returned to Chernigov heavy with sorrow. Svyatopolk escaped to Trepol' and there barricaded himself. He remained there till evening, and during the night departed for Kiev.

Upon perceiving their victory, the Polovcians scattered upon marauding expeditions (221) throughout the countryside, while others returned to Torchesk. This misfortune occurred on May 26, the day of the Ascension of our Lord Jesus Christ. Those who searched for Rostislav's body found it in the stream, and they brought it back to Kiev.

His mother wept over him, and the people pitied him greatly because of his youth. The bishops, the monks, and the priests assembled to sing the usual chants, and they laid him to rest beside his father in the Church of St. Sophia. While the Polovcians were beseiging Torchesk, the inhabitants resisted and fought boldly from the town, so that they killed many of the enemy. The Polovcians then began to press them hard and cut off their water supply, so that the inhabitants weakened from hunger and thirst. They thus sent messages to Svyatopolk to inform him that unless he sent them food supplies they would be obliged to surrender. Svyatopolk despatched the supplies, but because of the multitude of the besiegers it was impossible to introduce them into the town. When the enemy had thus beleaguered the town for nine weeks, they divided into two parties, one of which remained near the city to prosecute the siege, while the rest marched toward Kiev and scattered on raiding parties between Kiev and Vyshgorod. Svyatopolk sallied forth in the direction of Zhelan'[289] where the two forces advanced to the attack. When the battle-lines met, a fierce combat ensued, but our men fled before the pagans, and many perished, even a larger number than at Trepol'. Svyatopolk (222) arrived at Kiev with two companions, and the Polovcians returned to Torchesk. This sad event took place on July 23. Upon the next day, that is, on July 24, the festival of the holy martyrs Boris and Gleb, there was no joy in the city, but only lamentation, because of our manifold sins and unrighteousness and for the multiplication of our transgressions.

God sent the pagans upon us, not because he held them dear, but to chastise us that we might abstain from evil deeds. He thus punishes us by the incursions of the pagans (for they are the scourge of God) that we may perhaps repent and turn from our wicked way. For this reason, God visits us with affliction upon festal days, just as in this year the first catastrophe, which occurred at Trepol', took place on Ascension Day, while the second occurred on the feast of Boris and Gleb, which is a new festival in Rus'. It was thus that the prophet said, "I will change your feasts to mourning and your songs to lamentation" (*Amos, viii, 10*). For God caused great mourning in our land; our villages and our towns were desolated, and we fled before our foes.

As the prophet said, "Ye shall be slain before your enemies; they that hate you shall oppress you, and ye shall flee when none pursueth you. I will break the arrogance of your pride, and your strength shall be spent in vain. The sword of the stranger shall kill you, your land shall be desolate, and your courts laid waste. (223). For ye are worthless and contrary, and I will walk contrary to you also in anger, saith the Lord God of Israel" (*Lev.* xxvi, 17-33). For the malignant sons of Ishmael burned villages and granges, and consumed many churches with fire.

Let no one marvel at these misfortunes, for condign chastisement ensues wherever many sins are committed. For this reason the world shall ultimately come to its end. For this same reason, malice has now been spread abroad, and our own native land has fallen prey to torment; some of our compatriots are led into servitude, others are slain, and some are even delivered up to vengeance and endure a bitter death. Some tremble as they cast their eyes upon the slain, and others perish of hunger and thirst. Universal sorrow and universal chastisement prevail. Our people suffer many wounds, various woes, and awful torture. Some of them are bound and trampled underfoot, exposed to the chill of winter, and sorely wounded. And what is stranger and more terrible, it is among a Christian nation that this fear and terror and distress has been spread abroad.

Yet it is meet and right that we should be so chastised, and we suffer correction in proportion to our little faith. We have deserved to be delivered into the hands of an alien people, the most fearsome of all the world. Let us therefore cry aloud, "Righteous art thou, oh Lord, and righteous are thy judgments" (*Ps.*, cxviii, 137). Let us say like the thief upon the cross, "We receive the due reward of our deeds" (*Luke*, xxiii, 41). Let us exclaim with Job, "It hath been as the Lord appointed; blessed be the name of the Lord forever" (*Job,* i, 21). Through the incursions of the pagans and the torments which we suffer at their hands may we come to know the Lord whom we have angered. Though glorified by him, we have not glorified him; though honored by him, we have not honored him; though hallowed, (224) we have not understood it; though redeemed, we have not requited our redemption; reborn to righteousness, we have no revered our father. We are punished for our sins, we suffer in proportion to our misdeeds. All our cities are desolate, our villages are laid waste. We traverse the fields where horses, sheep, and cattle once grazed in herds, and behold them desolate. The meadows are grown wild, and have become the lairs of wild beasts. Yet we still hope in the mercy of God; for the Blessed Lord punishes us with kindly intent. "He hath not dealt with us after our sins, nor rewarded us according to our iniquities" (*Ps.*, ciii, 10). It is thus meet for the Blessed Lord to punish us not in strict proportion to the multitude of our iniquities, and even so has the Lord done unto us. For he restored his fallen creatures; he forgave the sin of Adam, and bestowed upon us the bath of purification when he shed his blood for us. When he beheld us living in unrighteousness, he brought upon us the present war and affliction so that even against our will we might find mercy in the life to come. For the soul that suffers in this world shall find in the next mercy and freedom from torment, for the Lord does not twice exact atonement for these transgressions. Ah, his ineffable love for humanity, when he beholds us returning to him even against our will! Ah, the depths of his love for us! Inasmuch as we voluntarily transgressed against his commandments, we must of necessity suffer chastisement against our will, and since we suffer against our will let us at least endure with resignation. When was sorrow known among us heretofore? Yet now our whole life is full of tears. When was sighing ever heard among us? Yet weeping is now spread abroad through all the streets because of the dead whom the infidels have slain.

The Polovcians harried widely, and (225) then returned to Torchesk. The inhabitants were weakened by hunger, and therefore surrendered to the enemy. The Polovcians, upon taking the city, destroyed it by fire, divided the inhabitants, and led them away among their tents to their relatives and kin. A multitude of Christian people were thus reduced to dire distress; sorrowing, tormented, weak with cold, their faces ravaged with hunger, thirst, and misfortune, their bodies black with blows, as they made their painful way, naked and barefoot, upon feet torn with thorns, toward an unknown land and barbarous races. In tears they made answer one to another, saying, "I was of this city," and others, "I came from that village." Thus they tearfully questioned one another, and spoke of their families, as they sighed and lifted up their eyes to the Most High, who knoweth all secrets.

Let no one venture to say that we are hated of God, lest it might be so. For whom does God love, as he has loved us? Whom has he so glorified as he has glorified and exalted us? None. So much the more have we incurred his wrath because, being honored of God before all the rest, we sinned more flagrantly than all the rest. Since we were enlightened before all other men, but knew the Lord's will and scorned it, we are chastised more severely for our correction than other men. For sinner that I am, I anger God much and often, and commit some transgression every day.[290]

On October 1 of this year, Rostislav, the son of Mstislav and the grandson of Izyaslav, passed away, and he was buried (226) on November 16 in the Church of the Holy Virgin of the Tithe.

6602 (1094). Svyatopolk made peace with the Polovcians, and took to wife the daughter of their prince Tugorkan.[291] In this same year, Oleg[292] arrived from Tmutorakan' before Chernigov with a force of

Polovcians. Vladimir fortified himself in the city. Oleg then approached and burned the environs, including the monasteries. Vladimir made peace with Oleg, and departed from Chernigov to occupy his father's throne in Pereyaslavl', while Oleg took possession of the city that had been his own father's. The Polovcians committed many depredations in the vicinity of Chernigov, and Oleg made no attempt to restrain them for the reason that he himself had inspired their raids. This was, in fact, the third time that he had led a force of pagans to attack Rus'. May God forgive his sin, for many Christians were destroyed, while others were taken captive and scattered throughout the lands.

On August 26 of the same year, a plague of locusts attacked Rus', and ate up all the grass and much grain. Such a visitation was unheard of in the early days of Rus', but in consequence of our sins, our eyes beheld it.

In this year, on April 27, at the sixth hour of the night, died Stephen, Bishop of Vladimir, who had formerly been Prior of the Crypt Monastery.[293]

6603 (1095). The Polovcians under the son of Diogenes attacked Greece, and devastated the Grecian territory. (227) The Emperor captured the son of Diogenes and had him blinded.[294] In the same year, the Polovcians Itlar' and Kÿtan came to Vladimir to sue for peace. Itlar' entered the city of Pereyaslavl', while Kÿtan remained between the ramparts with his soldiery. Vladimir gave his son Svyatoslav as a hostage to Kÿtan, while Itlar' remained in the city with an excellent escort. At this time, Slavyata was at Vladimir's court, whither he had come on a special mission from Svyatopolk in Kiev. The retainers of Ratibor[295] now urged upon Vladimir the advisability of massacring Itlar's troop. Vladimir, however, was unwilling to do this deed, and averred that it was unthinkable, since he had given them pledges of safety. But his followers replied, "Oh Prince, there is no sin entailed for you in this deed. They constantly swear oaths to you, and yet they bring incessant ruin on the land of Rus' and constantly shed Christian blood." Vladimir then adopted their advice, and on that same night, sent Slavyata out between the ramparts with a small escort and some Torks. They first stole Svyatoslav away, and then killed Kÿtan and slew his retinue. It was then Saturday night. Itlar' was passing the night in Ratibor's palace with his escort, completely ignorant of the fate of Kÿtan. On Sunday, the following day, about the hour of matins, Ratibor called his followers to arms, (228) and commanded them to heat a room. Vladimir then sent his servant Bandyuk to Itlar's troop with an invitation to join the prince after they had dressed in the heated room and breakfasted with Ratibor. Itlar' accepted the invitation. But when they had entered the heated room, they were locked in. The Russes then climbed atop it, and made a hole in the roof. Then Ol'beg, son of Ratibor, took his bow, and fitting an arrow to it, shot Itlar' through the heart. They also killed his whole escort. Thus Itlar' lost his life in evil fashion on February 24, the first Sunday in Lent, at the first hour of the day.

Svyatopolk and Vladimir summoned Oleg to join them in a foray against the Polovcians. After promising his aid, Oleg actually came, but did not follow the same route as the other princes. Svyatopolk and Vladimir arrived at the Polovcian encampment, captured it, and thus seized and led off to their own country the barbarians' cattle, horses, camels, and slaves. They then were wroth against Oleg because he had not joined their expedition against the pagans. They therefore sent to Oleg this message: "You did not accompany us upon our attack against the pagans who have brought ruin upon Rus'. You have a son of Itlar' at your court. Either kill him or deliver him up to us, for he is an enemy of Rus'." (229) Oleg paid no attention to this demand, and there was enmity between them.

In this same year, the Polovcians appeared before Yur'ev.[296] They besieged the city all summer and had almost reduced it when Svyatopolk succeeded in pacifying them. The Polovcians returned beyond the Ros', and the citizens of Yur'ev abandoned their town and fled to Kiev. Svyatopolk ordered that a town should be built on the hill of Vitichev, and he bade the Bishop Marinus settle there with the people from Yur'ev, Sakov,[297] and other refugees from various localities. The Polovcians then burned the deserted town of Yur'ev.

Toward the close of this year, David, the son of Svyatoslav, left Novgorod for Smolensk. The Novgorodians then went to Rostov in search of Mstislav, the son of Vladimir, and brought him to Novgorod as their prince, at the same time instructing David never to return. David thus returned to Smolensk and settled there, while Mstislav settled at Novgorod.[298] About the same time Izyaslav, the son of Vladimir, arrived at Murom from Kursk.[299] The people of Murom accepted him as their prince, and he took captive the regent of Oleg. On August 28 of this year, locusts came and covered the land to an extent which was terrible to behold. They then went on northward, eating up the grass and grain.

6604 (1096). Svyatopolk and Vladimir summoned Oleg to come to Kiev, that they might conclude a convention as to the defence of Rus' before the bishops and the priors and in the presence of the vassals of their fathers (230) and of the citizens, for the purpose of defending the country against the pagans. Oleg assumed an attitude of arrogance, and made reply that it was not proper for him to submit to the judgment of a bishop, or priors, or of the common people. He was unwilling to join his cousins, becasuse he heeded evil counsel. Svyatopolk and Vladimir then asserted, "You neither attack the pagans nor join us in counsel. You are plotting against us and desire to aid the pagans. God must judge between us."[300] Svyatopolk and Vladimir then marched forth against Oleg to Chernigov. Oleg fled from the city on Saturday, May 3. Svyatopolk and Vladimir accordingly pursued him. Oleg escaped to Starodub,[301] where he barricaded himself in the city. The other princes then laid siege to his position. The inhabitants made effective sallies from the town, while the beleaguers attacked it, so that the casualties were serious on both sides. The conflict thus raged fiercely. The besiegers remained before the town for thirty-three days, until the inhabitants weakened from hunger. Oleg then came forth from the city asking for peace. Svyatopolk and Vladimir granted his request, but directed him first to join his brother David, and then commanded that both of them should report in Kiev before the throne of their fathers and grandfathers, since it was fitting for them to gather and make their covenant at Kiev, the oldest city in the entire country. Oleg promised to follow these instructions, and confirmed his oath by kissing the cross.

(231) At this time, Bonyak and his Polovcians appeared before Kiev on a Sunday evening, and while ravaging the environs, they burned the prince's palace at Berestovo. Kurya and another band of Polovcians ravaged simultaneously the environs of Pereyaslavl', and burned Ust'e[302] on May 24.

Oleg departed from Starodub and arrived at Smolensk. The people of Smolensk would not receive him, so that he went on to Ryazan'. Svyatopolk and Vladimir returned each to his own domain.

In the same month, Tugorkan, the father-in-law of Svyatopolk, came to Pereyaslavl' and laid siege to the city. The inhabitants fortified themselves for resistance, while Svyatopolk and Vladimir advanced against him down the west bank of the Dnieper. They arrived at Zarub[303] and crossed the river without being detected by the Polovcians, for God protected them. They then marshalled their forces and advanced toward the city. When the inhabitants observed their approach, they rejoiced, and came forth to meet them, while the Polovcians were standing on the other bank of the Trubezh in battle array.

Svyatopolk and Vladimir immediately crossed the river to engage the Polovcians. Vladimir first intended to reform his troop, but they did not await his command, and instead spurred up their horses against their adversaries. When the Polovcians beheld their charge, they turned in flight, and our men pursued the foemen, cutting down their opponents. Upon this day the Lord performed a great deliverance. The aliens were thus conquered on July 19. (232) Their prince Tugorkan was killed, and many others of our enemies fell. On the morrow, they found the dead body of Tugorkan, and Svyatopolk, respecting him as his father-in-law even though he was a foe, brought him to Kiev and buried him at Berestovo, between the road to Berestovo and the road to the monastery.

On Friday, the twentieth of this same month, Bonyak, that godless, mangy thief and bandit, came suddenly to Kiev for the second time. The Polovcians almost entered the city, burned the suburbs about the town, and then attacked the monastery. After burning the monastery of Stephen and the villages of Germanus's monastery,[304] they came to the Crypt Monastery while we were resting in our cells after matins, and they howled about the monastery. They planted two standards before the monastery gates, and we fled, some of us behind the building of the monastery, and others to its various rooms. The godless sons of Ishmael slew the brethren in the monastery and wandered about among the cells, breaking down the doors, and they carried off whatever they could find in the various rooms. Then the set fire to the shrine of the Holy Virgin. Upon arriving before the church, they thus set fire to the south (233) and the north doors, and upon making their way into the chapel near the grave of Theodosius, they seized the eikons, burned the doors, and blasphemed against God and our faith. But God suffered their iniquities because their sins and their transgressions were not completed. Thus they said, "Where is their God? Let him come and deliver them," and they made other blasphemous remarks about the holy eikons, which they mocked, because they did not know that God punishes his servants by means of barbarian incursions that they may appear as gold which has been tried in the furnace. The Christians, by virtue of their many sufferings and oppressions, shall enter the Kingdom of Heaven, but these pagans and blasphemers, who in this world enjoy happiness and increase, shall suffer torment at the hand of the devil, since they are destined to everlasting fire.

Then they burned the red palace which the pious Prince Vladimir had constructed upon the hill called Vÿdobÿchi and consumed the whole of it with fire. Wherefore let us imitate the prophet David, and exclaim, "Oh Lord my God, make them as a whirling dust, as a fire before the face of the wind which consumeth the forests, so shalt thou pursue them with thy storm. Fill their countenances with shame" (*Ps.*, lxxxiii, 14-17). For they polluted and burned thy sacred dwelling, the monastery of thy Mother, and the relics of thy servants. The godless sons of Ishmael, (234) who had been sent as a chastisement to the Christians, even killed with the sword some of our brethren.

They came forth from the desert of Yathrib in the northeast. Four races of them issued forth: Torkmens, Pechenegs, Torks, and Polovcians. Methodius[305] relates concerning them that eight nations fled when Gideon massacred them; eight fled into the desert, and four he massacred. Others say[306] that they are the sons of Ammon, but this is not true, for the Caspians are the sons of Moab, while the Bulgars are the sons of Ammon. But the Saracens descended from Ishmael became known as the sons of Sarah, and called themselves *Sarakÿne,* that is to say, "We are descendants of Sarah." Likewise the Caspians and the Bulgars are descended from the daughters of Lot, who conceived by their father, so that their race is unclean. Ishmael begot twelve sons, from whom are descended the Torkmens, the Pechenegs, the Torks, and the Cumans or Polovcians, who came from the desert. After these eight races, at the end of the world, shall come forth the unclean peoples shut in the mountain by Alexander of Macedon.

I wish at this point to recount a story which I heard four years ago, and which was told to me by Gyuryata Rogovich of Novgorod: "I sent my servant," said he, "to the Pechera, a people who pay tribute (235) to Novgorod. When he arrived among them, he went on among the Yugra. The latter are an alien people dwelling in the north with the Samoyedes.[307] The Yugra said to my servant, 'We have encountered a strange marvel, with which we had not until recently been acquainted. This occurrence took place three years ago. There are certain mountains which slope down to an arm of the sea, and their height reaches to the heavens. Within these mountains are heard great cries and the sound of voices; those within are cutting their way out. In that mountain, a small opening has been pierced through which they converse, but their language is unintelligible. They point, however, at iron objects, and make gestures as if to ask for them. If given a knife or an axe, they supply furs in return. The road to these mountains is impassable with precipices, snow, and forests. Hence we do not always reach them, and they are also far to the north.'"

Then I said to Gyuryata, "These are the peoples shut up by Alexander of Macedon. As Methodius of Patara says of them, 'He penetrated the eastern countries as far as the sea called the Land of the Sun, and he saw there unclean peoples of the race of Japheth. When he beheld their uncleanness, he marvelled. They ate every nauseous thing, such as gnats, flies, cats, and serpents. They did not bury their dead, but ate them, along with the fruit of abortions (236) and all sorts of impure beasts. On beholding this, Alexander was afraid lest, as they multiplied, they might corrupt the earth. So he drove them to high mountains in the regions of the north, and by God's commandment, the mountains enclosed them round above save for a space of twelve ells. Gates of brass were erected there, and were covered with indestructible metal. They cannot be destroyed by fire, for it is the nature of this metal that fire cannot consume it, nor can iron take hold upon it. Hereafter, at the end of the world, eight peoples shall come forth from the desert of Yathrib, and these corrupt nations, which dwell in the northern mountains, shall also issue forth at God's command."[308]

But let us return to the topic we were discussing. When Oleg promised to join his brother David in Smolensk and to return to Kiev with him and there conclude a treaty of peace, he had no intention of keeping his promise, but as soon as he arrived at Smolensk, he gathered troops and went on to Murom, over which then ruled Izyaslav, the son of Vladimir.[309] When it became known to Izyaslav that Oleg was approaching Murom, he straightway summoned troops from Suzdal', Rostov,[310] and Beloozero,[311] and thus collected a large force. Oleg then sent envoys to Izyaslav with the message, "Return (237) to your own father's district in Rostov, for this is my father's territory here. I intend to abide here and settle my account with your father, for he expelled me from my father's city. Are you unwilling to let me eat my daily bread here?"[312]

Izyaslav relied on the number of his troops and paid no attention to this warning. Oleg counted, however, on his rights (for he was justified in his contention), and marched toward the city with his troops. Izyaslav took up his position on the plain before the town. Oleg then approached him with his force; the two parties met, and a fierce battle ensued. Izyaslav, the son of Vladimir and the grandson of Vsevolod, was thus slain on September 6. His followers fled, some through the forest and others into the city. Oleg entered the town and was well received by the citizens. They took up Izyaslav's body, and after laying him first in the Monastery of the Redeemer, they carried him thence to Novgorod, where they buried him in St. Sophia on the left side.

After the capture of the city, Oleg arrested the men of Rostov, Beloozero, and Suzdal', fettered them, and then marched on Suzdal'.

When he arrived there, the inhabitants surrendered to him. Oleg, after pacifying the city, seized some inhabitants, and banished others, confiscating their property. He then went on to Rostov, and the inhabitants surrendered to him. He thus won the whole district of Murom and Rostov, appointed regents in each city, and began to exact tribute.

Mstislav then sent messengers to him from Novgorod and bade him depart from Suzdal' to Murom, instead of settling in another's domain. Mstislav also promised to intercede with Vladimir (238) in Oleg's behalf so as to effect a reconciliation between the two princes. He added that Oleg's killing of his brother Izyaslav was not a matter for surprise, since both kings and commons meet their end in battles. Oleg by no means desired such a reconciliation, but rather had in mind the seizure of Novgorod as well. He therefore sent forth his brother Yaroslav[313] as an outpost, and took up his position on the plain by Rostov.

After deliberation with the men of Novgorod, Mstislav despatched Dobrÿnya, son of Raguel, before him as a vanguard. Dobrÿnya first seized Oleg's tax-collectors. When Yaroslav, who was stationed on the Medveditsa[314] as outpost, heard how he had seized these tax-collectors, he fled by night, and when he returned to Oleg in his flight, he informed him that Mstislav was on his way and that the tax-collectors had been seized. Oleg departed straightway for Rostov, and when Mstislav arrived at the Volga, he was duly informed of Oleg's departure thither. Mstislav then pursued him. Oleg went on to Suzdal', and upon hearing that Mstislav was on his trail, he directed that the city should be burned. Only the structure of the Crypt Monastery survived, together with the Church of St. Demetrius, which Ephraim had donated together with certain villages.[315] Oleg escaped thence to Murom, Mstislav eventually arrived at Suzdal', and while he was making a halt there, he sent envoys to Oleg and asked for peace, saying, "I am your junior. Send to my father and return to him the followers whom you seized. I will then obey you in every respect." Oleg replied to him with a pretence of peaceful intent. Mstislav accepted his pretence as sincerity, and scattered his retainers among the villages.

Then came the week of St. Theodore (239) just before Lent. On the Saturday of this week, while Mstislav was at dinner, he received news that Oleg was on the Klyaz'ma,[316] for he had approached undetected. Mstislav had had confidence in his word and had set no watches. But God knows how to save his pious followers from treachery. Oleg thus halted at the Klyaz'ma, expecting that Mstislav would flee. On that day and the next, Mstislav's retainers rallied about him, comprising men from Novgorod, Rostov, and Beloozero. Mstislav marshalled his troop and took his position before the city. Oleg did not advance against Mstislav nor did Mstislav advance against Oleg, and they stood over against each other for four days.

News then came to Mstislav that his father had despatched his brother Vyacheslav[317] with Polovcian support. Vyacheslav arrived on the Thursday after St. Theodore's week, and therefore during the first week of Lent. On Friday, Oleg marshalled his forces and approached the town, while Mstislav went out to meet him with men of Novgorod and Rostov. Mstislav entrusted Vladimir's standard to a Polovcian named Kunuy, and detailing some foot-soldiers to his command, posted him on the right wing. Kunuy took Vladimir's standard and led on his infantry. When Oleg beheld the standard, he was terrified, and fear beset him and his soldiery. They then joined battle against each other, Oleg against Mstislav and Yaroslav against Vyacheslav. Mstislav (240) crossed a burnt clearing with the men of Novgorod, and they clashed with the enemy at Kulachek.[318] The combat was violent, and Mstislav began to win the upper hand. When Oleg saw how the standard of Vladimir advanced, he began to fall back. He finally fled in terror, and Mstislav won the victory. Oleg escaped to Murom, and after fortifying Yaroslav there, he went on to Ryazan'.[319] Mstislav then arrived at Murom, made peace with the inhabitants, and after releasing his men from Rostov and Suzdal', pursued Oleg to Ryazan'.

Oleg escaped from that city, so that Mstislav on his arrival made peace with the inhabitants, and liberated those of his own subjects whom Oleg had thrown into prison. He then sent messages to Oleg, saying, "Flee no more, but rather approach your brethren with the request that they may not expel you from Rus'. I shall intervene with my father in your behalf." Oleg promised to act accordingly. Mstislav, upon returning again to Suzdal', departed thence to his own city of Novgorod, accompanied by the prayers of the reverend Bishop Nikita.[320] These events occurred at the close of the year 6604 (1096), the fourth of the indiction.[321]

(256) 6605 (1097). Svyatopolk, Vladimir, David son of Igor', Vasil'ko son of Rostislav, David son of Svyatoslav, and Oleg his brother met at Lyubech[322] to make peace, and said to one another, "Why do we ruin the land of Rus' by our continued strife against one another? The Polovcians harass our country in divers fashions, and rejoice that war is waged among us. Let us rather hereafter be united in spirit and watch over the land of Rus', and let each (257) of us guard his own domain; with Svyatopolk retaining Kiev, the heritage of Izyaslav, while Vladimir holds the domain of Vsevolod, and David,

Oleg, and Yaroslav between them possess that of Svyatoslav. Let the domains apportioned by Vsevolod stand, leaving the city of Vladimir in the hands of David, while the city Peremÿshl' belongs to Volodar' son of Rostislav, and Vasil'ko son of Rostislav holds Terebovl."[323] On this convention they took oath to the effect that, if any one of them should thereafter attack another, all the rest, with the aid of the Holy Cross, would be against the aggressor. Thus they all said, "May the Holy Cross and the entire land of Rus' be against him," and having taken oath, returned each to his domain. Accompanied by David, Svyatopolk arrived in Kiev, and all the people rejoiced. There was only the devil to be distressed by this display of affection.[324]

Satan now incited certain men to report to David son of Igor'[325] that Vladimir was conspiring with Vasil'ko against Svyatopolk and against himself. David gave credence to their false words, and endeavored to stir up Svyatopolk against Vasil'ko, saying, "Who killed your brother Yaropolk? Now he plots against me and against you, and has conspired with Vladimir. Take thought for your own head." Svyatopolk was thus perturbed, and wondered whether these allegations were true or false; he was uncertain, and replied to David, "If you speak aright, may God be your witness. But if you speak from motives of jealousy only God will punish you for it."

Svyatopolk was concerned for his brother and himself, and wondered whether the rumor were true. He finally believed David, who thus deceived Svyatopolk, and the two of them set out to plot (258) against Vasil'ko.[326] Now Vasil'ko and Vladimir were ignorant of this fact. David remarked, however, that if he and Svyatopolk did not seize Vasil'ko, Svyatopolk would not be sure of Kiev, nor he himself of Vladimir [Volÿnsk]. And Svyatopolk believed him.

Vasil'ko arrived on November 4, crossed over to Vÿdubichi, and went to make his reverence to St. Michael in the monastery, where he also supped. He pitched his camp on the Ruditsa. At evening, he returned to his camp. When it was morning, Svyatopolk urged him by messenger not to depart before his name-day. Vasil'ko refused, urging that he could not wait that long, or there would be disorder in his domain. Then David begged him not to depart, but rather to obey his elder cousin. Vasil'ko, however, was still reluctant to comply.

Then David remarked to Svyatopolk, "See, he sets no store by you, though he is in your power. If he departs to his domain, you shall see whether he does not seize your cities of Turov and Pinsk,[327] and other towns which belong to you; then you will perhaps remember my words. Call the men of Kiev and take him prisoner; then deliver him over to me." Svyatopolk followed his advice, and sent word to Vasil'ko, saying, "If you are unwilling to remain until my name-day, at least come and greet me now, and then we shall meet with David." Vasil'ko promised to go, and did not perceive the treachery which David was planning against him. Vasil'ko thus mounted his horse and rode off. One of his servants then met him and urged him not to go, because the princes were plotting to take him prisoner. But Vasil'ko heeded him not, as he thought (259) to himself, "How can they intend to take me prisoner? They have just sworn that if any one of us should attack another, the Holy Cross and all of us should be against him." Having thus reflected, he crossed himself, and said, "God's will be done."

He thus rode with a small escort to the Prince's palace. Svyatopolk came out to meet him, and they went into the hall. David entered, and all sat down. Then Svyatopolk begged Vasil'ko to remain until his name-day. Vasil'ko replied, "I cannot remain, cousin; I have already ordered my camp to move forward." David sat silent as if struck dumb, till Svyatopolk invited Vasil'ko to breakfast with them, and Vasil'ko accepted. Then Svyatopolk said, "Remain seated here a moment while I go out and make certain disposition." He thus went out, leaving David and Vasil'ko alone together. Vasil'ko tried to open a conversation with David, but there was no voice nor hearing in him, for he was afraid, and had treachery in his heart. After he had sat awhile, he inquired where his cousin was. The answer was given that he was standing in the vestibule. David then rose and asked Vasil'ko to remain seated while he sent in search of Svyatopolk. He thus stood up and went thence. When David had thus gone out, others seized upon Vasil'ko and fettered him with double fetters, setting guards over him by night. This treachery took place on November 5.

In the morning, Svyatopolk assembled the boyars and the men of Kiev and informed them of what David had told him, to the effect that Vasil'ko had been responsible for his brother's death, was plotting with Vladimir against him, and intended to kill him and seize his cities. The boyars and the populace replied, (260) "It behooves you, oh Prince, to protect your own life. If David spoke aright, let Vasil'ko suffer the penalty. If David has spoken falsely, let him suffer the vengeance of God and answer before God." When the priors heard of the circumstances, they interceded with Svyatopolk in Vasil'ko's behalf, but he protested that it was all David's affair.[328] When David heard of all this, he urged that Vasil'ko should be blinded, on the ground that if Svyatopolk did nothing and released Vasil'ko, neither he himself nor

Svyatopolk would be able to retain their thrones much longer. Svyatopolk was in favor of releasing him, but David kept close watch over him and would not consent.

During the night, they thus took Vasil'ko to Belgorod, which is a small town ten versts from Kiev. They transported him fettered in a cart, and after removing him from the vehicle, they led him into a small house. As he sat there, Vasil'ko saw a Tork sharpening a knife, and then comprehending that they intended blinding him, he cried out to God with loud weeping and groaning. Then came the emissaries of Svyatopolk and David: Snovid, the son of Izech, the squire of Svyatopolk, and Dmitr, David's squire, and they laid a rug upon the floor. After they had spread it, they seized Vasil'ko and endeavored to overthrow him. He offered a violent resistance, so that they could not throw him. Then others came and cast him down. They bound him, and laid upon his chest a slab taken from the hearth. Though Snovid, the son of Izech, sat at one end and Dmitr at the other, they still could not hold him down. (261) Then two other men came, and after taking a second slab from the hearth, they too sat upon him, and weighed upon him so heavily that his chest cracked. Then a Tork, Berendi by name, a shepherd of Svyatopolk, came up with his knife and though intending to strike him in the eye, missed the eye entirely and cut his face. This scar Vasil'ko bears to this day. Afterward, however, he struck him in one eye, and took out the pupil, and then in the other eye, and also removed the pupil of the latter.

At that moment Vasil'ko lay as if dead. They raised him in the rug, laid him fainting in the wagon, and carried him off to Vladimir. While he was being thus transported, they happened to halt with him at a market place after they had crossed the bridge at the town of Zvizhden'.[329] They took off his bloody shirt, and gave it to a priest's wife to wash. After she had washed it, the woman put it on him while the others were eating, and she began to weep, for he was as if dead. He heard her weeping, and inquired where he was. They replied that the town was Zvizhden'. He then begged for water. They gave him some, and after he had drunk the water, full consciousness returned to him. He remembered what had occurred, and feeling his shirt, he lamented, "Why did you take it from me? I had rather have met my death and stood before God in this bloody shirt."

When they had eaten, they rode on swiftly in the cart with him, and over a rough road, for it was then the month of Gruden, called November. They arrived with him at Vladimir (262) on the sixth day. David accompanied them, and behaved as if he had captured some prize. They quartered Vasil'ko in the Vakeev palace, and placed over him a guard of thirty men, as well as two servants of the Prince named Ulan and Kolchko.

When Vladimir learned that Vasil'ko was captured and blinded, he was horror-struck, and bursting into tears declared, "Such a crime as this has never been perpetrated in Rus' in the time of either our grandfathers or our fathers." Then he immediately sent messages to David and Oleg,[330] the sons of Svyatoslav, saying, "Come forthwith to Gorodets, that we may avenge this crime which has occurred in the land of Rus' among us kinsmen, and has cast a sword among us. If we do not avenge this deed, a greater crime will rise against us. Brother will begin to kill brother, so that the land of Rus' will perish, and our foes the Polovcians will come and take it."

When David and Oleg heard these words, they were deeply troubled and wept, saying, "Such a thing never before happened in our family." They straightway collected troops and joined Vladimir. While Vladimir and his troops remained in a forest, he and David and Oleg sent messengers to inquire of Svyatopolk, "What is this crime you have committed in the land of Rus', and thus have cast a sword among us? (263) Why have you blinded your cousin? If there was any charge against him, you should have accused him before us, and after properly convicting him you could then have treated him as he deserved. Now make plain this fault for which you so punished him."

Svyatopolk replied, "David, the son of Igor', said to me, 'Vasil'ko killed your brother Yaropolk, and likewise intends to kill you and seize your domain of Turov, Pinsk, Brest and the Pogorina.[331] He has sworn an oath with Vladimir that Vladimir shall reign in Kiev and he himself in the city of Vladimir.' I had to take my precautions, but it was David and not I who blinded him and carried him home." Then the envoys of Vladimir, David, and Oleg made answer, "Do not seek to excuse yourself for this crime on the ground that David did the actual blinding. Vasil'ko was not seized and blinded in David's city, but in your own." When they had thus spoken, they departed.

On the morrow, when the princes intended crossing the Dnieper to attack Svyatopolk, the latter planned to escape from Kiev. The inhabitants would not permit his departure, but sent Vsevolod's widow[332] and the Metropolitan Nicholas[333] to Vladimir with the plea, "We beseech you, oh Prince, and your brethren not to ruin the land of Rus'. For if you begin hostilities among yourselves, the pagans will rejoice and seize our country which was won by your sires and grandsires who, by waging war with great courage (264) throughout the land of Rus' added other territories to it. But you are in a fair way to destroy the whole country." The widow of Vsevolod and the Metropolitan came into the presence of Vladimir and made known their plea, expressing the prayer of the people of Kiev that he would conclude a peace, guard the land of Rus', and keep up the good fight against the pagans.

When Vladimir heard their request, he broke into tears and exclaimed, "Verily our fathers and our grandsires took thought for this land which we are trying to destroy." He inclined to the prayer of the Princess, and honored her as his mother out of pious memory of his father. For he had been very dear to his father, and never disobeyed him in any respect either during his lifetime or after his decease. Thus he obeyed her as he was bound to obey his mother, and he respected the Metropolitan as well (for he revered ecclesiastical rank), and did not disregard his plea. Vladimir was indeed considerate. He loved the metropolitans, the bishops, and the priors; and still more the monastic orders and the monks. Those who came to him in need he provided with food and drink as a mother aids her children. If he saw anyone uproarious or committing some excess, he did not condemn him, but rebuked all persons affably. But let us return to our subject.

When the Princess had visited Vladimir, she returned to Kiev, and recounted all his words to Svyatopolk and the inhabitants, announcing that there would be peace. The princes then exchanged communications, and agreed to suggest to Svyatopolk (265) that if David was responsible for the crime, then Svyatopolk should march against him and either capture him or drive him into exile. Svyatopolk accepted this proposal, so that all joined in an oath and thus made peace once more.

While Vasil'ko was at Vladimir [Volÿnsk] in the aforementioned place, and Lent was approaching, and while I was myself there at Vladimir, Prince David sent for me during a certain evening, and I entered his presence. His retainers sat around him, and he offered me a seat. He then remarked, "Vasil'ko spoke this evening to Ulan and Kolchko saying, 'I hear that Vladimir and Svyatopolk are marching against David. If David would take my advice, he would send an envoy to Vladimir and beg him to turn back.' For I know what he thus discussed with them. For that reason, I choose you, Vasiliy,[334] as my messenger. Go to your namesake Vasil'ko and bespeak him thus in my behalf: 'If you will send your messenger and Vladimir turns back, then I will give you any city you desire, either Vsevolozh', Shepol', or Peremil'."³³⁵ I then went to Vasil'ko and reported to him all the words of David. He replied, "As a matter of fact, I did not utter these words. But I hope in God, and shall indeed send a messenger, that they may not shed blood for my sake. I am indeed surprised that he promises me his own city, but Terebovl' is mine, my own domain, now and forever." Thus it came about that he soon recovered his domain. He then said to me, "Go to David and tell him to send Kul'mey to me; I will despatch him to Vladimir."

David did not heed his request, (266) but instead sent back word through me that Kul'mey was not there. Then Vasil'ko said to me, "Sit with me a little while." He thus bade his servant leave us, and as we sat together he remarked, "I hear that David wishes to surrender me to the Poles. He is not even satisfied with my blood, and desires the further satisfaction of delivering me up to them, for I have done the Poles much harm, and would gladly have done them still more to avenge the land of Rus'. Yet even if he does surrender me to the Poles, I do not fear death. But this much I tell you: verily God has brought all this upon me for my pride, since, when the news came to me that the Berendiches,³³⁶ the Pechenegs, and the Torks were approaching, I thought that, when they should all be subject to me, I might request my kinsmen Volodar' and David to lend me their younger retainers, while they themselves should drink and be happy. Then I hoped to invade Poland in winter and summer, subject the country of Poland, and thus avenge the land of Rus'. I also planned to overcome the Danube Bulgarians and subject them to my authority. After that, I intended to request Svyatopolk and Vladimir to allow me to attack the Polovcians, that I might either win fame or lay down my life for our country. There was no other thought in my heart against either Svyatopolk or David, and I swear by God and his judgment that I did not plan any evil in any respect against my kinsmen, and it is only for my pride that God has humbled and humiliated me."

(267) Thereafter, when Easter was come, David set out with the intention of seizing Vasil'ko's domains. Volodar', Vasil'ko's brother, met him at Buzh'sk.³³⁷ David did not dare to withstand him, but barricaded himself in Buzh'sk, while Volodar' laid siege to him in the city. Then Volodar' demanded, "Why have you done evil and why do you not repent? Bear in mind what crimes you have committed." Then David endeavored to pass the blame upon Svyatopolk with the excuse, "Did I commit this crime, or was it perpetrated in my city? I was afraid that they might seize me and deal with me in the same way.

I had to participate in their counsels since I was in their power." Volodar' replied, "God is witness to that. But now release my brother, and I will make peace with you."

David rejoiced, and sent for Vasil'ko. He thus led him forth and turned him over to Volodar', and made peace, after which they parted. Vasil'ko settled at Terebovl', while David went to the city of Vladimir, and when spring was come, Volodar' and Vasil'ko marched to attack David. They arrived at Vsevolozh', while David fortified his position at Vladimir. After laying siege to Vsevolozh', the princes captured the city by storm and set fire to it. As the inhabitants fled before the flames, Vasil'ko commanded that they should all be slain. Thus he took revenge upon innocent people, and shed innocent blood.

They arrived soon thereafter at Vladimir, where David was fortified, and laid siege to the city. (268) They then sent messages to the inhabitants, declaring, "We have not come to attack your city, nor yourselves, but our hostility is directed against our enemies Turyak, Lazar', and Vasiliy, for they gave evil advice to David, and in accordance with their counsel he has committed this crime. If you wish to take up arms in their behalf, we are ready to fight. But you would be better advised to surrender our enemies." The citizens, upon the receipt of this message, called an assembly, and demanded of David that he should surrendeer the fugitives. They made it clear that while they were willing to fight for him, they would not take up arms for the fugitives, and threatened to open the city gates, leaving him to shift for himself. David was thus under the necessity of surrendering the fugitives. He pointed out, however, that they were not in the city, as he had sent them to Lutsk. After they had gone to Lutsk, Turyak fled to Kiev, while Lazar' and Vasiliy returned to Turiysk.[338] When the inhabitants of Vladimir heard that they were in Turiysk, they cried out upon David, and demanded that he should yield up those men whom the princes desired of him, or else they would surrender the city. David then obeyed, and brought forth Lazar' and Vasiliy to deliver them up. On Sunday, peace was concluded, and at dawn on the following day Vasiliy and Lazar' were hanged. Vasil'ko's men shot at them with arrows, and then left the city. Thus Vasil'ko exacted a second revenge, which was not fair to do, since God was the avenger, and Vasil'ko should have entrusted his vengeance to God. For the prophet has said, "I will render vengeance to mine enemies, and will reward them that hate me" (*Deut*, xxxii, 41), even as he avenges and ever shall avenge the blood of his children, (269) and shall perform vengeance upon his enemies and them that hate him.

When the foemen had left the city, the inhabitants cut down the bodies and burned them. Since Svyatopolk had promised to expel David, he went to Brest for Polish aid. When David heard of his journey, he set out to visit Vladislav[339] in Poland in search of assistance. The Poles promised to aid him, and upon the receipt of fifty *grivnÿ* of gold, they proposed that he should go with them to Brest and surprise Svyatopolk while he slept, and thus effect a reconciliation between him and Svyatopolk. David followed their suggestion and accompanied Vladislav to Brest. Svyatopolk remained within the city, while the Poles stopped by the river Bug. Svyatopolk then made a compact with the Poles, and paid them large sums to turn against David. Vladislav thereupon informed David that Svyatopolk had not been amenable to his persuasion, and therefore recommended that he return home. David accordingly went back to Vladimir.

In accordance with his convention with the Poles, Svyatopolk moved on to Pinsk[340] after he had summoned his troops. He arrived at Dorogobuzh[341] and there waited his soldiery. He then marched against David in Vladimir. David fortified himself within the city, and expected help from the Poles against Svyatopolk, for they had promised to be his allies if the Russian princes attacked him. But they were deceiving him, since they had received gold from both David and Svyatopolk. Svyatopolk laid siege to the city and remained before it seven weeks. Then David entreated him to let him depart from the city. Svyatopolk gave him his promise to this effect, and after they had exchanged pledges, David left the city and went to Cherven.

Svyatopolk entered the city on Holy Saturday, and David fled into Poland. After expelling David, Svyatopolk seriously considered an attack upon Volodar' and Vasil'ko, on the ground that this was the domain of his father and his brother, and therefore marched forth against them. (270) When Volodar' and Vasil'ko heard of this action, they proceeded to meet him, carrying with them the cross upon which he had sworn that he had come only to attack David, but was desirous of maintaining peaceful and friendly relations with them. Svyatopolk, notwithstanding, violated his oath, since he trusted in the number of his troops. The two parties met on the Rozhne plain,[342] where both forces were drawn up, and Vasil'ko lifted up the cross, crying, "Here is the cross upon which you swore. First you stole the sight of my eyes, and now you desire to take my life as well. May this cross be between us!" They thus advanced to battle, and as the armies met, many pious men beheld the Cross lifted high above Vasil'ko's forces. Since the conflict was violent and the casualties numerous on both sides,

Svyatopolk, upon noticing that the combat was fierce, took to flight, and escaped to the city of Vladimir. After their victory, Volodar' and Vasil'ko remained on the spot and made no move, since they considered it advisable to remain within their boundaries.

Svyatopolk thus made good his escape to Vladimir, accompanied by his two sons, the two sons of Yaropolk, Svyatosha son of David Svyatoslavich,[343] and the rest of his retainers. Svyatopolk set up as prince in Vladimir Mstislav, who had been borne to him by a concubine, and then despatched Yaroslav among the Hungarians to incite them against Volodar', while he himself departed for Kiev. Yaroslav, the son of Svyatopolk, thus returned with Hungarian reinforcements, along with King Koloman[344] and two bishops, and they besieged Peremÿshl' on the Vyagro, while Volodar' fortified himself within the town.

At this time David, after returning from Poland, had left his wife with Volodar' and departed among the Polovcians. He was met by Bonyak, however, so David turned back, and the two of them attacked the Hungarians. While on their journey, they pitched a bivouac, and at midnight Bonyak arose and rode away from the troops. (271) He straightway began to howl like a wolf, till first one and then many wolves answered him with their howls. Bonyak then returned to camp and announced to David that on the morrow they would celebrate a victory over the Hungarians.

The next day Bonyak marshalled his troops; David had one hundred men and he himself three hundred. He divided them into three troops and attacked the Hungarians. He sent Altunopa as a vanguard with fifty men, stationed David under the standard, and split his own force into two parts with fifty in each section. The Hungarians were aligned in corps, for their number was one hundred thousand. Altunopa attacked the first corps, and after his troop had shot their arrows, they fled before the Hungarians, who gave chase. In their course, they passed in front of Bonyak, who wheeled and attacked them from the rear. Altunopa then faced about, and they did not allow the Hungarians to give ground, but thus killed a great number as they drove them back and forth. Bonyak divided his men into three sections and they drove the Hungarians hither and yon as a falcon drives magpies.

The Hungarians fled, and many were drowned, some in the Vyagro and others in the San. As they fled along the San toward the mountains, they jostled each other in their haste, and the enemy pursued them for two days as he cut them down. Their Bishop Kupan and many of their boyars there met their deaths, for it was commonly reported that forty thousand of them perished. Yaroslav[345] escaped to

Poland and arrived safely at Brest, while David, after taking Suteysk and Cherven, came suddenly and attacked the people of Vladimir.

Mstislav shut himself up in the city with his garrison, for he had with him men of Brest, Pinsk, and Vygoshev.[346] David persisted in his siege, and made frequent attacks. On one occasion, his troops advanced beneath the very towers of the city, while the inhabitants were fighting from the city wall, and as both sides shot at each other, (272) the arrows fell thick as rain. Just as Mstislav was drawing his bow, he was suddenly stricken under the arm-pit by an arrow which had come through a cranny in a board upon the wall. He was carried away, and died in the course of that same night. His retainers hid his body for three days, but on the fourth they reported his death to the assembly. The inhabitants then lamented, "Our prince is dead. If we surrender, then Svyatopolk will kill us all." They then sent a message to Svyatopolk, declaring, "Your son is slain and we ourselves are weak with hunger. If you do not relieve us, the people will surrender, since they cannot endure famine."

Svyatopolk then sent Putyata, his general, and Putyata marched with his followers to Lutsk to meet Svyatosha, the son of David [of Chernigov]. The latter had certain retainers of David [of Vladimir-Volynsk] there with him, for he had entered into a pact with David which entailed his promise to inform David if Svyatopolk should attack him. Svyatosha, however, did not keep his promise, but arrested David's retainers, and set out himself to attack David. Svyatosha and Putyata arrived at Vladimir on August 5, while David's forces were besieging the city. David was taking his noonday siesta, and they fell upon his army and cut it to pieces. The inhabitants thereupon sallied out from the city, and began a massacre of David's soldiery. Both David and Mstislav his nephew fled. Svyatosha and Putyata then took possession of the city, and appointed Vasiliy as Svyatopolk's regent. Svyatosha then returned to Lutsk and Putyata to Kiev.

David escaped to the Polovcians, among whom Bonyak received him. The two of them advanced to attack Svyatosha in Lutsk, but made peace after they had laid siege to him in his city. Svyatosha then left his city and journeyed to his father in Chernigov. David thereupon seized Lutsk, and then departed thence to the city of Vladimir. Vasiliy the Regent immediately took to flight, so that David (273) seized Vladimir and settled there as prince. In the following year, Svyatopolk, Vladimir, David, and Oleg won over to their cause David the son of Igor', but instead of assigning him the domain of Vladimir, they appointed him to Dorogobuzh, where he died. Thereupon Svyatopolk took possession of Vladimir, and established there as prince his son Yaroslav.

6606 (1098). Vladimir, David, and Oleg marched forth against Svyatopolk and halted at Gorodets,[347] where they made peace, as I mentioned in the account for the previous year.

6607 (1099). Svyatopolk advanced toward Vladimir [Volÿnsk] to attack David, and drove him into Poland. In this year, the Hungarians were defeated near Peremÿshl'. In this year, Mstislav, the son of Svyatopolk, was killed in Vladimir on July 12.

6608 (1100). On June 10, Mstislav[348] departed from David[349] to the seacoast. On August 10 of the same year, the cousins Svyatopolk, Vladimir and David, and Oleg concluded peace among themselves at Uvetichi.[350] At the same place, on the thirtieth day of the same month, the cousins Svyatopolk, Vladimir, David, and Oleg all met together, and David, the son of Igor', came before them and said, "Why have you summoned me? Behold, I am here. Who is dissatisfied with me?" Vladimir then answered him, "You have sent us this message: 'I desire, my cousins, to come before you and complain of my wrongs.' You now have come before us, and are seated upon the same rug with your cousins. Why do you not accuse any one of us against whom you have cause for complaint?" But David answered nought. All the kinsmen then mounted (274) their horses. Svyatopolk stood there with his retainers, and David and Oleg with theirs, at some little distance apart, while David, the son of Igor', sat by himself. They refused him further access to their presence, but considered him privately by themselves. After some consultation, they sent their messengers to David: Svyatopolk despatched Putyata, Vladimir detailed Orogost' and Ratibor, and David and Oleg deputed Torchin. These emissaries came to David and reported, "This is the decision of your cousins in your regard: they do not wish to grant you the domain of Vladimir, for the reason that you cast a sword among them in a fashion hitherto unknown in the land of Rus'. They will not take you prisoner or offer you any harm, but they grant you the privilege of settling in the fortress of Buzh'sk. Svyatopolk bestows upon you Duben and Chertorÿysk, while Vladimir pays you two hundred *grivnÿ,* and David and Oleg the same amount between them.[351] The princes then sent their deputies to Volodar' and Vasil'ko, with instructions that Volodar' should take Vasil'ko under his charge, and share with him the single domain of Peremÿshl'. They were to remain there together, but in case Vasil'ko was unfavorable to this arrangement, he was to rejoin the princes so that they might care for him. Volodar' was also instructed to return their slaves and peasants. Neither Volodar' nor Vasil'ko heeded these instructions. David, however, settled at Buzh'sk, and subsequently Svyatopolk gave him Dorogobuzh, where he died. The domain of Vladimir [Volÿnsk] he assigned to his son Yaroslav.

6609 (1101). Vseslav, the prince of Polotsk, died on Wednesday, April 14, at the ninth hour of the day.[352] In the same year, (275) Yaroslav, the son of Yaropolk prepared war at Brest. Svyatopolk advanced to attack him, besieged him in his city, and after capturing him, shackled him and brought him to Kiev. The Metropolitan and the priors interceded in his behalf, persuaded Svyatopolk to pardon him, and then conducted him to the tomb of Sts. Boris and Gleb, where they removed his shackles and released him. In the same year, all the cousins met at the Zolot'cha:[353] Svyatopolk, Vladimir, David, Oleg, and Yaroslav, the brother of the two last-mentioned.[354] The Polovcians sent messages from all their princes to the cousins with propositions of peace. The Russian princes replied that if they desired peace, a parley might be held at Sakov.[355] The Polovcians accepted the suggestion, and assembled at Sakov. Peace was there concluded with the Polovcians, and hostages were exchanged upon September 15, after which they parted company.

6610 (1102). Yaroslav, the son of Yaropolk, fled from Kiev on October 1. At the close of the same month, Yaroslav the son of Svyatopolk lured Yaroslav the son of Yaropolk into an ambush, captured him thus on the Nura,[356] and brought him before his father Svyatopolk. They thus laid him in chains. On December 20 of the same year, Mstislav, the son of Vladimir, arrived at Kiev with a suite of Novgorodians, since Svyatopolk had made an agreement with Vladimir whereby Svyatopolk should take over Novgorod and appoint his own son as prince there, while Vladimir was to appoint his own son prince in the domain of Vladimir. Mstislav thus arrived at Kiev, and settled in a house. The men of the city of Vladimir then called to Svyatopolk's attention that Vladimir had sent forward his son, and that the Novgorodians had already arrived. They therefore urged that the latter should take Svyatopolk's son with them and return to Novgorod, (276) while Mstislav should depart for Vladimir. The men from Novgorod then spoke up and declared to Svyatopolk, "We were sent to you, oh Prince, with positive instructions that our city does not want either you or your son. If your son has two heads, you might send him. But the fact is that Vsevolod assigned us Mstislav as our prince. We brought him up as one of us while you left us in the lurch." Svyatopolk then had a long argument with them, but in the end, since they could not agree, the Novgorodians took Mstislav and departed homeward.[357]

On January 29 of this year, there was a portent in the heavens visible for three days, resembling a fiery ray which proceeded from east, south, west, and north, and all night there was as much light as shines from the full moon. On February 5 of this year, there was a portent in the moon. On the seventh of the same month, there was a portent in the sun: it was surrounded by three rainbows, and there were other rainbows one above the other. At the sight of these portents, pious men with sighs and tears begged God that he should turn these portents to a good end. For some portents are of evil and others of favorable significance. During the following year, God inspired the princes of Rus' with a noble project, for they resolved to attack the Polovcians and invade their territory, and this project was actually realized. This event we shall describe under the coming year. In this same year, on August 11, Yaroslav, the son of Yaropolk, passed away. On November 16 of this same year, Sbÿslava, the daughter of Svyatopolk, was taken to Poland to marry Boleslav.[358]

(277) 6611 (1103). God inspired a noble project in the hearts of the Russian princes Svyatopolk and Vladimir, and they met for consultation at Dolobsk.[359] Svyatopolk with his retainers and Vladimir with his own took their seats in the same tent. The retainers of Svyatopolk began the discussion, and remarked that it was not advisable to open hostilities in the spring, since they would ruin the peasants and their fields. Vladimir then replied, "I am surprised, comrades, that you concern yourselves for the beast with which the peasant plows. Why do you not bear in mind that as soon as the peasant begins his plowing, the Polovcian will come, shoot him down with his bolt, seize his horse, ride on into his village, and carry off his wife, his children, and all his property? Are you concerned for the horse and not for the peasant himself?"

Svyatopolk's retainers could find no answer, and Svyatopolk himself arose, remarking that for his part he was ready to fight. Then Vladimir informed him that by so doing he would confer an inestimable benefit upon the land of Rus'. They then sent to Oleg and David and invited them to make a life-or-death stand against the Polovcians. David accepted, but Oleg opposed the campaign on the ground that he was unwell. Vladimir then embraced his cousin, and proceeded to Pereyaslavl', whither he was followed by Svyatopolk, David son of Svyatoslav, David son of Vseslav, Mstislav grandson of Igor', Vyacheslav son of Yaropolk,[360] and Yaropolk son of Vladimir. They advanced on horseback and by boat, arrived below the cataracts, and halted by the rapids (278) at the island of Khortitsa. They then mounted their horses, and when the foot-soldiers had disembarked from the boats, they traveled across country for four days, and arrived at Suten'.[361]

When the Polovcians learned that the Russes were on their way, they collected innumerable forces and began to deliberate. Urusoba proposed that the Polovcians should make peace with the Russes, since the latter would offer the nomads a violent combat in view of the fact that the Polovcians had done much scathe to Rus'. The younger chiefs replied to Urusoba that even if he was afraid of the Russes, they were not dismayed, for after conquering the Russes, they would invade their country and take their cities, and they wondered who would protect the Russes against them.

The princes of Rus' and all the soldiery offered their prayers to God and made their vows to God and to the Blessed Virgin; some promised presents of food, others alms to the poor, and others supplied for the monasteries. After they had prayed thus, the Polovcians advanced, and sent Altunopa in front as a vanguard, since he was celebrated among them for his courage. The Russian princes likewise sent forward their advance party. They thus surprised the vanguard of Altunopa, upon whom they fell, slaying him and his followers. Not one of them escaped, for the Russes slew them all. The nomad troops came on like the trees of the forest, and their mass was impenetrable. The Russes straightway advanced to meet them. Now God on high inspired an awful fear in the Polovcians, so that terror and trembling beset them at the sight of the Russian forces, and they wavered. Even their steeds possessed no more swiftness of foot. But our soldiery, both foot and horse, advanced joyously to the combat.

Upon beholding the effort (279) of the Russes against them, the Polovcians fled before the Russian troops without even waiting to meet them, and our men gave chase and cut them down. On April 4, God thus performed a great salvation and bestowed upon us a mighty victory over our foes. Upon this expedition twenty Polovcian princes were slain: Urusoba, Kchi, Arslanapa, Kitanopa, Kuman, Asup, Kurtek, Chenegrepa, Sur'bar', and many other princes. Beldyuz' was taken captive.

The cousins then rested, since they had overcome their foes. They brought Beldyuz' before Svyatopolk, and the Polovcian chief offered to pay gold and silver, horses and cattle as his ransom. Svyatopolk then sent him to Vladimir. When he stood before him, Vladimir inquired, "Have you noticed how your former oath has brought you to ruin?

Though you often gave pledges, you continued to harass the land of Rus'. Why did you not admonish your sons and your kinsmen not to violate their oaths by the shedding of Christian blood? Your blood be upon your own head." He then directed that the Polovcian should be killed, and they cut him to pieces.

Thereafter all the kinsmen gathered together, and Vladimir exclaimed, "This is the day that the Lord hath made, let us rejoice and be glad in it. For the Lord hath freed us from our foes, and put down our enemies, and crushed the serpents' heads. He hath given them as food to the men of Rus'." They thus seized sheep and cattle, horses and camels, tents with booty and slaves, and with the tents they captured Pechenegs and Torks. They then returned to Rus' carrying great spoil, with glory and a great victory won.

In this year, the locusts appeared on August 1. (280) On the eighteenth of the same month, Svyatopolk went forth and restored the town of Yur'ev,[362] which the Polovcians had burned. On March 4 of this year, Yaroslav[363] fought with the Mordva, and was overcome.[364]

6612 (1104). The daughter of Volodar' was taken to Tsar'grad on July 20 to become the wife of the son of the Emperor Alexius.[365] On August 21, of the same year Predslava, the daughter of Svyatopolk, was taken to Hungary to marry the king's son.[366]

In the same year, on December 6, the Metropolitan Nicephorus arrived in Russia. On the thirteenth of the same month, Vyacheslav, the son of Yaropolk, passed away.[367] On the eighteenth of this month, the Metropolitan was elevated to the throne.

We should also mention that at the close of this year Svyatopolk despatched Putyata to attack Minsk, while Vladimir sent his son Yaropolk on this same mission. Oleg, accompanied by David, the son of Vseslav, made an attack upon Gleb. They achieved no success, and returned home again.[368]

A son was born to Svyatopolk, and he named him Bryachislav.

In this year, a portent appeared. The sun stood in a circle; in the middle of the circle, a cross appeared, and the sun stood in the middle of the cross. Within the circle, on both sides, were seen two other suns, and outside the circle, above the sun, there appeared a rainbow with its horns to the northward. There was likewise a portent of the same aspect in the moon on February 4, 5, and 6, so that this portent was visible three days in the sun by day and three nights in the moon by night.

6613 (1105). The Metropolitan appointed Amphilochius as Bishop of Vladimir on August (281) 27. On November 12 of the same year, he appointed Lazarus in Pereyaslavl'. On December 13 of this year, he appointed Menas in Polotsk.

6614 (1106). The Polovcians raided in the vicinity of Zarechesk,[369] and Svyatopolk sent Yan son of Vyshata, his brother Putyata, and Ivan the Khazar, son of Zakhariy, to pursue them. They drove off the Polovcians and took some spoil. In the same year, Yan, that righteous ancient, died at a fair old age after a life of ninety years. Living as he did in the law of God, he was by no means inferior to the early saints. I heard from him many stories which I have set down in this chronicle as I heard them from his lips. His tomb is found in the chapel of the Crypt Monastery, where his body lies since its interment on June 24.

On December 6 of this year, Eupraxia, the daughter of Vsevolod, took the veil. In the same year, Zbygniew[370] took refuge with Svyatopolk. On February 17 of this year, Svyatopolk, the son of David and grandson of Svyatoslav, became a monk.[371] In this same year, the Zimegola defeated all the sons of Vseslav, and slew nine thousand of their followers.[372]

6615 (1107), first year of the indiction, the fourth year of the lunar cycle and the eighth of the solar cycle. On May 7 of this year, the wife of Vladimir passed away.[373] In the same month, Bonyak raided and seized many horses in the vicinity of Pereyaslavl'. In the same year, Bonyak and old Sharukan and many other princes came (282) and laid siege to Lubny.[374] Svyatopolk, Vladimir, Oleg, Svyatoslav, Mstislav, Vyacheslav, and Yaropolk[375] marched out to attack them at this town. At the sixth hour of the day, they crossed the Sula[376] and shouted at the foe. The Polovcians were terrified, and because of their fear could not even raise a standard, but seized their horses and fled, while their foot-soldiers took to flight also. Our men then began to cut them down as they pursued them, and took others captive. They drove them thus nearly to the Khorol.[377] They thus slew Taz, Bonyak's brother, while Sharukan barely escaped. On August 12, the Polovcians abandoned their camp, after the capture of which the Russian soldiery returned home with a great victory. Svyatopolk arrived before the Crypt Monastery at matins on the feast of the Assumption of the Blessed Virgin [August 15] and the brethren embraced him amid great rejoicing, because our enemies were overthrown through the prayers of the Holy Virgin and of our holy father Theodosius. For Svyatopolk,[378] before he went forth to war or on some other mission, made it a habit to kneel beside the tomb of Theodosius, and after receiving the blessing of the prior who was present, he proceeded with his errand.

On January 4 of this year, the Princess, Svyatopolk's mother, passed away.

During the same month of this year, Vladimir, David, and Oleg went forth to meet Aepa and his namesake and made peace. On January 12, Vladimir took (283) the daughter of Aepa son of Osen', to be the wife of Prince George, while Oleg took for his son the daughter of Aepa son of Girgen.[379]

6616 (1108). Upon July 11, the Church of St. Michael with the golden tower was founded by Prince Svyatopolk.[380] The refectory of the Crypt Monastery was completed under the Prior Theoctistus.[381] It had been constructed at the order of Gleb[382] who bore the expense of it. In this year, there was high water on the Dnieper, the Desna, and the Pripet'.

In this year, God brought inspiration to Theoctistus, the prior of the Crypt Monastery, and he proposed to Prince Svyatopolk that Theodosius might be inscribed in the synodikon. The prince welcomed the suggestion and promised to execute it. He directed the Metropolitan to inscribe Theodosius in the synodikon, and gave orders to all bishops that he should be thus inscribed.[383] They complied with pleasure, and promised to make mention of Theodosius at all the councils.

On July 25 of this year, Catherine, the daughter of Vsevolod, passed away.

In this year was completed the tower of the Church of the Holy Virgin in Klov, which had been founded by Stephen, former prior of the Crypt Monastery.[384]

6617 (1109). Eupraxia, the daughter of Vsevolod, died on July 10 and was laid in the Crypt Monastery by the southern portal. A chapel was built over her in which her body lies.[385]

On December 2 of this same year, (284) Dmitr, the son of Ivor, captured the Polovcian camp beside the Don.

6618 (1110). In the spring, Svyatopolk, Vladimir, and David marched forth to attack the Polovcians, but returned after reaching Voin'.[386]

On February 11 of this year, there was a portent in the Crypt Monastery. A fiery pillar appeared which reached from earth to heaven; lightnings illumined the whole countryside, and thunder was heard in the sky at the first hour of the night. The whole populace beheld the miracle. The pillar first stood over the stone refectory, so that its cross could not be seen. Then it moved a little, reached the church, and halted over the tomb of Theodosius. Then it rose, as if facing to the eastward, and forthwith became invisible.

This portent was not an actual pillar of fire, but an angelic manifestation. For an angel thus appears either as a pillar of fire or as a flame, even as David has said, "He maketh the winds his messengers and his ministers a flaming fire" (*Ps.* civ, 4). They are sent forth by the command of God, according to the desire of the Lord and Creator of all things. For an angel appears wherever there are blessed abodes and houses of prayer, and they there exhibit such portion of their aspect as it is possible for men to look upon. It is, indeed, impossible for men to behold an angelic form, even as the mighty Moses could not view the angelic being, for a pillar of cloud led the children of Israel by day, and a pillar of fire by night. This (285) apparition indicated an event which was destined to take place, and its presage was later realized. For in the following year, was not an angel the guide of our princes against our pagan foes, even as it is written, "An angel shall go before thee" (*Ex.* xxiii, 23), and again, "Thy angel be with thee?"[387]

In the hope of God's grace, I Sylvester, Prior of St. Michaels, wrote this Chronicle in the year 6624 (1116), the ninth of the indiction, during the reign of Prince Vladimir in Kiev, while I was presiding over St. Michael's Monastery. May whosoever reads this book remember me in his prayers.[388]

Appendix I

The Testament of Vladimir Monomakh[1]

(240 *ad fin.*) I, wretched man that I am, by my pious and glorious grandsire Yaroslav named at baptism Basil (Vasiliy) and with the Russian name Vladimir, surnamed Monomakh[2] by my beloved father and mother[3] ... (241) and for the sake of Christian people, for I was many times saved from all distress through his mercy and through the prayers of my father.

As I sat upon my sledge, I meditated in my heart and praised God, who has led me, a sinner, even to this day. Let not my sons or anyone else who happens to read this brief discourse laugh at its contents. But rather let any one of my sons take my words to heart and not be disposed to laziness, but labor zealously. First, for the sake of God and your own souls, retain the fear of God in your hearts, and give alms generously, for such liberality is the root of all good. If this document displeases anyone, let him not be angry, but rather let him believe that, in my old age, I talked nonsense as I sat upon my sledge. For emissaries from my cousins met me on the Volga with the message, "Join with us quickly, that we may expel the sons of Rostislav, and seize their possessions. If you do not join us, we shall act for our advantage, and you may conduct yourself as you deem best." I replied, "At the risk of your wrath, I cannot go with you or break my oath."[4]

When I had dismissed the emissaries, in my sorrow I took up the Psalter, and when I opened it, this passage struck my eye: "Why art thou cast down, my soul? Why dost thou disquiet me?" etc. (*Ps.* xliii, 5). I collected these precious words, and arranged them in order, and copied them. If the last passage does not please you, then accept the first. "Why art thou sorrowful, my soul? Why dost thou disquiet me? Hope in God, for I will confess to him" (*Ibid.*). "Rival not with evildoers, nor envy the doers of unrighteousness. For the evildoers shall be cut off, but those who wait upon the Lord shall not be; he shall seek his place and shall not find it. The meek shall inherit the earth. But yet a little while and the sinner shall inherit the earth, and shall rejoice in the abundance of peace. The sinner plotteth against the righteous, and gnasheth upon him with his teeth. The Lord shall laugh at him, and shall see that his day shall come. The wicked have drawn out the sword, they have bent their bow to cast down (242) the poor and the needy, and to kill the just of heart. The sword shall enter into their own hearts, and their bows shall be broken. A little that the righteous man hath is better than the riches of many wicked. The arms of the wicked shall be broken, but the Lord upholdeth the righteous. The wicked shall perish; but in his pity for the righteous he bestoweth gifts upon them. Those who bless him shall inherit the earth, but those that curse him shall be exterminated. The steps of man are ordered by the Lord. Though he fall, he shall not be utterly cast down, for the Lord upholdeth his hand. I have been young and now am old, yet have I not seen the righteous forsaken nor his seed begging bread. The righteous man is ever merciful and lendeth, and his seed is blessed. Depart from evil and do good; seek peace and pursue it, and dwell for evermore" (*Ps.* xxxvii, 1, 9-17, 19, 22-27).

"When men rose against us, they had swallowed us up quick; when their anger was kindled against us, then the waters had overwhelmed us" (*Ps.* cxxiv, 2-4). "Be merciful unto me, oh God, for man hath persecuted me, fighting daily he oppresseth me. My enemies have persecuted me, many were they who fought against me" (*Ps.* lvi, 1-2). "The righteous shall rejoice, when he seeth the vengeance; he shall wash his hands in the blood of the sinner, so that a man shall say, Verily there is a reward for the righteous, verily he is a God who judgeth in the earth" (*Ps.* lviii, 10-11).

"Deliver me from mine enemies, oh God, and defend me from those who rise up against me. Deliver me from the workers of iniquity, and save men from bloody men; for they have set snares for my soul" (*Ps.* lix, 1-3). "His anger endureth but a moment and in his favor there is life; weeping shall resound in the evening, and joy upon the morrow" (*Ps.* xxx, 5). "Because thy loving kindness is better than life, my lips shall praise thee. I will bless thee while I live, and in thy name will I lift up my hands." (*Ps.* lxiii, 3-4). "Hide me from the secret counsels of the wicked, and from the multitude of evildoers" (*Ps.* lxiv, 2). "Rejoice, all ye righteous in heart. I will bless the Lord at all times, his praise shall," etc. (*Ps.* xxxiv, 2).

It was thus that Basil, after gathering together young men who were pure in heart and untainted in body (243), inculcated in them a brief and a meek conversation and the word of God in right measure. He taught them to eat and drink without unseemly noise; to be silent in the presence of the aged; to listen to the wise; to humble themselves before their elders; to live in charity with their equals and their inferiors; to speak without guile, but to understand much; not to be immoderate in their language, nor to insult others in their conversation; not to laugh excessively; to respect the aged; to refrain from converse with shameless women; to cast their eyes downward and their souls upward; to pass the foolish by and not stir them up. He taught them to set no store by the powers honored of all men. If any one of you can render a service to another let him expect his recompense from God, and he shall thus enjoy eternal blessing.

Oh sovereign Mother of God! Take away pride and presumption from my poor heart, lest I be exalted in this empty life by the vanity of this world. Let the faithful learn to strive with pious effort. According to the word of the Gospel, learn to govern your eyes, to curb your tongue, to moderate your temper, to subdue your body, to restrain your wrath, and to cherish pure thoughts, exerting yourself in good for the Lord's sake. When robbed, avenge not; when hated or persecuted, endure; when affronted, pray. Destroy sin, free the oppressed, render justice to the orphan, protect the widow. "Come, let us reason together, saith the Lord; if your sins be as scarlet, I will make them white as snow, etc" (*Is.* i, 18).

The spring of fasting shall shine forth, and likewise the flower of repentance. Let us purify ourselves, my brethren, from every corporal and spiritual blemish, and, as we call upon our Creator, let us say, "Glory to thee, lover of mankind!" In truth, my children, understand how merciful, yea, how supremely merciful is God, the lover of mankind. Being of human stock, we are so sinful and mortal that, when anyone does us evil, we desire to destroy him and to shed his blood speedily. But our Lord, the ruler of life and death, suffers our sins to be higher than our heads, and yet he loves us all our lives as a father loves his son whom he chastens and then summons once more to his embrace.

Thus our Lord has promised us the victory over our enemies through three means of conquering (244) and overcoming them: repentance, tears, and almsgiving. My children, the commandment of God to conquer your sins by these three means and to be sure of the kingdom is not severe. But I implore you for God's sake, be not lazy, nor forget these three means. For they are not difficult of attainment. Not through solitude nor an ascetic life, nor by such fasting as other good men endure, but through easy efforts may you thus obtain the mercy of God.

"What is man, that thou art mindful of him?" (*Ps.* viii, 6). Great art thou, oh Lord, and wondrous are thy works. The reason of man cannot express thy miracles. And again we say: Great art thou, oh Lord, and marvelous are thy works, and blessed and praiseworthy is thy name forever throughout all the earth. Who fails to praise and magnify thy strength and thy great miracles and goodness that are made manifest on this earth: how the heaven was formed, the sun, the moon, the stars, the darkness of night and the light of day, and how the earth was set upon the waters, oh Lord, through thy devices, and how various creatures and birds and fishes were adorned by thy wisdom?

We marvel at this miracle, in that thou hast fashioned man out of clay and created the various aspects of human countenances, so that, if the whole world should come together, all would not be of one likeness, but each person in his own aspect through the wisdom of God. We wonder likewise that the birds of the air come from far climes and to our own land first of all. Yet they remain not in one region, for both weak and strong, by divine commandment, fly over the whole earth, to populate the forests and fields. All these blessings God has bestowed upon us for the delight, sustenance, and pleasure of mankind. Great, oh Lord, is thy mercy upon us, for that thou hast created these delights for the sinner. The birds of the air are inspired by thee, oh Lord, and when thou ordainest, they utter their songs and make men glad in thee; and when thou ordainest not, they are silent, though they possess tongues.

But blessed art thou, oh Lord, and greatly praised! Since thou hast made and created all goodness, may he be accursed who fails to praise thee, oh Lord, and to believe with his whole heart and (245) soul in the name of the Father and of the Son and of the Holy Ghost.[5]

As you read these words, my sons, praise God who has shown us his mercy and admonished you through the medium of my poor wit. Give heed to me, and accept an half of my instruction if you are not disposed to adopt it all. When God softens your hearts, shed tears for your sins, and pray, "As thou hast taken pity upon the adulteress, the thief, and the publican, have pity also upon us sinners," and utter these words both in the church and before you retire to rest.

If it is in any way possible, fail not one single night to kneel to the ground three times, in the case that you cannot do so more often. Forget not nor be remiss in this observance, for by his nightly worship and hymn man conquers the devil, and by this means expiates what sins he has committed during the day. When you are riding forth upon your horse, if you have no quarrel with any man and cannot utter some other prayer, then exclaim without ceasing "Kyrie eleison!"

within yourselves. This is the best prayer of all and infinitely better than thinking idle thoughts while riding. Above all things, forget not the poor, but support them to the extent of your means. Give to the orphan, protect the widow, and permit the mighty to destroy no man. Take not the life of the just or the unjust, nor permit him to be killed. Destroy no Christian soul even though he be guilty of murder.

When you speak either good or evil, swear not by the name of God, nor cross yourselves, for that is unnecessary. Whenever you kiss the Cross to confirm an oath made to your brethren or to any other man, first test your heart as to whether you can abide by your word, then kiss the Cross, and after once having given your oath, abide by it, lest you destroy your souls by its violation.

Receive with affection the blessing of bishops, priests, and priors, and shun them not, but rather, according to your means, love and help them, that you may receive from them their intercession in the presence of God. Above all things admit no pride in your hearts and minds, but say, "We are but mortal; today we live and tomorrow we shall be in the grave. All that thou hast given us is not ours, but thine, and thou hast but lent it to us for a few days." (246) Hoard not in the earth, for therein lies great sin. Honor the ancient as your father, and the youth as your brother.

Be not lax in the discipline of your homes, but rather attend to all matters yourselves. Rely not upon your steward or your servant, lest they who visit you ridicule your house or your table. When you set out to war, be not inactive, depend not upon your captains, nor waste your time in drinking, eating, or sleeping. Set the sentries yourselves, and take your rest only after you have posted them at night at every important point about your troops; then take your rest, but arise early. Do not put off your accoutrements without a quick glance about you, for a man may thus perish suddenly through his own carelessness. Guard against lying, drunkenness, and vice, for therein perish soul and body. When journeying anywhere by road through your domain, do not permit your followers or another's company to visit voilence upon the villages or upon the fields, lest men revile you. Wherever you go, as often as you halt, give the beggar to eat and to drink. Furthermore, honor the stranger, if not with a gift, at least with food and drink, whencesoever he comes to you, be he simple, or noble, or an emissary. For travelers give a man a universal reputation as generous or niggardly.

Visit the sick, and accompany the dead, for we are all but mortal. Pass no man without a greeting; give him a kindly word. Love your wives, but grant them no power over you. This is the end of all things; to hold the fear of God above all else. If you forget all my admonition, read this counsel frequently. Then I shall be without disgrace, and you shall profit thereby.

Forget not what useful knowledge you possess, and acquire that with which you are not acquainted, even as my father, though he remained at home in his own country, still understood five languages. For by this means honor is acquired in other lands. Laziness is the mother of all evil; what a man knows, he forgets, and what he does not know he does not learn. In the practice of good works, you cannot neglect any item of good conduct.

First of all, go to church; let not the rising sun find you in your bed. For this was my father's habit, and it is likewise the custom of all good and perfect men (247). After rendering praise to God at matins, as you look upon the rising sun, render praise to God with gladness once again, saying, "Thou hast lightened my eyes, oh Christ my God, thou hast given me thy bright light. Grant me increase, oh Lord, in the years to come, so that, as I repent my sins and order my life righteously, I may thus continue to praise God." Then sit and deliberate with your retainers, or render justice to the people, or ride out for hunting or for pleasure, or else lie down to sleep. Sleep is established by God for noonday repose, since birds and beasts and men then rest from their labors.

I now narrate to you, my sons, the fatigue I have endured on journeys and hunts for fifty-three years. First I rode to Rostov through the Vyatichians, whither my father had sent me while he himself went to Kursk.[6] Second, to Smolensk with Stavko the son of Gordyata; he then went to Brest with Izyaslav, and sent me to Smolensk. From Smolensk, I rode on to Vladimir.

In that same winter, my brethren sent me to Brest to the place which they had burned, and there I watched their city. Then I went to my father in Pereyaslavl', and after Easter, from Pereyaslavl' to Vladimir to make peace with the Poles at Suteysk.[7] Thence back to Vladimir again in the summer.

Then Svyatoslav sent me to Poland; after going beyond Glogau to the Bohemian forest, I traveled four months in that country.[8] In this year, my oldest child was born in Novgorod. Thence I went to Turov, in the spring to Pereyaslavl' again, and then back to Turov. Svyatoslav then died,[9] and I again went to Smolensk, and thence during the same winter to Novgorod, and in the spring to help Gleb.[10] In the summer, I went with my father to Polotsk, and in the next winter with Svyatopolk to Polotsk again, and the city was burned. He then went to

Novgorod, while I, supported by Polovcians, marched against Odresk, carrying on constant warfare, and thence traveled to Chernigov. Then, on my return trom Smolensk, I rejoined my father in Chernigov a second time.

Then Oleg arrived after his expulsion from Vladimir, and I invited him to dinner with my father at the Red Palace in Chernigov,[11] and I gave my father three hundred *grivnÿ* of gold (248). Upon leaving Smolensk, I fought my way through the Polovcian forces, and arrived at Pereyaslavl', where I found my father newly arrived from a raid. Then I rode with my father and Izyaslav to Chernigov to fight with Boris, and we conquered Boris and Oleg.[12] Then we went to Pereyaslavl', and remained in Obrov. Vseslav at that juncture fired Smolensk. I set forth with men from Chernigov with a spare horse each, but we did not catch him at Smolensk. On this pursuit of Vseslav, I burned the countryside and ravaged as far as Lukoml' and Logozhsk, then attacked Dryutesk, and returned to Chernigov.

In the winter of that year, the Polovcians devastated the whole of Starodub. I marched with men of Chernigov against the Polovcians. At the Desna, we seized the princes Asaduk and Sauk, and killed their followers. The next day, behind Novgorod, we scattered the powerful force of Belkatgin, and took their swords and all their booty.[13] We then went for two winters among the Vyatichians to attack Khodota and his son. The first winter, I went to Kordna and then to Mikulin in pursuit of the sons of Izyaslav, whom we did not catch. In that spring we joined with Yaropolk at Brodÿ.

The following summer, we chased the Polovcians beyond the Khorol, after they had captured Goroshin. During the autumn, in company with men of Chernigov, as well as Polovcians and Chiteeviches, we captured the city of Minsk and left in it neither slaves nor cattle. In that winter, we went to Brodÿ to join Yaropolk, and concluded an important pact of friendship. In that winter, my father set me up to rule in Pereyaslavl' in preference to all my cousins, and we crossed the Supoy.

While we were on our way to the town of Priluk, we suddenly encountered the Polovcian princes with eight thousand men. We were ready and willing to fight with them, but we had sent our equipment ahead with the baggage train, and we therefore entered the town. They thus captured alive only Semtsya[13a] and a few peasants. Our men, on the other hand, killed or captured a large number of them. They did not even dare to lead away their mounts, and during the night fled to the Sula. On the following day, which was Lady-Day, we arrived at

Appendix I 213

Bela Vezha. With the aid of God and of the Holy (249) Virgin, our troops killed nine hundred Polovcians, and captured the two princes Asin' and Sakz', the brothers of Bagubars, and only two men of their force escaped. We then pursued the Polovcians to Svyatoslavl', thence to Torchesk, and still further to Yur'ev. Then again, on the east bank of the Dnieper, we once more defeated the Polovcians near Krasno. In company with Rostislav, we subsequently captured their camp at Varin. I then went to Vladimir and set up Yaropolk as prince, but he soon died.[14]

After the death of my father,[15] under Svyatopolk we fought until evening with the Polovcians at the Sula in the vicinity of Khalep, and then made peace with Tugorkan and other Polovcian chiefs.[16] We took from Gleb's followers all their troops. Oleg subsequently attacked me in Chernigov with Polovcian support; my troops fought with him for eight days by the small entrenchment and would not let him inside the outworks. I took pity on the souls of our Christian subjects, and upon the burned villages and monasteries, and said, "It is not for the pagans to boast." I therefore gave my cousin his father's place, and retired myself to my father's domain of Pereyaslavl'. We left Chernigov on the day of St. Boris, and rode through the Polovcians in a company of not more than a hundred together with the women and children. The Polovcians showed their teeth at us, as they stood like wolves at the fords and in the hills. But God and St. Boris did not deliver us up to them as their prey, so we arrived at Pereyaslavl' unscathed.[17]

I remained in Pereyaslavl' three summers and winters with my retainers, and endured great distress through war and famine. We attacked the Polovcian forces behind Rimov, and God stood by us, so that we defeated them and took many captives. We overthrew the troops of Itlar', and after marching beyond Goltav, we captured their camp. We now attacked Oleg at Starodub,[18] because he had made common cause with the Polovcians. In pursuit of Bonyak, we advanced to the Bug and later beyond the Ros' in company with Svyatopolk. After reaching Smolensk, we became reconciled with David.

We set out a second time from Voronitsa. At this juncture, the Torks and the Chiteeviches came from among the Polovcians to attack us, so that we advanced against them to the Sula. (250) We then returned again to Rostov for the winter, and three winters later I returned to Smolensk. Thence I went to Rostov.

A second time, Svyatopolk and I pursued Bonyak, but the nomads escaped and we did not catch them. Thereupon we again followed

Bonyak beyond the Ros', yet did not overtake him. During the winter, I traveled to Smolensk, but left there after Easter. George's mother passed away. In the summer, I went to Pereyaslavl', and assembled my kinsmen together. Bonyak with his entire force of Polovcians approached Ksnyatin, and we sallied forth from Pereyaslavl' to meet them as far as the Sula. God helped us, and we conquered their forces and captured their best princes. After Christmas, we were able to make peace with Aepa,[20] and after receiving his daughter in marriage, we proceeded to Smolensk. Thence we journeyed to Rostov. On departing thence, I again attacked the Polovcians under Urusoba in company with Svyatopolk, and God aided us. Then I again attacked Bonyak at Lubno, and God again vouchsafed us his aid. In company with Svyatopolk, I set out once more upon a campaign.[21] With Svyatopolk and David, I later went as far as the Don, and God granted us his aid.[22]

Aepa and Bonyak had approached Vÿr' with the intention of capturing it. I advanced to meet them as far as Romnÿ with Oleg and my sons. When the nomads learned of our coming, they fled.[23] Then we marched to attack Gleb at Minsk, because he had captured our retainers. God aided us, and we accomplished our purpose.[24] Thereupon we marched to attack Yaroslav son of Svyatopolk at Vladimir, since we were no longer disposed to endure his malice.[25] On one occasion, I rode at full speed from Chernigov to join my father in Kiev in one day before Vespers.[26] Among all my campaigns, there are eighty-three long ones, and I do not count the minor adventures.

I concluded nineteen peace treaties with the Polovcians with or without my father's aid, and dispensed much of my cattle and my garments. I freed from their captivity the best Polovcian princes, including two brothers of Sharukan, three brothers of Bagubars, four brothers of Ovchin, and one hundred of their foremost leaders. Of other chieftains whom God delivered alive into my hands, I took captive, killed, and had cast into the river Slavlya Koksus' and his son, Aklan, the son of Burch, Azguluy Prince of Tarev, and fifteen other young chieftains, (251) and at the same time not less than two hundred of the leading prisoners were likewise killed, and cast into the same river.

I devoted much energy to hunting as long as I reigned in Chernigov. Since I left Chernigov, even up to the present time, I have made a practice of hunting a hundred times a year with all my strength, and without harm, apart from a certain hunt after bison, since I had been accustomed to chase every sort of game in my father's company.

At Chernigov, I even bound wild horses with my bare hands or captured ten or twenty live horses with the lasso, and besides that, while riding along the Ros', I caught these same wild horses barehanded. Two bisons tossed me and my horse on their horns, a stag once gored me, one elk stamped upon me, while another gored me, a boar once tore my sword from my thigh, a bear on one occasion bit my kneecap, and another wild beast jumped on my flank and threw my horse with me. But God preserved me unharmed.

I often fell from my horse, fractured my skull twice, and in my youth injured my arms and legs when I did not reck of my life or spare my head. In war and at the hunt, by night and by day, in heat and in cold, I did whatever my servant had to do, and gave myself no rest. Without relying on lieutenants or messengers, I did whatever was necessary; I looked to every disposition in my household. At the hunt, I posted the hunters, and I looked after the stables, the falcons, and the hawks. I did not allow the mighty to distress the common peasant or the poverty-stricken widow, and interested myself in the church administration and service.

Let not my sons or whoever else reads this document criticize me. I do not commend my own boldness, but I praise God and glorify his memory because he guarded me, a sinful and a wretched man, for so many years in these (252) dangerous vicissitudes, and did not make me inactive or useless for all the necessary works of man. As you read this screed, prepare yourselves for all good works, and glorify God among his saints. Without fear of death, or war, or of wild beasts, do a man's work, my sons, as God sets it before you. If I suffered no ill from war, from wild beasts, from flood, or from falling from my horse, then surely no one can harm you and destroy you, unless that too be destined of God. But if death comes from God, then neither father, nor mother, nor brethren can hinder it, and though it is prudent to be constantly upon one's guard, the protection of God is fairer than the protection of man.

Appendix II

A. *Letter of Vladimir Monomakh to Oleg, Son of Svyatoslav*[1]

(252) Oh long-suffering and wretched man that I am! My soul, long hast thou wrestled with my heart, and thou hast conquered it. For being but mortal, I reflect how I may stand before the dread Judge ere we have done penance and become reconciled with one another. "For if any man say, I love God, and love not his brother, it is a lie" (*John,* iv, 20). Likewise, "If ye do not forgive your brother's trespasses, neither will your heavenly Father forgive you" (*Matt.,* vi, 15). The Prophet says, "Fret not thyself because of evildoers, nor be thou envious against the workers of iniquity" (*Ps.* xxxvii, i). "Behold how good and how pleasant it is for brethren to dwell together in unity!" (*Ps.* cxxxiii, 1).

But the teaching of the devil prevails everywhere. There were wars in the days of our wise grandsires and our righteous and blessed sires. For the devil, who desires no good to the race of man, continues to incite us.

I have written these words because my son, whom you christened, and who lives near you, influenced me to do so.[2] He sent to me a messenger with letters, saying, "Let us make peace and be reconciled. Judgment has been visited upon my brother. Let us not set ourselves up as avengers, but rather trust in God. The criminals shall stand before the bar of God. But let us not bring ruin upon the land of Rus'." I observed the humility of my son, and in the fear of God, I said, "In his youth and his inexperience he is humble (253) and trusts in God, while I am a man sinful before all his fellows." I heeded the words of my son, and wrote this letter. I shall discern from your answer whether you received it with favor or scorn. For with these words I have forestalled you in the action to which I expected humility and repentance would impel you, just as I myself desire God's forgiveness for my former sins. Our Lord is not a mere man, but God of the whole universe. Yet though he can, if he so desire, perform any miracle in the winking of an eye, he submitted himself to reviling, to spitting, and to blows, and even delivered himself up to death, though he was Lord of both life and death. But what are we, sinful men? Today alive, tomorrow dead; today in glory and honor, tomorrow in the grave and unremembered, while others divide our treasures.

Look, my cousin, upon our sires. What did they carry away with them, or what did they profit by their promises? Only as much as they had done for their souls. Would that you, my cousin, had been the first to write, and had forestalled me in these utterances! When my son was slain, and you beheld his blood and his mutilated corpse as he lay like a withered flower or a slaughtered lamb, you might have stood over him and said, as you read the secret thoughts of your soul, "Alas, what have I done? Without considering his inexperience, I have brought crime upon myself through the perversity of this vain world, and have brought tears upon his father and his mother." You could have lamented like David, "I know my sin, it is ever before me" (*Ps.* li, 3).

Without shedding of blood, David, the Lord's anointed, committed adultery. But when he cast dust upon his head and wept bitterly in that hour, God remitted his sins. You might have repented also. You might have sent me a letter of consolation, and returned to me my daughter-in-law (for in her there is no harm), that I might embrace her and mourn her husband and her marriage, instead of uttering joyous songs. For because of my sins I did not behold their joy of other days nor their betrothal. But now, for God's sake, send her to me quickly with your first (254) answer, so that I may mourn with her unceasingly and set her in the station that befits her: so may she sit languishing like a dove on the dry tree, and I shall be consoled in God!

Our sons and our fathers have trod this same path. Judgment came to my son from the hand of God, not at your hand. But if you had satisfied your desire, and had taken Murom instead of Rostov, a message to me would have reconciled us. But consider which was fitting, that I should write to you, or you to me. If you had bidden my son to write to his father, I should have sent conciliatory messages ten times over.[3]

It is strange that a man should have perished in war? Better men have died ere this even in our own family. You should not have coveted another's domain, nor brought me to shame and sorrow, for slaves have learned to steal for themselves, but they have won evil thereby. If therefore you repent before God, you will make me of good cheer. Send me your messenger or a bishop, and write a letter with just intent. Then you shall receive your domain with my good wishes, you will turn our hearts toward each other, and we shall be better off than before. I am not malicious or revengeful. I did not desire to see your blood shed at Starodub. May God grant that I should not see blood shed by your hand or at my command, or through the instigation of any kinsman of mine! If I lie, may God and the Holy Cross judge me!

Perhaps I sinned when I attacked you in Chernigov[4] because of the pagans. But I repent of my action, and I have said so aloud to my cousin, and confessed it repeatedly, for after all I am but human. If this seems good, let it be so: if ill, let your godson sit with his little brother, eating his uncle's bread, while you possess your domain, and make your own decision in this regard. If you purpose to kill them both, they are in your power, for I wish no ill, but I desire rather the good of my kinsmen and of the land of Rus'. If you are thinking to use violence, remember that out of friendly regard for you we restored to you your inheritance at Starodub. But God is witness that we have come to an agreement with your brother, (255) but it does not avail us to make any terms without your adherence. We have done no evil, nor have we asked him to send for you before we are reconciled. If one of you does not wish good or peace to Christian men, let him receive no repose for his soul at God's hand in the life to come! It is not by compulsion that I address you, nor am I in any wise distressed, but you hear me speak from God's inspiration. My soul is dearer to me than aught else in this world. At the last judgment, I count myself without accusers.

B. *Prayer Attributed to Vladimir Monomakh*[5]

Master of wisdom, bestower of knowledge, chastiser of the thoughtless and protector of the needy, confirm my heart in wisdom, oh Lord! Give me a fatherly word, for thou hast not hindered me from raising my cry unto thee, Merciful Father, have pity upon a weak mortal. God is my hope, Christ my refuge, the Holy Ghost my protection. Oh my hope and my fortress, scorn me not, blessed one! Since I possess thee as my helper in sorrow and in sickness and against all adversities, I glorify thee, Exalted Being.

Understand and see that I am God, who test your hearts and know your minds, who reveal your deeds, punish your sins, and render justice to orphans and to the poor and the needy.

Incline, oh my soul, and consider thy deeds that thou hast done; bring them before thine eyes, shed tears from thine eyes and confess openly all thy actions and thought to Christ, and be purified. Holy Andrew, thrice blessed father, shepherd of Crete, cease not to intercede for us who honor thee, that we may escape from all malice, all sorrow, pollution, sin, and misery, faithfully honoring thy memory.

Pure Virgin Mother, preserve thy city, which through thy help endures in faith, that we may be strengthened by thee and hope in thee, and conquer all obstacles, overthrowing our enemies and living in obedience.

Oh exalted (256) Mother, who didst bear the Word that exceeds all holiness, accept this present oblation and protect us from present evils and future torments, now that we call upon thee! We thy servants entreat thee and kneel before thee with prayerful hearts. Incline thine ear, pure one, and save us, who are constantly beset by misfortune, and guard thy city, oh Mother of God, from every captivity of its foes!

Oh God, spare thy heritage, look not upon our sins, since we on earth pray to thee, who, through thy pity for this world, wast born unbegotten, and didst reign, oh Christ, to clothe thyself in flesh.

Spare us, oh Saviour, who wast born and preserved immaculate her who bore thee, even when thou dost come, sinless and merciful, to judge our deeds as God and lover of mankind.

Immaculate Virgin, who didst not know marriage, delight of God, guide of the faithful, save me as I perish and call upon thy Son. Have mercy upon me, oh Lord, have mercy when thou shalt judge. Judge me not with fire nor accuse me in thine anger! The Holy Virgin, who bore thee, intercedes with thee, oh Christ, in company with the angelic host and the army of martyrs. Through Jesus Christ our Lord, to whom be honor and glory, to Father, Son, and Holy Spirit, now and forever, world without end.

Notes to Introduction

1. For descriptions of the MSS, see the introductions to the latest editions of the text: for the Laurentian, in *Polnoe Sobranie Russkikh Letopisey*, I (2d ed., Leningrad, 1926), and for the Hypatian, in *P.S.R.L.*, II (3rd ed., Leningrad, 1923), as well as the phototype reproductions of the Laurentian (Spb., 1872) and the Hypatian (Spb., 1871). The interrelation of these redactions and the subordinate compilations connected with them is conveniently discussed by A. A. Shakhmatov, *Povĕst' Vremennÿkh Lĕt*, I (Spb., 1916), xlii-lvii. In the Laurentian MS., the *Povest'* is followed by accounts of the Rostov and Suzdal' areas extending to 1305, while the Hypatian supplies a detailed treatment of events at Kiev during the twelfth century, followed by a South-Russian chronicle covering the period 1201-1292. Cf. also Likhachev (*infra*, n. 2a), II, 149-181.

2. *Chronica Nestoris* (textum slovenicum edidit F. Miklosich, Vienna, 1860).

2a To this must be added the latest critical edition of the Laurentian text, supplied with a Russian translation by D. S. Likhachev, *Povest' Vremennÿkh Let*, 2 vols. (Moscow-Leningrad: Academy of Sciences, 1950).

3. The evolution or this passage is as follows: L^2, I: *se povĕsti vremyan'nÿkh lĕt otkudu est' poshla russkaya zemya;* H^3, 2: *povĕst' vremennÿkh lĕt chernoriztsa Fedoseva monastÿrya Pecherskago otkudu est' poshla Russkaya zemlya; Khleb.* (var. quoted H^3, I): *povĕst' vremennÿkh lĕt Nestera chernoriztsa monastÿrya Pecherskago otkuda est' poshla russkaya zemlya.* "[These are] the tale(s) of bygone years of (Nestor [*Khleb.*]) a monk of the Theodosian Crypt Monastery [*Khleb.*-Hyp.] whence came the land of Rus'." A. Norrbach, *Nestors Krönekan* (Stockholm: P. A. Norsledt and Söners Forlag, 1919).

4. V. N. Tatishchev, *Istoriya Rossii*, I (Spb., 1768), 51-60.

5. V. Yakovlev, *Pamyatniki Russkoy Literaturÿ XII-XIII Vĕkov* (Spb., 1872), p. cxxix: *Nester zhe, izhe napisa lĕtopisets;* p. cxxxv: *yako zhe blzhnÿy Nester v lĕtopistsĕ napisa o blazhennÿkh ottsĕkh, o Dam'yani, Ieremĕi, i Matfeĕ, i Isakii.* The most modern edition of the *Paterikon* is D. I. Abramovich *Paterik Kievskogo Pecherskogo Monastÿrya* (Spb., 1911). Cf. also, V. M. Istrin, *Ocherk po Istorii Drevney Russkoy Literaturÿ* (Leningrad, 1922), pp. 199-208; S. A. Bugoslavsky, "Kharakter i Ob'ëm Literaturnoy Deyatel'nosti prep. Nestora," in *Izv. Otd. Russk. Yaz. i Slov.*, XIX (Spb., 1914), No. 3, 190 ff.

6. For the text of the Nestorian *Life of Boris and Gleb*, cf. I. I. Sreznevsky, *Skazaniya o Svyatÿkh Borisĕ i Glĕbĕ* (Spb., 1860), pp. 1-40, with beautiful lithograph reproduction of the text in the fourteenth-century *Silvestrovskiy Sbornik*. Cf. also, V. M. Istrin, *Ocherk*, pp. 118-127; Bugoslavsky, *loc. cit.*, pp. 131 ff.; Shakhmatov, *Razÿskaniya o Drevnĕyshikh Russk. Lĕtopisnÿkh Svodakh* (Spb., 1908) pp. 29-97; *Povĕst' Vremennÿkh Lĕt*, pp. lxvi-lxvii; E. Shchepkin, "Zur Nestorfrage," *Arch. Slav. Phil.*, XIX (Berlin, 1897), 529, 530.

7. For text of Nestor's *Life of Theodosius,* cf. Yakovlev, *op. cit.,* pp. ix-lxxii.

8. A survey of the earlier literature (to 1850) may be found in M. I. Sukhomlinov's article, "Posobiya pri izuchenii Nestorovskoy Lětopisi," reprinted in *Sbornik Otd. Russk. Yaz. i Slov.,* LXXXIII (Spb., 1908), 238-245, with which should be compared the bibliographical material in K. Bestuzhev-Ryumin, *Russkaya Istoriya,* I (Spb., 1872), 18-19 n.

9. Sreznevsky, *Stat'i o Drevnikh Russkikh Lětopisyakh* (1853-1866, reprint, Spb., 1903), p. 111.

10. N. Kostomarov, *Istoricheskiya Monografii,* XIII (Spb., 1881), 4-8.

11. Bestuzhev-Ryumin, "O Sostavě Russkikh Lětopisey do Kontsa XIV Věka," in *Lětopis' Zanyatiy Arkheograficheskoy Kommissii,* vol. XIV (Spb., 1868).

12. This introduction is reprinted in Shakhmatov, *Povest' Vremennÿkh Lět,* pp. 361-364. Cf. Shakhmatov, "Predislovie k Sofiiskomu Vremenniku i Nestorova Lětopis'," in *Iz. Otd. Russk. Yaz. i Slov.,* XIII (Spb., 1908), I.

13. *Povest' Vremennÿkh Lět,* I, i-lxxx.

14. *Razÿskaniya o Drevněyshikh Russk. Lětopisnÿkh Svodakh* (Spb., 1908).

15. Viz., Nestor's *Life of Theodosius* (Yakovlev, *op. cit.,* p. xviii).

16. *Archiv f. Slav. Philol.,* XLI (Berlin, 1927), 49.

17. Cf. Istrin, "Zamechaniya o Nachale Russkogo Letopisaniya," in *Izv. Otd. Russk. Yaz. i Slov.,* XXVI (Leningrad, 1921), 45-102; XXVII (Leningrad, 1922), 207-251; *Ocherk,* pp. 135-152; *Khronika Georgiya Amartola v Drevnem Slavyanskom Perevode,* 2 vols. (Leningrad, 1920-1922), especially II, 348-363.

18. *Razÿskaniya,* pp. 455, 456. As a matter of fact Shakhmatov's postulation of a Bulgarian source for portions of his supposed text of 1039 is an excellent example of the defects of his method. He constantly exhibits a tendency to imagine that any item in the *Povest'* not directly connected with Kiev must have been derived from a foreign source. In this particular instance he traces the items of 969-972 on Svyatoslav's Danubian campaigns to a Bulgarian source. There is, however, no evidence that such a thing as a native Bulgarian chronicle ever existed prior to the fourteenth century.

19. It should be noted, however, that Istrin's theory of the development of a chronograph *po velikomu izlozheniyu* ("according to the long text") from a Russian translation of Georgius Hamartolus is not acceptable mainly because there is no proof whatever that this translation was actually made in Russia at the period alleged. Istrin's idea that the prototype of the *Povest'* was based on the Russian data originally contained in such a chronograph cannot be viewed as anything but an ingenious invention without even a shadow of fact behind it. Cf. M. Weingart, *Byzantské Kroniky v Literatuře Cirkevneslovanské,* II, ii (Bratislava 1923), pp. 520, 521.

20. Editions: E. von Muralt, *Georgii Monachi Chronicon* (Spb., 1859) and in Migne, P. G. CX (1863); K. de Boor, *Georgii Monachi Chronicon* (Leipzig, 1904); Istrin, *Khronika Georgiya Amartola,* I (Leningrad, 1920), II (Leningrad, 1922). The best modern analysis is found in Weingart, *op. cit.,* II, i, 112-142; cf. the bibliography of earlier works, *ibid.,* pp. 112-118. Cf. also J. B. Bury: *History of the Eastern Roman Empire* (London, 1912), 453-459.

21. Cf. A. Brückner in *Archiv f. Slav. Philol.,* XLI (1927), 50, 51.

22. M. I. Sukhomlinov, "O Drevney Russkoy Lětopisi kak Pamyatnike Lit-

eraturnom," (Spb., 1856), reprinted in *Sbornik Otd. Russk. Yaz. i Slov.*, LXXXV (Spb., 1908), i ff. For the Creed, see pp. 70-77 of reprint. The original Greek may be found both in Sukhomlinov's study and in Montfaucon, *Bibliotheca Coisliniana olim Segueriana* (Paris, 1715), pp. 90-93; cf. also J. A. Fabricius, *Bibliotheca Graeca*, X (Hamburg, 1721), 220. The Slavic text also in N. K. Nikol'sky, "Materialÿ dlya Istorii Drevnerusskoy Dukhovnoy Literaturÿ," in *Sbornik Otd. Russk. Yaz. i Slov.*, LXXXII (Spb., 1907), pt. 4, pp. 21-24.

23. Sukhomlinov, *op. cit.,* pp. 70-71.

24. Cf. N. S. Tikhonravov, *Pamyatniki Otrechennoy Russkoy Literaturÿ*, II (Moscow, 1863), 213-283; *Sochineniya*, I (Moscow, 1898), 229, 230, and n. 34; Istrin, *Otkrovenie Mefodiya Patarskago* (Moscow, 1897); E. Sackur, *Sibyllinische Texte und Forschungen* (Halle, 1898), pp. 5 ff.; P. O. Potapov, in *Russkiy Filologicheskiy Věstnik*, LXV (Warsaw, 1911), 81-110; Istrin, in *Izv. Otd. Russk. Yaz. i Slov.*, XXIX (Leningrad, 1924), 379-381; and most recently S. H. Cross, in *Speculum*, IV (Cambridge, 1929), 329-339.

25. For the *Paleya,* cf. Weingart, *Byzantské Kroniky,* I (Bratislava, 1922), 18-31. The use of the term *Paleya* to designate the Old Testament is well exemplified by the Old-Slavic translation of Georgius Hamartolus in the following passage (von Muralt, p. 432, 11. 15 ff.) «σαφῶς διὰ τούτων καὶ δι' ἄλλων πολλῶν . . . κηρύττει ἡ παλαιὰ διαθήκη,» rendered as follows: (Istrin, I, 345; II, 20, 21) "yavě bo sikh radi iněmi mnogimi . . . paleya propovědaiet." Cf. also *infra,* Text, nn. 92, 93.

26. Edition: *Paleya Tolkovaya po Spisku Sdělannomu v g. Kolomně v 1406 g. Trud Uchenikov N. S. Tikhonravova* (Moscow, 1892) The earliest text of the *Paleya* is the Alexandro-Nevskiy parchment of the fourteenth century.

27. It should be noted that Istrin ("Zaměchaniya o Sostavě Tolkovoy Palei," in *Izv. Otd. Russk. Yaz. i Slov.*, II [Spb., 1897], 175 ff., 845 ff.: III [1898], 472 ff.) assigns the origin of the *Paleya* to the thirteenth century, which would preclude its use as a source by the compiler of the *Povest'* in the early twelfth. Shakhmatov, however, in his article, "Tolkovaya Paleya i Russkaya Lětopis" (in *Stat'i po Slavyanovědeniyu* I [Spb., 1904], 199-272), concludes that the *Paleya* is derived from a Bulgarian source dating from the period and originating in the circle of St. Methodius (late ninth century). The Bulgarian original was, in his opinion, known in Russia by the close of the eleventh century, and influenced the *Povest'* in the manner outlined by Sukhomlinov. Shakhmatov likewise holds that the investigations of Istrin do not appreciably weaken the source relation between the *Paleya* and the *Povest'* which Sukhomlinov endeavored to establish.

28. Von Muralt, *ed. cit.,* pp. 404, 474, 499, 506, 528, 611, and 665.

29. *Photii Epistolae* (ed. R. Montacutius, London, 1651), pp. 3 ff.

30. Texts in F. Pasternek, *Dějiny Slovanských Apostolů Cyrilla a Methoda s Razborem a Otiskem Hlavních Pramenů* (Prague, 1902); and in P. Lavrov, "Materialÿ po Istorii Vozniknoveniya Drevneyshey Slavyanskoy Pis'mennosti," *Trudÿ Slavyanskoy Komissii,* I (Leningrad: Acad. of Sc., 1930); French translation in F. Dvornik, *Les légendes de Constantin et Méthode vues de Byzance* (Prague, 1933); basic analysis by V. Jagić, *Zur Entstehungsgeschichte der altkirchenslav. Sprache* (2nd ed., Berlin, 1913), pp. 1-130; cf. also *idem,* "Conversion of the Slavs," in *Camb. Med. Hist.,* IV (1923), chap. 8 b; Brückner, *Die Wahrheit über die Slavenapostel* (Tübingen, 1913); H. von Schubert, *Die sogenannten*

Slavenapostel Constantin und Methodius (Heidelberg. Sitz.-Ber. Phil.-hist. Kl., 1916), i; Bury, *History of the Eastern Roman Empire*, pp. 392-401.

31. Cf. Jagić, *Enstehungsgeschichte*, pp. 182-247; idem "Glagolicheskoe Pis'mo," in *Entsiklopediya Slavyanskoy Filologii*, III (Spb., 1911), 51-229.

32. Cf. S. Gedeonov, *Varyagi i Rus'* (Spb., 1876), pp. 282-285; V. Sergeevich, "Grecheskoe i Russkoe Pravo v Dogovorakh s Grekami X Věka," in *Zhur. Min. Nar. Prosv.*, (Spb., Jan. 1882), p. 82; A. Dimitriu, "K Voprosu o Dogovorakh Russkikh s Grekami," in *Vizantiyskiy Vremennik*, II (Spb., 1895), 3; Shakhmatov, *Povest'*, p. xxiv; Istrin, *Zamechaniya O Nachale Russkogo Letopisaniya* (*Izv. Otd. Russk. Yaz. i Slov.*, XXVI), 76, 77; idem, "Dogovorȳ Russkikh s Grekami," in *Izv, Otd. Russk. Yaz. i Slov.* XXIX (Lenigrad, 1924), 382-393; J. Kulischer, *Russische Wirtshaftsgeschichte* (Jena, 1925), I, 20-30. There appears, in the main, to be very little probability that a translation of each of these treaties was made into either Norse or Old Russian at the time of their negotiation, though the presence of Bulgarian interpreters in Constantinople during the tenth century is not unlikely.

33. Shakhmatov considers (*Povest'*, p. xxxix) that the compiler of his hypothetical *Povest'* text of 1118 was a monk originally belonging to the Crypt Monastery, who spent some time in Novgorod with Vladimir's son Mstislav, and was possibly his confessor. Upon Mstislav's return to the south (according to the Hypatian text, Mstislav took over Belgorod in 1117), Shakhmatov thinks that this learned monk was intrusted by Mstislav with the edition of the supposed 1118 text. Shakhmatov also supposes that Mstislav, as oldest son of Vladimir Monomakh, had in his possession not only the *Pouchenie* but also a copy of Vladimir's letter to Oleg, son of Svyatoslav, which had been written in 1096 after Vladimir's younger son Izyaslav had lost his life in a battle against Oleg at Murom. Shakhmatov thus adopts the view that the *Pouchenie* instead of being composed in its entirety by Vladimir himself shortly before his death in 1125, was actually written by him as early as 1100-1101, and that the account of Vladimir's campaigns was continued down to 1117 by Mstislav when he turned the document over to the compiler of the *Povest'* redaction of 1118. These highly ingenious combinations unfortunately lack any real factual basis.

34. Istrin, *Zamechaniya* (*Izv. Otd. Russk. Yaz. i Slov.*, XXVII), 227-228.

35. Editions: Nikol'sky, *Materialȳ*, pp. 28-55; V. Sreznevsky, in *Musin-Pushkinskiy Sbornik* (Spb., 1893), pp. 32-74. Cf. Shakhmatov, *Razȳskaniya* p. 147; Istrin, *Ocherk*, pp. 127-135. The work is commonly referred to as the *Slovo o Zakone i Blagodati*.

36. For the text of the Jacobean *Eulogy*, cf. V. Sreznevsky, *op. cit.*, pp. 1-32. On the traditional elements in the *Povest'* narrative, cf. Shakhmatov, *Razȳskaniya*, pp. 10-38, 133-161. The textual history of the various biographies of Vladimir presents in itself a highly complicated problem. Cf. E. Golubinsky, *Istoriya Russkoy Tserkvi*, I (Moscow, 1901), 105-254; P. Serebryansky, *Drevne-Russkie Knyazheskie Zhitiya* (Moscow, 1915), pp. 43-81, and Texts, pp. 14-26.

37. Text of both in Sreznevsky, *Skazaniya o Svyatȳkh Borisě i Glěbě* (Spb., 1860).

38. *Svědeniya i Zamětki o Maloizvěstnȳkh i Neizvěstnȳkh Pamyatnikakh*, vol. I (Spb., 1867), no. 25.

39. For the sources of still another legend, that of St. Andrew's journey up the

Dnieper, cf. Golubinsky, *op. cit.*, I, 19-34. The legend of St. Andrew in Rus' developed in Kiev during the eleventh century and is referred to *ca.* 1075 in a letter of the Emperor Michael VII Dukas to Prince Vsevold I Yaroslavich of Kiev; cf. V. G. Vasil'evsky, *Trudÿ*, II (Spb., 1909), 49-51; A. Sedel'nikov, "Drevnyaya Kievskaya Legenda ob Apostole Andree," *Slavia*, III (Prague, 1924), 316-335, the latter with reference to sixteenth-century Western tradition. The legend evolved from an expansion of Greek lives recounting that St. Andrew taught in the Caucasus and in the Crimea.

40. The analogy of this account with the *Orvar-Odds Saga* has been frequently noted. Cf. R. C. Boer's ed. of the latter (Halle, 1892), chaps. 2, 3, 4, and especially A. I. Lyashchenko's interesting article: "Letopisnÿya Skazaniya o Smerti Olega Veshchego," in *Izv. Otd. Russk. Yaz. i Slov.*, XXIX (Leningrad, 1925). 254-288, together with the literature there cited; cf. A. Stender-Petersen, *Die Varägersage als Quelle der altruss. Chronik* (Leipzig, 1934), pp. 176-209. Lyashchenko's conclusion (pp. 287-288) may be quoted: "Comparing the details of the *Chronicle* accounts of Oleg with the narratives of the sagas of Scandinavian heroes, we have noted features of resemblance between them. This similarity is explained by the cultural exchanges between Russes and Varangians during the first centuries of the historical life of Rus'. It is difficult to determine what traditions are borrowed by Russes from Scandinavians, and *vice versa*. But the influence of Russian narratives on Scandinavian is unquestionable . . . The tale of the death of Oleg by the sting of a serpent crawling out of his horse's skull, was transferred to Russia from Norway. The Russian influence is much more strongly felt in those Scandinavian sagas treating the more recent period, viz., Olga, Vladimir, and the time of Yaroslav." Cf. F. Braun, "Das historische Russland im nordischen Schrifttum des X-XIV. Jahrhunderts," in *Festschrift für Eugen Mogk* (Halle, 1924), pp. 150-196; Cross, "Yaroslav the Wise in Norse Tradition," in *Speculum*, IV (1929), 177-197.

41. In the case of Olga, it seems clear that an early biography of the princess actually existed. It related mainly to her conversion and remnants of it are preserved only in Serbian and North-Russian texts of late date. Cf. Serebryansky, *op. cit.*, pp. 1-11.

42. Cf. Shakhmatov, *Razÿskaniya*, pp. 477-488; Sukhomlinov, *op. cit.*, pp. 248-273; N. Kostomarov, "Predaniya Pervonachal'noy Russkoy Lětopisi," in *Istoricheskiya Monografii*, XIII (Spb., 1881), 3-207.

43. "Iskhodnaya Tochka Lětochisleniya *Povesti Vremennÿkh Lět*," in *Zhur. Min. Nar. Prosv.*, CCCX (Spb., 1897), i, 217-222.

44. K. de Boor, *Nicephori archiepiscopi Constantinopolitani opuscula historica* (Leipzig, 1890), pp. 83, 84, 102; M. Weingart, *op. cit.*, I, 56, 57; N. V. Stepanov, "Lětopisets Nikifora v Novgorodskoy Kormchey," in *Izv. Otd. Russk. Yaz. i Slov.*, XVII (Spb., 1912), ii, 250-293, iii, 256-320.

45. "Khronologiya Drevněyshikh Russkikh Lětopisnÿkh Svodov," in *Zhur. Min. Nar. Prosv.*, I (Spb., 1897), 463-482.

46. *Ibid.*, p. 464.

47. Von Muralt, *ed. cit.*, p. 816: «κδ΄ τοῦ Σεπτεμβρίου μηνὸς τιμᾶται Ῥωμανὸς τῇ τοῦ Καίσαρος ἀξίᾳ»; Istrin, I, 552: *V k̄ i d̄ dn sentevria mtsa pochten bÿst Rōman Kesarevom sanom;* von Muralt, *ibid.*,: «καὶ Ἰανουαρίου ς΄ τῇ τῶν ἁγίων φωτῶν ἡμέρᾳ στέφει Θεοδώραν τὴν γυναῖκα αὐτοῦ;»

Istrin, I, 553: *V lě suki indikta ī genouaria mtsa v s stẏ bgoyavlenii dn'*, *věnchaet tsr feodorou . . . tsrtseyu.* Cf. E. de Muralt: *Essai de chronographie byzantine* Spb., 1855), pp. 497, 498. It is obvious that the Bulgarian translator of Hamartolus here had before him a Greek text in which this date was given; it appears, in fact, among von Muralt's variants. It should be noted in general that von Muralt's text is unscientific and highly unsatisfactory, and is employed in this study solely for reasons of convenience. Cf. K. de Boor's trenchant remarks on this point (*ed. cit.*, I, x). Though the accretions to Hamartolus after 843 are derived from Symeon the Logothete, they are here conventionally referred to as belonging to the Hamartolus text, since the Russian Chronicle doubtless regarded them as such.

48. Cf. K. de Boor, "Der Angriff der Rhos auf Byzanz," in *Byz. Zts.*, IV (Leipzig, 1897), 444-466; F. Cumont, *Anec. Brux.*, I (Ghent, 1894), 33.

49. Cf. von Muralt, p. 736, variant 4: «τῷ θ' αὐτοῦ ἔτει ἐκστρατεύει κατὰ τῶν 'Αγαρηνῶν.»

50. Shakhmatov (*loc. cit.*, pp. 455-456, 470-477) explains this error by the assumption that the author of an hypothetical basic chronicle text which he dates as of *ca.* 1073 knew the correct date of Michael's accession (842), but misread the Slavic translation of Hamartolus to the extent of mistaking the chapter heading IB ([12], Istrin, I, 511, 1, 7) for the twelfth year of Michael's reign, and thus succeeded in dating the raid as of 854. The compiler of the first redaction of the *Povest'* (1116) in his turn mistook 854 for the date of Michael's assession, and thus according to Shakhmatov, moved the raid forward to 866. Finally, the compiler of a second redaction of the *Povest'* (1118), being, in Shakhmatov's opinion, the first to have at his disposal a translation of Nicephorus, corrected the accession of Michael to 852, but kept the date of 866 for the raid, changing "twelfth" to "fourteenth" in accordance with his previous correction. Shakhmatov subsequently modified his theory as to primitive texts prior to 1116 by attributing the hypothetical compilation of 1073 to the monk Nikon (*supra*, p. 94), and basing the latter upon his equally hypothetical "most ancient" (*drevněyshiy*) Kiev text of 1039. In his restoration of the supposed Nikonian text (*Razẏskaniya*, pp. 539-610), he admits no dates at all before 978 (6486, the accession of Vladimir), and likewise assumes (*ibid.*, pp. 97-108) that the chronological framework was introduced only in the hypothetical text of 1095. This important change of view between 1897 and 1908 is but one of the many revisions to which Shakhmatov subjected his own hypotheses concerning the evolution of the *Povest'*, and suggests that Slavists who unquestionably accept Shakhmatov's later views as a basis for further investigation are building on a by no means sound foundation.

51. For a brief survey of the early views on Slavic origins, cf. L. Niederle, *Manuel de l'antiquité slave*, I (Paris, 1923), 1-12. The evolution of scholarship in this field is analyzed in greater detail in the same author's *Slovanské Starožitnosti*, I (2d ed., Prague, 1925), pt. I, pp. 1-65. The development of Slavic philology is broadly treated in Jagić, *Istoriya Slavyanskoy Filologii* (Spb., 1910).

52. Cf. Niederle, *Slov. Star.*, I (Prague, 1925), pt. 4, pp. 72-81, and sources there cited; G. Vernadsky, *Ancient Russia* (New Haven, 1946).

53. J. Marquart, *Osteuropäische und ostasiatische Streifzüge* (Leipzig, 1903), p. 111.

54. Cf. Niederle, *Slov. Star.*, II, I, 120 n. The name *Slav* first appears in a source of the early sixth century (Pseudo-Caesarius of Nazianzus [Migne, *Patr. Gr.*, XXXVIII, 847], and then frequently from Procopius and Jordanes forward. By the seventh century, certainly, it was the generic term for members of this race. The original form *Slověnin*, plural *Slověne* corresponds, except for the inserted *ķ* and *t*, to the Greek and Latin Σκλαβηνοί, Στλαυηνοί, *Sclaveni, Stlaueni*, and it has been suggested that the shorter forms Σκλάβοι, Σθλάβοι, *Sclavi, Stlavi* are imitated from the numerous characteristic proper names ending in *–slav*. The origin of the *ķ* is dubious, though it may be remarked that the initial combination *sl* occurs in no native Greek word, while *skl*, of which the sound is identical to an unpracticed ear, was familiar from σκληρός and its cognates, and *stl* occurs in στλεγίς, etc. The Arabic forms which include the *ķ* (*Asqālab*, *Saqāliba*) would thus appear to depend originally on these Greek forms. Popular etymology rapidly developed a legendary derivation from *slava*, "glory", while numerous competent scholars, including Dobrovsky and Šafařík, have accepted the derivation from *slovo*, "word", this interpreting *Slověne* to mean "speakers of the same language." This derivation is, however, suspect, in view of the fact that *–ěnin* (plur. *–ěne*) is invariably a suffix denoting origin from a place or locality. The most recent attempt to etymologize *Slověnin* is offered by A. Brückner in *Slavia*, III (Prague, 1924), 199-203, who characterizes it as a nickname derived from pregerm. *slaiwa=Eng. *slow*, which he connects with Goth. *slawan*, "be silent." Apart from the fact that the relation of *slawan* to *slaiwa is questionable (not recognized by S. Feist, *Etym. Wtb. d. got. Sp.*, 2d. ed. [Halle, 1923], s.v., nor by *NED*, s.v., "slow"), it remains to be shown at what juncture this Germanic nickname was applied to the Slavs, and to what particular branch of the latter. A certain parallelism between this derivation and the Slavic use of *němets* ("dummy") for *German* is apparent.

55. Slavic paganism is conveniently discussed in Niederle, *Manuel*, II (Paris, 1925), 127-168, and *Slov. Star.*, II, pt. I (2d ed., Prague, 1924). Cf. also F. Mansikka, *Religion der Ostslaven* (Helsinki, 1921); A. Brückner, "Mythologische Thesen," in *Arch. Slav. Philol.*, XL (1925), 1-22; *Mitołogja Słowianska* (Cracow, 1918); L. Léger, *La Mythologie slave* (Paris, 1901); A. Sobolevsky, "Zametki po Slavyanskoy Mifologii," in *Slavia*, VII (Prague, 1928), 174-178; C. Clemen, *Religionsgeschichte Europas* (Heidelberg, 1926) I, 368-377; J. Máchal, "Slavic Mythology," in *Mythology of All Races* (Boston, 1918), III, 222-361, bibliography *ibid.*, pp. 389-398. – Taking oath by Perun is again mentioned at the ratification of the treaty of 945, while at the accession of Vladimir I it is recorded that "he set up idols on the hill outside the castle with the hall: one of Perun . . . and others of Khors, Dazh'bog, Stribog, Simar'gl, and Mokosh'." It has been suggested in the latter instance that the *Povest'* is in error, because in the cases of the well-known Slavic pagan shrines at Akrona, Garz, and Stettin, only one image was found in any one shrine (Brückner, *Thesen*, p. 10). Though Perun is habitually conceived as the pagan East Slavic god of thunder and lightning, there is no evidence for a native Slavic deity of this name. Perun 'the striker' (from root **per–*) is better regarded as the Slavic equivalent of the Norse Thor, imported by the Varangians. Dazh'bog, "the god who brings gifts", seems to have been

the general Slavic sun-god. Though Stribog is usually interpreted as the god of the whistling winds, he may be viewed more properly as a vegetation spirit. Khors has never been satisfactorily explained. Simar'gl seems to be a copyist's combination of the two deities, Sim, a household spirit, and Rogl, a spirit of the harvest. Folkloristic survivals indicate that Mokosh' was a female house spirit associated with women's tasks; she has been identified with Astarte, whose cult may have reached the Dnieper valley through oriental channels. Volos (Veles) was originally the god of the dead; his attribute as god of flocks results from a late assimiliation to St. Blasius.

56. For the Khazars, cf. *Camb. Med. Hist.*, IV, 188-192; Bury, *Eastern Roman Empire*, pp. 402-408; H. Kutschera, *Die Chasaren* (Vienna, 1910); Niederle, *Slov. Star.*, I, pt. 4, 51-53, also *Manuel*, I, 178, 196, and *Původ a Počátky Slovanů Východních* (Prague, 1925), pp. 51-53; V. Parkhomenko, "Kievskaya Rus' i Khazariya," *Slavia*, VI (1927), 380-387; G. Vernadsky, *Opyt Istorii Evrazii* (Berlin, 1934), pp. 51-57; J. Brutzkus, *Encycl. Jud.*, art. "Chasaren", V, 341; Vernadsky, *Ancient Russia* (New Haven, 1946), chaps. V-VII. A Turko-Tartar tribe, the Khazars appears at the beginning of the seventh century as settlers on the lower Volga. After the dissolution of Kubrat's Bulgar khanate (from 642), they overran the Bulgar territory about the Sea of Azov, and their movement apparently stimulated a migration of the Bulgars partly westward toward the Danube and partly northeastward toward the Kama. The Khazar domain centered between the Donets, the Kuban', and the lower Volga, extending at its maximum across the steppes from the Volga to the Dnieper. They rapidly increased in wealth and influence through their control of the trade-routes along the Don and the Volga; and they were, in the eighth century, in close diplomatic contact with the Eastern Empire whose constant allies they were in their common struggle against the Caliphate. Their principal eastern center was the city of Itil, on the lower Volga, near modern Astrakhan, but, in the ninth century, Byzantine engineers built for the Khagan the fortified town of Sarkel, usually identified with the city mentioned in the *Povest'* as Běla Věža, designed to resist the attacks or the nomad Pechenegs and the raids of the Russes (cf. K. V. Kudryashov, "O Mestonakhozhdenii Khazarsk. Gor. Sarkela," *Izvestiya Akad. Nauk. SSSR.*, Ser. ist. fil. 1947, 6; Marquart, *Streifzüge*, pp. 1 ff., endeavored to establish that *Bela Vezha* actually referred to Itil). The Emperor Michael III sent Constantine (St. Cyril) on a mission to the Khazars in 851, but the influence of Judaism, proceeding from the Jewish communities both in the Crimea and in Caucasia, was momentarily stronger than either Christianity or Islam. In the ninth century, therefore, Judaism thus became the official faith, until overshadowed by Islam which was adopted by the Khazar ruler about 950 to ensure Khwarezmian aid against the invading Turks (Marquart, *op. cit.*, p. 4). At this time, the decline of the Khazar State had already begun. It was hard pressed by the Pechenegs, while the Slavic tribes, especially after they fell under the leadership of the Varangian element, rapidly achieved independence from the weakish Khazar rule. Its fall was signalized by the reduction of the fortress, of Bela Vezha by Svyatoslav I of Kiev in 965.

57. Cf. L^2, 19: "Izgnasha Varyagi *za* more ... idasha *za* more k Varyagom k Rusi."

58. Venerunt autem legati Graecorum a Theophilo imperatore directi ...

quos imperator xv. kal. Iunii in Ingulenheim honorifice suscepit . . . Misit [Theophilus] etiam cum eis quosdam qui se, id est gentem suam, Rhos uocari dicebant, quod rex illorum, chacanus uocabulo, ad se amicitiae, sicut asserebant, causa direxerat, petens per memoratam epistolam, quatenus benignitate imperatoris redeundi facultatem atque auxilium per imperium suum tuto habere possent, quoniam itinera, per quae ad illum Constantinopolim uenerant inter barbaras et nimiae feritatis gentes immanissimas habuerant, quibus eos, ne forte periculum inciderent, redire noluit. Quorum aduentus causam imperator dilligentius inuestigans comperit eos gentis esse Sueonum."

59. Luidprand, *Antapodosis,* I (ed. L. Becker, Hannover, 1915), 11: "Constantinopolitana urbs, quae prius Byzantium, Noua nunc dicitur Roma, inter ferocissimas gentes est constituta. Habet quippe ab aquilone Hungarios, Pizenacos, Chazaros, Rusios, quos alio nos nomine *Nordmannos* appellamus." *Ibid.,* V, 15: "Gens quadam est sub aquilonis parte constituta quam a qualitate corporis Greci vocant Rusios, nos vero a positione loci nominamus *Nordmannos.* Lingua quippe Teutonum *nord* aquilo *man* autem dicitur homo, unde et Nordmannos aquilonares homines dicere possumus. Huius denique gentis rex uocabulo Inger erat, qui collectis mille et eo amplius nauibus Constantinopolim uenit."

60. *De administrando imperio* ix., in *Corp. Script. Hist. Byz.,* IX, 74-79.

61. The exact connotation of Λενζανινοί is a subject of dispute. Cf. G. Ilinski, "Kto bÿli Λενζανινοί Konstantina Bagryanorodnogo," in *Slavia,* IV (Prague, 1925), 314-319.

62. Cf. W. Thomsen, *op. cit.,* pp. 52 ff.; Niederle, *Slov. Star.,* I iv, 107-110; T. J. Arne, *Le Suède et l'Orient* (Uppsala, 1914), p. 11; K. Muka, "Prohi Dnjepra a městne miena z X l.," in *Časopis, LXVIII* (Prague, 1916), 84-89; H. Pipping, "De skandinaviska Dnjeprnamnen," in *Stud. i Nord. Filil.,* vol. II (Helsingfors, 1911), no. 5.

63. *Theophanis Continuati,* VI, 39 (*Corp. Script. Hist. Byz.,* XXXII, 423): «Δεκάτης καὶ τετάρτης ἰνδικτιῶνος Ἰουνίῳ μηνὶ ἑνδεκάτῃ, κατέπλευσαν οἱ Ῥῶς κατὰ Κωνσταντινουπόλεως μετὰ πλοίων χιλιάδων δέκα, οἱ καὶ Δρομῖται λεγόμενοι, οἳ ἐκ γένους τῶν Φράγγων καθίστανται.» Also Symeon Magister, *De Leone Basilii,* 14 (*ibid.,* p. 707). A. Krumbacher (*Byz. Litt.-gesch.,* pp. 124-126) remarks that Symeon used the former work as a source; hence the identity in terms of the two passages.

64. Arne, *op. cit.,* p. 61.

65. F. Braun, "Das historische Russland im nordischen Schrifttum des X-XIV. Jhdts," in *Festschrift für Eugen Mogk* (Halle, 1924), pp. 163, 164.

66. Cf. F. Braun, *op. cit.,* and Cross, "Yaroslav the Wise in Norse Tradition," in *Speculum,* IV (Cambridge, 1929), 177-197; also Cross, "La tradition islandaise de St. Vladimir," *Revue des Etudes Slaves,* XI (Paris, 1931).

67. The survival at a late date of precisely these names is in itself significant. Without exception, these cities lie on recognized trade-routes (Novgorod, Polotsk, Smolensk), or at the headwaters of the Volga and its tributaries (Rostov, Murom, Suzdal'). They were thus familiar stages on the old trade-routes to the Orient and the Black Sea. The emphasis on Novgorod rather than Kiev also points to the existence of a body of information which originated at the moment when Novgorod was the principal point of Scandinavian contact with the Eastern Slavic world.

68. Cf. Cross, *Speculum*, IV, 177-197, and the texts there cited.
69. Arne, *op. cit.*, pp. 220-231.
70. Marquart, *Streifzüge*, XXXI, 24-25, 160-206.
71. For Ibn Rustah, cf. D. A. Khvolson, *Izvěstiya o Khazarakh*, etc. (Spb., 1869). For Al Bakrī, cf. E. Kunik-A.Rosen, "Izvěstiya Al-Bekri i drugikh Avtorov o Rusi i Slavyanakh," in *Prilozheniya k XXXIIomu Tomu Zapisok Imp. Akad. Nauk* (Spb., 1878), no. 2; Barthold, "Otchet o Poězdkě v Srednyuyu Aziyu," in *Zapiski Imp. Akad. Nauk* (Spb., 1897), series 8, vol. I, no. 4.
72. Cf. F. Westberg, "K Analizu Vostochnȳkh Istochnikov o Vostochnoy Evropě," in *Zhur. Min. Nar. Prosv.*, n.s., XIII (Spb., 1908), 364-371.
73. In De Goeje, *Bibl. géograph. arabe*, VI (Leyden, 1889), 15: "Les Russes qui appartiennent aux peuples slaves se rendent des régions les plus éloignées de Çaklaba (le pays des Slaves) vers la mer romaine, et y vendent des peaux de castor et de renard noir, ainsi que des épées."
74. Quoted by Westberg, *Zhurn. Min. Nar. Prosv.*, n.s., XIV (1908), 25.
75. Quoted by Marquart, *Streifzüge*, p. 102.
76. A. Harkavi, *Skazaniya Musul'manskikh Pisateley o Slavyanakh i Russkikh* (Spb., 1870), p. 130.
77. V. Vasil'evsky, editor, in *Lětopis' Arkheograficheskoy Kommissii*, IX (Spb., 1893), xli, cxvi ff., ccxcv, and particularly 66-67: «ἔφοδος ἦν βαρβάρων τῶν 'Ρῶς· ἔθνους, ὡς πάντες ἴσασιν, ὠμοτάτου καὶ ἀπηνοῦς καὶ μηδὲν ἐπιφερομένου φιλανθρωπίας λείψανον. Θηριώδεις τοῖς τρόποις, ἀπάνθρωποι τοῖς ἔργοις, αὐτῇ τῇ ὄψει τὴν μιαιφονίαν ἐπιδεικνύμενοι, ἐπ' οὐδενὸς τῶν ἄλλων, ὧν πεφύκασιν ἄνθρωποι, χαίροντες ὡς ἐπὶ φονοκτονίᾳ. τοῦτο δὴ τὸ φθοροποιὸν καὶ πρᾶγμα καὶ ὄνομα, ἀπὸ τῆς Προποντίδος ἀρξάμενον τῆς λοίμης, καὶ τὴν ἄλλην ἐπινεμηθὲν παράλιον, ἔφθασεν καὶ μέχρι τῆς τοῦ ἁγίου πατρίδος, κόπτον ἀφειδῶς γένος ἅπαν καὶ ἡλικίαν πᾶσαν, οὐ πρεσβύτας οἰκτεῖρον, οὐ νήπια παρορῶν, ἀλλὰ κατὰ πάντων ὁμοῦ τὴν μιαίφονον ὁπλίζον χεῖρα, τὸν ὄλεθρον ἔσπευδεν διαβῆναι ὅση δύναμις».
78. Vasil'evsky, *op. cit.*, p. 100: "po smerti zhe svyatago malo lět minou, priide rat' velika rouskaa iz Novagrada knyaz' Bravlin silen zělō. Plěni ot Korsounya i do Korza. s mnogoyu siloyu priide k Surozhu. za 10 d'niy bisha zlě mezhou sebe." For a discussion of the literature on this passage, which has provoked extensive comment, cf. Vasil'evsky's survey of the literature, pp. clii-clxvi.
79. E. Kunik, *Die Berufung der schwedischen Ruodsen durch die Finnen und Slaven* (Spb., 1844); also the article "Begannen die Russischen Handelsfahrten u. Raubzüge auf dem Schwarzen u. Caspischen Meere zur Zeit Mohammeds oder Ruriks?" in Dorn's *Caspia* (Spb., 1875), pp. 221-256. W. Thomsen, *op. cit.*, p. 94.
80. *Die Germanen* (Berlin, 1928), p. 144.
81. Shakhmatov, "Skazanie o Prizvanii Varyagov," in *Izv.*, IX (Spb., 1904), 340.
82. Efforts have been made to connect 'Ρῶς with the Iranian name of the Volga, *Raha='Pā in Ptolemy (so F. Knauer, *O Proiskhozhdenii Imeni Rus'* [Moscow, 1901]), 'Ρῶς in Agathemerus (*Arriani Periplus* [ed. A. Hoffmann, Leipzig, 1842], p. 367), Mordvin *Raws*. While the alleged connection of 'Ρῶς with the *Rosh* of Ezekiel, xxxviii, 2, and xxxix, 1, was criticized by G. F. Müller as early as 1760 (*Sammlung russischer Geschichte*, V, 390 ff.), it is considered not improbable by Marquart (*op. cit.*, p. 355) and has been revived once more by

V. A. Brim, "Proiskhozhdenie Termina Rus'," *Rossiya i Zapad,* I (Leningrad, 1923); A. Florovsky, "Knyaz' Rosh u Proroka Ezekiila," *Sbornik v Chest na V. N. Zlatarski* (Sofia, 1925); M. Syuzyumov, "K Voprosu o Proiskhozhdenii Slova 'Ρῶς, 'Ρωσία, Rossiya," *Vestnik Drevney Istorii,* II (1940). Most recently Prof. Vernadsky has come out with an interesting theory which derives the name *Rus'* from the Roxolani (possibly, Rukhs-As, "Light Alans"), which tribe may have been spoken of by the Patriarch Proclus (434-447), when he referred, in one of his sermons on the Hunnic invasion, to Ezekiel's prophecy concerning the Prince of Rosh (indeed as 'Ρῶς; this is reported by Nicephorus Callistus in the fourteenth century), and by Zacharias Rhetor (sixth century), as Hros (='Ρῶς); *Ancient Russia,* esp. pp. 87-88, 96-97, 108, 138-139, 257-260, 275-278. It can, however, be replied by the defenders of the *Ruotsi* > *Rus'* theory that, although the derivation of 'Ρῶς (Hros) from biblical *Rosh* appears indeed satisfactorily indicated, the application of that Greek term to Ezekiel's Rosh, to the Roxolani (?), and to Rus' need in no way imply that any connection exists between these ethnic groups themselves. That term was merely an archaic near-homophone of *Rus';* hence: ου>ω. The recurrence of river-names like Ros' (*not* Rus) in Eastern Europe may indeed be due to the conjectural Aryan term *ronsa* ("moisture, water") cf. Russ. *rosa* (cf. Vernadsky, p. 97).

83. C. M. Frähn, *Ibn Foszlans und anderer Berichte über die Russen* (Spb., 1823), pp. 177-179, 182, 183.

84. *Ibid.,* pp. 196, 197.

85. *Hrafnkelssaga Freysgoða* (Reykjavík, 1911), p. 16.

86. *Njalssaga* (Reykjavi'k, 1910), p. 185: "Kolskeggr tók skírn í Danmörku, enn nam þar þó eigi yndi ok fór austr í Garðaríki, ok var þar einn vetr. Þa fór hann þaðan út í Miklagarð, ok gekk þar á mála. Spurðist þat til hans, at hann kvangaðist þar ok var höfðingi fyrir Væringjarliði, ok var þar til dauða-dags." The extant text of this saga is, however, not older than 1250.

87. The word *Vaeringjar* itself is conventionally regarded as of Norse origin, cognate with Old-English *wǣrgenga,* "one who seeks protection, a stranger," and thus derived from ON. *várar,* "solemn vow, oath," and *ganga.* An unexplained difficulty lies in the fact that the Slavic, Greek, and Arabic forms all point without exception to an unumlauted original, though in such cases *i*–umlaut is supposed to have taken place in ON. before A.D. 700 (A. Noreen, *Altisl. u Altnord. Gram.* [4th ed., Halle, 1923], pp. 61 ff.). The query may therefore be put forward whether the derivation of the word should not rather be sought in its connection with Med. Lat. *vargus, varganeus* (see Ducange *s. vv.*) and an initial corruption of *vagrans vagrantes* to **vargans vargantes,* later transformed by popular etymology in the Germanic dialects to the extant forms now usually accepted as primitives. Cross proposed to return to this topic in a later study.

88. Cf. V. A. Mošin, "Normannÿ v Vostochnoy Evrope," *Byzantinoslavica,* III (Prague, 1931), 33-58, 285-301; T. D. Kendrick, *A History of the Vikings* (New York, 1930), pp. 143-178; Vernadsky, *Ancient Russia* (New Haven, 1946), chaps. VII, VIII. For early commerce, cf. also Vasiliev, "Economic Relations between Byzantium and Old Russia," *Journal Econ. and Hist.,* IV (1932), 314-334.

Notes to the Russian Primary Chronicle

1. The passage in italics is derived from the *Chronicle* of Georgius Hamartolus, for which source, cf. *supra* Introduction: Sources. The geographical names corrupted in the Old-Russian text are corrected to accord with the Greek original.

2. Though related to Hamartolus, ed. von Muralt, p. 39, Istrin, p. 58, the story of the Tower of Babel is also based on the Slavic translation of John Malalas (sixth-century Byzantine chronicler; cf. K. M. Obolensky, *Lětopisets Pereyaslavlya Suzdal'skago* [Moscow, 1851], p. xix), and likewise affected by the *Paleya,* for which, cf. *supra* Introduction: Sources.

3. The Croats (*Khorvatÿ*) were a remnant of the South Slavic tribe of the same name who remained in Bukovina and East Galicia after the main body of the tribe had moved farther southward. They are not to be identified as a Russian tribe, but were the object of conquest by Oleg in 907 and by Vladimir I in 992; cf. Niederle, *Pův. Slov. Vy'chodních,* pp. 154-156 with literature.

4. *Lyakh* (cf. Lith. *leñkas,* Magyar *lengyel,* "a Pole," Turk. *Lekhistan,* "Poland"), though not preserved in Polish texts, where it is replaced by forms derived from *pole,* "field," (*Polska, Polak*), is the common designation for a Pole in the earliest Russian sources, and is still used in the Polish highland districts. The derivation from *lyada,* "meadow," would indicate a division of the population into those who lived by cattle-raising and hunting as opposed to the *polyane,* "field-dwellers, husbandmen," who practiced agriculture; cf. Niederle, *Původ a Počátky Slovanů Západních* (Prague, 1919), pp. 228-229.

5. Tsar'grad "Imperial City"=Constantinople.

6. Cf. *supra,* Introduction, n. 39.

7. Cf. *infra,* n. 94.

8. For the Khazars, who lived on the Volga till the beginning of the seventh century and did not appear in Southern Russia until after the breakup of the Bulgar State of Kubrat, subsequent to 642, cf. *supra,* Introduction, n. 56. The Bulgars themselves were probably the remnant of the Huns which remained in the east after the overthrow of the Goths (375). In 482, some thirty years after Attila's death, outposts of the Bulgars appeared on the Byzantine frontier, and were enlisted by the Emperor Zeno as allies against the Visigoths; cf. Niederle, *Pův. Slov. Východních,* pp. 48-51; V. N. Zlatarski, *Istorijata na bulgarskata důržava,* I (Sofia, 1918), 22-37; S. Runciman, *History of the First Bulgarian Empire* (London, 1930), pp. 3-10. Though the "White Ugrians" are sometimes identified with the Khazars, they are more probably an offshoot of the Bulgars, presumably the so-called Onogunduri; cf. Zlatarski, p. 83 ff., Runciman, pp. 15-16. Heraclius (*regn.* 610-641) campaigned against the Persians in 622-628; cf. A. A. Vasiliev, *History of the Byzantine Empire* (Madison, 1952), pp. 197-199. Before the Bulgars arrived in the Balkans, the Avars, a Mongolian tribe originating in the modern Bokhara and Turkestan, shook off the Turkish yoke and moved

westward, reaching the northern Caucasus in 558. Expelling or subjecting the Bulgars of the steppes and the Slavs of the Dnieper basin, they occupied the Dobrudzha in 562 and within four years were settled in Pannonia (Hungary) and Syrmia, from which movement rise the traditions of their oppression of the Slavs; cf. J. Marquart, *Streifzüge,* pp. 43, 45-6; Zlatarski, I, 72; Vernadsky, *Opÿt Istorii Evrazii,* pp. 32, 36-39. The mention of their attack on Heraclius is from Hamartolus, von Muralt, pp. 565-566, Istrin, I, 434. During the early seventh century, the Avars succumbed to concerted Frankish, Slav, and Bulgar pressure, and their power on the Danube was eliminated by 650; cf. Likhachev, *Povest' Vrem. Let,* II, 223-229. Cf. also Vernadsky, *Ancient Russia,* chaps. IV, V, VI.

9. The Dulebians, not mentioned in the Chronicle after 907, were a Volhynian tribe on the northern Bug; cf. M. Hrushevsky, *Stat'i po Slavyanovĕdeniyu,* I (Spb., 1904), 317; *Kievskaya Rus',* I (Spb., 1911), 247-249.

10. The Pechenegs (Patzinaks), a Turko-Tartar tribe and the most threatening nomad foe of the Kievan principality prior to 1034, moved into the steppes from the area between the Volga and the Yaik early in the ninth century, driving the Magyars before them into the Danube basin. Their first contact with the princes of Kiev occurred in 915; cf. Niederle, *Pův. Slov. Vých.,* pp. 53-54. The Magyars (here referred to as "Black Ugrians") are found on the Don in contact with the Khazars by 833, and under Pecheneg pressure reached the lower Danube by 860. Their chronological association with Oleg (*infra.,* under 888-898) points to their ultimate movement into Hungary via the Carpathians; Niederle, *op. cit.,* pp. 36-38. While akin to the Polovcians (*Polovtsÿ*), they were not identical with them (contrary to Bury, *Eastern Roman Emp.,* p. 411, n. 4).

11. In the corresponding passage of the Hypatian redaction (*PSRL,* II, 3rd edition, col. 10), the *Ulichi* and *Tivertsÿ* are located along the southern Bug and the Dnieper, while the earliest Novgorod chronicle (Synodal codex: *Novgorodskaya Lĕtopiś po Sinodal'nomu Spisku* [Spb., 1888], p. 7) reports under 922 that the Ulichi resisted attempts by Igor' to reduce them to tribute; one city, Peresechen', held out for three years. Under pressure the Ulichi transferred their residence to the area between the Bug and the Dniester, but eventually became tributary to Kiev. These tribes are an example of the thrust of the Eastern Slavs toward the Black Sea which was repeatedly interrupted by nomadic incursions. They were thus unable to withstand the successive onslaughts of Magyars and Pechenegs, and withdrew into Transylvania and Hungary during the tenth and eleventh centuries. They consequently appear to have been the ancestors of the modern Subcarpathian Russians. Of the Tivertsÿ little is known beyond their situation as neighbors to the Ulichi. For extensive literature on these minor Slavic elements, cf. Niederle, *op. cit.,* pp. 157-162 and nn.; Hrushevsky, *Kievskaya Rus',* I, 240-247.

12. Reading *umÿkivachu uvodÿ,* "carried off by capture," instead of *u vodÿ,* "by the water"; *uvodÿ* is instrum. plur. Survivals of marriage by capture persisted in Russian peasant practice almost to the present day; cf. D. Zelenin, *Russische Volkskunde* (Berlin, 1927), pp. 305-319. The present interpretation is thoroughly justified by Brückner, "Wzory Etymołogji i Krytyki Zródłowej," *Slavia,* V (1927), 420-421.

13. While cremation rapidly gave way to the tradition of Christian burial, once conversion had taken place, it is still attested for the Eastern Slavs of the

tenth century both by Byzantine and Arabic sources (notably Leo Diaconus, X, 6, in connection with Svyatoslav's campaign in Bulgaria; cf. also Harkavi, *Skazaniya Musul'manskikh Pisateley, passim*).

14. From Georgius Hamartolus, von Muralt, pp. 26-28; Istrin, pp. 57-58.

15. For the Khazars, cf. *supra*, Introduction, n. 56.

16. The indiction was originally a fifteen-year tax-assessment period, and came to be used in all Byzantine secular chronology; cf. V. Gardthausen, *Griech. Paläographie*, II (Leipzig, 1913), 454-467. The Byzantine era customarily reckons from Creation as of 5508 B.C., hence, any date of the Christian era may be obtained by deducting 5508 from the Byzantine date. The Byzantine year was usually counted as beginning on September 1. The Russians, however, used the March calendar until the fourteenth century. The January calendar from the birth of Christ was first adopted by Slavs in close contact with Catholicism, e.g., Bosnia (1189), Smolensk (treaty with Riga, 1229), and frequently in Western Russia from the fourteenth century. Dates of both systems appear in Muscovite documents only from the second half of the fifteenth century. The Christian era from January 1 was not officially adopted in Russia until 1700 under Peter the Great.

17. For the problem of the chronology of the *Povest'*, cf. *supra*, Introduction: Chronology.

18. From Hamartolus, von Muralt, pp. 732-733, Istrin, p. 508.

19. For a summary of the Varangian controversy, cf. *supra*, Introduction: The Traditional Origin of Rus'.

20. The Hypatian red. (*PSRL*, II, 3rd. ed., col. 15) here preserves a divergent story. . . . "They took with them all the Russes and came first to the Slavs (*Slověne*), and they built the city of Ladoga. Rurik, the eldest, settled in Ladoga, Sineus, the second, at Beloozero, and Truvor, the third, in Izborsk. From these Varangians the land of Rus' received its name. After two years Sineus died, as well as his brother Truvor, and Rurik assumed the sole authority. He then came to Lake Il'men' and founded on the Volkhov a city which they named Novgorod, and he settled there as prince, assigning cities. . . ." etc. This account reflects an earlier tradition of Swedish settlement in close accord with archaeological evidence as to the direction of Swedish penetration from the Sea-coast. Ladoga (now Staraya Ladoga) is on the right bank of the Volkhov river, 12 kilometers above its opening into Lake Ladoga; the town was known to the Scandinavians as Aldeigjuborg, and figures frequently in Old Norse sources dealing with the eleventh century. The name *Novgorod* (lit. 'Newton") suggests that it was founded later than some other place, e.g., Ladoga. The Norse name for Novgorod was Hólmgarðr; in historical times (to the twelfth cent.) part of the town was still known in Old Russian as the *Holm* (*Nov. Chronicle*, Synodal codex, pp. 126-127, *ad* 1134, and p. 135, *ad* 1144), or "hill," and the Norse name derives from this fact, though *holmr* in ON means "island." The identification of the Rurik of the Chronicle with Roricus of Jutland and, in general, the problem of the historicity of Rurik, Sineus, and Truvor, remains until today a subject of learned controversy. At present, however, the majority of writers on the subject seem inclined to accept the above identification; cf. N. T. Belyaev, "Rorik Yutlandskiy i Ryurik Nachal'noy Letopisi," *Seminarium Kondakovianum*, III (1929); Kendrick, *History of the Vikings*; Vernadsky, *Ancient Russia*, pp. 333-344. Also F. Kruse,

"O Proiskhozhdenii Ryurika," *Zhurn. Min. Nar. Prosv.,* IX (1936); A. Kunik, "Remarques critiques sur les antiquités russes," *Bull. Acad. Imp. Sc.,* VII (1850); G. Gedenov, *Varyagi i Rus'* 1891); Thomsen, *op. cit.;* C. F. Keary, *The Vikings in Western Civilization* (1891); W. Vogel, *Die Normannen und das frankische Reich* (1906). But Rurik's brothers seem apocryphal, cf. Vernadsky, 339, 340.

21. The account of this raid is from Hamartolus, von Muralt, pp. 726-737, Istrin, p. 511. It actually took place 18 June, 860; cf. Vasiliev, *The First Russian Attack on Constantinople in 860-61* (Mediaeval Academy of America, 1946); Bury, *Eastern Roman Empire,* pp. 419-423, with indication of other Byzantine sources. The motives for the ascription of this raid to the "fourteenth year" of Michael are uncertain; cf. *supra,* Introduction: Chronology. For an elaborate theory regarding Askold, cf. M. de Taube, *Rome et la Russie avant l'invasion des Tatars (IXe-XIIIe siècle),* I (Paris, 1947).

22. In the light of subsequent chronology, it is doubtful whether Igor' was Rurik's son, since he is stated to have married Olga in 903; though the birth of Svyatoslav, his own son, is set in 942; cf. Vernadsky, *Ancient Russia,* p. 366.

23. The Hungarian hill(*Ugorskaya Gora*)at Kiev is traditionally located on the west bank of the Dnieper just north of the Crypt Monastery and beyond Berestovo, some two kilometers south of the Podol, or riverside section of the city; cf. N. Zakrevsky, *Opisanie Kieva* (Moscow, 1868), pp. 191-198.

24. St. Irene's, constructed by Yaroslav the Wise *ca.* 1040, was situated slightly southwest of the extant Cathedral of St. Sophia. Its ground plan has been established by excavation; cf. Alpatov-Brunov, *Altrussische Kunst* (Augsburg, 1932), p. 17, with literature. One column is still preserved.

25. Prior to the importation from the German of the word *funt,* "pound," a *grivna* indicated, at least in theory, a pound of silver; the basic weight used was the so-called Kufic (or Iraq) pound (408 gr.), but the weight of the *grivna* was reduced as the price of the metal appreciated. The Kiev *grivna* was an hexagonally cast lump of silver, with two sides shorter than the other four, so that it possessed an elongated aspect. The *grivna* in varying form served as the highest token of exchange until the introduction of the ruble in the fourteenth century. The primitive *grivna* was divisible fractionally into 20 *nogatÿ,* 26 *kunÿ,* or 50 *rezanÿ;* these words themselves indicate various furs which were used as monetary tokens, just as the *grivna kun* was the fur equivalent of a silver *grivna.* During the eleventh century, the *kuna* itself (originally a marten-skin) was the equivalent of a Byzantine *keration* (one-half of a *miliaresion*) and worth about 17 cents; a silver *grivna* was thus worth about $4.25. The silver *grivna* of 1000-1050 A.D. contained approximately half a pound of silver; cf. Niederle, *Život Starých Slovanů,* III, ii (Prague, 1925), 469-470; Klyuchevsky, *Kurs Russkoy Ist.,* I, 261-264.

26. Probably a dirhem. As proved by abundant archaeological discoveries, dirhems circulated extensively in Russia before native coinage began under Vladimir I, and for fractional currency they were occasionally cut into bits as small as one fortieth (cf. Klyuchevsky, *loc. cit.*). The word *skŭlędzĭ,* Old Russ. *shch'lyag,* was probably introduced into general Slavic from West-Germanic toward the close of the eighth century, when Frankish trade with the Slavs attained considerable proportions; cf. Cross, "Gothic Loan-Words in the Slavic Vocabulary," *Harvard Studies and Notes,* XVI (1934), 42.

27. The accession dates of Byzantine emperors under 867-868 and 886-887 were computed by the compiler from the continuation of Hamartolus. The authentic text of the latter stops at 843 (death of Michael III) but was supplemented by transcriptions from Symeon the Logothete to the death of Romanus I Lecapenus in 948 (cf. Bury, *East. Rom. Emp.*, pp. 453-459).

28. Though the Magyars appear in the South Russian steppes from 835 forward, their concerted movement into Central Europe did not ensue until 889, cf. *Reginonis Chron.*, ed F. Kurze (Hanover, 1890), pp. 131-132, stating that this movement was the direct result of Pecheneg (Patzinak) pressure.

29. This mention of the Slavs settled among the Vlakhs points to the presence of at least isolated groups of Slavs on the Danube as early as the first and second centuries A.D., and is a reflex of Trajan's Dacian compaigns of 101-102 and 105-106; cf. Niederle, *Puvod a Počátky Slovanů Jižnich* (Prague, 1906), 141-146, also *Manuel de l'antiquité slave*, I, 50-59. The term *Vlakhi, Vlasi* used in early Slavic sources for the Italians persists in the modern West-Slavic name for Italy, cf. Czech. *Vlachy*, Pol. *Włochy*.

30. Derived, with modifications of later Bulgarian origin, from the so-called *Pannonian Lives* of SS. Constantine (Cyril) and Methodius; cf. *supra* Introduction: Sources and n. 30. Since St. Cyril died at Rome, whither the two brothers had repaired to have their work authorized by the Pope, in 869, he cannot have taught in Bulgaria. It was Methodius alone who, not only found the support of the Holy See, but was also, in 869-870, consecrated Archbishop of Sirmium and sent as Papal *legatus a latere* to the Slavic lands (cf. P. J. Alexander, "The Papacy, the Bavarian Clergy, and the Slavonic Apostles," *The Slavonic Year-Book* [1941], pp. 268-269). The tradition of the preternaturally fast translation of the Scriptures is apocryphal. There was no complete Slavic translation of the entire Bible until the fifteenth century, though the earliest manuscripts of Slavic translations of the New Testament belong to the tenth. The mediaeval Russians derived their notions of Old Testament history from the so-called *Paleya* (for which, cf. *supra*, Introduction: Sources), originating in Bulgaria at the least as early as the tenth century. For the elevation by the Pope of Constantine (Cyril) to the episcopate, cf. S. Sakač, "De dignitate episcopali S. Cyrilli Thessalonicensis," *Orientalia Christiana periodica*, XVI (1950), 238-266.

31. From Hamartolus, von Muralt, p. 772, Istrin, p. 529. For the background and sequence of events, cf. Vasiliev, *History*, pp. 315-316; Runciman, *History of the First Bulgarian Empire*, pp. 144-152. Cf. also, *supra*, Introduction: Chronology.

32. Hagiographical tradition characterized Olga as of Scandinavian origin and of non-noble birth; Makariy, *Istoriya Russkoy Tserkvi*, I, 3rd ed. (Spb., 1889), 268; Golubinsky, *Ist. Russ. Tserkvi*, I, i, 74.

33. The historicity of this attack is seriously questioned by G. Laehr, *Die Anfänge des russischen Reiches* (Berlin, 1930), pp. 95-99, on the ground of the complete absence of corroborative data in Greek or other sources. Vasiliev and Ostrogorsky, however, think that this account of the Russian chronicler, not devoid of legendary details, is based on actual historical events; Vasiliev, "The Second Russian Attack on Constantinople," *Dumbarton Oaks Papers*, VI (1951), 161-225; and *History*, pp. 320-321; G. Ostrogorsky, "L'expédition du prince Oleg contre Constantinople," *Annales de l'Institut Kondakov*, XI (1940), 47-62. Some traces of a reference to such a Russian raid about 904-907 seem to have been pre-

served in a passage of Pseudo-Symeon; cf. Symeon Magister, *De Leone Basilii*, Bonn ed. pp. 706-707; R. J. H. Jenkins, "The Supposed Russian Attack on Constantinople in 907," *Speculum*, XXIV (1949). Contrary to R. Trautmann, *Die altrussische Nestor-Chronik* (Leipzig, 1931), p. 242, the ensuing treaty is to be regarded as authentic, and represents a *modus vivendi* preceding the longer instrument of 911 (so also Vasiliev, *loc. cit.*, on the basis of John Tzimiskes's reference to previous agreements preserved in Leo Diaconus, VI, 10, Bonn ed., p. 106, and Laehr, p. 99). Cf. H. Grégoire "La légende d'Oleg et l'expédition d'Igor," *Bulletin de la Classe des Lettres . . . de l'Académie royale de Belgique*, XXIII (1937), 80-94, attributing this legendary account of Oleg's expedition to Russian misunderstanding of the Bulgarian title ὀλγου τραχανοῦ and expressing doubt as to the historicity of Prince Oleg himself; for a refutation of this fanciful theory and of similar other theories, cf. Vasiliev, "The Second Russian Attack," pp. 214-219.

34. St. Mamas's was on the Golden Horn outside the Byzantine walls just beyond the Blachernae and near the modern Eivan-Serai Kapÿ. It was approached from the city through the gate known as the Xyloporta; there was at this point a landing place known as the port of St. Mamas (Golubinsky, *op. cit.*, I, 73, n. 1).

35. For the pagan Russian pantheon, cf. *supra*, Introduction, p. 38.

36. *Pavolochitÿ* (adj. from *pavoloki*, "palls, brocade"), a Byzantine silk fabric of the tenth through the twelfth century, usually with a geometrical pattern, as compared with the so-called *aksamitÿ* (from Gk. *hexamitos*), still more expensive with an animal pattern: cf. O. v. Falke, *Kunstgeschichte der Seidenweberei*, II (2nd edition, 1913), 6 and plates; *Slovo o Polku Igoreve*, ed. S. Shambinago and V. Rzhiga (Moscow, 1934), pp. 244-251, and plates 5-10 incl.; ed. V. P. Adrianova-Perets (Moscow-Leningrad, 1950), pp. 13, 401. The word *kropin'nÿya* rendered "silken," refers to a lighter silk such as might be used for garments; cf. Bulg. *koprina*, "silk."

37. From Hamartolus, von Muralt, p. 797, Istrin, p. 541.

38. These names, greatly contaminated in the text, are restored as far as possible to their Scandinavian forms; cf. Thomsen, *Origin*, pp. 71-72.

39. There is no evidence that this and other treaties of the period (945-971) were executed simultaneously in Old Russian (or Old Bulgarian) as well as in Greek; in fact, the crabbed character of the texts points to the opposite conclusion, since in the tenth century there were numerous Bulgarians capable of making a perfectly clear translation from a Greek original; cf. A. Dimitriu, *K Voprosu o Dogovorakh Russkikh s Grekami*, p. 3; Istrin, *Dogovorÿ Russkikh s Grekami*, pp. 382-393; *supra*, Introduction, n. 32. It will be noted that this is the only fully dated treaty (Sept. 2, 912); that of 971 simply gives the month as July.—Likhachev (II, 279) rejects the emendation of *ivanovÿm* to *kinovarevÿm*.

40. Unique example of the transfer of Russian folklore material to Scandinavia; cf. *supra*, Introduction, n. 40. According to other traditions, Oleg went north and died in Ladoga, where he was buried, in one instance with the addition that he was on his way overseas to Scandinavia; Shakhmatov, *Razÿskaniya*, pp. 333-334.

41. Italicized passage from Hamartolus, von Muralt, pp. 333-335, Istrin, pp. 304-306.

42. For the dating of this item, cf. *supra*, Introduction: Chronology.

43. For the dating of the two items on Symeon of Bulgaria, cf. *ibid.*

44. From Hamartolus cont., von Muralt, pp. 104-105, and nn.; Istrin, p. 552.

45. Hamartolus, cont., von Muralt, p. 816, Istrin, p. 557-559. For the dating of Symeon's campaign, cf. *supra*, Introduction: Chronology.

46. From Hamartolus cont., von Muralt, p. 840; Istrin, p. 566. For the dating of the Magyar attack, cf. *supra*, Introduction: Chronology.

47. From Hamartolus cont., p. 841; Istrin, p. 567. For the dating of the Russian attack on Constantinople, cf. *supra*, Introduction: Chronology. The account of the attack is from the same source. Cf. Laehr's valuable excursus "Die Quellen zu Igors Zug nach Byzanz," *op. cit.*, pp. 99-103. The Russes appeared on the Bosphorus on June 11 and remained on the Bithynian coast until September. Cf. Theophanes continuatus, Bonn ed., pp. 423-426; Cedrenus. Bonn ed., II, 316-317; *Vita Basilii Junioris*, ed. A. N. Veselovsky, "Razÿskaniya v Oblasti Russkago Dukhovnago Stikha," *Sbornik Otd. Russk. Yaz. i Slov.*, XLVI (1890), supplement p. 65 ff.

48. The death of Symeon is misdated in accordance with the Russian compiler's previous chronology; cf. *supra*, Introduction: Chronology. The attack on Constantinople took place in 926 (Runciman, p. 176).

49. From Hamartolus cont., von Muralt, p. 844, Istrin, p. 568. The Magyars raided into the Balkans in the spring of both 934 and 943. Since Ham. cont. speaks specifically of a "second attack," the raid of the latter year is referred to, and in view of the assignment of the event in the same source to the first indiction, the Russian compiler, in accordance with his previous system, dated it correctly as 6451 (943). Cf. *supra*, Introduction: Chronology. With the exception of the treaties, this date concludes the items of chronology demonstrably derived from Greek sources. In 943 also took place the best-known Russ campaign in Transcaucasia; for it and other similar raids, unrecorded in the *Povest'*, cf. Dorn, *Caspia;* V. Barthold, *Mesto Prikaspiyskikh Stepey v Istorii Musul'manskogo Mira* (Baku, 1925). In his *Studies in Caucasian History* (London, 1953), Professor V. Minorsky brings to light the Arabic work of the *Münejjim-bashÿ* (Astronomer Royal) Ahmad ibn Lutfullāh (died in 1702), entitled *Jāmi' al-duwal* (Top-Kapÿ Library MS. 2951), which has hitherto been known only in an abridged Turkish translation. This work is largely based on the *Ta'rīkh al-Bāb*, a local history of Derbent, Shirvan, and Arran, composed *c.* 1075/1106 and now lost; Minorsky, *op. cit.*, pp. 3-5. The new text reveals the hitherto unknown Russ incursions and activities in Caucasia in the years 987, 989, 1030, and 1031 (or 1032); Minorsky, pp. 76-77.

50. Practically all modern investigators consider Igor's second expedition unhistorical, e.g., Shakhmatov, *Razÿskaniya*, p. 395: "Igor's expedition of 944 after the attack of 941 appears clearly as invented to cover up the inglorious event of which the annalist learned from the continuator of Hamartolus." So also Hrushevsky, *Istoriya Ukrainÿ-Rusi*, I (Kiev, 1913), p. 442-ff; and Laehr, *op. cit.*, pp. 101-103. Vasiliev, however, *Hist.*, p. 322, accepts the chronicle account. In view of the terms of the treaty of 945, which makes no reference whatever to a war-like prelude, and the manifest effort of the annalist to place Igor' on a par with his descendants as a match for the Greeks, the item of 944 is best regarded as an invention. The names of the Byzantine sovereigns (Romanus, Constantine, and Stephen) indicate that, though the treaty may have been ratified in Kiev after March 1, 945, the preliminary negotiations took place before December 16, 944,

on which date Romanus Lecapenus was deposed by Constantine VII Porphyrogenitus (son of Leo the Wise and Romanus' son-in-law) and Romanus' two sons Constantine and Stephen (who had been co-emperors since December 25, 925). It will be recalled that Constantine VII Porphyrogenitus excluded the sons of Romanus from participation in the sovereignty on January 27, 945, but had previously taken little interest in affairs up to the time when it became clear that Romanus was deliberately pushing him into the background in favor of his own sons.

51. Cf. *supra,* n. 38. The wording of the opening paragraph indicates that Igor's authority was not admitted by the cities outside Kiev to the extent of permitting him the exclusive conduct of foreign relations, since his tributaries named their own delegates, who were also accompanied by a number of agents sent by merchants interested in trade between the Dnieper valley and Byzantium.

52. This item contains the first provision for military aid to be supplied on demand from Kiev to Byzantium, and is aimed against the Pechenegs and the Magyars.

53. Christians among the Russes are mentioned in this treaty for the first time; no such reference to them was made in the instrument of 911. Cosmas of Prague attests to their presence in Kiev (*MGH, NS.,* II, xxii, 44). These Varangian Christians belonged more likely to the Latin rite than to the Byzantine (cf. M. Jugie, *Le schisme byzantin* [Paris, 1941] pp. 173-175, 180-181; also, *infra,* nn. 64, 92). The location of the church of St. Elias (which was probably a wooden structure) can be only approximately defined. From the phrase "above the creek" it would appear that the church stood on a hill above the former Pochayna creek, and therefore near the site of St. Michael's (demolished in 1935). The "Pasÿncha square and the quarter of the Khazars" are a relic of the tributary relation of Kiev to the Khazar khagans; *Pasÿncha* is probably derived from the Khazar-Turkish *bash,* "head, chief," and an unidentified suffix; cf. Cross, "The Earliest Mediaeval Churches of Kiev," *Speculum,* XI (1936), 478.

54. The two chief towns of Dereva were Iskoroten' and Ovruch, both in the region of the Usha, a tributary of the Pripet' and thus northwest of Kiev.

55. There is some doubt whether the Derevlian prince's name was actually *Mal.* H. Pipping, *De Skandinaviska Dnjeprnammen,* pp. 27-29 (supported by S. A. Korff, "Den drevljanske forsten Mal," *Stud. i Nordisk Filol.,* II, Helsingfors, 1911) attributes its origin to a misunderstanding of the Scandinavian formula *giptas maeþ mund ok maeli,* "to marry with dowry and contract." Brückner, on the other hand, *Wzory etymołogji,* pp. 206-207, explains the origin of the name from a misunderstanding of the Derevlians' proposal that Olga should marry their *za mal,* in other words, as his principal, or legal, wife in distinction from other less formal alliances.

56. The *Borichev uvoz* or *spusk* was the path from the old citadel of Kiev to the riverside. Until early in the nineteenth century, the creek Pochayna, which drains some small ponds on the northern edge of Kiev and now enters the Dnieper north of the Petrovskiy section of the city, extended as a respectable stream much farther south, and was separated from the Dnieper by a sandpit which continued to a point opposite the southern extremity of the modern Podol district. The Pochayna is thus the stream referred to as flowing "below the heights," the hills on which the older town was situated. The "city" referred to is the smaller inclosure as it existed prior to the extensions of Yaroslav (*ca.* 1037).

It lies to the northeast of the Cathedral of St. Sophia, and includes the sites of the Church of the Three Saints, St. Andrew's and the *Desyatinnaya*. The "Palace of the Cantors" was situated near the west end of the *Desyatinnaya* (Church of the Blessed Virgin of the Tithe) see *infra*, n. 105. Of the exact location of the other residences mentioned, nothing is known beyond their proximity to the churches named.

57. The legendary account of Olga's triple revenge is complicated by the introduction of the "incendiary bird" motive, fairly common elsewhere; cf. H. M. Cam, "The Legend of the Incendiary Birds," *Eng. Hist. Rev.*, XXXI (1916), 98-101; F. Lot and H. Bédier, *Légendes épiques*, 2nd ed., IV (1921), p. 59, ff.; A. Stender-Petersen, *op. cit.*, pp. 127-155. The legend obviously came into Russia from Scandinavia; cf. Snorri Sturluson, *Heimskringla*, ed. F. Jensson (Copenhagen, 1922), pp. 450-451; also *Heimskringla*, trans. E. Monsen (New York: Appleton, 1932), p. 509; and for a similar exploit by Harold Hardrade in Sicily, and a corresponding stratagem by Fridelev before Dublin; see *Saxo Grammaticus*, ed. A. Holder (Strasbourg, 1886), p. 119. Cf. A. Stender-Petersen, "Et Nordisk Krigslistmotivs historie," *Edda*, XXIX (1929), 145-164.

58. For Vÿshgorod, cf. *infra*, n. 83.

59. The Msta flows from the northeast into Lake Il'men' near Novgorod, while the Luga rises west of Novgorod and flows into the Gulf of Finland just east of the Bay of Narva.

60. Ol'zhichi was situated on the south bank of the river Desna at the junction of the Chertorÿya and near the confluence of the former with the Dnieper; cf. N. P. Barsov, *Ocherki Russkoy Istor. Geografii*, 2nd ed. (Warsaw, 1885), p. 143; and M. Hrushevsky, *Ocherk Ist. Kievskoy Zemli* (Kiev, 1891), p. 21 and n. 3.

61. Constantine Porphyrogenitus, *regn.* 912-959; succeeded by his son Romanus II (*regn.* 959-963). Theophano, the widow of Romanus, married Nicephorus II Phokas (*regn.* 963-969), who was murdered at the instigation of his wife by her lover John Tzimiskes (*regn.* 969-976). The latter strengthened his position by marrying Theodora, sister of Romanus II. Romanus himself left the following children, Basil II and Constantine VIII, Anna (later wife of Vladimir I of Kiev) and, possibly, Theophano (later wife of Otto II).

62. Olga's reception at Byzantium is related by Const. Porph. himself, *De ceremoniis*, II (Bonn ed., pp. 594-598). Since Constantine places the official receptions of Olga on Wednesday, September 9, and Sunday, October 18, the actual date of Olga's visit was 957; cf. Laehr excursus, "Olga und das Christentum," *op. cit.*, pp. 103-106. While Constantine refers to Olga only by her pagan Scandinavian name Helga, he also mentions a domestic chaplain named Gregory in her suite, which, together with the fact that he makes no reference to her baptism, would indicate that her conversion took place elsewhere. One Greek source (Cedrenus, Bonn ed., II, 329; he was, however, a contemporary of Alexius I Comnenus, *regn.* 1081-1118) makes the explicit statement that Olga was indeed baptized at Constantinople; this is corroborated by the *Continuator Reginonis* (ed. F. Kurze, Hanover, 1890, p. 170, *ad* 959). Since the continuator was probably Adalbert of Trier, who went to Russia himself and must have known Olga personally, this evidence may be important. The fact that she assumed in baptism the name of Helena, which was also that of the wife of Constantine VII, is no proof that her baptism took place in Constantinople: St. Vladimir took the baptismal name of Basil, in honor of the Emperor Basil II, and he was not bap-

tized in the Imperial capital. The Chronicle, of course, states that she took the name of St. Helena, Constantine the Great's mother. The Kievan monk James (writing *ca.* 1075) likewise says in his *Eulogy of Vladimir,* (text in Golubinsky, I, i, 241) that Olga was baptized in Constantinople, but (*ibid.,* p. 242), setting her death on July 11, 6477 (969), remarks that she had been a Christian for fifteen years previous; which means that she became one in 954, three years before her trip to Constantinople. It is probably because of this statement that the annalist computed Olga's visit to have taken place *ca.* 6463 (955). Cf. Golubinsky, I, i, 73-84; cf. A. M. Ammann, *Abriss der ostslawischen Kirchengeschichte* (Vienna, 1950), p. 12.

63. For the Pochayna, cf. *supra.* n. 56.

64. The answer of Olga indicates that she had some reason to be piqued at her reception. And, soon afterwards, in 959, she turned to the West, asking Otto I for priests and a bishop (*Cont. Reg., loc. cit.;* cf. Golubinsky, *loc. cit.*). The monk Adalbert of Trier (later Archbishop of Magdeburg) was consecrated Bishop of the Russians. His mission, however, was fruitless, owing to pagan opposition. He returned in 962 (*Cont. Reg.,* p. 172). Cf. Ammann, *Ostsl. Kirchengesch.,* p. 13. St. Olga herself, like the early Varangian Christians of Russia, may have been of the Latin rite (Jugie, *op. cit.,* p. 174).

65. The motives of Svyatoslav's attack on the Khazars are well established. With the diversion of Byzantine attention to Syrian campaigns against the Emir of Aleppo and an expedition of 960-961 against Crete, the Greek protectorate in the Crimea lost much of its efficacy. At the same time, the decline of the Khazar power was marked by a relapse of many of the subject elements in the Khazar complex to a stage of nomadic barbarism. The unprovoked raids of these groups upon the Gothic districts of the southern Crimea induced the Goths to apply to Svyatoslav for protection. A mission for this purpose visited Kiev in the late autumn of 962 and returned to Gothia in January, 963. Svyatoslav's campaign against the Khazars began the following spring and culminated with the fall of Bela Vezha (Sarkel) at the mouth of the Don. His protectorate over Gothia continued until his defeat in Bulgaria by John Tzimiskes in 971. The date (965) supplied by the Chronicle probably applies not to Svyatoslav's Crimean adventure, but to subsequent operations against Alans, Cherkesses, and Volga Bulgars. For bibliography and full interpretation of the sources, see Vasiliev, *The Goths in the Crimea* (Cambridge: Mediaeval Academy of America, 1936), pp. 119-131.

66. The Russian annalist places Svyatoslav's campaigns against the Yasians and Kasogians (Ossetians and Cherkesses) in the Kuban district prior to his attack on the Khazars. From Arabic sources, however, we learn that he continued his operations as far as Semender (on the Caspian north of Derbent), then attacked Itil, the Khazar metropolis at the mouth of the Volga, and finally overthrew the Bulgar capital of Bolgarÿ, near the junction of the Kama and Volga; cf. Ibn Hauqal, etc., quoted by C. M. Frähn, *Ibn Foszlans und anderer Araber Berichte über die Russen älterer Zeit* (Spb., 1823), pp. 63-67. The operations in the Kuban are thus to be interpreted as occurring after the reduction of Bela Vezha, and it is probable that the second campaign against the Vyatichians, in the upper Don basin south of modern Ryazan', took place after the attack on Bolgarÿ. It will be noted that by these campaigns Svyatoslav made himself master of all the important contemporary trade routes between the Volga and the Dnieper.

67. Vyatichians, cf. *infra,* n. 85.

68. For accounts of Svyatoslav's campaign, cf. Zlatarski, *Istorija*, I, ii, 567-588; Runciman, *First Bulgarian Empire*, pp. 200-202; Laehr, *Anfänge*, pp. 61-64. Nicephorus Phokas actually instigated Svyatoslav's invasion by a bribe of 108,000 gold *solidi* (present value approx. $550,000), hoping with his aid to keep the Bulgarians in subjection and the Magyars quiescent while Byzantine forces were engaged against the Arabs (Leo Diaconus, Bonn ed., IV, 63). The Greek sources know of Svyatoslav's return to Kiev, but do not give the reason (Cedrenus, Bonn ed., II, 372). Pereyaslavets is "Little Preslav," in the Danube delta, as opposed to "Great Preslav" on the river Tutsa, some sixty miles inland and westward from Varna.

69. Vladimir, as the son of Malusha, Olga's stewardess, was not a son of the same mother with Yaropolk and Oleg, and there is a good possibility that Malusha was also Scandinavian; Stender-Petersen, *Die Varägersage*, pp. 14-16; cf. *infra*, n. 114.

70. July 11, 969, cf. *supra*, n. 62.

71. This is the first indication of the dominance of Kievan influence in Novgorod, apart from Olga's excursions to that vicinity (cf. item of 947).

72. The Chronicle account of Svyatoslav's second campaign in Bulgaria is so far contaminated with legendary accretions as to have little historical value, since the facts regarding his ultimate defeat are entirely disguised. Vasiliev, *History*, pp. 319, 322-323, gives only a cursory summary of these events; detailed narrative in Zlatarski, *op. cit.*, pp. I, ii, 593-624; Runciman, *op. cit.*, pp. 65-73 and, for chronology, pp. 106-110. Both Zlatarski and Runciman date Svyatoslav's final defeat as of 972, though F. Dölger, "Die Chronologie des grossen Feldzuges des Kaisers Joh. Tzimiskes gegen die Russen," *Byz. Zts.* XXXII (1932), has since shown, on the basis of the Greek sources, and in spite of certain contradictions which they contain, that 971 is the correct date. Svyatoslav appeared at the mouth of the Danube late in the summer of 969. Capturing Great Preslav, the capital, he crossed the Haemus Mountains in the spring of 970 and overran Adrianople. During the previous winter (10 December, 969), Nicephorus Phokas had been assassinated and succeeded by John Tzimiskes, who fruitlessly endeavored to make terms with the invader. He then began training special troops, and in the autumn of 970 defeated the Russians and their allies before Arcadiopolis (Lule Burgas), but without following up his advantage, and it was not until the spring of 971 that the Byzantines resumed an aggressive campaign. After their defeat at Arcadiopolis, the Russians had withdrawn north of the Haemus, contenting themselves with irritating raids into Thrace. Sending his fleet to block the Danube mouths, Tzimiskes pushed across the mountain passes during Holy Week and took by surprise the Russian garrison at Great Preslav, which fell on Good Friday. The survivors fled to join Svyatoslav in Silistria. By the end of April, Tzimiskes was besieging Silistria, where Svyatoslav offered a stubborn resistance until the last week in July, when he was forced to capitulate. The Greek sources for those events are Leo Diaconus, Bonn ed., IV-V, 61 ff.; Cedrenus, II, 372 ff.; Zonaras, IV, 87 ff.; cf. also G. Schlumberger, *Un empereur byzantin au Xe siècle. Nicéphore Phocas*, Paris, 1890; *L'épopée byzantine*, I, (Paris, 1896).

73. During Svyatoslav's historic interview with Tzimiskes after his defeat, he had asked the Emperor's good offices in securing safe conduct from the Pechenegs for his return passage up the Dnieper through the territory which they occupied (Cedrenus, II, 412), but the Pechenegs refused to commit themselves on this point

when approached by the Greeks. "Belobereg (Beloberezh'e)" designates the Black Sea coast at the mouth of the Dnieper.

74. Vladimir's relations with Scandinavia are attested by the Norse tradition that Olaf Tryggvason (King of Norway, 995-1000) stayed in Russia at Vladimir's court in 977-986. Olaf's mother's brother Sigurd is stated by the Norse sources to have occupied a responsible position under Vladimir at Norgorod. At the moment when he discovered Olaf after the latter had been sold into slavery by Esthonian pirates who had captured Olaf and his mother Astrid, Sigurd is represented as being on an expedition to collect taxes payable by the Esthonians to the Prince of Novgorod. In view of the chronology, it is possible that Sigurd's expedition was related to Vladimir's plans for collecting means to attack Yaropolk. For an analysis of the Norse sources, cf. F. Braun, *Das historische Russland im nordischen Schrifttum des X-XIV Jhdts.,* p. 179 ff.; Cross, "La tradition islandaise de Saint Vladimir," pp. 133-148; N. de Baumgarten, "Olaf Tryggwison, roi de Norvège, et ses relations avec Saint Vladimir de Russie," *Orientalia Christiana,* XXIV (1931); E. A. Rÿdzevskaya, "Legenda o Knyaze Vladimire v Sage ob Olave Tryuggvasone," *Trudÿ Otd. Drevne-Russk. Lit.,* II (Moscow, 1935), 5-20. The assassination of Yaropolk and Vladimir's occupation of Kiev should probably be dated as of 978, since the latter died in 1015 after a reign of 37 years. The date of his victorious entry into Kiev is also fixed as of 11 June, 978 by the Monk James's Eulogy, cf. Golubinsky, *op. cit.* I, i, 245.

75. Both names are Scandinavian, i.e., *Ragnheiðr* and *Rognvalðr;* it should be noted that the latter is specifically characterized as an immigrant from overseas. Rogned's death in 1000 is mentioned by the chronicle. She was unceremoniously put away by Vladimir at the time of his marriage to the Byzantine princess Anna (989). There are two subsequent traditions in the Russian annals concerning Rogned, one that Vladimir, upon his marriage to Anna, suggested Rogned should marry some Russian boyar, whereupon she indignantly refused, became converted, and took the veil under the name of Anastasia (*PSRL.,* II, 258). The other (Laurentian *PSRL,* I, ii, 2nd ed., 299-300) recounts that Vladimir nicknamed Rogned *Gorislava,* and that she resented Vladimir's relations with other women to the point where she attempted to stab him as he slept. Vladimir then intended to kill her, but was dissuaded by his boyars out of consideration for Rogned's young son Izyaslav. This legend is recounted as an explanation of the subsequent hostility which prevailed between the princely houses of Polotsk and Kiev. But cf. M. v. Taube in *Jahrbücher f. Gesch. u. Kult. d. Slaven,* IX (1935).

76. Dorogozhich was apparently the flat elevation extending between the present northwestern section of Kiev known at Luk'yanovka and the locality of St. Cyril's Monastery (Zakrevsky, *Opisanie,* pp. 300-342). Kapich (for no indicated reason) is believed by the same authority to have been the site of the modern village of Belichi, about ten kilometers west of Kiev on the highway to Belgorodka, (*ibid.,* p. 560); the town contains traces of an old entrenchment.

77. Rodnya, south of Kiev, on the west bank of the Dnieper where it is joined by the Ros' river, near the later town of Kanev.

78. She had formerly been a nun, and was presumably brought back to Kiev by Svyatoslav after his first Bulgarian campaign; cf. Golubinsky, *Istoriya,* I, 2, 92, n. i, and *supra,* under 977.

79. In view of the purely approximate chronology of this section of the Chronicle, one is tempted to see in this report of the wholesale departure of

Varangians for Constantinople a reflex of Vladimir's despatch of 6000 Varangians to aid his future brothers-in-law Basil II and Constantine VIII in repressing the revolt of Bardas Phokas during the summer of 988; cf. *infra*, n. 93.

80. For the pagan Slavic pantheon, cf. *supra*, Introduction, p. 38.

81. The site of this church, supposed to have been of wood and thus probably destroyed in the conflagration of 1017, cannot be determined with certainty, though it is traditionally identified with that of the modern church of the Three Saints (*Trëkhsvyatitel'skaya*). It stood, at any rate, within the old citadel; cf. Cross, "The Earliest Mediaeval Churches of Kiev," p. 481.

82. The brook Lÿbed' rises in the western section of modern Kiev and follows substantially the track of the modern railway from the central station to the point where the brook joins the Dnieper just south of the monastery at Vÿdubichi. It was formerly a more considerable stream, since there are records of mills run by it in the seventeenth century (cf. Zakrevsky, *Opisanie*, p. 438). Predslavino cannot be located beyond its proximity to this creek.

83. Vÿshgorod, on the Dnieper some 15 km. north of Kiev. The town was surrounded with six concentric ramparts and a moat of which traces are still visible. Belgorod (mod. Belgorodka), on the river Irpen' about 25 km. southwest of Kiev. The Chronicle states that Vladimir founded it in 991, but the implication of the present passage is that the village existed prior to that date, so that this item would then refer to Vladimir's fortifying it as an outpost against the Pechenegs. On the site have been identified the ruins of two stone churches founded by Prince Rurik Rostilavich in 1187; cf. Niederle, *Pův. Slov. Východn.*, p. 274. Berestovo, now a section of the modern city of Kiev, is situated on the bluffs overlooking the Dnieper just north of the Crypt Monastery. The remains of Vladimir's residence on this site have recently been excavated, and the locality also contains the Church of the Redeemer in Berestovo, dating from the first quarter of the twelfth century.

84. Peremÿshl'=mod. Przemyśl, on the Vyagro river in Eastern Galicia (now Polish). Cherven, now the unimportant Polish village of Czermo, northeast of Przemyśl and some 22 km. south of Hrubieszów. The capture of the cities implies control over the dependent districts and reflects Vladimir's desire to possess an assured route into the Vistula basin. Other towns on this area are Buzh'sk, Belz, and Volÿn' (all on the Western Bug). Their importance declined with the rise in prestige of the newly founded city of Vladimir Volÿnsk, 20 km. south of Volÿn'. These cities remained under Kievan control until 1018, when they were temporarily retaken by Bolesław Chrobry of Poland during the strife accompanying the change of sovereignty after Vladimir I's death.

85. The Vyatichians, momentarily subjected to tribute by Svyatoslav *ca.* 965, were the furthest northeastern Slavic tribe in the tenth century, and populated the district at the headwaters of the Oka, south of modern Moscow. They thus bordered on the Finns of the Volga basin, and were accordingly among the first Slavic colonists in the districts of Rostov and Suzdal'.

86. The Yatvingians (in med. Lat. sources *Jaczwingi, Jadzwingi*), a Lithuanian tribe, lived at this period north of the Pripet' and between the lower western Bug and the upper Niemen. Their proximity to the Slavic settlements in the Bug basin (cf. *supra*, n. 84) made it necessary for Vladimir to subdue the Yatvingians in order to assure his communications with these western towns. Similarly, in 1034, Yaroslav was obliged to campaign once more against the Yatvingians after

he had retaken the towns along the Bug in 1031. As a result of their defeat by Yaroslav, the main body of the Yatvingians moved northwest toward the Narev into the southern portion of the East Prussian lake district, while the Yatvingian remnants on the Niemen were absorbed either by the Lithuanians themselves or by new Russian settlements east of modern Brest-Litovsk during the twelfth and thirteenth centuries. A considerable number of place-names in the upper Niemen basin (e.g., near Nowogródek, Nieśwież, Lida, and Grodno) testify to the early localization of the Yatvingians in this area; cf. Barsov, *Ocherki Russk. Istor. Geografii,* pp. 39-41, 231, 232, 233-236.

87. While Shakhmatov, *Razÿskaniya,* p. 145, believes this account of the Varangian martyrs to be derived from an extraneous source, it is an open question to which the priority belongs: to the Chronicle or to the Prolog (short saint's life) for July 12, in which this same episode is narrated. In any case, the latter establishes the son's name as Ivan and the father's as Turÿ; cf. Shakhmatov, "Kak Nazÿvalsya Pervÿy Russkiy Khrist. Muchenik," *Izvěstiya Akad. Nauk,* 6th series (1907), pp. 261-264. Continuing this line of thought, S. Rozhnetsky has endeavored to prove that the Norse original of the father's name was Ottarr; "Kak Nazÿvalsya Pervÿy Russkiy Muchenik," *Izv. Otd. Russk. Yaz. i Slov.,* XIX (1914), iv, 94-98; cf. also N. Nikol'sky, *Materialÿ dlya Povremennago Spiska Russkikh Pisateley i ikh Sochineniy (X-XI věka)* (Spb., 1906), p. 406.

88. Pishchan', mod. Peshchan', a tributary of the river Sozh' east of Mogilev.

89. Since the eighteenth century, doubt has existed as to whether this raid was directed against the Bulgars on the Volga or those south of the Danube. Later Russian annalistic compilations (e.g., the *Nikonovskaya,* [*PSRL,* IX, 42, 66], sixteenth century), specifically locate upon the Volga the Bulgars attacked by Vladimir. Karamzin (*Ist. Gos. Ross.,* I, 125) applied the reference to the Balkan Bulgarians, and his interpretation has, until recently, been widely accepted. It was rejected, however, by Hrushevsky, *Istoriya Ukr.-Rusi,* I, 486, also by Laehr, *op. cit.,* pp. 143-144, and still more lately by D. A. Rasovsky, "Pecheněgi, Torki, i Berenděi na Russii i v Ugrii," *Seminarium Kondakovianum,* VI (1933). 7. Against Solov'ëv, one need merely urge that such a raid into Balkan Bulgaria just at the moment when Tsar Samuel was making his repeated incursions into Thessaly which culminated in the capture of Larissa in 986 (Zlatarski, *Ist.,* I, ii, 660-661) — a series of events followed with close attention in Byzantium—could hardly have escaped notice in the Greek sources.

90. The Torks (of Turkish extraction like the Pechenegs) are identical with the Uzes of the Byzantine historians (cf. the literature cited by Rasovsky, *op. cit.,* p. 3, n. 11). At the end of the ninth century, the Torks were on the upper Don, east of the Pechenegs. The latter in Vladimir's day were already moving into Hungary, and as they left the east bank of the Dnieper, the Torks filtered into the area they had left. Since the Torks were in constant hostilities with the Pechenegs, they were the logical allies of Vladimir against the latter. They were occasionally restive, however (cf. Vsevolod's campaign against them in 1054), and were eventually expelled from the steppes south of Kiev in 1060 (cf. Rasovsky, pp. 7-9).

91. Since the Russian annalist knew of the conversion of the Balkan Bulgars (cf. the entry *ad* 869; Boris of Bulgaria had himself been baptized in September, 865), the reference is to the Volga Bulgars. The summary of the Mohammedan doctrine is derived from the *Paleya;* cf. Shakhmatov, *Tolkovaya Paleya i Russkaya Lětopis',* p. 230. The text of Marvazi (eleventh-twelfth cent.), recently discovered

and published by Prof. V. Minorsky (*Sharaf al-Zamān Ṭāhir Marvazi on China, the Turks and India,* The Royal Asiatic Society, 1942), makes mention of Vladimir's negotiations with the King of Khwarezm regarding Islam and his subsequent conversion to it (*op. cit.*, pp. 23/36; cf. 118-119). This information contains, in an exaggerated form, an indication of Islamic proselytism in Rus'. The Volga Bulgars were close allies of Khwarezm; cf. S. Tolstov, *Po Sledam Drevnekhorezmiyskoy Tsivilizatsii,* Moscow-Leningrad, 1948, pp. 250-265.

92. The apocryphal version of the conversion of St. Vladimir, inserted here in the Chronicle, was formed, in part at least, under the influence of Byzantine polemical attacks on Rome (for which, cf. *infra*, n. 98). It is an obvious anachronism to represent Byzantine Christianity before 1054 as a different religion (as different as Judaism or Islam) from Catholic Christianity. All that Vladimir could at all have considered was the question of which *rite* (Latin or Byzantine) of the Church to adopt and, consequently, which patriarchal jurisdiction *in* it to follow. Likewise, the method of choosing the faith described in this narrative is quite unlikely. It is completely unknown to Hilarion (*Discourse*), to the *Eulogy* attributed to the Monk James, or to the Nestorian *Life* of SS. Boris and Gleb (for these sources, cf. *supra*, Introduction: Authorship; Sources). Regarding this version, Golubinsky I, 1, 105 has the following to say: ". . . the inexorable duty of the historian compels us to state that this tale contains no truth and that it is a later invention, and, at that, in all probability, not even a Russian, but a Greek invention. . . . Being a later interpolation into the Chronicle and inserted into it without any connection with what precedes it, it tells the following story. . . ." (Cf. pp. 105-187.) This story may have been inspired also by the memories of Muslim proselytizing in Rus', attested to by Marvazi (cf. *supra*, n. 91) as well as of Vladimir's political contacts with the Byzantines (cf. *infra*, n. 94). Actually, once a member of the Church, Vladimir entertained normal relations with the Papacy. The *Nikonovskaya* compilation (PSRL., IX, 57) reports the arrival of a Papal embassy to Vladimir while he was at Kherson after capturing the city. Another mission from the Pope to Vladimir is reported by the chronicle in 991 (*ibid.*, p. 64). Both these missions must have been sent by John XV (985-996). Still another such embassy was sent to Kiev in 1000, this time accompanied by the envoys of the rulers of Bohemia and Hungary (*ibid.*, p. 68). This one must have come from Silvester II (999-1003). It is also recorded that Vladimir sent answering embassies to Rome in 994 and 1001 (*ibid.*, pp. 65, 68). Earlier, in the reign of Yaropolk I and probably in connection with the Christians already then in Kiev (cf. *supra*, n. 53), the same source reports as of 979 the arrival of an embassy from the Pope (*ibid.*, p. 39); the actual year may result from a mistake in chronology derived in the *Nikonovskaya* from the *Primary Chronicle* as a source. It is far more difficult to suppose that the compilers of the *Nikonovskaya* invented these items (found in some other sources as well) than to admit their suppression in the *Primary Chronicle.* Cf. N. de Baumgarten, "Chronologie ecclésiastique des terres russes du Xe au XIIIe siècle," *Orientalia Christiana,* XVII (1930); "Saint Vladimir et la Conversion de la Russie," *ibid.,* XXVII (1932); Ammann, *op. cit.,* p. 17. For the various theories regarding the early jurisdiction of the Kievan Church, cf. *infra,* n. 171. Cf. also *infra,* n. 238.

93. As is evident from the present narrative, the story of Vladimir's conversion and baptism as related by the Chronicle represents the fusion of two elements:

one a tradition according to which Vladimir was converted by a Greek missionary, the climax of whose argument consisted in the exhibition of an eikon with a realistic depiction of the Last Judgment, and the other supplying an account of his baptism at Kherson in connection with his marriage to the Byzantine princess Anna. The combination of the two stories is further indicated by the express remark that there was a diversity of opinion as to precisely where Vladimir was baptized. The deliberations of Vladimir at the close of the scholar's oration and the interpretation of his mission to Constantinople as purely religious in purpose also serve to unite the two traditions. The Byzantine background of these events is important: upon the death of John Tzimiskes in 976, he was succeeded by Basil II and Constantine VIII, the youthful sons of Romanus II. In October, 987, a military conspiracy proclaimed as Emperor Bardas Phokas, nephew of Nicephorus Phokas (murdered 969), and a former trusted aid of Tzimiskes. Gaining control of the Asiatic themes, Bardas even occupied Chrysopolis (Scutari) early in 988. To quote the best Arabic source of the period, Yaḥya ibn Saʿīd of Antioch (first half of the eleventh cent.), trans. by I. Kratchkovsky and A. A. Vasiliev, *Patr. Orient.,* XXIII, iii (Paris, 1932), 423-424: "La situation était devenue grave et l'empereur Basile en était préoccupé à cause de la force de ses troupes [i.e., Bardas'] et de l'avantage qu'il [Bardas] avait sur lui. Les caisses étaient vides. Dans ce besoin pressant, [Basile] fut contraint de demander secours au roi des Russes, qui étaient ses ennemis. Le [Russe] y acquiesça; après quoi ils firent une alliance de parenté, et le roi des Russes épousa la soeur de l'empereur Basile à la condition qu'il se ferait baptiser avec tout le peuple de sons pays. Le grand peuple des Russes n'avait à cette époque aucune loi ni aucune foi religieuse. Peu après, l'empereur Basile lui envoya des métropolites et des évêques qui baptisèrent le roi et tout le peuple de son pays; en même temps il lui envoya sa soeur qui fit bâtir plusieurs églises dans le pays des Russes. La question du mariage ayant été conclue entre eux, les troupes russes arrivèrent aussi, et après s'être jointes aux troupes des Grecs, qui étaient avec Basile, se mirent en marche tous ensemble pour attaquer Bardas Phocas par terre et par mer, vers Chrysopolis, [ces troupes] vainquirent Phocas. . . ." The arrival of Russian auxiliaries is mentioned briefly by Psellus, *Chronographia,* I, 13 (ed. E. Renaud, Paris, 1926, p. 9), while Cedrenus (Bonn ed., II, 444) mentions the aid of the Russian before Chrysopolis and the marriage of Vladimir with Anna: ἔτυχι γὰρ [ὁ βασιλεὺς] συμμαχίαν προσκαλησάμενος ἐξ αὐτῶν [i.e., the Russes] καὶ κηδεστὴν ποιησάμενος τὸν ἄρχοντα αὐτῶν Βλαδιμηρὸν ἐπὶ τῇ ἑαυτοῦ ἀδέλφῃ Ἄννῃ; so also Zonaras, IV, 114. None of these Greek sources mentions the conversion. Among the Russian sources, apart from the Chronicle, the *Eulogy* of the monk James (Golubinsky, *op. cit.,* I, i, 224) places Vladimir's conversion and baptism prior to his expedition against Kherson. Of the early *Lives* of Vladimir among the Russian *vitae sanctorum,* the shortest states that Vladimir was baptized at Kherson, but shows indications of being influenced by the narrative of the Chronicle; cf. N. Serebryansky, *Drevnerusskie Knyazheskie Zhitiya* (Moscow, 1915), texts, p. 15. The story of the impression produced upon Vladimir by the picture of the Last Judgment at the close of the scholar's discourse must be regarded as apocryphal. It was derived from a Bulgarian source, as suggested by Shakhmatov, *Razÿskaniya,* pp. 152-153, since there is a strikingly similar tradition according to which Prince Boris of Bulgaria was converted (in 865) after beholding a mural of the Last Judgment by a monk-artist named

Methodius; cf. Runciman, *First Bulgarian Empire*, pp. 102-103; sources: Theophanes Cont., Bonn ed., pp. 163-164; Cedrenus, Bonn. ed., II, 152-153. The summary of Old Testament history supplied by the scholar is derived principally from the *Paleya*, for which, cf. *supra*, Introduction: Sources. For the anti-Catholic references, cf. *supra*, n. 92; *infra*, n. 98.

94. Kherson (Gk. Chersonesus; Old R. Korsun'), on the Crimean coast facing north at a point some three kilometers west of modern Sebastopol, and founded as a colony of Heraclea Pontica (hence Dorian) about the fifth century B.C. It is not mentioned by Herodotus, and must therefore have been founded after his time. It lies on a promontory between two inlets, to the west the so-called Khersonesskaya, and to the east the inlet now known as Quarantine Bay, which was the ancient harbor. In the fourth century A.D. a place of exile for personages in disfavor at Byzantium, it became in the seventh a pawn of diplomacy in Byzantine relations with the Khazars. The mediaeval trade of the city consisted in exporting hides and wax to Byzantium from the hinterland and in selling luxury products up-country both to the nomads and to the Russians. It is not clear from the Old Russian text whether Vladimir proceeded against Kherson by land or by sea. The clause *ide Volodimer s voi na Korsun'* means literally "Vladimir went with warriors against Kherson," but it is generally believed that he came by water; cf. A. L. Berthier de la Garde, "Kak Vladimir Osazhdal Korsun'," *Izv. Otd. Russk. Yaz. i Slov.*, XIV (1909) 38, with a full bibliography, and more recently Vasiliev, *Goths*, pp. 132-134. The harbor beside which Vladimir landed was the modern Quarantine Bay, and his object of attack was presumably the vulnerable northeast corner of the city, since at this point the water supply enters the town; cf. E. H. Minns, *Scythians and Greeks* (Cambridge, 1913), pp. 493-534; esp. Plan VII and Map VIII. Golubinsky thinks, however, that Vladimir landed in Round Bay, some distance west of Kherson (I, i, 227, n. 1), but Berthier de la Garde shows (p. 249) that this is improbable. The capture of Kherson took place in the summer of 989. The approximate date is determinable by juxtaposition of the Greek and Arabic sources (esp. Yaḥya ibn Saʿīd). Leo Diaconus, X, 10 (Bonn ed., p. 175) remarks that fiery pillars appeared in the heavens as a presage of the capture of Kherson by the Russes and of Berrhoea (in Macedonia) by the Bulgars, and further notes that a comet gave warning of a subsequent earthquake in Constantinople. The celestial phenomena are accurately dated by Yaḥya (*ed. cit.*, pp. 432-433) a pillar of flame was seen at Cairo on 27 Ḍū-l-ḥijja, 378 Heg.=April 7, 989, while a comet was visible for twenty days starting from 19 Rab. I, 379 Heg.=July 27, 989. Hence Kherson was taken between these dates (the earthquake in question took place, acc. to Yaḥya, p. 428, in the fourteenth year of Basil's reign, i.e., 379 Heg.=989, and other sources show that it occurred on October 25; cf. Vasil'evsky, cited below, pp. 102-105). This fact was first established by Vasil'evsky by comparison of the passage in Leo Diaconus with the data supplied by the Arabic compiler Al-Makīn, who used Yaḥya as a source; "K Istorii 976-986 godov," *Trudÿ*, II (Spb., 1909), 98-105; cf. also Laehr's excursus, "Die Quellen über die Taufe Wladimirs," *op. cit.*, pp. 110-115. The *Eulogy* of the Monk James (Golubinsky, *op. cit.*, I, i, 245) states that Vladimir took Kherson in the *third* year after his baptism. Yet, it may be significant that the same source (p. 244), regardless of Vladimir's previous favorable attitude toward conversion, indicates that the Prince's *active* steps to introduce Christianity were directly connected with the Kherson expedition. The chronology for the whole

episode may thus become clear. Vladimir's negotiations with Basil and Constantine took place during the Winter of 987-988. The auxiliary corps was sent to Constantinople in the Spring of 988, after Vladimir (probably as early as the latter part of 987) had agreed to accept baptism in return for the hand of the Porphyrogenita Anna. Since the Emperors Basil and Constantine took no steps to execute their part of the bargain, once the victory over Bardas had been won with Russian help, Vladimir attacked Kherson in the Spring of 989 (thus actually in the *third* year after his initial decision). Vladimir's mission to Constantinople, actually a summation to the Byzantines, was attributed in the above version of the story of his conversion (cf. *supra*, n. 92) to the wholly apocryphal intention of inspecting the "Greek faith." The Byzantines were then forced to carry out their promises in the Autumn of 989. Just as Olga seems to have taken the baptismal name of Helena (same as that of Constantine VII's wife), so Vladimir was now, in 989 or 990, baptized as Basil (in honor of Basil II). This tradition of Vladimir's baptism in Kherson thus appears justified by the historical evidence, though it cannot be confirmed with entire certainty. Cf. Ammann, *op. cit.*, pp. 15-17.

95. The churches of this period at Kherson were for the most part basilicas roofed with wood; the basilica in the baptistry of which Vladimir was baptized (if this event actually took place in Kherson) was probably discovered by Uvarov in 1851, it was built in the seventh century (restored in the ninth) and is adjoined by a baptistry of trefoil shape, cf. Minns, *op. cit.*, pp. 509-510, and fig. 140, p. 511; also Tolstoy-Kondakov, *Russkiya Drevnosti*, IV (SPB., 1891), 15-18, and fig. 10.

96. On the Stugna, about 35 km. southwest of Kiev, now Vasil'kov.

97. The first sentence cites the Nicene creed (not quoted in full); the second is a somewhat condensed translation of the Λίβελλος περὶ τῆς ὀρθοδόξου πίστεως of Michael Syncellus (ninth century), of which a Slavic text is also contained in the *Sbornik* of Prince Svyatoslav (1073); Greek text, Slavic text from the *Sbornik*, and the text as rendered in the Chronicle, in M. I. Sukhomlinov, "O Drevney Russkoy Lětopisi kak Pamyatnikě Literaturnom," *Sbornik Otd. Russk. Yaz. i Slov.*, LXXXV (1908), 71-74; cf. also Nikol'sky, *Materialÿ*, pp. 16-19.

98. The source of the material in the paragraphs on the Oecumenical Councils is not exactly determinable, though it has been referred to the *Paleya*, to Georgius Hamartolus, and to the Epistle of Photius to Boris of Bulgaria; cf. Sukhomlinov, pp. 74-77; Nikol'sky, pp. 27-34; Shakhmatov, *Razÿskaniya*, p. 156. The author of these paragraphs was obviously using various related sources, some of which gave topics of the various councils, while others contained Byzantine polemical writings directed, in the tradition of Photius and Cerularius, against Rome. Typical of these writings, then flooding Russia, is the apocryphal story of Peter the Stammerer (*Gugnivÿy*), intended to insinuate that Rome had lost her original position. It has been suggested (cf. A. Lilov, *O Tak-Nazÿvaemoy Kirillovskoy Knigě* [Kazan, 1858] pp. 190-191) that the name "Peter the Stammerer" was invented in connection with that of St. Peter the Apostle, though, doubtless, it also evoked the memories of the Monophysite Peter Mongus (μουγγός). Later, together with other pieces of similar Byzantine anti-Catholic polemic (for Byzantine propaganda in Russia, cf. A. Pavlov, *Kriticheskie Opÿtÿ po Istorii Drevněyshey Grekorusskoy Polemiki protiv Latinyan* [Sbp., 1878]; Golubinsky, pp. 86-89, 796 ff.; A. Palmieri in *Acta Acad. Velehrad.* [Prague, 1912]; cf. also *supra*, n. 92), this

story was incorporated into the so-called *Kormchaya Kniga* (= Πηδάλιον, i.e., *Corpus juris canonici* of the Russian Church). The mention of the eikon painted by St. Luke may be from Hamartolus, von Muralt, p. 633. In the Laurentian codex (p. 114) the translated quotation from St. Basil is mutilated to read *ikona* [*na*] *pervÿy obraz prikhodit* ("the eikon resembles the original image"), here corrected to accord with the Greek ἡ γὰρ τῆς εἰκόνος τιμὴ ἐπὶ τὸ πρωτότυπον διαβαίνει, i.e., *chest' obraza prikhodit na pervoobraznoe*, and the passage is therefore so rendered as to accord with the correct citation (Basil, *On the Holy Ghost* [to Amphilochius of Iconium], Migne, *P. G.*, XXXIV, 119).

99. Constantine (Cyril), later one of the proto-apostles of the Slavs, passed the winter of 860 at Kherson. Here, according to the *Pannonian Life* of Constantine (French translation in Dvornik, *Les légendes de Constantin et de Méthode*, p. 359), he discovered the relics of Pope St. Clement I (third successor of St. Peter; *ca.* 91-99), who is alleged by hagiographical tradition to have been exiled to the Crimea and to have met a martyr's death there (cf. J. Lebreton and J. Zeiller, *History of the Primitive Church*, Eng. trans. [New York, 1949], I, 389). As has been pointed out, however, this tradition is open to suspicion, since Kherson was not subject to the Roman Empire in Trajan's day and because the tradition in question is found in some Greek *Acts*, which are not earlier than the fourth century (Funk, *Patrum apostol. opera* [Tübingen, 1901] II, 28-45; cf. *Hist. Prim. Church, loc. cit*). There is no doubt that Constantine actually discovered some relics, which Dvornik (p. 193) conjectures may perhaps have been those of a local martyr named Clement whom subsequent tradition confused with the early Pope. Later Russian annals, reporting a Papal mission to Vladimir while he was at Kherson (*PSRL.*, IX, 57; cf. *supra*, n. 92) add that the envoys brought him "relics of the saints." *The Pannonian Life* (Dvornik, p. 378) asserts that in 867 Constantine (Cyril) presented to Pope Adrian II the relics of Pope St. Clement, so that Golubinsky suggests (I, i, 223, n. 2) either that Constantine did not take all of St. Clement's relics to Rome or that John XV sent back to Vladimir these relics. However this may be, Vladimir seems to have dedicated a chapel to this saint in the church of Our Lady of Tithe, which he built in 989 ff., and in 1147 Clement of Smolensk was consecrated Metropolitan of Kiev "by the head of St. Clement, even as the Greeks appoint by the head of St. John" (Hypatian Chronicle, *PSRL.*, II [1843], 30). Furthermore, Thietmar of Merseburg, ed. F. Kurze, VIII, 74, p. 237, states that Vladimir was buried "in eccclesia Christi martiris et papae Clementis iuxta predictam coniugem suam" (i.e., Anna), again obviously referring to a chapel of St. Clement in the Desyatinnaya, where Vladimir was actually entombed (cf. *infra*, n. 115). Phoebus (Slav. *Fif*), the disciple, is not identifiable.

100. Cf. *supra*, n. 56.

101. A tradition also existed (repeated in Gizel's *Synopsis*, an uncritical historical compilation of the seventeenth century, ed. 1823, p. 50) that Vladimir's sons were baptized at Kiev in the Kreshchatik spring (their baptism, without location, is mentioned in *PSRL*, IX, 57), which was situated in a grove near the Dnieper at the junction of what is now the Ul. Revolyutsii and the riverside road north from the Chain Bridge. While there was formerly a monument on this spot, the tradition is thoroughly unhistorical (cf. Zakrevsky, *Opisanie*, pp. 420-429).

102. Cf. *supra*, n. 81.

103. The assignment of Vladimir's progeny to various outlying principalities reflects his policy of consolidating the dominance of Kiev. Whatever independent Varangian principalities had previously existed (e.g., Rogvold in Polotsk and Turÿ in Turov, cf. *supra,* the item under 980) were now subjected. After Kiev, Novgorod is recognized as the most important center. Vladimir's campaigns against the Vyatichians and the Bulgars had established his authority in the upper Volga basin, as indicated by his control of Rostov and Murom. His operations against the Croats and the Polish marches gave him mastery of the Volhynian cities, now dominated by Vladimir-Volÿnsk. Later annalistic compilations also mention his son Stanislav in Smolensk and Sudislav in Pskov (*PSRL.,* VII, 313, V, 120). Vsevolod seems to have died in 995, and to have been replaced in Vladimir-Volÿnsk by Pozvizd, another son; cf. A. Presnyakov, *Knyazhoe Pravo v Drevney Rusi* (Spb., 1909), p. 31, n. 2. The mention of Tmutarakan' (cf. *infra,* n. 147) is problematic; there is no mention in the Russian sources of any Kievan operations in the eastern Crimea in Vladimir's day, so that some authorities degrade to rumor or legend all early Russian references to Tmutorakan', e.g., V. Smirnov, "Chto takoe Tmutorakan'," *Viz. Vrem.,* XXIII (Petrograd, 1923), 48-51. However, some indication of Russian interest in the area is supplied by Cedrenus' report (Bonn ed., II, 464), that in January, 1016, Basil II sent a detachment to the Crimea for an operation against the Khazars in which the Byzantine force was victorious, thanks to the cooperation of an otherwise unknown Sphengos (Norse *Sveinki*), characterized as brother of Vladimir (cf. Vasiliev, *Goths,* p. 134); cf. *infra,* n. 147.

104. Of the rivers mentioned, the Desna, Oster', Trubezh, and Sula join it from the west. Since no towns are specifically mentioned, the reference is presumably to border fortresses set up as protection against Pecheneg raids.

105. This church is the Desyatinnaya, or Church of the Blessed Virgin of the Tithe; cf. Cross, "The Earliest Mediaeval Churches in Kiev," pp. 481 ff.; D. Ainalov, *Russische Monumentalkunst der vormoskovitischen Zeit* (Berlin, 1932), pp. 9-11; Brunov-Alpatov, *Altrussische Kunst* (Augsburg, 1932), pp. 9-10. The Desyatinnaya suffered so severely in the fire of 1017 that it was rebuilt and then rededicated in 1039. It was destroyed upon the capture of Kiev by the Tartars in 1240. The site was formerly occupied by an undistinguished modern church, demolished in 1935, but a portion of the primitive structure (apses and north side) were excavated by D. V. Mileev, cf. *Otchetÿ Imp. Arkheograficheskoy Kommissii* (Spb., 1912), pp. 132-158. As constructed by Vladimir, the Desyatinnaya was (as far as one can judge by surviving remains) a basilica with a wooden roof. Since Kherson was taken only in 989, the church can hardly have been begun before 990-991.

106. Cf. *supra,* n. 83.

107. Cf. *supra,* n. 3.

108. As Pereyaslavl' is mentioned in both the treaties of 911 and 945, it must have been founded before Vladimir's day.

109. The Desyatinnaya was dedicated on May 12, which is thus the first Russian festival introduced into the *Prolog* (collection of readings and saints' lives for church festivals); cf. Nikol'sky, *Materialÿ,* pp. 41-42.

110. Cf. *supra,* n. 96.

111. In view of its rapid construction, this church was apparently of wood, and may be compared with the so-called *obÿdennÿe tserkvi* (one-day churches)

built, as their name indicates, in one day by communal labor in historical times (from the fourteenth century forward) in execution of vows to banish plagues and epidemics; cf. D. Zelenin, *Russische Volkskunde*, p. 335, Makariy, *Ist. Russkoy Tserkvi*, I, 51. The Transfiguration was August 6, and the Assumption of the Blessed Virgin August 15.

112. These princes are: Bolesław Chrobry of Poland (*regn.* 992-1025); St. Stephen I of Hungary (*regn.* 997-1038); and Udalrich of Bohemia (*regn.* 1012-1034).

113. Cf. *supra*, n. 83.

114. As stated by the Chronicle under 970, Vladimir was the son of Malusha, sister of Dobrynya (a distinguished boyar) and stewardess of the princess Olga. While Vladimir was characterized as a "slave's son" by Rogned in 975, this epithet is not to be taken seriously in view of Dobrynya's influential position. Stender-Petersen, *Die Varägersage*, p. 15, thus identifies Malmfrid with Malusha, supposing Vladimir to have been of pure Scandinavian ancestry.

115. This item refers primarily to the ceremonial interment of the relics of the Princess Olga in the Desyatinnaya. As the Chronicle recounts under 969, Olga had requested only a simple funeral, and even later compilations, which dwell at length on her life and virtues (e.g., the *Stepennaya Kniga* and its sources) retain no tradition of the place of her first burial. As there were no other Russian saints at the moment, it is to be assumed that the relics of Pope St. Clement (cf. *supra*, n. 99) were translated to the Desyatinnaya at the same time with those of Olga. Shakhmatov (*Razyskaniya*, p. 162) considers the word *svyatii*, "saints," an error for *si*, "these," and interprets the passage to mean that the previously-mentioned deceased relatives of the princely house were entombed in the Desyatinnaya. Like many other suggestions of the same scholar, this conjecture is by no means conclusive.

116. Prior to Vladimir's day, the authority of the Kievan princes had been purely patriarchal, but with the delegation of authority over outlying areas, centrifugal tendencies soon developed of which Yaroslav's insubordination is the first conspicuous example. It is likely, however, that the assignment of Poltosk to Rogned's son Izyaslav (who died in 1001; cf. *supra*, n. 75, and *PSRL*, I, ii, 2nd ed., 299-300) reflects a similar movement by an outlying principality toward independence from Kiev. This movement is later reflected in the efforts of Izyaslav's son Bryachislav to seize control of Novgorod. It should also be noted that in Vladimir's day there was as yet no express system of seniority among the subordinate princes. Yaroslav's relations with Vladimir cannot have been particularly cordial, as is indicated by his original assignment to the distant and unimportant district of Rostov. His official assignment to Novgorod took place only subsequent to the death of his oldest brother Vysheslav and also after another elder brother, Svyatopolk, had fallen into disfavor for intriguing with Bolesław Chrobry of Poland (cf. *infra*, n. 119), a further example of an effort by another of Vladimir's sons to escape central control. It would also appear, from Vladimir's insistence on Boris' presence with him toward the close of his life, that he intended to designate the latter as his heir.

117. The following 28 lines are taken by Cross from *Hyp.* p. 115.

118. In this eulogy to Vladimir, especially the words "If we had been zealous . . . God . . . would have glorified him," there is manifestly a reference to some delay either in Vladimir's official canonization, or in general recognition of the

saintly qualities which distinguished at least the latter part of his life, whatever may have been its pre-Christian phase. During the first part of the eleventh century, the latter was clearly remembered (cf. Thietmar of Merseburg's epithet, VIII, 72), and it is only toward the end of the reign of Yaroslav, especially in Hilarion's *Discourse on Law and Grace* (*Slovo o Zakone i Blagodati, ca.* 1050) that a tendency developed to concentrate on Vladimir's virtues which culminates in the Eulogy of the monk James. Vladimir was thus recognized as a saint at least after the middle of the eleventh century, and Golubinsky's assertion that he was not canonized till the thirteenth is not conclusive (*op. cit.*, I, i, 185; cf. Serebryansky's refutation, *Knyazheskie Zhitiya,* pp. 56-58). Prisëlkov's explanation for the non-canonization of Vladimir by supposed Greek hostility because he allowed the newly-founded Russian Church to be subject to Ochrida, in Bulgaria (*Ocherki po Tserkovno-politicheskoy Istorii Kievskoy Rusi* (Spb., 1913), p. 303) lacks the slightest factual basis.

119. Svyatopolk married a daughter of Bolesław Chrobry of Poland, who arrived in Russia accompanied by Bishop Reinbern of Colberg, and adopted the Latin rite. When Vladimir heard rumors that Svyatopolk was conspiring with Bolesław, he threw Svyatopolk, his wife, and the Bishop into prison. Thietmar who relates the whole episode (VIII 72-73, ed. Kurze, pp. 236-237) adds that Svyatopolk escaped from prison upon his father's death and fled to Poland, leaving his wife behind. This account cannot be reconciled with the Chronicle unless it is supposed that Svyatopolk escaped during Vladimir's last illness, and returned immediately after assuring himself of Bolesław's support in seizing the principate.

120. The Al'ta (L'to) is a confluent of the Trubezh, an eastern tributary of the Dnieper below Kiev.

121. For Vÿshgorod, cf. *supra,* n. 83. Nothing is known of the church mentioned beyond the tradition that it was built by Vladimir and burned *ca.* 1020 (Makariy, *Ist.,* I, 51-52).

122. The Smyadÿn', a small stream joined the Dnieper near Smolensk.

123. There are two other early accounts of the murder of Boris and Gleb: one by the monk James, who wrote the *Eulogy* of Vladimir, and the other by Nestor, to whom the *Povest' Vremennÿkh Let* has often been attributed; texts of both in Sreznevsky, *Skazaniya o Svyatÿkh Borisĕ i Glĕbĕ;* cf. *supra,* Introduction: Authorship.

124. In the original *vo dvorĕ Poromoni;* this enigmatic phrase is identified as a corruption of the Old Norse *farmanna garpr,* "the court of the overseas merchants," and indicates that the Swedish traders frequenting Novgorod possessed their corporate centers in the town even at this early period; cf. A. Bugge, "Die nordeuropäischen Verkehrswege im frühen Mittelalter," *Vtljhrsch. f. Soz.—u. Wirtschaftsgeschichte,* IV (1905-1906), 244-251. These Varangians are the mercenaries collected by Yaroslav in 1015 (see *supra*) in expectation of Vladimir's attack after Yaroslav had suspended payment of the annual tribute.

125. Rokom, mod. Rakoma, on the northeastern shore of Lake Il'men' south of Novgorod.

126. While these figures are doubtful, independent evidence of a further enrolment of Varangian auxiliaries is found in the *Saga of Eymund son of Hring* (*Eymundarpáttr Hringssonar*) preserved in the *Flateyarbók,* an Icelandic compilation of the late fourteenth century, but containing considerable material from

earlier sources now lost. Eymund was the great-grandson of Harald Fair-Hair, King of Norway (died in 933). A close friend of Olaf Haraldsson (King of Norway 1016, killed at Stiklastadir in 1030), Eymund was unwilling to fight against Olaf when the latter had overthrown Eymund's father Hring, and he apparently took service with Yaroslav after the massacre of the Varangians by the men of Novgorod. He played an active part in the engagement at Lyubech. Text of the *þáttr* in *Flateyarbók* II (Oslo, 1862), 118-135, also *Fornmanna Sögur*, V, 267-298, and C. C. Rafn, *Antiquités russes*, II, (Copenhagen, 1825), 173-211, with Latin and French trans. and notes; cf. F. Braun, *Mogk Festschrift*, pp. 179-182; Cross, "Yaroslav the Wise," pp. 186-190.

127. Svyatopolk's alliance with the Pechenegs has been interpreted as indicating that the Varangian domination in Kiev was not firmly established by Vladimir and that Yaroslav's rivalry with Svyatopolk was a phase of the Varangian struggle for mastery against a party of the local inhabitants supported by the nomads of the steppes; cf. V. Parkhomenko, 'Rus' i Pechenegi,' *Slavia*, VIII (1929), 138-144.

128. While the account would seem to refer to Lyubech, on the west bank of the Dnieper north of the confluence of the Pripet', this town belonged to the Chernigov area and was not a dependency of Kiev. Barsov *Ocherki Russk. Istor. Geografii*, p. 143, therefore considers that a town of the same name here referred to was located on the east bank of the Dnieper some five miles northeast of Kiev.

129. The "crooked-shanks" was Yaroslav himself, who, according to tradition, had been lame from birth (*PSRL.*, II, 1st ed., 258); the same legend has it that he never even walked until Vladimir's conversion, which is of course impossible if he had been 28 years in Novgorod in 1016-1017 (see n. *infra*, 132). The Hypatian text (*PSRL.*, II, 3rd ed., [Leningrad, 1923], 129) here reads 18.

130. The position between two lakes accords with Barsov's theory on the location of Lyubech. There was formerly a body of water known as the Dolobskoe lake on the east bank a short distance northeast of Kiev. The topography of this district has subsequently been so modified by floods and alluvial deposits that the exact location of this pond or bayou is no longer determinable. A similar small body of water known as the Podlyubskoe lake is probably the second one referred to, and derives its name from the town Lyubech (Barsov, *ibid.*). The preceding sentence, noting that frost was setting in, places the campaign in late fall or winter. Since Vladimir died on July 15, 1015, it is not likely that Yaroslav could have collected Varangian auxiliaries in time to arrive before Kiev by August 15-30, 1015, which would be required if the final engagement took place as early as November 15-30, 1015, at the onset of winter frosts after a stalemate of three months. Hence Yaroslav's movement southward must have taken place late in 1016.

131. The Hypatian text (*ibid.*) here reads "entered into Kiev." Since the annalist is using the March calendar, this event can have taken place only after March 1, 1017. Barring an unexplained corruption of the text, it is necessary to assume either that Yaroslav returned to Novgorod before entering Kiev or that the decisive engagement with Svyatopolk did not occur at least until the end of February, 1017.

132. When Yaroslav died in 1054 he was 76 years old and was thus born in 978. If he had been 28 years at Novgorod in 1016, this fact would indicate that Yaroslav had lived at Novgorod even since Vladimir in 987-988 had made up his

mind to accept conversion and marry a Byzantine princess. It is scarcely to be supposed that Yaroslav was made Prince of either Rostov or Novgorod while still a mere boy. See *supra,* n. 129.

133. The fire of 1017 is corroborated by Thietmar of Merseburg, IX, 32, ed. Kurze, p. 257. The church referred to by Thietmar in this passage as "sanctae monasterium Sophiae" is probably the Desyatinnaya.

134. The intervening events are described by Thietmar, VIII, 59 ff., pp. 229 ff. During the summer of 1017, Henry II had attacked Nimptsch in Silesia, and Bolesław Chrobry had invaded Bohemia. After recovering Kiev, Yaroslav also raided Bolesław's borders (*ibid.,* VIII, 65, p. 232) to attack Brest Litovsk (Synodal text, p. 89). Bolesław hastened to make peace with Henry in order to have his hands free for a Russian campaign: a treaty was concluded at Bautzen on January 30, 1018 (*ibid.,* IX, p. 239). The preceding November Henry had been informed by Yaroslav of his accession and attack on the Polish borders. He supplied a force of 300 troops to Bolesław for his invasion of Russia (*ibid.,* IX, 33, p. 258).

135. The battle on the Bug took place July 22, 1018 (Thietmar, IX, 31, p. 257). Yaroslav's troops failed to hold the ford they were defending and made no concerted stand against the Poles once the latter had crossed the river. On Volÿn', cf. *supra,* n. 84.

136. Upon Bolesław's arrival before Kiev, the Pechenegs joined his standards, and the city fell on August 14, 1018, cf. Thietmar, *ibid.,* S. M. Solov'ëv's notion (*Ist. Ros.,* I, 4th ed. [Moscow, 1888] 221) that the Pecheneg attack preceded by some months Bolesław's occupation of the city does not accord with the account of Thietmar, who had friends among Bolesław's German allies.

137. On the basis of the values quoted *supra* in n. 25, these contributions amounted respectively to 68 cents, $42.50, and $76.50, showing a considerable accumulation of individual wealth in Novgorod.

138. While not mentioned by the Chronicle, part of the Novgorod policy for the restoration of Yaroslav to the Kievan principate was an alliance with Olaf Skotkonung, king of Sweden (*regn.* 995-1022), to be sealed by the marriage of Yaroslav to the latter's daughter Ingigerd, as is indicated by the fact that Rognvald of West Gautland, a Swedish jarl who accompanied Ingigerd on her marriage journey to Novgorod in 1019, was guaranteed under the marriage contract the principality of Ladoga (Snorri Sturluson, *Heimskringla,* p. 258); cf. Cross, "Yaroslav the Wise," pp. 183; F. Braun, *loc. cit.,* p. 182. Ingigerd received the Russian name of Irene and died in 1050. It will be noted that since Constantine the *Posadnik* of Novgorod, was Dobrÿnya's son, and since Dobrÿnya was Vladimir's maternal uncle, Constantine was an older cousin of Yaroslav. The marriage of Ingigerd with Yaroslav should be taken as occurring before the latter's successful attack on Kiev.

139. Thietmar (IX, 32, p. 258) adds the detail that after the capture of Kiev, Bolesław's foreign auxiliaries (300 Germans, 500 Hungarians, and 1000 Pechenegs) were allowed to return home because Svyatopolk reported that the Russians were flocking to his standards and appeared loyal.

140. This Anastasius may be identified with the Anastasius who betrayed Kherson in 989 (see *supra,* item for 988), accompanied Vladimir to Kiev, and was placed in charge of the Desyatinnaya (see item of 989). He also figures in Thietmar (*ibid.*) as an emissary from Bolesław to Yaroslav to negotiate an exchange of prisoners. In the light of the conclusive Norse evidence for Yaroslav's marriage to

Ingigerd in 1019, Thietmar's report that Yaroslav's wife was at Kiev when Bolesław captured it would appear erroneous, the more so since Thietmar in the same passage refers to eight sisters (or half-sisters) of Yaroslav, though the Chronicle knows of but two.

141. Cf. *supra,* n. 84.

142. Cf. *supra,* n. 120.

143. Brest-Litovsk (Polish, Brześć-Litewski), on the northern Bug.

144. This phrase, interpreted by Karamzin (ed. Suvorin [Spb., 1888], II, 14) as "in the Bohemian wastes" and by Solov'ëv, *op. cit.,* I, 224, literally as here translated, was alleged by O. E. Senkovsky, "Skandinavskiya Sagi," *Biblioteka dlya Chtenya,* I (Spb., 1834),iii, 66 ff, as the equivalent of the Polish phrase *między Czechy i Lechy,* meaning "heaven knows where."

145. Izyaslav, a brother of Yaroslav, died in 1001 (*q.v.*) and his domain passed directly to his posterity (even during Vladimir's lifetime) without any visible opposition from Kiev. Polotsk, at the headwaters of the southern Dvina, controlled the portage from the latter to the Dnieper and thus possessed some commercial importance. It was also *de facto* independent of Kievan influence. Bryachislav's effort to wrest Novgorod from Kiev indicates not only commercial rivalry but also a spirit of particularism among the regional princes which had already been exemplified by Yaroslav's projected revolt against his father. For the legendary explanation of the traditional hostility between Polotsk and Kiev, cf. *supra,* n. 75; see also A. Presnyakov, *Knyazhoe Pravo v Drevney Rusi,* pp. 32-33.

146. The Sudomir' (Sudoma) river, southwest of Novgorod, is a small stream rising east of Pskov and itself a tributary of the Shelon', which in turn flows into Lake Il'men' from the west. Yaroslav thus travelled some 500 miles in seven days to meet Bryachislav.

147. Tmutorakan' (Gk. Tamatarcha), probably on the site of ancient Hermonassa, modern Taman', near ancient Phanagoria, on the south shore of the Bay of Taman', which extends eastward from the Strait of Kerch; V. F. Gaydukevich, *Bosporskoe Tsarstvo* (Moscow-Leningrad, 1949), pp. 208-209; I. P. Kozlovsky, "Tmutarakan' i Tamatarkha-Matarkha-Taman'," *Izvestiya Tavrichesk. Obshch. Ist. Arkh. i Etnogr.,* II, 58-72. Its history is uncertain. Smirnov, *Chto takoe Tmutorakan',* pp. 15-73, concluded that Tmutorakan' designated some "distant unfamiliar region extending from the Strait of Kertch to the river Kur, into which from time to time the Russian princes with their retainers made fierce raids for booty from the various Kasogians, Khazars, and similar barbarous minor tribes, but they never founded there any town, much less any principalities" (ibid., pp. 72-73). On the other hand, V. Parkhomenko, *U Istokov Russkoy Gosudarstvennosti* (Leningrad, 1924), finds in Tmutorakan' a late survival of extensive Slavic settlements about the Sea of Azov. As the Chronicle itself later indicates (see below, 1023-1024, and the next note), there was in the early eleventh century a Russian settlement at Tmutorakan' connected by dynastic tradition with Chernigov. Cf. D. Bagaley, *Istoriya Sěverskoy Zemli* (Kiev, 1882), pp. 26-28. Karamzin (*op. cit.,* II, 15), identifies Mstislav with the Russian prince Sphengos (characterized by Cedrenus, II, 464, as brother of Vladimir I; cf. *supra,* n. 103) who in January, 1016, cooperated with the Byzantines under Mongos in a campaign against the Khazars led by George Tzulos. The legendary account of Mstislav's combat with Rededya is connected by A. Stender-Petersen, *Varägersage,* pp.

163-164, with a similar duel in the *Bjarnarsaga Hitdoelakappa,* but this rapprochement is impossible save with complete disregard of the chronology, unless one assumes that the story of the combat became an item of Varangian tradition and was gratuitously introduced by the composer of the *Bjarnarsaga* when it was written down at the close of the twelfth century (cf. Cross, "Tradition islandaise de St. Vladimir," pp. 138-141). The Kasogians are the Cherkesses of the Northern Caucasus. For Tmutorakan' cf. Vernadsky, *Ancient Russia, passim.*

148. Mstislav's intimacy with Cherkesses and Khazars again testifies to the close contact prevailing between such Slavic settlements as existed in the region east of the Dnieper and the other ethnic units in the same territory (cf. *supra,* n. 127).

149. Chernigov, on the Desna some 75 miles northeast of Kiev, is one of the oldest Russian cities, being mentioned in the treaties of 907 and 945 and known to Constantine Porphyrogenitus. It is associated with the tribal group of the Severians, on the right bank of the Dnieper, who were tributary to the Khazars until subjected by Oleg in 884 (*q.v.*). This district is not mentioned again until 907, when the Severians are stated to have participated in Oleg's (questionable) attack on Constantinople. Chernigov does not figure among the cities allotted to Vladimir's sons, presumably because the Severian area at that time was closely affiliated with Kiev (cf. Bagaley, *op. cit.,* p. 47).

150. Suzdal' (here mentioned for the first time), about 100 miles northeast of Moscow in territory originally occupied by the Finns, but subjected to early Eastern Slavic colonization. The first settlement in this area was Rostov, a colony of Novgorod (cf. V. S. Ikonnikov, *Opÿt Russkoy Istoriografii,* II, i [Kiev, 1908], 856 and n. 5).

151. Cf. a similar episode in Rostov under 1071. While some scholars have inclined to regard these magicians as Finnish shamans, they may equally well be debased survivors of the Slavic pagan cult in a remote border district (cf. Mansikka, *op. cit.,* 100-103).

152. The Kama Bulgars, cf. *supra,* Introduction, n. 56.

153. Though all the basic MSS read *slěpŭ* "blind," Karsky, *PSRL.,* I, ii, 148, still suggests the correction *bě Akun s' lěpŭ,* "this Haakon was handsome." The tradition of Haakon's blindness is however, preserved in the *Kievo-Pecherskiy Paterik* (thirteenth cent.), ed. D. Abramovich (Kiev, 1931), p. 1: "There was in the Varangian land a prince Afrikan, brother of Haakon the Blind, who fled out of his golden cloak while fighting in battle array behind Yaroslav against Mstislav the Fierce." Cross agrees with R. Trautman, *Nestorchronik,* p. 246, that the MS. reading must thus stand.

154. Listven', north of Chernigov, some eight miles from modern Gorodnya.

155. On the east bank of the Dnieper at its junction with the Desna.

156. Bel'z, one of the so-called cities of Cherven now in Poland, near the border between Galicia and Volhynia (cf. *supra,* n. 84). Upon the death of Bolesław Chrobry in 1025, his more powerful neighbors (Knut the Great of Denmark, Stephen I of Hungary, the Emperor Conrad II) all endeavored to wrest his conquests from his weak son Mieszko II (1025-1034).

157. This campaign against the Finnish tribes of Estonia resulted from the ambitions of the rulers of Novgorod to control the south shore of the Gulf of Finland and the river-routes leading to it. The Chuds (Ests) attacked by Yaroslav lay to the north and west of Lake Peipus, thus blocking the routes to the Gulf

of Finland and the Gulf of Riga, in distinction from those Chuds who lived north and east of Novgorod, and had been on good terms with the Slavic settlers from earliest times (cf. Barsov, *Ocherki,* pp. 46-48). Yur'ev (mod. Dorpat, in Esthonian Tartu) is on the river Embach, in Esthonia.

158. The disorders mentioned took place not after the death of Bolesław Chrobry in 1025, but upon that of his successor Mieszko II in 1034, which was followed by a tumultuous six-years' interregnum. Mieszko had been obliged to abdicate in favor of his brother Otto in 1031, but after the latter's death in 1032 Mieszko II made his submission to Conrad II and returned to Poland. When Mieszko II died insane in 1034, he was succeeded by his minor son Casimir under the regency of the latter's mother Richeza, niece of Otto III, but a popular revolt compelled them to flee the country. Conrad II himself died in 1039, and the following year, with the aid of Henry III, Casimir was able to regain his throne, which he held until his death in 1058. The sources on the reign of Casimir are extremely scanty (cf. J. Szujski, *Dzieje Polski,* I [Cracow, 1895], 83-90).

159. The Ros' joins the Dnieper from the west some 60 miles below Kiev; it was the natural line of defense against the Pechenegs and was fortified by a rampart on its northern shore; cf. Hrushevsky, *Kievskaya Zemlya,* pp. 30-31.

160. The Cathedral of the Redeemer in Chernigov, begun about 1034 and probably completed by Yaroslav's son Svyatoslav, who was prince of Chernigov after his father's death; cf. Golubinsky, *op. cit.,* II, 1, 304. This edifice is the first Russian example of the five-domed Church with three naves and apses; cf. D. Ainalov, *op. cit.,* pp. 33-36; Brunov-Alpatov, *op. cit.,* pp. 17-19.

161. Born in 1020.

162. Joachim, the first Bishop of Novgorod, had died in 1030; *PSRL.,* III, 121; IX, 79. He designated as his successor his pupil Ephrem, who was *locum tenens* for five years; A. I. Ponomarev, *Pamyatniki Drevne-Russkoy Tserkovno-Uchitel'noy Literaturÿ,* I (Spb., 1894), 17. Yaroslav, however, disregarded Joachim's wishes and finally in 1036 appointed Luka Zhidyata to the see, which he held for nineteen years. In 1055, however, after the death of his patron Yaroslav, Luka was accused of improper conduct, summoned to Kiev by the Metropolitan Ephrem, deprived of his see, and thrown into prison, where he lay for three years. Upon Ephrem's death he was released and sent back to his diocese, but died during the return journey on October 15, 1059; *PSRL.,* IX, 91. There is extant, and probably from his pen (Golubinsky, I, i, 812, gives no cogent resason for his supposition that Luka did not compose it himself) a brief admonition to his "brethren," of which the content indicates that it was his farewell communication upon his ill-fated departure for Kiev.

163. This passage supplies the classic motive for believing that the Cathedral of St. Sophia was not begun until 1037; cf. Cross, "The Earliest Mediaeval Churches of Kiev," p. 490 ff.

164. The Setoml' was a small stream which formerly flowed into the Pochayna across the northern part of the Podol', or lowland riverside section of Kiev; cf. Zakrevsky, *Opisanie,* p. 560.

165. Mentioned elsewhere only under 988, together with his release, which is mentioned as having taken place in 1059, and his death in 1063.

166. Yaroslav's citadel inclosed the plateau lying to the southwest of the smaller primitive citadel dating from the days of Olga and Vladimir, and extending westward as far as the modern Ul. Podval'naya (formerly Yaroslavov Yar), while

on the south the boundary of the citadel followed the edge of the plateau overlooking the central part of the modern city (above and to the northwest of the Ul. Vorovskogo, formerly Kreshchatik). The ruins of the Golden Gate are found in a park at the junction of the Ul. Sverdlova and Korolenko. The portion now visible, however, is (according to the opinion of S. H. Cross) not the gate itself, but a remnant of the Church of the Annunciation over the gate, and some excavation on the side would be rewarding. The ruins themselves show the *opus mixtum* characteristic of the eleventh century.

167. St. Sophia was not consecrated until 4 November, 1061 or 1067, since it is impossible that so complicated a structure, begun only in 1037, should have been sufficiently far advanced to permit consecration in 1039, as some scholars have believed (cf. *infra,* n. 170; and N. P. Sÿchov, "Drevneyshiy Fragment Russko-Vizantiyskoy Zhivopisi," *Seminarium Kondakovianum,* II (1928), 90-104. St. Sophia as at first erected was a cruciform church with five apses and naves and thirteen cupolas, together with one-story lateral arcades on the north and south sides. It was constructed of red granite from neighboring quarries fixed in courses of pink cement. Later in the eleventh century (perhaps before its consecration), a masonry narthex and the northwest staircase tower were added, and the original arcades were supplemented by a second story. The third primary stage of construction (also eleventh century) consisted in the addition of a further one-story arcade and the southwest tower which was designed to provide additional access to the internal galleries and which is connected with the second story of the arcade by a special bay. The church as it now stands is the result of two eighteenth-century restorations which resulted in adding a second story to the outermost arcade and the construction of six additional cupolas (two over the towers and two over the middle and over the east ends of the lateral arcades). While the external decoration and aspect is thus Ukrainian Baroque, the interior (apart from the west front, which was badly dilapidated in the later middle ages) is well preserved. The eleventh-century Greek mosaics of the Blessed Virgin *orans,* the Eucharist, and the Fathers of the Church in the altar apse, the Annunciation at either side of the main arch, and the Pantocrator and the Archangels in the central cupola are among the great artistic products of the period. The process of cleaning the primitive frescos (which were painted over), though progressing slowly, has also produced valuable results. Cf. Ainalov, *op. cit.,* pp. 12-24; Brunov-Alpatov, op. cit., pp. 10-17; L. Réau, *L'art russe dès origines à Pierre le Grand* (Paris, 1921), pp. 102-109; D. R. Buxton, *Russian Mediaeval Architecture* (Cambridge, England, 1934), pp. 10-16 (elementary); Cross, "The Earliest Mediaeval Churches of Kiev," pp. 490-493; K. J. Conant, in *Speculum,* XI (1936), pp. 493-499; with brilliant restoration drawings and the best available modern photographs.

168. The monastery of St. George and the convent of St. Irene, with the accompanying churches, bear the names of the patron saints of Yaroslav and his consort. These edifices were located within Yaroslav's citadel south of St. Sophia. A column from St. Irene's still stands in the Ul. Korolenko, but the disappearance of the ruins of the edifices is doubtless explicable by the use of stone from them for the restoration of St. Sophia itself. A wooden church of St. George was erected on the site in 1674, and replaced by a stone church in 1744 during the reign of the Empress Elizabeth. There is a tradition that Hilarion was consecrated as metropolitan in Yaroslav's St. George's on the 5th of November,

1051, the same day on which the church was dedicated (Zakrevsky, *Opisanie*, pp. 264-265). The early church of St. George was first investigated by Mileev in 1910 (Brunov-Alpatov, *op. cit.*, pp. 06-17). For St. Irene's, cf. *Otchetÿ Arkheologicheskoy Kommissii* (1918), pp. 167-168.

169. Cf. *supra*, n. 86.

170. The reference is to the Desyatinnaya (cf. *supra*, n. 105), which was damaged in the fire of 1017 (cf. *supra*, n. 133) and rebuilt by Yaroslav. As Sÿchov points out (*loc. cit.*, p. 101), the Desyatinnaya was not dedicated to any particular festival of the Blessed Virgin (e.g., the Assumption), but to Our Lady herself, as is the case with several mediaeval Roman churches (e.g., S. Maria Maggiore, S. Maria in Ara Coeli, etc.). The rededication of the Desyatinnaya took place on October 4 (Sÿchov, *ibid.*).

171. In view of the formal mention of Yaroslav's founding the metropolitan church of St. Sophia in 1037 (*q.v.*) and of the fact that neither the Laurentian nor the Hypatian redactions, nor (indeed) the Synodal text of the annals of Novgorod (which antedates both the former by some two centuries), name any metropolitan in Kiev prior to Theopemptos (1039), serious doubts have been expressed whether any metropolitanate existed before the reign of Yaroslav. These doubts are intensified by the presence of divergent traditions in later texts as to the predecessors of Theopemptos. One tradition, typified by the so-called *Sofiyskiy Vremennik* (2nd ed., *PSRL.*, V [Leningrad, 1925], 72) states that in 991 Vladimir received the metropolitan Leo from Constantinople, while the *Stepennaya Kniga* (*PSRL.*, XXI [Spb., 1908,] 102) mentions that the first metropolitan sent out by Byzantium was Michael, and that he was succeeded by Leo in 991 (*ibid.*, p. 113). It is curious, in any case, that both these texts mention Photius as the patriarch to whom Vladimir applied, though Photius had been dead since 891. However, the *Stepennaya* correctly connects with Leo the patriarch Nicholas Chrysoberges, who had succeeded Antonius in 984, and died himself in 991, to be succeeded by Sisinnius Magister (996-998), Sergius (1001-1019), Eustathius (1019-1025), Alexius (1025-1043), and Michael Cerularius (1043-1059). Two late eleventh-century texts (the *Lives of Boris and Gleb* by Nestor and the monk James. ed. I. I. Sreznevsky, *Skazaniya o Svyatÿkh Borisě i Glěbě*) mention (cols. 25-29, 72-74) a metropolitan John before Theopemptos, though in both texts he is referred to more frequently as "Archbishop," but sometimes as "Metropolitan," and it will be recalled that when Bolesław Chrobry and Svyatopolk entered Kiev on August 14, 1018, they were received, according to Thietmar of Merseburg (IX, 32, p. 257), by the "archiepiscopus civitatis illius cum reliquiis sanctorum." Several theories have been formulated regarding the origin of the Russian Church. I.—M. D. Prisëlkov suggested (*Ocherki po Tserkovno-politicheskoy Istorii Kievskoy Rusi* [Spb., 1913]) that the Church of Vladimir's realm was under the jurisdiction, not of the See of Constantinople, but of the Patriarchate (from 1018, Archbishopric) of Ochrida in Bulgaria. This Bulgarian theory has been contested by M. Jugie (*Le schisme byzantin*, p. 185), E. Honigmann ("Studies in Slavic Church History," *Byzantion*, XVII [1945]), and G. Vernadsky (*Kievan Russia*, p. 67). - II. The Western origin and early affiliation of the Kievan Church have been indicated by N. de Baumgarten (*Saint Vladimir et la Conversion de la Russie;* "Olaf Tryggwison, roi de Norvège et ses relations avec Saint Vladimir de Russie," *Orientalia Christiana*, XXIV [1931], 1-37 and M. Jugie (*op. cit.*, pp. 172-186), but rejected by G. Ostrogorsky (*Geschichte des byzantinischen*

Staates [Munich, 1952], p. 244) and Honigmann (*op. cit.*, pp. 130-131). - III. G. Vernadsky is the proponent of the theory according to which the original primate of the Russian Church was the presumably autocephalous Archbishop of Tmutorakan' dating supposedly from the days of Photius's mission of 867 ("The Status of the Russian Church during the first half-century following Vladimir's Conversion," *The Slavonic Year-Book,* 1941; *Kievan Russia,* pp. 67-68); this has been challenged by Honigmann (*op. cit.*, pp. 131-132; but cf. Vernadsky *Kievan Russia,* p. 67, n. 49). - IV. Recently, N. Zernov has expanded Golubinsky's suggestion (*op. cit.*, I, i, 264) that the Kievan Church was autocephalous from the beginning ("Vladimir and the Origin of the Russian Church," *Slavonic and East European Review,* LXX [1949], 123-138 and LXXI [1950], 425-438). Zernov's theory rests on a shaky foundation: its argument is from silence—the complete silence of the available sources regarding two things proposed by the author and essential for his theory, viz., the episcopal dignity of Anastasius of Kherson and St. Vladimir's insistence on autocephaly, and, *a fortiori,* regarding that autocephaly itself. - V. Finally, the Constantinopolitan theory of the origin of the Kievan Church has been again defended by Ostrogorsky (*op. cit.*) and Honigmann (*op. cit.*). In this connection the use of the title of Archbishop for the early Metropolitans of Kiev has been interpreted as implying their autocephaly (Golubinsky) or their Western affiliation (Jugie); the two terms are regarded as interchangeable by Honigmann (*op. cit.*, p. 141). Some confusion in these various theories is perhaps due to the projection of post-Cerularian conditions to antecedent epochs, when only the question of patriarchal and other autocephalous jurisdictions *within* the Church was involved and not that of different Churches. Cf. Ammann, *op. cit.*, pp. 15-28.

172. Yaroslav's campaigns against the Lithuanians (according to the *Nikonovskaya* compilation, *PSRL.,* IX, 83, a second attack upon them was made in 1044) were connected with his operations against the Yatvingians and probably intended to protect the frontiers of the Turov district and to assure communication westward along the Pripet'.

173. The Mazovians occupied the northeastern section of mediaeval Polish territory about the junction of Vistula and Bug, hence near modern Warsaw. The Mazovians were in constant warfare with the Prussians, Lithuanians, and Yatvingians, and Yaroslav's attack upon them at this time was probably intended, like his campaign against the Lithuanians in the previous year, to maintain order in the northwestern marches along the Pripet'.

174. The Yam' were a Finnish tribe occupying at this period the region between Lake Ladoga and the Northern Dvina, into which they seemed to have been forced by the pressure of Slavic colonization. In the thirteenth and fourteenth centuries they appear in Southern Finland, but the prevalence of place-names with the element *häm* "damp, watery" to the northeast of Lake Ladoga, indicates their previous residence in the latter locality (cf. Barsov, *Ocherki,* pp. 57-60, 241-243).

175. The Byzantine sources for this attack are Cedrenus, II, 551-555, and Psellus, *Chronographia* (an eyewitness account), ed. E. Renauld, II (Paris, 1928), pp. 8 ff., with French translation. Cf. also V. G. Vasil'evsky *Trudÿ,* I, 303-308; Prisëlkov, *op. cit.,* pp. 88-92. According to Cedrenus (p. 551), the Russian expedition, which appeared before Constantinople in June, was provoked by an attack on some Russian merchants at the Imperial capital in which a noble Russian lost

his life. Psellus, however, attributes it to a long-standing Russian resentment against the Byzantines which was checked by a wholesome respect for Basil II as long as he was alive, but was translated into military preparations as soon as the decline in Imperial prestige after his death became evident, especially during the reigns of Michael IV and Michael V (1034-1042). Prisëlkov (p. 92), in connection with his theory of the origin of the Kievan Church (cf. *supra*, n. 171), considers this resentment to have been caused by the "pretensions" of the Greek hierarchy after the establishment of the Kievan metropolitanate in 1037. In any case, Constantine IX (*regn*. 1042-1055) was caught ill-prepared and twice endeavored to negotiate. This failing, he organized an attack upon the Russian fleet which was rendered successful by an effective charge of triremes, the use of Greek fire, and a rising wind. After heavy losses, the Russians withdrew northward up the coast toward Bulgaria. Here they succeeded in surprising 24 Byzantine triremes sent in pursuit, and captured four, among them the ship of the Byzantine commanding officer. On the subsequent journey homeward the Russian armada put in near Varna, where they were attacked by the local commander and suffered large casualties, including the loss of 800 prisoners who were sent back to Byzantium. The capture of Vyshata doubtless took place in this engagement. He was released from captivity and returned to Kiev three years later (Shakhmatov, *Razÿskaniya*, p. 584).

176. Casimir's marriage to Yaroslav's sister Dobronega-Maria was a union of policy intended to strengthen the Polish prince's position after his restoration; cf. *supra*, n. 158, also Gallus, in Bielowski, *Mon. Pol. Hist.*, I, 417; Annalista Saxo, *MGH., SS.*, VIII, 683 (under 1039). Yaroslav's son Izyaslav also married Casimir's sister, cf. *infra*, n. 213. Dobronega-Maria's mother, St. Vladimir's last wife, was the third daughter of Count Cuno of Oeningen and of Richlint, daughter of Otto the Great; Baumgarten, "Le dernier mariage de Saint Vladimir," *Orientalia Christiana*, XVIII (1930), 165-168.

177. Yaropolk was killed in 980 (*q.v.*, but cf. *supra*, n. 74); Oleg in 977 (*q.v.*).

178. Cf. *supra*, nn. 75 and 145.

179. *Yazveno* (here translated "caul") is taken by other recent translators (C. W. Smith, *ar;* A. Norrback, *sår;* Trautmann, *Wunde*) to signify "sore, wound," but Sreznevsky, *Materialÿ*, col. 1645, identifies the word with *yazv'no*, "skin," and renders it with mod. Russian *plënka, kozhitsa,* "membrane," hence "caul," which is better adapted to the phrase *se yazveno navyazhi na n'*, "bind this *yazveno* upon him," in which the accusative *na n'* can scarcely apply to bandaging a wound. Trautmann's rendering of *yazveno* as "wound" in one sentence and as "bandage" (*Binde*) in the next only increases the confusion. The meaning was also misunderstood by early copyists; cf. the gloss *yazveno yama* in *Sofiysk. Vrem.* (*PSRL.*, V, 129).

180. I.e., Vladimir son of Yaroslav. Consecrated in 1052, St. Sophia of Novgorod was constructed to replace a wooden church with thirteen cupolas erected by Joachim, the first Bishop of Novgorod, which was destroyed by fire in 1045. Built of local grayish-yellow stone, St. Sophia is a modified example of the five-nave church of inscribed-cross type. It was not stuccoed externally until 1152. It has three apses and five cupolas, exclusive of the cupola surmounting the staircase tower on the west front. The low arcade on the south, together with the narthex, was added in the twelfth century, the northern arcade in the nineteenth. Apart from this northern arcade and an extra chapel added at the east and in the

sixteenth century, St. Sophia thus retains substantially its primitive aspect. The interior has galleries on three sides, and the central apse is decorated with mosaic panels of rich geometrical design. Of the original frescoes little is preserved save the Pantokrator in the main cupola and the recently discovered Prophets in its drum. The so-called Chersonian doors of the west front are actually Saxon work of the middle twelfth century, having been made at Magdeburg, *ca.* 1152. Cf. Ainalov, *op. cit.,* pp. 40-42; Brunov-Alpatov, *op. cit.,* pp. 28-31; Réau, *op. cit.,* pp. 124-128; Golubinsky, *op. cit.,* I, ii, 107-112; and for the doors, A. Goldschmidt, *Die Bronzetüren von Novgorod und Gnesen* (Marburg, 1932).

181. The resistance of the Mazovians was the principal disturbing element in the early part of Casimir's reign; cf. Gallus, in *Mon. Pol. Hist.,* I, 417-418; Kadłubek, *ibid.,* II, 284.

182. For Ingigerd-Irene, cf. *supra,* n. 138.

183. It would have been exceptional—if the theory of Constantinopolitan origin and affiliation of the early Kievan Church be admitted—for a Metropolitan of Kiev to be selected and consecrated outside Constantinople. Beside Hilarion there is only one other Russian who was thus appointed in the pre-Mongol period, i.e., when the Metropolitan Michael had left Kiev in 1145, Prince Izyaslav II Mstislavich, in July 1147, appointed Clement Smolyatich, a Russian monk, to succeed him without consulting the Patriarch of Constantinople (cf. Golubinsky, *op. cit.,* I, i, 300-311, also L. K. Goetz, *Staat u. Kirche in Altrussland* [Berlin, 1908], pp. 82-92). This question forms an integral part of the controversy regarding the initial stages of the Russian Church, for which, cf. *supra,* n. 171.

184. The Monastery of the Crypts, or Catacombs (Pecherskaya Lavra), still one of the chief sights of Kiev and before the revolution a noted goal of pilgrimage. It is situated on a bluff overlooking the Dnieper at the southeastern extremity of the modern city. For Berestovo, cf. *supra,* n. 83.

185. Cf. *supra,* n. 128.

186. In 1054 (*q.v.*), succeeded by his eldest surviving son Izyaslav I (1054-1068, then deposed, restored in 1069, deposed again in 1073, restored in 1077, killed near Chernigov, October 3, 1078; cf. *infra,* nn. 215-220).

187. In 1062 (Golubinsky, *op. cit.,* I, ii, 297); Barlaam acc. to Nestor (*Life of Theodosius,* in V. Yakovlev, *Pamyatniki Russkoy Literaturÿ XII i XIII věkov,* p. xxvii), was a nobleman's son and later visited both Jerusalem and Constantinople. The location of the Monastery of St. Demetrius is not known with certainty, though Golubinsky (*ibid.,* p. 298) supposes that Svyatopolk, son of Izyaslav (Prince of Kiev, 1093-1113) either rebuilt Izyaslav's monastery or included it in his own. Professor H. V. Morgilevsky of Kiev, the greatest authority on the archaeology of the Kievan period, suggested to Professor Cross, in personal conversations, that the monastery and church of St. Michael (the church demolished in 1935 to make way for a government building), at the eastern end of the Pl. Krasnÿkh Geroev Perekopa, was actually St. Demetrius' enlarged and renamed by Svyatopolk for his own patron saint (Michael). This hypothesis is supported by the prominence given in this church to an excellent mosaic of St. Demetrius, Izyaslav's patron.

188. According to Nestor (*ibid.,* pp. iii-xi), Theodosius was born in Vasil'ev (cf. *supra,* n. 96) and for some years was prevented from following his pious inclinations by his mother.

189. The dates of George's metropolitanate are not known, but he was the

second successor of Hilarion. He was present in Kiev in 1072 and absent at Byzantium in 1073 (*q.v.*). The Studion Monastery in Constantinople had been, since the days of St. Theodore, its most famous abbot (died in 826), not only a center of monastic reform but also a nucleus of opposition to caesaropapism, and Theodore himself took a bold stand against the iconoclastic movement (cf. Bury, *Eastern Roman Empire*, pp. 65, 70-73, 208). It is however, reported elsewhere (Nestor's *Life of Theodosius*, Yakovlev, *op. cit.*, p. XXI) that Theodosius sent one of his monks to Constantinople to secure a copy of the rule of Studion.

190. This passage may be regarded as an essential bit of evidence that Nestor was not the author or compiler of the *Primary Chronicle;* cf. *supra*, Introduction: Authorship.

191. Born in 1020 (*q.v.*); he was the eldest son from the second marriage; cf. Baumgarten, "Généalogies et mariages occidentaux des Rurikides russes, du Xe au XIIIe siècle," *Orientalia Christiana*, IX (1927), 7-8.

192. The above item of the *Povest'* ("by the Greek Princess"=*ot tsaritsě gr' kÿně*) and the surname of her son Vladimir II induced some historians to assume that Vsevolod I was married to a *daughter* of Constantine IX Monomachus. Actually, all that one is warranted to deduce from these indications is that the princess in question was of the house of Constantine IX, even perhaps only descended from it in the female line. While the marriage of Vsevolod is dated by B. Lieb (*Rome, Kiev et Byzance à la fin du XIe siècle* [Paris, 1924], p. 169) as of 1046 (following V. S. Ikonnikov, *Opÿt Russkoy Istoriografii*, II, i, 141), there is no basis for this attribution. Prisëlkov, on his part (*op. cit.* p. 110) places it as late as 1052-1053, supposing the marriage to have been a means of inducing Yaroslav not to insist on the recognition of the Russian Hilarion as Metropolitan by Constantinople (for Prisëlkov's views, cf. *supra*, n. 171). Vsevolod himself was born in 1030. His son by the Byzantine princess, Vladimir II Monomakh (died in 1125), was the husband of the Anglo-Saxon princess Gytha (cf. *infra*, n. 373).

193. Yaroslav had six sons by Ingigerd: Vladimir (1020-1052); Izyaslav (born 1025), Svyatoslav (born 1027), Vsevolod (born 1030), Vyacheslav (1036-1057), Igor' (born after 1036, died 1060). There is, however, a possibility that Igor' was older than Vyacheslav, as the Chronicle mentions him first in the list of Yaroslav's sons (cf. A. Presnyakov, *Knyazhoe Pravo*, p. 44).

194. Vladimir-Volÿnsk.

195. The obvious purpose of Yaroslav's arrangement was to avoid a dissolution of the patrimony accumulated by Vladimir I and himself. There is no indication that he wished to set up an order of succession with reference to the various districts, though it appears that he had in mind the succession of his sons to the Kievan throne in the order of their age, with the idea that harmony should prevail under the leadership of his oldest living son (cf. A. Presnyakov, *op. cit.*, pp. 34-42).

196. Cf. *supra*, n. 90. Voin' was eight miles south of Pereyaslavl' on the east bank of the Dnieper.

197. The movement of the Pechenegs into the Balkans during this decade was hastened by the pressure of a kindred Turkish nomadic tribe, the Polovcians (Cumans, Kipchaks), who here make their first appearance, but become the most serious menace experienced by the Kievan principality prior to the incursion of the Tartars eighty years later. The Torks attacked by Vsevolod, Prince of

264   *The Russian Primary Chronicle*

Pereyaslavl', were in all likelihood subject to the Khan of the Polovcians whose raid was thus retaliatory (cf. D. A. Rasovsky, *Pechenĕgi, Torki, i Berendĕi*, pp. 8-9. The Polovcians seem to have followed the same procedure in 1061. Cf. *infra*, n. 256.

198. The *Golyad'*, or Galindians, were a Lithuanian remnant residing on the river Porotva, a tributary of the river Oka in central Russia, west of Serpukhov and south of Moscow. There are still a few place-names in the vicinity of Moscow and Kaluga reminiscent of this tribe (cf. Barsov, *Ocherki*, p. 44; Niederle, *Pův. Slov. Vych.*, pp. 42, 45).

199. Cf. *supra*, n. 165.

200. Cf. *supra*, n. 168.

201. Vseslav of Polotsk (cf. *supra*, nn. 179 and 145) son of Bryachislav; since Bryachislav was son of Izyaslav, and the latter a son of Vladimir I by Rogned, Vseslav was Vladimir I's great-grandson.

202. Though a son of the deceased Vladimir (the eldest son of Yaroslav by Ingigerd, died at Novgorod in 1052), Rostislav was apparently excluded by his uncles from all participation in Yaroslav's inheritance. The intention of Yaroslav's three eldest sons to concentrate the chief districts under their joint control is reflected by the transfer of Igor' from Vladimir-Volÿnsk to Smolensk upon the death of Vyacheslav in 1057, thus leaving Vladimir-Volÿnsk in the hands of the three elder princes. Then, upon Igor's own death in 1060, Smolensk also fell into their possession. The flight of Rostislav to Tmutorakan' and his expulsion thence of Prince Gleb, the son of Svyatoslav of Chernigov, would seem to be a result of the aggressive policy of the three surviving sons of Yaroslav. For the traditional attachment of Tmutorakan' to Chernigov, cf. *supra*, n. 147.

203. For the Setoml', cf. *supra*, n. 164; this is one of seven passages in the whole *Primary Chronicle* in which the narrator recounts an episode in the first person.

204. These portents were culled from Georgius Hamartolus; von Muralt, pp. 208, 281, 540, 554, 653; Istrin, pp. 200, 262, 421, 428, 479; cf. *supra*, Introduction: Authorship.

205. Byzantine authority in the Crimea, having suffered both from Svyatoslav's eastern campaigns and from Vladimir's capture of Kherson, was restored during the second decade of the eleventh century as far east as Bosporus and Kerch (Vasiliev, *Goths*, pp. 134-135). While the Polovcians became a power in the Crimea after 1050, it is probable that the Byzantines endeavored to maintain control of the chief coastal cities, and resented the expansion of Rostislav's authority in the Kuban district. There is evidence elsewhere of considerable Russian activity at Tmutorakan' after 1060. Early in 1061, Nikon, a distinguished inmate of the Crypt Monastery (whom Prisëlkov would identify with Hilarion, supposing him to have taken the monastic habit after his deposition from the metropolitanate about 1051, *op. cit.*, pp. 181-184), having made himself unpopular with Izyaslav, went to live at Tmutorakan', where he founded a monastery and a church of the Blessed Virgin in an open field near the city (*Pecherskiy Paterik*, ed. Abramovich, p. 36; cf. Prisëlkov, *op. cit.*, p. 206). According to the same source, after Rostislav was poisoned by the Byzantine *katepano* on the 3d of February, 1067 (the Chronicle dates the year 1066, according to the March calendar), the inhabitants of Tmutorakan' requested Nikon to be their emissary to Svyatoslav for the sake of having Gleb restored as their prince (*Paterik*,

p. 45). Nikon therefore arrived north at Chernigov and Kiev in the midst of the events described by the Chronicle under 1067. The dominance of material not directly related to Kiev in this section of the Chronicle and the knowledge of events in Tmutorakan' displayed by the annalist led Shakhmatov to suppose that Nikon, later Abbot of the Crypt Monastery (1077-1088), was intimately concerned with the compilation of the Chronicle itself (*Razÿskanya*, pp. 431-437).

206. Karamzin (II, 49) understood the Nemiza as the Niemen. Solov'ev, however (II, 405) states that there is a stream named Nemiza at Minsk and that a town of the same name was located between Orsha and Drutsk. He therefore supposes that the princes were on their way back to Smolensk when they encountered Vseslav.

207. The town of Orsha (Rsha), on the Dnieper west of Smolensk, belonged to the principality of Polotsk, and was not attached to Smolensk until 1116 (Hypatian, *PSRL.*, II, i, 3rd ed. (1923), 279). Solov'ev, on account of the phrase *na Rshe*, "on the Orsha," which refers to a stream, implies that the locality referred to may not have been Orsha itself, but the hamlet Orshanskiy Yan, nearer Smolensk (II, 406).

208. Cf. *supra*, n. 120.

209. This excerpt is from the *Sermon on Divine Chastisements* (*Pouchenie o Kaznyakh Bozhiikh*) attributed to Theodosius, the great prior of the Crypt Monastery (cf. Nikol'sky, *Materialÿ*, pp. 170-178; Sukhomlinov, *O Letopisi*, pp. 84-89, gives the chronicle text parallel with one derived from the Lenin Library (form. Rumyantsev Museum) *MS. 435*, fols. 340-342. The discourse was not entirely original with Theodosius, since a similar text, the *Slovo o Vedre i o Kaznyakh Bozhiakh*, is known in twelfth-century Bulgarian literature, and one of its sources is a sermon of Gregory the Theologian (cf. Mansikka, *op. cit.*, pp. 106-108, with references). Parallels to these early comments on popular superstitions are frequent well down into the seventeenth century. For a collection of related texts, cf. Mansikka, *op. cit.*, pp. 106-241, esp. p. 215, an anonymous sixteenth century sermon from Novgorod, with warnings against superstitious belief "in meeting, sneezing, and the song of birds."

210. The following events are conventionally referred to in modern historical literature as "the first Kievan revolution," a term originated by Hrushevsky used also by Prisëlkov, and more lately by Vernadsky, *Political and Diplomatic History of Russia* (Boston, 1936), p. 57. It could be objected, however, that no permanent alteration of the administrative system took place.

211. The thousand-man (*tÿsyatskiy*) was the commander of the militia (citizen troops) of a given district. There is no evidence that this soldiery was divided into regiments of 1000 men, as the name might indicate (cf. Presnyakov, *Knyazhoe Pravo*, pp. 167-173). The *veche*, or popular assembly, is to be conceived as taking place in the lower town (Podol), whence the participants mounted the hill and penetrated into both the old citadel and that of Yaroslav.

212. The bridge in question seems to have crossed a small ravine on the southwest side of the old citadel, facing toward St. Sophia and connecting the old citadel with the extension of Yaroslav. As the text implies, both the prison and the residences of Constantine and Bryachislav (Vseslav's father, who had died in 1044) were outside the old citadel and near St. Sophia. Izyaslav and Vsevolod are represented as living in the old citadel (cf. Zakrevsky, *Opisanie*, p. 551).

213. The ruling prince of Poland (not crowned king till 1076) was now

Bolesław Śmiały, "the Bold," eldest son of Casimir, who succeeded the latter in 1058 and reigned until 1080. Since Bolesław's mother was Izyaslav's aunt Maria (married to Casimir in 1038; cf. Baumgarten, *Généalogies,* pp. 7-8), Bolesław was Izyaslav's cousin. Furthermore, since Izyaslav had also married Casimir's younger sister Gertrude (Baumgarten, *op. cit.,* pp. 7, 9), Izyaslav was simultaneously Bolesław's uncle by marriage. Bolesław's wife was also a Rurikid princess: Výsheslava, a daughter of Svyatoslav of Chernigov (Baumgarten, pp. 18, 20).

214. The river Snov' flows into the Desna east of Chernigov, and Snovsk was probably at the junction (cf. Barsov, *Ocherki,* pp. 172-173; Solov'ëv, II, 407, n. 48).

215. Some hint of hostility to Izyaslav on the part of the community in the Crypt Monastery is evident in this passage. It is also reflected in a later passage of the Chronicle (cf. *Pecherskiy Paterik,* p. 186), where it is stated that when Izyaslav eventually returned from his first exile, he was angry with Antonius, the founder of the Crypt Monastery, "on account of Vseslav," so that Antonius prudently retired to Chernigov before Izyaslav's arrival.

216. Cf. *supra,* n. 83.

217. The meaning of this somewhat ambiguous statement seems to be that the Kievans, while regretting their revolt against their legitimate sovereign, also feared Izyaslav and his Polish allies, and felt that, if Svyatopolk and Vsevolod would not intervene to mitigate the hardships of a Polish occupation, they would rather migrate than experience it. They doubtless placed their hopes on Svyatoslav, who had just demonstrated his energy by his defeat of the Polovcians on the Snov' in 1068.

218. An effort is subsequently made to attribute the responsibility for this drastic procedure not to Izyaslav but to his son Mstislav.

219. In view of the fact that the account of Izyaslav's sending the Poles out to forage and of their being attacked repeats almost literally the sequence of events reported concerning Bolesław Chrobry's stay in Kiev in 1018, it is safe to say that in this respect the present narrative is rather of doubtful historicity. The Polish sources for Bolesław Śmiały's relations with Russia are of trifling value, as even Karamzin perceived (II, notes 121-125). Bolesław stayed in Kiev for the remainder of 1069, and on his way home attacked Przemyśl, in Galicia (Karamzin, *ibid.,* n. 123).

220. In the light of the rebellious activity of the *veche* held in the market-place which preceded Izyaslav's first exile, this measure was doubtless intended to facilitate a more immediate princely supervision of such assemblages. In the middle of the twelfth century, however, the market-place is once more found in the Podol (Hrushevsky, *Kievskaya Zemlya,* p. 74).

221. In the *Sofiysk. Vrem., (PSRL.,* V, 2nd ed., 137-138; also *Nikon.,* PSRL., IX, 96) after the item concerning Vseslav's expulsion from Polotsk, we read: "Prince Gleb with the men of Novgorod defeated Prince Vseslav at the Kzemlya at the sixth hour of the day on Friday, October 23, the festival of St. James, the brother of Our Lord; great was the carnage of the *Vozhane,* and the next day was found in the gallery of St. Sophia the cross of Prince Vladimir, which Prince Vseslav had taken in St. Sophia during the hostilities." Gleb son of Svyatoslav had been only recently heard of at Tmutorakan', but apparently had been transferred to Novgorod after Izyaslav's exile to guard against possible raids by Vseslav. The latter's attack on Novgorod was evidently an act of retaliation

against the princes who had momentarily driven him out of Polotsk. The *Vozhane* were a Finnish tribe with whom Vseslav took refuge (cf. Solov'ëv, II, 408). The enthronement of Svyatopolk in Polotsk after Mstislav's death signifies only that Polotsk was added to Izyaslav's domain (Kiev).

222. The monastery at Vydubichi is situated on the western shore of the Dnieper about 1½ miles south of the Crypt Monastery. The church was dedicated in 1088. Though still extant in part, its eastern portion was undermined in the sixteenth century by a freshet which washed away the edge of the bluff (protected against this contingency by a retaining wall as early as 1199) and allowed the apse end to collapse. The church as restored in the seventeenth century thus has only a fraction of its original length and is a two-story structure (cf. a full account of its entire history in Zakrevsky, *Opisanie*, pp. 225-254).

223. South of Kiev and just west of Yur'ev, on the Rastavitsa, a tributary of the Ros', which itself flows into the Dnieper at Kanev.

224. Yaropolk, eldest son of Izyaslav of Kiev. The location of Golotichesk is not determinable beyond the probability that it lay on the road between Chernigov and Polotsk.

225. Yan, son of Vyshata, was the brother of Putyata, later a general of Svyatopolk, and is not to be confused with the *starets* Yan whom the annalist mentions as dying in 1106 at the age of 90.

226. The magicians of Egypt referred to in *II Tim.*, iii, 8 and *Exodus*, vii, 2.

227. In the new wooden church erected in their honor at Vyshgorod; this church was finally replaced by a stone church consecrated in 1115, no longer extant (*Hyp.*, PSRL., II, 3rd (1923), 176). The observances of 1072 are described at some length by Nestor in his *Life of Boris and Gleb*, ed. Sreznevsky, cols. 31-33, who relates that the Metropolitan George had been sceptical of the sanctity of these Russian saints and was convinced only by the saintly fragrance of their remains.

228. The date should be May 20, as the Laurentian mistakenly reads $\overline{B}$ (2) for $\overline{K}$ (20), the correct reading of *Hyp.* col. 170, and the Nestorian *Life*, col. 33.

229. Izyaslav's unpopularity in Kiev was plainly so aggravated by his liquidation of Vseslav's partisans that he was unable to secure the support of the populace against Svyatoslav and Vsevolod. The latter had taken no part in Izyaslav's restoration beyond warning him not to bring his Polish auxiliaries into the city and to conduct himself with moderation. The Kievan populace themselves had, moreover, been obliged to accept Izyaslav at the point of a foreign spear. In the light of these facts, there may well have been some truth in Izyaslav's alleged intrigue with Vseslav. Izyaslav had lost Polotsk, while his brother Svyatoslav was in control of Novgorod through the presence there of his son Gleb since 1069. An alliance between Izyaslav and Vselav would have presented the familiar spectacle (cf. Yaroslav and his brother Mstislav) of a conflict between parties representing the opposite sides of the Dnieper (west: Kiev-Polotsk; east: Chernigov-Pereyaslavl').

230. The exact course of Izyaslav's adventures in Poland is not clear. From the fact, however, that he did not appear at the court of Henry IV in Mainz until January, 1075, he must have remained some time with Bolesław. In the *Testament* of Vladimir Monomakh (son of Vsevolod) there are obscure references to war-like operations near Brest-Litovsk and Vladimir-Volynsk just after Izyaslav's departure which would indicate that Bolesław at least made some attempt either

to help Izyaslav or to regain the Volhynian cities lost to Yaroslav forty years previous. Vladimir specifically mentions a peace made with the Poles at Suteyska, in Volhynia (cf. Barsov, *Ocherki*, p. 267), after Easter, 1074. There is thus some fact behind Długosz's highly imaginative account of Bolesław's operation in Volhynia during 1074, among them a six months' siege of Volÿn' (ed. A. Przeździecki, II, 311-313). When Izyaslav left Poland (possibly during the summer of 1074), Bolesław appropriated much of the wealth which Izyaslav had brought with him from Kiev, and we have Pope St. Gregory VII's letter of April 20, 1075 to Bolesław directing the Polish sovereign to make restitution (E. Caspar, *Reg. Greg. VII*, 1, 235: "... inter omnia servanda vobis est caritas, quam, quod inviti dicimus, in pecunia, quam regi Ruscorum abstulistis, violasse videmini. Quapropter ... vos rogamus et ammonemus, ut ... quicquid sibi a vobis vel vestris ablatum est, restitui faciatis"). Bolesław's reasons for suspending his Russian campaign were connected with his interests in Hungary, where he was involved in the contemporary dynastic quarrel on the side of Géza, who was opposing King Solomon, Henry IV's brother-in-law and protégé. Upon arriving in Germany, Izyaslav, together with his son Yaropolk, enjoyed the hospitality of the Margrave Dedi of Lower Lusatia, who presented him to Henry IV at Mainz in January, 1075 (cf. Lambert of Hersfeld, ed. O. Holder-Egger [Hanover, 1894] p. 202). Cf. *infra*, n. 238. Henry IV was to marry, later, in 1089, Izyaslav's niece, Eupraxia (Adelheid) (cf. Baumgarten, *Généalogies,* pp. 22, 24; *infra*, n. 385).

231. This passage reflects the hostility toward Svyatoslav entertained by the Crypt Monastery, which was loyal to Izyaslav in spite of its previous support of Vseslav (cf. *supra*, n. 215). When Svyatoslav took over Kiev in 1073, the Prior Theodosius emphatically refused a dinner invitation from the Prince, and even wrote him a letter containing the words, "The voice of your brother's blood calls out to God, even as Abel's did against Cain." Svyatoslav is thus reported to have said that he envied Izyaslav such devoted adherence (*Pecherskiy Paterik*, ed. Abramovich, pp. 66-67).

232. Dedicated to the Assumption of the Blessed Virgin and consecrated in 1089, this edifice was originally a six-column church with one cupola and three naves and apses. It was seriously damaged by fire in 1482 and 1718, but restored during the third decade of the eighteenth century in ornate Ukrainian baroque. The church was built by Greek architects imported for the purpose, and is the starting-point for the one-cupola church of simple design which became the standard type of church architecture in the principalities of the northeast (Vladimir-Suzdal'); cf. Ainalov, *op. cit.*, pp. 24-27; Brunov-Alpatov, *op. cit.*, pp. 20-22.

233. According to the Byzantine calendar, the Easter fast begins on the Monday after Quinquagesima with a preliminary week of abstinence; the feast of Saint Lazarus falls on the Saturday before Palm Sunday.

234. Placing a dying person on a sled was an old Russian custom. Another such custom, that became a part of the old Russian burial ritual, was to transport the dead body by sled to its burial place. (Cf. Likhachev, *Pov. Vrem. Let,* II pp. 433-434).

235. That Nicholas' character was unfavorably judged with reason is indicated by the anecdote recounted in the *Pecherskiy Paterik* (*ed. cit.*, pp. 75-76), according to which he stole a casket of money which had been entrusted by a layman to another inmate of the monastery named Conon. Of Ignatius nothing is known.

236. A village on the Al'ta river in the vicinity of Pereyaslavl' (so Trautmann,

p. 134), hence either identical with or near the so-called *Letskoe pole* ("Al'ta field," cf. 1019 above), the scene of the murder of Vladimir's son Boris and of the final clash between Yaroslav and Svyatopolk in 1019. (Cf. Barsov, *Ocherki,* pp. 165-166).

237. While Theodosius requested Svyatoslav's support for Stephen in the priorate, he was not able to retain the confidence of his community, and about the time of Svyatoslav's death he was obliged to quit the Crypt Monastery (*Pecherskiy Paterik, ed. cit.,* p. 77; cf. Prisëlkov, *op, cit.,* p. 219). He secured financial assistance from wealthy partisans, however, and founded another monastery at Klov (on lower ground closer to the citadel of Kiev), where he raised a church dedicated to Our Lady of the Blachernae (*Paterik, ibid.*). He was succeeded in the priorate by Nikon, who returned from Tmutorakan' after Svyatoslav's death, hence in 1077 (for Nikon and his identity, cf. *supra,* n. 205). Stephen later became Bishop of Vladimir, and died in 1094.

238. Impressed by Izyaslav's claims, Henry IV sent as envoy to Svyatoslav Bishop Burchard of Trier "agere cum illo de iniuriis, quas fratri intulerat, et commonere, ut regno, quod iniuste invasisset, ultro decederet, alioquin auctoritatem et arma Teutonici regni propediem experturum fore" (Lambert, *loc. cit.*). Burchard's half sister (by another marriage of Count Etheler) was Svyataslav's wife; his other half-sister (by the same mother) was Oda of Stade, who had been married to Vladimir (died in 1052), son of Yaroslav (Baumgarten, *Généalogies,* pp. 7, 8-9. Formerly, Svyatoslav was believed to have married Oda). While the mission was on its way, Izyaslav continued to enjoy the Margrave Dedi's hospitality. Burchard returned in July, 1075, carrying such a load of gifts that Izyaslav's offerings were paltry in comparison. By this time, in any case, Henry IV was menaced by the Saxon rebellion, and, as Lambert dryly observes (*ed. cit.,* p. 226): "intestinis ac domesticis bellis occupatus ad externa tamque remotis gentibus inferenda bella nullo modo vacabat," while Sigebert of Gembloux adds: "gravissima in imperio Romano orta dissensio monebat magis sua tueri quam aliena adquirere" (*MGH., SS.,* VI, 362). Without waiting for Burchard's return, Izyaslav sent his son Yaropolk to Rome to win the support of Gregory VII, who on April 17, 1075, replied as follows (Caspar, *Reg. Greg. VII,* I. 236-237):

Gregorius episcopus servus servorum Dei Demetrio regi Ruscorum et regine uxori eius salutem et apostolicam benedictionem.

Filius vester, limina apostolorum visitans, ad nos venit et, quod regnum illud dono sancti Petri per manus nostras vellet optinere, eidem beato Petro apostolorum principi debita fidelitate exhibita devotis precibus postulavit indubitanter asseverans illam suam petitionem vestro consensu ratam fore ac stabilem, si apostolice auctoritatis gratia ac munimine donaretur. Cuius votis et petitionibus, quia iusta videbantur, tum ex consensu vestro tum ex devotione poscentis tandem assensum prebuimus et regni vestri gubernacula sibi ex parte beati Petri tradidimus ea videlicet intentione atque desiderio caritatis ut beatus Petrus vos et regnum vestrum omniaque vesta bona sua apud Deum intercessione custodiat et cum omni pace honore quoque et gloria idem regnum usque in finem vite vestre tenere vos faciat et huius militie finito cursu impetret vobis apud supernum regem gloriam sempiternam. Quin etiam nos paratissimos esse noverit vestre nobilitatis serenitas, ut, ad quecumque iusta negotia huius sedis auctoritatem pro sua necessitate petierit, procul dubio continuo petitionum suarum consequetur effectum. Preterea, ut hec et alia multa, que litteris non continentur, cordibus vestris artius infigantur, misimus hos nuntios nostros, quorum unus vester notus est et fidus amicus, qui et ea que in litteris sunt diligenter vobis exponent et que minus sunt viva voce explebunt. Quibus pro reverentia beati Petri, cuius legati sunt, vos mites et affabiles prebeatis et, quicquid vobis dixerint ex parte nostra, patienter audiatis atque indubitanter credatis et, que ibi ex auctoritate apostolice sedis negotia tractare voluerint et statuere, nullorum malo ingenio turbare permittatis, sed potius eos sincera caritate favendo iuvetis. Omnipotens Deus mentes vestras illuminet, atque per temporalia bona faciat vos transire ad gloriam sempiternam. Data Rome XV Kalendas Maii, Indictione XIII.

Cf. *supra*, n. 230 for the Pope's communication addressed to Bolesław Śmiały. Izyaslav-Demetrius (*supra*, n. 187) placed Russia under the protection of the Holy See and expressed his fidelity to the Pope; he elso enjoyed the friendship and admiration of the monks of the Crypt Monastery of Kiev, a leading center of Russian religious life (cf. *supra*, n. 231, *infra*, n. 251). This, together with various other facts, such, e.g., as the numerous marriages contracted by the Rurikids with Catholics down to the thirteenth century in connection with which no question of religious difference appears ever to have been raised (cf. Leib, *op. cit.*, pp. 143-178; Baumgarten, *Généalogies*), can only indicate that, whatever the attitude of the Greek hierarchs in Russia, that country's definitive drift into the Byzantine schism occurred considerably later than 1054. Cf. *supra*, n. 92; also N. Kondakov, *Izobrazheniya Russk. Kn. Sem'i v miniat. XI v.* (Spb., 1906).

239. According to the *Testament* of Vladimir Monomakh, he spent four months in Bohemia, apparently in the Summer of 1076. The Saxon resistance was not yet liquidated, and Henry IV's conflict with Gregory VII was at its peak. Bolesław allied himself with Henry's Saxon foes, and was encouraged in his independent attitude by the Pope, who allowed him to be crowned king on December 25, 1076 (Lambert *ed. cit.*, p. 284; Holder-Egger here dates the coronation as 1077, which is unlikely, cf. Szujski, *Dzieje Polski*, I, 93-95; the Polish chroniclers are themselves uncertain as to the date). With general attention focussed on the Saxon rebellion and the conflict between Pope and King, together with the obvious weakening of Henry IV's prestige in consequence of these developments, it is natural that Bolesław Śmiały should both have asserted his independence and operated against Henry IV wherever possible. The same factors, however, condition the silence of German sources as to Bolesław's precise activities in the eastern marches during 1075-1076. Giesebrecht is doubtless right in assuming (*Geschichte der deutschen Kaiserzeit*, III, i, 5th ed. [Leipzig, 1890], 320, 378) that Henry's raids on Meissen and into Bohemia in 1075 and 1076 were conditioned by the fear that Adela of Meissen might easily be persuaded to make common cause with Bolesław. Vladimir's presence in Bohemia may thus be associated with Bolesław's cooperation with the Saxon rebels and his attacks upon Vratislav of Bohemia, Henry's loyal ally. Cf. A. V. Florovsky, *Chekhi i Vostochnÿe Slavyane*, I (Prague, 1935), 50-57.

240. Cf. *supra*, n. 160.

241. In spite of Długosz's long and fabulous account of Bolesław's stay in Kiev and the excesses which he and his suite committed there (II, 319-320), it is unlikely that Bolesław visited Kiev at all on this expedition. The silence of the Russian annals in this respect, after dealing circumstantially with his presence in 1069, seems to be conclusive evidence that the Polish king was not a participant in the adventure. It is curious, however, that Bolesław, after temporarily

Notes to the Russian Primary Chronicle 271

allying himself with Svyatoslav to secure Russian aid against Bohemia (cf. *supra*, n. 239), should have made common cause with Izyaslav again immediately after Svyatoslav's death. Bagaley (*Ist. Sěversky Zemli*, pp. 164-165) explains this reversal of intent by Tatishchev's report (*Ist. Ross.*, II, 130) that Bolesław was annoyed by the insistence of Vladimir and Oleg upon continuing the Bohemian adventure after Bolesław himself had concluded peace with Vratislav of Bohemia, and that therefore Bolesław transferred his support to Izyaslav once more.

242. Boris was the son of Yaroslav's son Vyacheslav, who had died at Smolensk in 1057 (*q.v.*). Tatishchev (II, 131), adds that Boris was expelled from Chernigov by Vladimir Monomakh. Boris' seizure of Chernigov was in any case the attempt of a dispossessed nephew to secure a respectable domain. Roman was the son of the late Svyatoslav of Chernigov, and had apparently been established by his father in Tmutorakan' after Rostislav died in 1066 or after Gleb was transferred to Novgorod *ca.* 1069.

243. During his reign at Kiev, Svyatoslav had also set up his son Oleg at Vladimir-Volÿnsk, whence he was removed at the return of Izyaslav. In his *Testament* (*PSRL.*, I, 247), Vladimir Monomakh recalls having invited Oleg to dinner with him and his father Vsevolod in Chernigov after Oleg's removal from the Volhynian principality. The removal of Oleg indicates the intention of Izyaslav and Vsevolod to control the chief dependent principalities by setting up their sons in each. Vsevolod's occupation of Chernigov (in addition to his domain of Pereyaslavl') reflects the same policy.

244. *Zavoloch'e* generally means the country beyond a watershed or portage (*volok*) and specifically the White Sea basin north and east of the great lakes, occupied by Finnish tribes. While it would seem natural that Gleb, as son of the late Svyatoslav, should have been expelled or transferred from Novgorod upon Izyaslav's return, there is evidence to the contrary. The *Pecherskiy Paterik* (ed. cit., p. 126), speaking of the gift of second-sight of the monk Nikita (later Bishop of Novgorod), reports that he announced to Izyaslav the death of Gleb before the news had regularly arrived, and suggested that Izyaslav's son Svyatopolk should be sent immediately to Novgorod.

245. Eldest son of Izyaslav, who had been the latter's emissary to Pope St. Gregory VII (cf. *supra*, n. 238), and built in Kiev the Church of St. Peter Apostle.

246. Vladimir Monomakh, son of Vsevolod (cf. *supra*, n. 192).

247. Oleg and Boris evidently endeavored to take Chernigov from the north, since the Sozh' is a tributary joining the Dnieper north of Lyubech. Their attack was successful and Vsevolod sought refuge in Kiev.

248. *Nezhatina Niva*, associated with the modern town of Nezhin on the Oster river (Barsov, *Ocherki*, p. 308). The death of Izyaslav took place on October 3.

249. Izyaslav's interest in the expulsion of Oleg and his partisans from Chernigov lay not only in the fact that the pretender princes were supported by the nomads but also in the circumstance that he had seized Oleg's original principality of Vladimir-Volÿnsk.

250. A suburb of Kiev, on the Chertorÿya creek, on the east bank of the Dnieper just south of the confluence of the Desna.

251. Cf. *supra*, nn. 205, 215, and 231. While the Crypt Monastery had favored Vseslav of Polotsk against Izyaslav, this religious center had consistently taken the latter's part against his brothers, and, as is evident from the parallel drawn

between Svyatoslav and Hezekiah under 1075 (*q.v.*), had no particular love for the latter, even though he had saved Antonius from Izyaslav's resentment. Nikon had now returned from Tmutorakan' and become prior (cf. *supra,* n. 231). In view of his friendliness toward Izyaslav, Prisëlkov (*op. cit.,* pp. 224-225) suggests that the present (exceptionally lengthy) eulogy on Izyaslav derives from a funeral oration pronounced for Izyaslav by Nikon himself. An obvious effort is made to mitigate Izyaslav's unpopularity among the local population, e.g., by shunting to Mstislav the responsibility for the massacre of Vseslav's partisans in 1069.

252. As the last surviving son of Yaroslav, Vsevolod combined under his control practically all the Russian districts associated with Kiev. Leaving Izyaslav's son Svyatopolk at Novgorod, he assigned Vladimir-Volÿnsk with Turov (on the Pripet') to the latter's brother Yaropolk (cf. *supra,* n. 245), and retained control of Chernigov and Pereyaslavl' through his son Vladimir Monomakh. Though he thus satisfied Izyaslav's surviving sons, the remaining fifteen years of his reign were disturbed by recurrent quarrels with his other nephews, who were not included in the appointment of major domains (the sons of Svyatoslav and Igor', and those of Rostislav son of Vladimir [eldest son of Yaroslav by Ingigerd, died at Novgorod in 1052], cf. *supra,* n. 202).

253. Cf. supra, n. 196.

254. During Oleg's stay in Constantinople, he married Theophano of the house of Muzalon; G. Schlumberger, *Sigillographie de l'empire byzantin* (Paris, 1884), p. 342; Kh. Loparev, "Vizantiyskaya Pechat' s Imenem Russkoy Knyagini," *Viz. Vrem.,* I (1894), 159-166.

255. A small seal bearing on the obverse a portrait of St. Nicholas and on the reverse the inscription *ot Ratibora* (from Ratibor), in eleventh-century characters, was found near Yenikale in 1872, and seems to have belonged to Vsevolod's lieutenant. Cf. Tolstoy-Kondakov, *Russkie Drevnosti,* IV (Spb., 1891), 172.

256. Cf. *supra,* n. 197. In 1060, the three sons of Yaroslav had made a successful attack upon the Torks which drove most of them toward the Danube and into the Balkans. There, at Byzantine instigation, they were violently attacked by the Bulgars and Pechenegs, so that some remnants of the Torks were settled in Macedonia (Rasovsky, *loc. cit.,* p. 9). Other detachments succeeded in returning across the Danube, and settled peaceably in the steppes along the lower Dnieper. It is the Torks of these settlements who now attack Vsevolod's territory.

257. Cf. *supra,* nn. 202 and 252. David's father Igor' (son of Yaroslav) had died in 1060, and Volodar' was the son of Igor's nephew Rostislav (the son of Yaroslav's son Vladimir, d. 1052). Rostislav had been poisoned by a Greek emissary at Tmutorakan' in 1066 (*q.v.*).

258. Since Oleg was son of Svyatoslav (died in 1076), long Prince of Chernigov, he had a more legitimate claim to Tmutorakan', a dependency of that principality, than his two cousins (actually Volodar' was his first cousin once removed, since he was Oleg's junior by a generation, Volodar's father Rostislav having been Oleg's own cousin), who had never been assigned to any important principality.

259. After their expulsion from Tmutorakan' by Oleg in 1083, Vasil'ko and Volodar', his brother, had apparently taken up their residence with Yaropolk at Vladimir-Volÿnsk (cf. *supra,* n. 252), but profited by his absence in Kiev to seize the principality.

260. Oleshki (otherwise Olesh'e), mod. Aleshki, near the mouth of the Dnieper.

261. Dorogobuzh, on the Gorÿn', in Volhynia, near Rovno. While the Laurentian Chronicle reads *Gr'kÿ*, "Greeks," the other texts have *Greehnikÿ*, "merchants faring to Greece," which is intrinsically more probable. David thus made a raid upon the major trade-route.

262. From the fact that the *Testament* of Vladimir Monomakh (*PSRL.*, I, 248) mentions a campaign against "the *sons* of Izyaslav' (*po Izyaslavichikh*), there is some likelihood that Svyatopolk of Novgorod was also involved in these intrigues. Yaropolk's mother was the sister of Casimir, Duke of Poland (1040-1058), and since the ruling prince of Poland, Duke Władysław Herman (1080-1102), was Casimir's younger son (who succeeded Bolesław Śmiały in 1080, ruled till 1102) Yaropolk was his cousin. Cf. *supra*, n. 213.

263. Lutsk, on the river Stÿr', 51 miles southeast of Kowel, midway between Vladimir-Volÿnsk and Rovno.

264. The location of this convent and church is uncertain; Zakrevsky (*Opisanie*, p. 189), supposes it to have stood between the Desyatinnaya and the Trekhsvyatitel'skaya. It was devastated at the time of the Tartar conquest of 1240.

265. No metropolitan has now been mentioned since 1073 (*q.v.*, cf. *supra*, n. 189) when it was stated that the metropolitan George was absent from Kiev. It has frequently been believed that the next metropolitan, John Prodromus here mentioned, was appointed before 1077, since other sources mention the regular appointment of bishops (Rostov and Novgorod) in that and the following year (Golubinsky, I, i, 286 and nn. 3-4; *PSRL.*, V, 147). There is, however, some evidence for a severance of ecclesiastical and even diplomatic relations between Kiev and Constantinople in the years 1073-1076. Two letters are preserved from the Emperor Michael VII Dukas Parapinakes (*regn.* 1071-1078; texts in K. Sathas, *Bibliotheca graeca medii aevi*, V, 385-392, cf. V. G. Vasil'evsky, "Dva Pis'ma Mikhaila VII Duki," *Trudÿ*, I [Spb., 1908], 3-55, with Russ. trans. of the letters, pp. 8-14) to Vsevolod of Pereyaslavl' offering the latter a marriage between one of his daughters and Michael's brother Constantine, on condition that Vsevolod should be Michael's ally and protect the Byzantine northern frontier. The letters were written while Svyatopolk was Prince of Kiev, 1073-1076, and it would seem unlikely that Vsevolod should thus have been addressed by Michael if intimate relations had prevailed between Svyatoslav and himself. Furthermore, under 1089 (*q.v.*) mention is made of a Metropolitan Ephrem in Pereyaslavl', which is striking, in view of the fact that the Metropolitan John of Kiev is mentioned as dying the same year and as being replaced by a successor of the same name brought from Constantinople by Vsevolod's daughter Yanka. The Chronicle implies that Ephrem carried the title of Metropolitan only *honoris causa*, "since there had previously been a metropolitanate in Pereyaslavl'." The second letter of Michael VII refers pointedly to other princes who do not share the same divine service, which Prisëlkov (*op. cit.*, p. 132-133) interprets as pointing at Svyatoslav, thus concluding that after the departure of the Metropolitan George there was a definite break between Byzantium and Kiev, and that the subsequent agreement between Michael VII Dukas and Vsevolod entailed the appointment of a metropolitan in Pereyaslavl', who was probably Leo, otherwise known for his Greek polemical work against the Latins on the subject of clerical marriages. Leo probably lived until 1077 (*ibid.*, p. 140), when he was succeeded by

John Prodromus, the uncle of Theodore Prodromus, who speaks of his uncle as τῆς 'Ρωσικῆς πρόεδρος, ἁδρὸς ἐν λόγοις, (Migne, *P.G.,* CXXXIII, 1412; cf. Golubinsky, *loc. cit.*).

266. One of Yanka's sisters was Eupraxia - Adelheid second wife of the Western Emperor Henry IV, who married her in 1089; after a checkered career in Germany, she returned to Russia, took the veil in 1106, and died in 1109. In the first letter of Michael VII Dukas to Vsevolod (cf. preceding note), mention is made of a projected marriage between one of Vsevolod's daughters and the son of Michael's previous co-ruler. Vasil'evsky (*loc. cit.,* pp. 43-44) supposes that this marriage between Vsevolod's granddaughter Maria (dau. of Vladimir Monomakh) and a son of Romanus IV Diogenes (*regn.* 1067-1071) actually took place, but that Yanka was betrothed to Constantine Dukas, the brother of Michael VII. The latter marriage did not occur, however, in view of the overthrow of Michael VII, the brief three years' reign of Nicephorus III Botaniates (1078-1081), and the accession of Alexius I Comnenus. Yanka, who apparently took the veil when her marriage failed to materialize, was in good standing at the court of Alexius, since she visited Constantinople in 1089 (*q.v.*) and selected a metropolitan to succeed John Prodromus. Cf. Baumgarten, *Généalogies,* pp. 22, 24-25.

267. Not to be confused with Zvenigorod south of Kiev, but here a town in Galicia, near modern Lemberg (Barsov, *Ocherki,* p. 280, Karamzin, II, n, 148, p. 56).

268. Yaropolk's wife, mentioned as brought back to Kiev after her husband's revolt against Vsevolod in 1085, was Cunigundis, daughter of Otto, Count of Weimar-Orlamünde, later Margrave of Meissen, and his wife Adela (cf. *supra,* n. 239). On Otto's death, Adela married the Margrave Dedi of Lower Lusatia who was host of Izyaslav and Yaropolk on their flight to Germany in 1075 (cf. *supra,* nn. 230, 238; *Annalista Saxo, MGH., SS.,* VI, 693, 737, 738; T. Ediger, *Russlands älteste Beziehungen zu Deutschland, Frankreich, u. der rom. Kurie,* diss. [Halle, 1911], pp. 49-55). Cunigundis returned to Germany after Yaropolk's death and married (1) Kuno of Beichlingen and (2) Wipprecht of Groitsch. Cf. Baumgarten, *Généalogies,* pp. 10, 11.

269. Turov had been a portion of Yaropolk's principality (cf. *supra,* n. 252). Upon Yaropolk's defection in 1085, Vladimir-Volÿnsk had been assigned to David son of Igor', so that a parcellation of Yaropolk's territory was thus being carried out.

270. Cf. *supra,* nn. 205 and 251.

271. Murom, on the Oka, about 90 miles southwest of Gor'kiy (Nizhni Novgorod). One of the oldest Slavic colonization points of the northeast, it figures in the Norse sagas as Móramar (Braun, *loc. cit.,* p. 170), and the presence of Scandinavian graves also shows it to have been a Viking settlement (*ibid.,* p. 154).

272. Cf. *supra,* n. 265.

273. The successor of Nikon as Prior of the Crypt Monastery was John, who held the office until 1108, when he was succeeded by Theoctistus. The latter was succeeded in 1113 by Prokhor (*Pecherskiy Paterik, ed. cit.,* pp. 210-211). To John, Shakhmatov (*Razÿskaniya,* pp. II, 421) attributes the continuation of Nikon's annalistic activities. The transfer of the relics of Theodosius to the Cathedral of the Transfiguration in the Crypt Monastery seems to have been deliberately planned to take place between the death of the Metropolitan John the Castrate and the appointment of his successor (Nicholas, who apparently did not arrive

until 1096), at the time when there was no foreign head of the Kievan hierarchy to oppose the glorification of a saintly national figure. This account represents the second distinctive use of the first person in the narrative of the Chronicle (cf. 1065), and is important not only for the evidence it supplies as to the authorship of the *Povest'* and its various components but also for its implication of a strong national feeling emanating from the Crypt Monastery and exemplified by the reverence in which the great prior was held. Shakhmatov (*Pov. Vrem. Lět.* [Petrograd, 1916], pp. xxv-xxvi) assigns this narrative of the discovery of the relics of Theodosius to Nestor himself; cf. the account attributed to Nestor in the *Pecherskiy Paterik* (ed. cit., p. 78-81), with the statement that he, the sinful Nestor, was favored with first becoming a witness of his relics at the Prior's command. There is thus a strong probability that the *Paterik* narrative reproduces the source from which the *Povest'* account is derived.

274. At Klov, cf. *supra*, n. 237.

275. Cf. *infra*, the item on Yan's death, 1106.

276. Shakhmatov (*op. cit.*, p. xxvi) notes that this eulogy does not belong to Nestor (if he wrote the previous passage, especially since the author speaks of himself as Theodosius's' "sinful servant and disciple," and it appears to be a portion of a eulogy pronounced over the relics of Theodosius after their transfer to the cathedral. Some case might be made for the contention that the author was the Prior John himself.

277. There was actually a solar eclipse on the 21st of May, 1091.

278. Cf. Mansikka, *Religion der Ostslaven,* pp. 92-94. Mansikka attributes the popular belief in the dangerous activities of evil spirits to the manifestations of the plague mentioned below, especially its sudden onset in individual cases. The drought and the epidemic may well have been related.

279. All three towns were in the principality of Pereyaslavl': Pesochen on the Sula river, and Perevolok and Priluk on its tributary, the Uday (Barsov, *Ocherki,* pp. 163, 166).

280. Rurik's father Rostislav (poisoned in Tmutorakan', 1066) was the son of Yaroslav's son Vladimir (died in 1052). Rurik himself was Prince of Przemyśl, in Galicia.

281. According to the Byzantine calendar, St. Philip's Day falls on the 14th of November.

282. With the exception of Yaroslav, no other prince of the time had been buried in St. Sophia. This privilege can scarcely be attributed to Vsevolod's popularity, since during his reign the principality was impoverished by constant war against the nomads, and his administration was not distinguished by efficiency. His policy toward his nephews (except for the sons of Izyaslav) had been neither far-sighted nor generous, and his military successes were invariably the work of Vladimir Monomakh. The emphasis upon Vsevolod's devotion to the Church would rather indicate that his interment in St. Sophia depended on his good standing with the hierarchy, including the Crypt Monastery. His close relations with Constantinople guaranteed him the favor of the Greek party, and the present sympathetic estimate of his character implies that he also won the respect of the more or less Graecophobe Crypt Monastery.

283. Vsevolod I was only 63 when he died, having been born in 1030. He was a man of some culture, since his son Vladimir Monomakh mentions that,

though he had never been abroad, he still understood five languages (*Testament, PSRL.*, I, 246, see *infra*).

284. Svyatopolk, formerly Prince of Novgorod, but residing in Turov at Vsevolod's death, was the son of Vsevolod's elder brother Izyaslav I. If Izyaslav was married *ca.* 1043, Svyatopolk may have been several years older than Vladimir Monomakh, who was born in 1053. Vladimir did not, however, specifically recognize Svyatopolk's seniority on that basis, but simply avoided a conflict with him.

285. Torchesk signifies "the town of the Torks," and was apparently a settlement resulting from the subjection of the Torks in the principate of Izyaslav. It was the last border town on the edge of the Polovcians, and was probably situated on the Torch', a small stream flowing into the river Ros' (Barsov, *Ocherki*, pp. 138-139). Other investigators have placed it on the Stugna (cf. Hrushevsky, *Kievskaya Zemlya*, pp. 27-29 and nn.).

286. St. Michael's at Vÿdubichi, the monastery built by Vsevolod, cf. *supra*, n. 222.

287. Trepol', on the west bank of the Dnieper at the confluence of the Stugna, some 30 miles below Kiev.

288. When St. Bruno of Querfurt visited St. Vladimir in 1007 on his way to missionary activity among the Pechenegs, he found that there was a rampart two days' journey below Kiev. Cf. *Mon. Pol. Hist.*, I, 224-225: "Senior Ruzorum duos dies exercitu duxit me ipse usque ad regni sui terminum ultimum, quem propter vagum nostem firmissima ac longissima sepe undique circumclausit." There are traces of three ramparts in the Stugna district: one along its northern shore, another on its southern shore, and the outermost one on the north shore of the river Krasna, which flows south of the Stugna. It has been supposed that the rampart on the north bank of the Stugna is the one referred to by Bruno, while the others were constructed as settlements moved further south (cf. Hrushevsky, *op. cit.*, pp. 26-27).

289. The precise location of Zhelan' is unknown; Barsov (*op. cit.*, p. 144) places it west of Kiev in the direction of Belgorod, while Zakrevsky locates it considerably closer to the mediaeval town and even within the limits of the modern city, between the Lÿbed' and the site of St. Cyril's Monastery, now an insane asylum (*Opisanie*, p. 311).

290. Obviously an excerpt from a sermon suggested by Theodosius's *Pouchenie o Kaznyakh Bozhiikh* (cf. *supra*, n. 209); the authorship is unknown, but might be reasonably attributed to the Prior John himsef, together with the pious reflections ("Let no one venture . . . commit some transgression every day") (cf. Prisëlkov, *op. cit.*, p. 301). C. W. Smith (*Nestors Russiske Kronike* [Copenhagen, 1869], pp. 310-311) thought that the passage: "For the malignant sons of Ishmael . . . the infidels have slain" is an interpolation dating from the period of the Tartar incursions, but there seems to be no motive for separating this section from the beginning of the discourse, since the author, by his description of the flight of the inhabitants of Torchesk after their city was burned, shows himself possessed of an eloquent and effective style.

291. Tugorkan (Tugorkhan) and Bonyak (mentioned under 1096) also figure prominently in Byzantine history of the period. During the reign of Alexius I Comnenus (1081-1118), the rebellious Bogomiles in Bulgaria summoned the aid of the Pechenegs, who in 1091 penetrated even to the very gates of Constantinople, and in combination with the Seljuq threat placed the Byzantine

Empire in one of the most critical situations of its entire history. Alexius despaired of the issue when the day was saved by the arrival of the Polovcians under Tugorkan and Bonyak, whose aid was purchased by Alexius so that, on the 29th of April, 1091, they administered a crushing defeat to the Pechenegs. The captives from this battle were mercilessly slaughtered by the Greek soldiery during the same night, a bloodthirsty act which so terrified the Polovcians that they precipitately retired without claiming the promised rewards, which had to be sent after them, and their next exploits took place in Hungary (cf. Vasil'evsky, "Vizantiya i Pechenegi," *Trudÿ*, I, 96-107). Though Svyatopolk and Vladimir scarcely realized it at the time, they were thus fighting against two nomad chiefs whom modern historians class as "the saviors of the Byzantine Empire" (Vasil'evsky, p. 107; cf. also Vasiliev, *Hist. of the Byz. Emp.*, p. 385).

292. Oleg, son of Svyatoslav of Chernigov (died 1076), had returned from Byzantium to Tmutorakan' in 1083 (*q.v.*). Vladimir's eventual surrender of Chernigov indicates that he recognized the priority of his cousin's rights to that domain over his own, since Oleg's father had been older than Vsevolod, Vladimir's father. The principality of Pereyaslavl' had been vacant since the death of Vladimir's brother Rostislav at Trepol' on the 26 of May of the previous year.

293. Cf. *supra*, n. 237.

294. Romanus IV Diogenes (1067-1071) was supplanted by Michael VII Dukas Parapinakes (1071-1078), who was followed by Nicephorus III Botaniates (1078-1081) and Alexius I Comnenus (1081-1118). About 1090, a base-born soldier appeared to claim he was the son of Romanus, though of the two sons of Romanus whom the pretender could impersonate, one (Leo) had been killed in battle with the Pechenegs and the other (Constantine) fell while fighting the Turks before Antioch. The pretender was eventually captured and imprisoned at Kherson. Here he entered into communication with the Polovcians, and with their aid escaped to the steppes in 1092. Though the nomads under Tugorkan (Svyatopolk's father-in-law) tried to conceal their intentions, their plans to support the pretender on an invasion of the Balkans soon became known to Alexius Comnenus. The nomads laid siege to Adrianople for seven weeks, and in one sally by the inhabitants Tugorkan almost lost his life. Alexius eventually succeeded in luring the pretender away from the Polovcians; he was thus captured and blinded in the fortress of Chorlu. Under Alexius's command, the Byzantines then turned on the Polovcians inflicting upon the latter near Adrianople a crushing defeat in which 7000 nomads fell. The chief Greek source for these events is Anna Comnena (Vasil'evsky, *loc. cit.*, pp. 109-117).

295. Lieutenant of Vsevolod in Tmutorakan', 1079-1081.

296. Yur'ev was probably on the north shore of the Ros' river near the confluence of the Rut'; cf. Barsov, *Ocherki*, p. 298, Hrushevsky, *Kievskaya Zemlya*, pp. 36-37.

297. Vitichev, on the west bank of the Dnieper just below Trepol'; Sakov, on the east bank, between Trepol' and Kiev.

298. Svyatopolk himself had been Prince of Novgorod until transferred to Turov in 1088. He was replaced by David, his son, and Mstislav. Mstislav was born in 1076, and his mother was Gytha, daughter of the Saxon King Harold who fell at Hastings in 1066. Mstislav's first wife was Christina, daughter of Inge Steinkelson, King of Sweden; she died in 1122; he became Great Prince of Kiev in 1125; cf. Baumgarten, *Généalogies*, pp. 22, 24.

299. Kursk lies in Severian territory some 200 miles east of Chernigov and is here mentioned in the Chronicle for the first time. It would appear that Vladimir's son Izyaslav had seized this town, normally under the control of the princes of Chernigov, as a midway point for a campaign of annexation directed at the northeastern districts of Ryazan' and Murom.

300. These negotiations are presented from the Kievan standpoint. Oleg had never received any favors from Vladimir's father Vsevolod, and Vladimir's son Izyaslav had just appropriated Oleg's domains of Kursk and Murom. Oleg could hardly expect to be amicably judged by any elements of the Kiev population, especially since he was regarded as primarily responsible for the raids of the Polovcians, though the latter were the only allies at his disposal.

301. Starodub, about 100 miles northeast of Chernigov.

302. Ust'e, presumably at the confluence of the Trubezh with the Dnieper west of Pereyaslavl'.

303. Zarub, on the west bank of the Dnieper below the junction of the Trubezh. There was a ford at this point.

304. The monastery of Stephen is that of Our Lady of the Blachernae at Klov (cf. *supra*, n. 237); the other is that of the Redeemer in Berestovo.

305. The compiler is citing by memory from the *Revelations* of Pseudo-Methodius, originally composed in Syria during the seventh century, later translated into Greek and finally into Slavic (cf. E. Sackur, *Sibyllinische Texte u. Forschungen* (Halle, 1898), p. 5 ff.; M. Kmosko, "Das Rätsel des Pseudo-Methodius," *Byzantion*, VI (1931), 273-296; V. M. Istrin, *Otkrovenie Mefodiya Patarskogo* (Moscow, 1897); Cross, "Earliest Allusion in Slavic Literature to the *Revelations* of Pseudo-Methodius," *Speculum*, IV (1929), 329-339). The related passage is: οὗτος γὰρ ὁ Γεδεὼν κατέκοψε τὰς παρεμβολὰς αὐτῶν καὶ ἐδίωξε καὶ ἐξήνεγκεν αὐτοὺς ἐκ τῆς οἰκουμένης γης εἰς τὴν ἔρημον Ἐτριμβον ἐξ ἧς ἐτύγχανον, καὶ οἱ ὑπολειφθέντες δώδεκα γενεαὶ συνθήκας ἔθεντο εἰρήνην ἐν τοῖς υἱοῖς Ἰσραὴλ καὶ ἐξῆλθον ἐπὶ τὴν ἔρημον τὴν ἐξωτέραν ἐννέα φυλαί. μέλλουσι δὲ ἐξιέναι ἔτι ἅπαξ καὶ ἐρημῶσαι πᾶσαν τὴν γῆν. (Istrin; *ibid.*, "Texts," p. 14; Cross, *loc. cit.*, pp. 334-335).

306. This may refer to Georgius Hamartolus; Shakhmatov, "'Povest' Vremennÿkh let i ee istochniki," *Trudÿ ODRL*, IV (1940), 58.

307. The Pechera and the Yugra, together with the Perm' and the Yam' (Yem') were the tributary Finnish tribes in the White Sea basin, the region known as Zavoloch'e (cf. *supra*, n. 244). The narrative indicates that the Yugra themselves had only recently made contact with the Samoyedes, who are represented as living to the east of the northern Urals. Though of Ural-Altaic stock, they differ somewhat in physical aspect from the Finns, and seem originally to have been driven far to the north by the Turko-Tartars. At the present time their settlements are scattered along the Arctic coast from the Yenisei river to the White Sea.

308. Cf. *supra*, n. 305. The Greek original for the passage quoted may be found in Istrin, *op. cit.*, "Texts," pp. 89-90 or Cross, *loc. cit.*, pp. 336-337, with translation. Cf. also A. R. Anderson, *Alexander's Gate, Gog and Magog, and the Inclosed Nations* (Cambridge: Mediaeval Academy of America, 1932), pp. 89-90.

309. Murom had been seized by Izyaslav in 1096 after his capture of Kursk (cf. *supra*, n. 299).

310. Cf. *supra*, n. 150.

311. Beloozero, "White Lake," midway between modern Vologda and Lake Onega, connected with the Volga by the Sheksna river.

312. Implying that while Murom-Ryazan' properly belonged to Chernigov, Rostov-Suzdal' were momentarily attached to Pereyaslavl'.

313. Yaroslav (son of Svyatoslav of Chernigov) died in 1129.

314. The Medveditsa, a tributary of the Volga, and border between the principalities of Suzdal' and Novgorod.

315. The Kievan Crypt Monastery had a dependency at Suzdal' which developed into an independent monastery before the early thirteenth century (Golubinsky, *op. cit.*, II, i, 760). The church of St. Demetrius was apparently a wooden structure, since the first stone churchly edifice in this city was the Cathedral of Our Lady, constructed by Vladimir Monomakh, and replaced by a new building in 1222-1225 (*ibid.*, p. 323). Bishop Ephraim of Rostov was originally a monk of the Kievan Crypt Monastery (*Paterik, ed. cit.*, p. 103), and occupied the see 1090-1119 (*ibid.*, p. 221; Golubinsky, *op. cit.*, I, i, 677).

316. The Klyaz'ma rises east of Moscow and flows into the Oka about fifty miles of Gor'kiy (Nizhni Novgorod).

317. Vyacheslav (son of Vladimir Monomakh) died in 1154.

318. Kulachek is apparently a locality in the vicinity of Suzdal', and is probably connected with the river Koloksha, which enters the Klyaz'ma from the south a short distance above Vladimir.

319. Ryazan', 110 miles southeast of Moscow, on the river Trubezh a little over a mile from its junction with the Oka.

320. Nikita, originally a monk in the Crypt Monastery (cf. *Paterik, ed. cit.*, pp. 124-127), Bishop of Novgorod 1096, died November 30, 1108 (Golubinsky, *op. cit.*, II, i, 672).

321. The Laurentian Chronicle preserves here, as an interpolation (*PSRL.*, I, 252-255) the Testament of Vladimir Monomakh (*infra*, Appendix I) and a personal letter written by Vladimir to Oleg at Mstislav's suggestion (*infra*, Appendix II). The letter seems inspired by an honest desire to make peace, since Vladimir protests that he would gladly have restored Murom to Oleg at the latter's request. On the other hand, Vladimir had been equally responsible with Svyatopolk for Oleg's expulsion from Chernigov the previous May (1096), so that Oleg mistrusted his assurances of peaceful intent.

322. Svyatopolk (son of Izyaslav), Prince of Kiev; Vladimir Monomakh, Prince of Pereyaslavl'; David (son of Igor'), Prince of Dorogobuzh in 1084, of Vladimir-Volÿnsk in 1085; Vasil'ko (son of Rostislav, poisoned at Tmutorakan' in 1066), Prince of Terebovl' (Galicia); David (son of Svyatoslav and brother of Oleg), Prince of Smolensk; Oleg (son of Svyatoslav), originally Prince of Tmutorakan', and during the previous year operating against Mstislav son of Vladimir in the northeast. Lyubech, on the Dnieper west of Chernigov, and in the territory of the latter principality.

323. Terebovl' on the Gnezda on the borders of Volhynia and Galicia.

324. The settlement at Lyubech momentarily consecrated the *status quo*: Svyatopolk, as son of Izyaslav, retained Kiev with Turov and the Gorÿn' basin, while Vladimir Monomakh continued to hold what had belonged to his father Vsevolod, i.e., Pereyaslavl' with Rostov-Suzdal', Smolensk and Novgorod. The former domain of Svyatoslav of Chernigov was divided among his sons: David received Chernigov, Oleg received Novgorod-Seversk (on the Desna east of

Chernigov and now a principality for the first time), while Yaroslav, the youngest brother, was assigned to Murom-Ryazan'. The former patrimony of Yaropolk (son of Izyaslav) in Volhynia and Galicia was divided so that David son of Igor' received Vladimir-Volÿnsk, while the sons of the late Rostislav, Vasil'ko and Volodar', were guaranteed the possession of Terebovl' and Przemyśl respectively. It would seem from this arrangement that the principle of succession in one family was to apply to Kiev as well as to the other principalities, though the action of popular preference nullified this principle upon the death of Svyatopolk in 1113. It will be noted, however, that the convention of Lyubech left Vladimir Monomakh at the constant mercy of a combination of Svyatopolk with Oleg and his brothers (cf. Presnyakov, *Knyazhoe Pravo*, pp. 55-60; Hrushevsky, *Ist. Ukrainÿ-Rusi*, II, ii, 90-91, 101-131; *Kievskaya Zemlya*, pp. 107-109; Bagaley, *Ist. Sěverskoy Zemli*, pp. 176-178.

325. David son of Igor', Prince of Vladimir-Volÿnsk.

326. As Vladimir Monomakh was in control of Novgorod which strictly speaking belonged to the original domain of Izyaslav, Svyatopolk's father, there was enough probability in David's allegations to arouse Svyatopolk's suspicions, since Monomakh might try to realize his designs on Kiev (if he entertained any) by promising Vasil'ko compensation in the west at the expense of David (Vladimir-Volÿnsk) and Svyatopolk (Turov and the Gorÿn' district).

327. Turov on the river Pripet' and Pinsk on the Pina, near Brest-Litovsk.

328. Svyatopolk's consultation of the *veche* (popular assembly) shows him to have been on good terms with both boyars and masses in Kiev, and also gave him an opportunity to shift the responsibility to David. On the other hand, the protest of the priors indicates the presence of a party friendly to Monomakh in Kiev. After the blinding of Vasil'ko, the indignant protests of the Prior John of the Crypt Monastery were so violent that Svyatopolk imprisoned him in Turov, though he was later obliged to restore him to his dignity by the instance of Vladimir Monomakh (*Paterik, ed. cit.*, pp. 153-154).

329. Zvizhden', on the river Zvizh', joining the Teterev from the south; thus northwest of Kiev.

330. David, now Prince of Chernigov; Oleg, of Novgorod-Seversk.

331. Pogorina, the district along the Gorÿn' river in eastern Volhynia and the westernmost section of the principality of Kiev. Its three most important towns were Dorogobuzh on the Gorÿn' itself, Peresopnitsa on the Stubel', a small tributary of the Gorÿn', and Ostrog at the confluence of the Gorÿn' and the Velya.

332. Vsevolod had originally been married *ca*. 1052 to a relative of Constantine IX Monomachus (cf. *supra*, n. 192). She died in 1067, and Vsevolod married a Polovcian princess by whom he had a son Rostislav (drowned while fighting the Polovcians, 1093) and several daughters (Ikonnikov, *Opÿt*, II, i, 141, n. 2). The widow of Vsevolod mentioned here is thus his second wife. Cf. Baumgarten, *Généalogies*, pp. 7, 9.

333. Nicholas arrived in Kiev *ca*. 1096 (cf. *supra*, n. 273), and was succeeded by Nicephorus in 1104 (*q.v.*, cf. Golubinsky, I, i, 287). The truce described is again mentioned under 1098.

334. For this lengthy eyewitness account of the otherwise unknown Vasiliy, which has been interpolated into the Chronicle, cf. *supra*, Introduction: Sources.

335. Towns on the border of Volhynia and Galicia. The exact location of Vsevolozh' is unknown, though apparently close to the district of Terebovl';

Notes to the Russian Primary Chronicle 281

Peremil' (mod. Peremel') and Shepol' (mod. Shepel') are both near Lutsk.

336. The Berendichi (Berendei) were a Turkish tribe related to the Torks and apparently migrated westward with them. Their name is definitely Turkish (*bëren, börön*), so that they cannot be justly characterized as either Iranian or Japhetite. They appear not only in Galicia and Volhynia, but also in the Rostov-Suzdal' area. Cf. Rasovsky, *Pechenĕgi, Torki i Berendĕi*, pp. 11-12.

337. Buzh'sk (mod. Busk), on the upper western Bug southwest of Lutsk. Terebovl' is on the Seret' further south.

338. Turiysk, on the river Turya near Kowel.

339. Władysław Herman (youngest brother of Bolesław Śmiały), Duke of Poland 1080-1102.

340. Cf. *supra*, n. 327.

341. Cf. *supra*, n. 331.

342. Rozhnepole, between Terebovl' and Zvenigorod (cf. Barsov, *Ocherki*, p. 290). Zvenigorod was near mod. Lwów (Lvov, Lemberg).

343. The princes mentioned are: (1) sons of Svyatopolk: Yaroslav and Mstislav; (2) sons of Yaropolk (Svyatopolk's brother; they were both sons of Izyaslav of Kiev, and Yaropolk had been assassinated in 1086, *q.v.*): Yaroslav (Prince of Brest) and Vyacheslav (died in 1104); Svyatosha Svyatoslav, son of David of Chernigov.

344. Koloman (Kalman I), *regn*. 1095-1116. These events are again referred to under 1099. Yaroslav was married to a Hungarian princess, daughter of St. Ladislaus; Baumgarten, *Généalogies*, pp. 10, 11.

345. Yaroslav son of Yaropolk (cf. *supra*, n. 343).

346. Vygoshev was a town of the principality of Brest, near that city and Pinsk (cf. mod. Wyżówka; Barsov, *Ocherki*, pp. 291-292). The death of Mstislav natural son of Svyatopolk) is referred to and dated under 1099.

347. Gorodets, north of Kiev on the east bank of the Dnieper, at the junction of the Desna.

348. This Mstislav was son of Vsevolod and grandson of Igor', hence the nephew of David son of Igor' (of Vladimir-Volÿnsk). Solov'ëv (III, 61) says that David sent Mstislav to the coast "to intercept merchants," following Karamzin, II, n. 200, who gives no reason for the statement. Mstislav had been with David in his next to last attack upon Vladimir-Volÿnsk which was broken up by the arrival of Svyatosha and Putyata.

349. David of Chernigov (son of Svyatoslav).

350. Uvetichi was located southwest of Kiev, near Vasil'ev (Barsov, *Ocherki*, pp. 144, 301) probably on the stream Veta, which flows into the Dnieper on the west bank north of the Stugna.

351. After his successful attack upon David son of Igor' at Vladimir-Volÿnsk, Svyatopolk had stirred up trouble for himself by a project for enlarging his domains at the expense of Volodar' and Vasil'ko. The latter put up a stiff resistance, and were soon joined by David with Bonyak and his Polovcians. Even with Hungarian support, Svyatopolk's son Yaroslav made no head against this combination, which laid siege to his other son Mstislav at Vladimir itself, where the latter met his death. David's designs on Vladimir were momentarily checked by the intervention of Svyatosha (son of David of Chernigov) who raised David's siege of Vladimir and held it for Svyatopolk. After Svyatosha had left Vladimir, however, David returned from among the Polovcians, among whom he had

taken refuge, drove out Svyatopolk's viceroy from Vladimir, and remained in possession of the city. Svyatopolk's plans for controlling all the western principalities were thus checked, and he therefore combined with David (Chernigov) and Oleg (Novgorod-Seversk), as well as with Vladimir Monomakh to force David son of Igor' out of Vladimir-Volÿnsk. The upshot of the conference at Uvetichi is thus the transfer of David from Vladimir-Volÿnsk to Buzh'sk with compensation including two other small districts in the same area and an indemnity of 400 grivnÿ.

352. Cf. 1067, 1068, 1069.

353. The Zolot'cha was a small inlet from the Chertorÿya creek on the east bank of the Dnieper opposite Kiev.

354. Cf. *supra,* n. 313; Yaroslav had cooperated with Oleg in his operations in the northeast against Mstislav of Novgorod in 1096.

355. Cf. *supra,* n. 297.

356. The Nura is a tributary of the Western Bug.

357. The removal of David son of Igor' from Vladimir-Volÿnsk, coupled with Svyatopolk's designs against Vasil'ko and Volodar', and now his forcing upon Vladimir Monomakh a plan to exchange Vladimir-Volÿnsk for Novgorod, indicate that as long as Svyatopolk was backed by the princes of Chernigov he was independent of Monomakh. The failure of his plan to gain control of Novgorod resulted more from the opposition of its inhabitants than from any protest by Vladimir.

358. Bolesław Krzywousty ("the Wrymouthed," son of Władysław Herman), *regn.* 1102-1138. His deceased brother Mieczysław had married Svyatopolk's sister Eudoxia (Leib, p. 161, Naruszewicz, *Ist Nar. Polsk,* ed. Turowski [Cracow, 1859], II, 101-106), and a Papal dispensation from Paschal II was required before Bolesław's marriage to Sbÿslava could take place, in view of the canonical prohibition of consanguineous unions to the seventh degree (cf. also Solov'ëv, II, 418, n. 162). Cf. *supra,* n. 238.

359. Dolobsk, on the east bank of the Dnieper opposite Kiev; cf. *supra,* n. 130.

360. Son of Yaropolk (Izyaslav's son), assassinated in 1086.

361. A not otherwise identifiable locality in the steppe country. It is possible, however, that this was the old name of the river Molochnaya (cf. K. V. Kudryashov, *Polovetskaya Step'* [Moscow, 1948], pp. 91-94).

362. Cf. *supra,* n. 296.

363. Son of Svyatoslav of Chernigov, and brother of David and Oleg.

364. Under the agreements reached by the Council of Lyubech (cf. *supra,* n. 324 above) the youngest of the sons of Svyatoslav, the Yaroslav here named, received the principality of Murom-Ryazan'. This district bordered at its northwestern extremity on the seats of the Finnish tribes along the Volga, of which the Mordva were one. Their original home seems to have lain along the southern shore of the Oka.

365. Irene, daughter of Volodar' of Przemyśl, married the Sebastocrator Isaac Comnenus, younger son of the Emperor Alexius I and father of the Emperor Andronicus I (died in 1185); Baumgarten, *Généalogies,* pp. 15, 16.

366. Predslava married Almos (died *ca.* 1129), son of Géza I of Hungary; Baumgarten, *Généalogies,* pp. 10, 11.

367. Cf. *supra,* n. 343.

368. In the Novgorod Chronicle (Syn. text, p. 119), this unmotivated cam-

paign against Polotsk is dated as of 1103. It will be noted that Vseslav's son David took part of the southern princes against his brother Gleb.

369. Zarechesk (Zaretsk), at the western border of the Kiev area, on the Stubel' river south of Peresopnitsa.

370. Zbygniew, the brother of Bolesław Krzywousty, had been the latter's bitter opponent ever since his accession in 1102. In view of Zbygniew's effort to overthrow his brother in 1106 with the aid of the rebellious Pomeranians, it would appear likely that Zbygniew's flight to Russia was connected with the failure of his projects in that quarter. He cannot have received much comfort from Svyatopolk, however, as the Polish sources report Russian aid to Bolesław in his further operations against Pomerania (Naruszewicz, *op. cit.,* pp. 119-122).

371. Referred to as Svyatosha during the Volhynian campaigns against David son of Igor' (cf. *supra*, n. 343).

372. The Zimegola (cf. Semigallien) were an eastern branch of the Lithuanians, living on the east bank of the Dvina between Polotsk and Pskov and the Finnish Esthonians; the name is supposedly derived from Lith. *ziemes galas,* "end of the [Lithuanian] land." The sons of Vseslav of Polotsk (died in 1101), apart from David, who made common cause with the southern princes, were Roman, Gleb, Boris, Rogvold, Svyatoslav, and George; Baumgarten, *Généalogies,* pp. 32, 34.

373. Two Norse sources (*Fagrskinna,* ed. P. A. Munch and C. R. Unger [Oslo, 1847], p. 144, and *Morkinskinna,* ed. C. R. Unger [Oslo, 1867], p. 169) state that Gytha, the daughter of Harald of England, who fell at Hastings, married Vladimir, the son of Yaroslav. As Vladimir son of Yaroslav died at Novgorod in 1052, the Vladimir referred to must be Vladimir Monomakh, son of Vsevolod and grandson of Yaroslav. Saxo Grammaticus, ed. A. Holder (Strasbourg, 1886), p. 370, also remarks with similar confusion of identity: "Cuius [Haraldi] filii duo confestim in Daniam cum sorore migrarunt. Quos Sueno paterni eorum meriti oblitus consanguinee pietatis more except, puellamque Rutenorum regi Waldemaro, qui et ipse Iaroslauus a suis est appellatus, nuptum dedit."

374. Lubnÿ, on the Sula, due east of Pereyaslavl'.

375. These princes may be identified as follows: Svyatopolk of Kiev, Vladimir Monomakh of Pereyaslavl', Oleg of Novgorod-Seversk, Mstislav son of Vsevolod and grandson of Igor' (cf. *supra,* n. 343), and three sons of Vladimir Monomakh: Vyacheslav, Svyatoslav and Yaropolk.

376. The Sula enters the Dnieper from the east bank south of the junction of the Ros' from the opposite shore.

377. A tributary of the Psël, east of the Sula.

378. Svyatopolk was the son of Izyaslav (son of Yaroslav the Wise), his mother was Gertrude, sister of Casimir of Poland (died in 1058) and daughter of Mieszko II (died in 1034), who had married Izyaslav *ca.* 1043; cf. *supra,* n. 213.

379. George, son of Vladimir Monomakh, is the prince known as Yuriy Dolgorukiy (George Long-Arm), subsequently ruler of Suzdal'-Vladimir, who died in 1157. The son of Oleg who married the daughter of Aepa was Svyatoslav.

380. Cf. *supra,* n. 187.

381. Prior of the Crypt Monastery 1108-1113; cf. *supra,* n. 273.

382. Gleb, son of Vseslav, Prince of Polotsk; cf. *supra,* n. 372. He was Svyatopolk's nephew by marriage, since he married the latter's niece Anastasia, daugh-

ter of Izyaslav's son Yaropolk (cf. *PSRL.*, ii, 82). Both Yaropolk and Gleb and his wife made large gifts to the monastery.

383. The Metropolitan in question was Nicephorus, who had arrived to succeed Nicholas (cf. *supra,* n. 273) on December 6, 1104 (*q.v.*) and died in 1121.

384. Cf. *supra,* n. 237.

385. Eupraxia (or Praxedis) was married, first, to Henry the Long, Margrave of the Nordmark (died in 1087) and, after his death, in 1089, to the Western Emperor Henry IV (died 7 August, 1106). In the West she was known as Adelheid. She took the veil four months after Henry's death (cf. *supra, ad* 1106). Cf. Baumgarten, *Généalogies,* pp. 22, 24; *supra,* n. 266.

386. Cf. *supra,* n. 196.

387. In the Hypatian redaction (*PSRL.*, I, ii, 259-261), these reflections on the portent of 1110 are greatly expanded, and serve as an introduction to an expedition undertaken by Vladimir and Svyatopolk against the Polovcians in 1111. It has been supposed that these reflections were also present in the prototype of the Laurentian redaction, but that several leaves were lost at the conclusion, while the colophon of Sylvester was on a separate leaf or on the binding, and was thus preserved.

388. For the relation of Sylvester, Prior of St. Michael's in Vydobichi, to the text of the *Povest',* cf. *supra,* Introduction: Composition.

Additional Note. The passage from 6390 (882) through 6428 (920) is lacking in the Laurentian text and is restored from the Hypatian text as having probably belonged to the original *Povest'*.

Appendix I

Notes to Testament of Vladimir Monomakh

1. As noted in the text, the Testament (*Pouchenie*) follows immediately after the items for 1096 in the Laurentian manuscript and is not preserved in any other codex. The extant text opens with excerpts from the Psalter and from patristic works (particularly the *Asketika* and *Discourses* of St. Basil the Great), followed, first, by extensive admonitions to Vladimir's sons, and finally, by a somewhat incomplete summary of Vladimir's campaigns and adventures in approximate diary form, beginning in 1073 and ending in 1117. There is considerable likelihood that the text as we have it represents a fusion of at least two intrinsically unrelated documents. A comparison of the Chronicle itself with the *Pouchenie* also reveals that, during the forty-five years covered by Vladimir's account, military activity against the nomads was more strenuous and constant than the annals themselves would indicate.

The *Pouchenie* was apparently composed shortly before Vladimir's death on May 19, 1125, since the phrases *na dalechi puti* (literally "on a far journey," but signifying figuratively "in your old age") and *na sanĕkh sĕdya* ("sitting on my sledge") obviously refer to advancing years and weakness. The occurrence of the *Pouchenie* in the Laurentian codex defies entirely satisfactory explanation. The fact that it fails to appear either in the Hypatian codex or in the two other texts (the Konigsberg-Radziwiłł and Moskovsko-Akademicheskiy), both of which derive either from the same prototype as the Laurentian or from a text closely related to this prototype, would even indicate that it was possibly inserted as late as the fourteenth century. For this problem, cf. N. V. Shlyakov, "O Pouchenii Vladimira Monomakha," *Zhurn. Min. Nar. Prosv.* (1900), May, p. 96 ff; June, p. 209 ff.; A. A. Shakhmatov, *Povĕst' Vremennÿkh Lĕt*, pp. xxxviii-xxxix; P. V. Vladimirov, *Drevnyaya Russkaya Literatura Kievskago Perioda* (Kiev, 1900), pp. 244-247, also App. iii; I. M. Ivakin, *Knyaz' Vladimir Monomakh i Ego Pouchenie*, I (Moscow, 1901); Istrin, "Zamechaniya o Nachale Russkogo Letopisaniya." *Izv. Otd. Russk. Yaz. i Slov.*, XXVII (1922), pp. 227-228; *Ocherk Istorii Drevnerusskoy Literaturÿ* (Leningrad, 1922), pp. 162-170; and recently M. P. Alekseev, "Anglo-saksonskaya Parallel' k Poucheniyu Vladimira Monomakha," *Trudÿ Otdela Drevne-russkoy Literaturÿ*," II (Moscow, 1935), 39-80, an extremely valuable study including a parallel drawn with the *Faedar Larcwidas* of the Exeter Book (cf. J. Gollanez, *The Exeter Book*, EETS., orig. ser., CIV, 300-305).

2. Vladimir, born in 1053, was the son of Vsevolod I by a Byzantine princess, a relative of the Emperor Constantine IX Monomachus. He was married in 1074-1075 to Gytha, daughter of Harald of England; cf. *supra*, nn. 192, 373; also Alekseev, *loc. cit.*, pp. 50-53.

3. Lacuna of four and one half lines.

4. The reference is to Svyatopolk's project of 1099-1100 for the attack upon Volodar' and Vasil'ko after he had seized Vladimir-Volÿnsk from David son of Igor'. This occurrence has nothing to do with the date when the *Pouchenie* was composed, but simply motivates the Psalter excerpts.

5. It has been suggested that the selections from the Psalter and from the rule of St. Basil, as well as the address to the Blessed Virgin ("Oh sovereign Mother of God . . . white as snow") and the section "What is man . . . of the Holy Ghost" do not belong to the original *Pouchenie* (cf. Alekseev, *loc. cit.*, p. 72).

6. When Izyaslav fled to Poland in 1073, cf. *supra*, n. 213.

7. In 1074: cf. *supra*, n. 230.

8. Apparently in the summer of 1076, cf. *supra*, n. 239. The year is ascertainable from the date of the birth of Vladimir's first son Mstislav.

9. On December 27, 1076.

10. Apparently the Spring of 1078, since Gleb was killed in the northern marches during that year and buried in Chernigov on July 23.

11. Oleg was at Chernigov during the winter of 1077-78 and fled to Tmutorakan' on April 10, 1078.

12. The reference is to the battle of the Nezhatina plain in 1078. The Chronicle supplies no data on the subsequent operations against Vseslav.

13. This operation would seem to refer either to Roman's raid with Polovcian allies in 1079 or the attack upon Rus' made in 1080 by the Torks of Pereyaslavl'.

13a. For an interpretation of *semtsyu* as signifying "younger member of a family" or "servant," cf. Likhachev, II, 446.

14. Yaropolk died on November 22, 1086. The Lady-Day was the Assumption (15 August) or the Nativity (8 September) of Our Lady.

15. Vsevolod died on April 13, 1093.

16. The Chronicle reports that in 1094 Svyatopolk made peace with the Polovcians and married Turgorkan's daughter.

17. The corresponding events are described by the Chronicle under 1094.

18. Oleg's flight from Chernigov to Starodub took place on May 3, 1096.

19. Vladimir's first wife died on May 7, 1107.

20. The Chronicle itself dates this peace with the Polovcians as of January 12, 1007.

21. According to the Chronicle, this campaign took place in 1110.

22. The expedition to the Don ended in a Russian victory over the nomads on March 24, 1111 (*PSRL.*, II, 3rd ed., 263).

23. Svyatopolk died on April 16, 1113, and Vladimir arrived at Kiev on April 22. The Polovcians advanced on the Vÿr' as soon as they heard of Svyatopolk's death (*PSRL.*, II, 3rd ed., 271-273).

24. The operations of Vladimir against Gleb are dated by the Laurentian codex as of 1115 (*PSRL.*, I, ii, 2nd ed., 290-291) and by the Hypatian as of 1116 (*P.S.R.L.*, II, 3rd ed., 279).

25. Vladimir's campaign against the Prince of Vladimir-Volÿnsk, Yaroslav son of Svyatopolk, is dated by the Laurentian codex as of 1118 (*PSRL.*, II, 2nd ed., 291) and by the Hypatian as of 1117 (*PSRL.*, II, 3rd ed., 280-281).

26. The distance from Chernigov to Kiev is about seventy miles.

Appendix II

1. This letter follows immediately after the *Testament* of Vladimir Monomakh in the Laurentian codex (fol. 83r). E. F. Karsky (*PSRL.*, II, i, 2nd ed., 252) indicates a lacuna at the top of fol. 83v (though there is no evidence for it in the manuscript), and would thus begin the letter with the words "but the teaching of the devil prevails everywhere." On the other hand, the passage "I reflect now I may stand before the dread Judge ere we have done penance and become reconciled" at the bottom or fol. 83r obviously belongs to the content of the letter rather than to the *Pouchenie*, which ends logically with the reflection that "the protection of God is fairer than the protection of man."

2. At the instance of Vladimir's son, Mstislav, Prince of Novgorod, this letter was written to Oleg son of Svyatoslav after the latter had defeated Mstislav's younger brother in a battle fought near Murom on September 6, 1096, in which the young prince met his death.

3. There is a certain inconsistency between Vladimir's letter and the facts as recounted by the Chronicle. Vladimir reproaching Oleg with not taking diplomatic steps to secure Murom instead of Rostov. The Chronicle recounts that Oleg actually did request Izyaslav to withdraw to Rostov.

4. Vladimir had surrendered Chernigov to Oleg in 1094. Two years later, after Oleg had refused to make any pact with his cousins, Svyatopolk and Vladimir laid siege to Chernigov, whereupon Oleg fled to Starodub on May 3, 1096. When the allies appeared before Starodub, Oleg sued for peace, and was directed to join his brother David in Smolensk. There the inhabitants refused to admit him, so that he went on to Ryazan', from which he launched his offensive against Izyaslav.

5. This prayer follows immediately after Vladimir's letter to Oleg, on fol. 84v of the Laurentian codex. As Shlyakov has shown (*op. cit.*, pp. 227-237), the euchological passages from which it is compiled derive entirely from the services of the Byzantine rite for Shrovetide and the first week of Lent.

Selected Bibliography

I. SOURCES

A. RUSSIAN.

For the versions and editions of the Russian Chronicles, cf. *supra,* Introduction: Manuscripts and Editions.

James the Monk, *Pamyat' i Pokhvala Vladimiru,* ed. V. Sreznevsky, in *Musin-Pushkinskiy Sbornik.* St. Petersburg, 1893.
———. *Skazanie Strastey Sv. Borisa i Gleba,* ed. I. Sreznevsky, *Skazaniya o Sv. Borisě i Glěbě.* St. Petersburg, 1860.
Khronika Georgiya Amartola v Drevnem Slavyanorusskom Perevode, ed. V. M. Istrin, 2 vols. Leningrad, 1920, 1922.
Hilarion, Metropolitan of Kiev, *Slovo o Zakone i Blagodati,* ed. N. K. Nikol'sky, "Materialÿ dlya Istorii Drevnerusskoy Dukhovnoy Literaturÿ," *Sbornik Otd. Russk. Yaz. i Slov. Akad. Nauk,* LXXXII (St. Petersburg, 1907); V. Sreznevsky, in *Musin-Pushkinskiy Sbornik* (St. Petersburg, 1893).
Nestor, *Chtenie o Zhitii i o Pogublenii Borisa i Gleba,* ed. I. Sreznevsky, *Skazaniya o Sv. Borisě i Glěbě.* St. Petersburg, 1860.
———. *Zhitie Prep. Feodosiya,* ed. D. Abramovich, *Paterik Kievo-Pecherskogo Monastÿrya,* cf. *infra.*
Paterik Kievo-Pecherskogo Monastÿrya, ed. D. Abramovich (Pamyatniki Slavyano-Russkoy Pis'mennosti). St. Petersburg, 1911, and Kiev, 1931.
Slovo o Polku Igoreve, ed. S. Shambinago and V. Rzhiga (Moscow, 1933); ed. V. P. Adrianova-Perets (Moscow-Leningrad, 1950).
Stepennaya Kniga, ed. *Polnoe Sobranie Russkikh Lětopisey,* XXI (St. Petersburg, 1908).

B. BYZANTINE.

Constantine VII Porphyrogenitus, *De ceremoniis.* Bonn, 1819.
Georgius Cedrenus, *Synopsis historion.* Bonn, 1838.
Georgius Monachus, *Universal History,* ed. von Muralt (St. Petersburg, 1859), and Migne, *PG.* CX; ed. de Boor (Leipzig, 1904).
Joannes Malalas, *Chronographia,* ed. Migne, *PG.* XCVII.
Michael VII Dukas, Letters to Vsevolod I of Kiev, *ca.* 1073-6, ed. K. Sathas, *Bibliotheca graeca medii aevi,* V; cf. V. K. Vasil'evsky, *Trudÿ* I (St. Petersburg, 1908).
Michael Psellus, *Chronographia,* ed. and French transl. E. Renauld, 2 vols. Paris, 1928.
Nicephorus I, Patriarch of Constantinople, *Opuscula historica,* ed. de Boor. Leipzig, 1890.

Symeon, Magister and Logothete (Ps. Simeon), *Chronicon*. Bonn, 1838.
Theophanes, *Chronographia*, ed. de Boor. Leipzig, 1887.
Theophanes Continuatus. Bonn, 1838.

C. Western.

Annales Bertiniani, ed. G. Waitz. Hanover, 1883.
St. Bruno of Querfurt, Letter of 1007 to the future Emperor Henry II, ed. A. Bielowski, *Monumenta Poloniae historica*, I. Lemberg-Cracow, 1864.
Continuator Reginonis, ed. F. Kurze. Hanover, 1890.
Cosmas Pragensis, *Chronicon Bohemorum, MGH, NS., II*.
Długosz, Joannes, *Historia polonica*, ed. A. Przeździecki: *Joan. Dlugossi . . . Opera, II*. Cracow, 1867.
Eymundarpáttr Hringssonar, in *Flateyarbók*, II. Oslo, 1862.
Fagrskinna, ed. P. A. Munch and C. R. Unger. Oslo, 1847.
Fornmanna Sögur, in *Flateyarbók*, V. Oslo, 1862.
Gallus Anonymus, *Chronicon*, ed. A. Bielowski, *Monumenta Poloniae historica*, I. Lemberg-Cracow, 1864.
St. Gregory VII, Pope, Letters of 17 April 1075 to Izyaslav (Demetrius) I of Kiev and of 20 April 1075 to Bolesław II Śmiały of Poland, ed. E. Caspar, *Das Register Gregors VII.*, I. Berlin, 1920.
Kadłubek, Vincent, *Historia polonica*, ed. A. Bielowski, *Monumenta Poloniae historica*, II. Lemberg, 1872.
Lambert of Hersfeld, *Annales*, ed. O. Holder-Egger. Hanover, 1894.
Liudprand, Bishop of Cremona, *Antapodosis*, ed. L. Becker. Hanover, 1915.
Morkinskinna, ed. C. R. Unger. Oslo, 1867.
Orvar-Odds Saga, ed. R. C. Boer. Halle, 1892.
Pannonian Lives of SS. Cyril and Methodius, ed. P. A. Lavrov, "Materialÿ po Istorii Vozniknoveniya Drevneyshey Slavyanskoy Pis'mennosti," *Trudÿ Slavyanskoy Komissii* of the Academy of Science, I (Leningrad, 1930); ed. F. Pasternek, *Dějiny Slovanských Apoštolů Cyrilla a Methoda* (Prague, 1902).
Rafn, C. C., ed. *Antiquités russes d'après les monuments historiques des Islandais*. 2 vols. Copenhagen, 1850-1862.
Reginonis Chronicon, ed. F. Kurze. Hanover, 1890.
Saxo Grammaticus, *Gesta Danorum*, ed. A. Holder. Strasbourg, 1886.
Snorri Sturlesson, *Heimskringla*, ed. F. Jensson. Copenhagen, 1922.
Thietmar, Bishop of Merseburg, *Chronici libri VIII*, ed. F. Kurze. Hanover, 1889.

D. Islamic.

Marvazi, ed. V. Minorsky; *Sharaf al-Zamān Ṭāhir Marvazi on China, the Turks and India*. London: The Royal Asiatic Society, 1942.
Yahya ibn sa'īd of Antioch, *Annals*, ed, and French transl. I. Kratchkovsky and A. A. Vasiliev, *Patrologia Orientalis*, XXIII, iii (Paris, 1932).

II. WORKS

Ainalov, D., *Russische Monumentalkunst der vormoskowitschen Zeit*. Berlin, 1932.
Alexander, P. J., "The Papacy, the Bavarian Clergy, and the Slavonic Apostles," *The Slavonic Year-Book*, 1941.
Ammann, A., *Abriss der ostslawischen Kirchengeschichte*. Vienna, 1950.
Alpatov, M. and Brunov, N., *Altrussische Kunst*. Augsburg, 1932.

Anderson, A. R., *Alexander's Gate, Gog, Magog, and the Inclosed Nations.* Cambridge: Mediaeval Academy of America, 1932.
Arne, J. J., *Les relations de la Suède et de l'Orient pendant l'âge des Vikings.* Le Mans, 1910.
———. *Le Suède et l'Orient.* Uppsala, 1914.
Bagaley, D., *Istoriya Sěverskoy Zemli.* Kiev, 1882.
Barsov, N. P., *Ocherki Russkoy Istoricheskoy Geografii.* Warsaw, 1885.
Barthold, V., *Mesto Prikaspiyskikh Stepey v Istorii Musul'manskogo Mira.* Baku, 1925.
Baumgarten, N. de, "Généalogies et mariages occidentaux des Rurikides russes, du Xe au XIIIe siècle," *Orientalia Christiana,* IX (1927).
———. "Chronologie ecclésiastique des terres russes du Xe au XIIIe siècle," *Orientalia Christiana,* XVII (1930).
———. "Le dernier mariage de Saint Vladimir," *Orientalia Christiana,* XVIII (1930), 165-168.
———. "Olaf Tryggwison, roi de Norvège, et ses relations avec Saint Vladimir de Russie," *Orientalia Christiana,* XXIV (1931).
———. "Saint Vladimir et la conversion de la Russie," *Orientalia Christiana,* XXVII (1932).
Belyaev, N., "Rorik Yutlandskiy i Ryurik Nachal'noy Letopisi," *Seminarium Kondakovianum,* III (1929).
Berthier de la Garde, A. L., "Kak Vladimir Osazhdal Korsun'," *Sbornik Otd. Russk. Yaz. i Slov. Akademii Nauk,* XIV (1909).
Bestuzhev-Ryumin, K. N., *O Sostavě Russkikh Lětopisey do Kontsa XIV v.* St. Petersburg, 1868.
———. *Russkaya Istoriya,* I. St. Petersburg, 1872.
Boor, K. de, "Der Angriff der Rhos auf Byzanz," *Byz. Zts.,* IV (1897).
Braun, F., "Das historische Russland in nordischen Schrifttum des X-XIV. Jahrhunderts," *Festschrift für Eugen Mogk,* Halle, 1924.
Brim, V. A., "Proiskhozhdenie Termina Rus'," *Rossiya i Zapad,* I (Leningrad, 1923).
Brückner, A., *Die Wahrheit über die Slavenapostel.* Tübingen, 1913.
———. *Mitołogja Słowianska.* Cracow, 1918.
———. "Wzory Etymołogji," *Slavia,* III (1924.
———. "Mythologische Thesen," *Archiv f. Slav. Philologie,* XL (1925).
———. "Wzory Etymołogji i Krytyki Żródłowej," *Slavia,* V (1927).
Bugge, A., "Die nordeuropäischen Verkehrswege im frühen Mittelalter," *Vtljhrsch. f. Soz.–u. Wirtschaftsgeschichte,* IV (1905-1906).
Bury, J. B., *A History of the Eastern Roman Empire.* London, 1912.
Buslaev, F., *Istoricheskie Ocherki Russkoy Narodnoy Slovesnosti i Iskusstva.* St. Petersburg, 1861.
Bugoslavsky, S. A., "Kharakter i Ob'ëm Literaturnoy Deyatel'nosti Prep. Nestora," *Izv. Otd. Russk. Yaz. i Slov. Akademii Nauk,* XIX (1914).
Buxton, D. R., *Russian Mediaeval Architecture.* Cambridge, England, 1934.
Cherepnin, L. V., "Povest' Vremennÿkh Let," *Istoricheskiya Zapiski,* XXV (Moscow-Leningrad, 1948.
Cross, S. H., "Yaroslav the Wise in Norse Tradition," *Speculum,* IV (1928).
———. "Earliest Allusion in Slavic Literature to the Revelation of Pseudo-Methodius," *Speculum,* IV (1929).

Selected Bibliography

―――――. *Slavic Civilization through the Ages.* Cambridge: Harvard University Press, 1948.

―――――. "The Russian Primary Chronicle," *Harvard Studies and Notes in Philology and Literature,* XII. Cambridge: Harvard University Press, 1930.

―――――. "La tradition islandaise de Saint Vladimir," *Revue des études slaves,* XI (1931).

―――――. "Gothic Loan Words in the Slavic Vocabulary," *Harvard Studies and Notes in Philology and Literature,* XVI (1934).

―――――. "The Earliest Mediaeval Churches of Kiev," *Speculum,* XI (1936).

Dimitriu, A., "K Voprosu o Dogovorakh Russkikh s Grekami," *Vizant. Vremennik,* II (1895).

Dölger, F., "Die Chronologie des grossen Feldzugs des Kaisers Johannes Tzimiskes gegen die Russen," *Byz. Zts.,* XXXII (1932).

Dorn, B., "Caspia," *Mém. Acad. Imp. des Sci.,* XXIII. St. Petersburg, 1875.

Dvornik, F., *Les légendes de Constantin et Méthode vues de Byzance.* Prague, 1933.

Ediger, T., *Russlands älteste Beziehungen zu Deutschland, Frankreich und der röm. Kurie.* Diss. Halle, 1911.

Florovsky, A V., "Knyaz' Rosh u Proroka Ezekiila," *Sbornik v Chest na V. Zlatarski.* Sofia, 1925.

―――――. *Chekhi i Vostochnÿe Slavyane.* Prague, 1935.

Frähn, C. N., *Ibn Fozslans und anderer araber Berichte über die Russen älterer Zeit.* St. Petersburg, 1823.

Fribler, K., *Das russische Reich: eine Gründung der Franken.* Marburg, 1923.

Gaydukevich, V. F., *Bosporskoe Tsarstvo.* Moscow-Leningrad, 1949.

Gedeonov, G., *Varyagi i Rus'.* St. Petersburg, 1876.

Goetz, L. K., *Staat und Kirche in Altrussland.* Berlin, 1908.

Goldschmidt, A., *Die Bronzetüren von Novgorod und Gnesen.* Marburg, 1932.

Golubinsky, E., *Istoriya Russkoy Tserkvi,* 2nd ed. Moscow, 1901.

Golubovsky, P., "Khronika Ditmara kak Istochnik dlya Russkoy Istorii," *Kievskie Universitetskie Izvéstiya* (Kiev, 1878).

Grégoire, H., "La légende d'Oleg et l'expédition d'Igor." *Bulletin de la classe des Lettres et des Sciences morales et politiques de l'Académie royale de Belgique,* XXIII (1937), 80-94.

Grekov, B. D., *Kievskaya Rus'.* Moscow-Leningrad, 1939.

Harkavi, A., *Skazaniya Musul'manskikh Pisateley o Slavyanakh i Russkikh.* St. Petersburg, 1870.

Honigmann, E., "Studies in Slavic Church History," *Byzantion,* XVII (1945).

Hrushevsky, M., *Ocherki Istorii Kievskoy Zemli.* Kiev, 1891.

―――――. *Stat'i po Slavyanovědeniyu.* St. Petersburg, 1904.

―――――. *Kievskaya Rus'.* St. Petersburg, 1911.

―――――. *Istoriya Ukrainÿ-Rusi.* Kiev, 1913.

Ikonnikov, V. S., *Opÿt Russkoy Istoriografii,* II. Kiev, 1908.

Istrin, V. M., *Otkrovenie Mefodiya Patarskago.* Moscow, 1897.

―――――. "Zamechaniya o Nachale Russkogo Letopisaniya," *Izv. Otd. Russk. Yaz. i Slov. Akademii Nauk,* XXVI (1921), XXVII (1922).

―――――. *Ocherki po Istorii Drevney Russkoy Literaturÿ Domongolskogo Perioda.* Leningrad, 1922.

———. "Dogovorÿ Russkikh s Grekami," *Izv. Otd. Russk. Yaz. i Slov. Akademii Nauk,* XXIX (1924).

———. "Otkrovenie Mefodiya Patarskogo i Letopis'," *Izv. Otd. Russk. Yaz. i Slov. Akademii Nauk,* XXIX (1924).

Ivakin, I. M., *Knyaz' Vladimir Monomakh i Ego Pouchenie.* Moscow, 1901.

Jagić, V., *Zur Entstehungsgeschichte der altkirchenslav. Sprache,* 2nd. ed. Berlin, 1913.

Jenkins, R. J. H., "The Supposed Russian Attack on Constantinople in 907," *Speculum,* XXIV (1949).

Jugie, M., *Le schisme byzantin.* Paris, 1941.

Karamzin, N. M., *Istoriya Gosudarstva Rossiyskago.* St. Petersburg, 1888.

Keary, C. F., *The Vikings in Western Civilization.* London, 1891.

Kendrick, T. D., *A History of the Vikings.* New York, 1930.

Khrushchov, I. P., *O Drevnerusskikh Istoricheskikh Pověstyakh i Skazaniyakh.* Kiev, 1878.

Klyuchevsky, V., *Kurs Russkoy Istorii.* Moscow, 1904.

Kmosko, M., "Das Rätsel des Pseudomethodius," *Byzantion,* VI (1931).

Kondakov, N. P., *Izobrazheniya Russkoy Knyazheskoy Sem'i v Miniatyurakh XI v.* St. Petersburg, 1906.

Korff, S. A., "Den drevljanske forsten Mal," *Stud. i Nordisk Filologi* II (Helsingfors, 1911).

Kozlovsky, I. R., "Tmutarakan' i Tamatarkha-Matarkha-Taman'," *Izvestiya Tavricheskogo Obshchestva Istorii, Arkheologii i Etnografii,* II.

Krug, P., *Forschungen in der alteren Geschichte Russlands.* St. Petersburg, 1848.

Kruse, F., "O Proiskhozhdenii Ryurika," *Zhurnal Minist. Narodnago Prosv.* 1836.

———. *Chronicon Nortmannorum.* Hamburg, Gotha, and Dorpat, 1851.

Kudryashov, K. V., "O Mestonakhozdenii Khazarskogo Goroda Sarkela," *Izvestiya Akademii Nauk,* Ser. Ist Fil. 1947.

———. *Polovetskaya Step'.* Moscow, 1948.

Kulischer, J., *Russische Wirtschaftsgeschichte.* Jena, 1925.

Kunik, E., *Die Berufung der schwedischen Ruodsen durch die Finnen und Slaven.* St. Petersburg, 1844.

———. "Remarques critiques sur les antiquités russes," *Bull. Acad. Imp. des Sciences,* VII. St. Petersburg, 1850.

Laer, G., *Die Anfänge des russischen Reiches.* Berlin, 1930.

Lebreton, J. and Zeiller, J., *The History of the Primitive Church.* Eng. transl. New York, 1949.

Léger, L., *La mythologie slave.* Paris, 1901.

Leib, B., *Rome, Kiev et Byzance à la fin du XIe siècle.* Paris, 1924.

Likhachev, D., "Kul'tura Kievskoy Rusi pri Yaroslave Mudrom," *Istoricheskiy Zhurnal,* VII (1943).

Lilov, A., *O Tak-Nazÿvaemoy Kirillovskoy Knigě.* Kazan, 1858.

Loparev, Kh., "Vizantiyskaya Pechat' s Imenem Russkoy Knyagini," *Vizant. Vremennik,* I (1894).

Lot, F. and Bédier, H., *Légendes épiques.* 2nd ed. IV (Paris, 1921).

Lyashchenko, A. I., "Letopisnÿe Skazaniya o Smerti Olega Veshchego," *Izv. Otd. Russk. Yaz. i Slov. Akademii Nauk,* XXIX (1924).

Makariy, *Istoriya Russkoy Tserkvi.* St. Petersburg, 1889.

Mansikka, F., *Religion der Ostslaven.* Helsinki, 1921.

Selected Bibliography

Marquart, J., *Osteuropäische und ostasiatische Streifzüge*. Leipzig, 1903.
Minns, E. H., *Scythians and Greeks*. Cambridge, England, 1913.
Minorsky, V., *Studies in Caucasian History* (*Cambridge Oriental Series No. 6*). London, 1953.
Mošin, V. A., "Normannÿ v Vostochnoy Evrope," *Byzantinoslavica*, III (1931).
Muka, K., "Prohi Dnjepra a městne miena z XI.," *Časopis*, LXVIII (Prague, 1916).
Muralt, E. de, *Essai de chronographie byzantine*. 2 vols. St. Petersburg, 1855, 1871.
Naruszewicz, A., *Istorja Narodu Polskiego*. Cracow, 1859.
Niederle, L., *Původ a Počátky Slovanů Jižních*. (*Slovanské Starožitnosti*, II) Prague, 1906-1910.
———. *Původ a Počátky Slovanů Západních*. (*Slovanské Starožitnosti*, III). Prague, 1919.
———. *Manuel de l'Antiquité slave*. 2 vols. Paris, 1923, 1926.
———. *Život Starých Slovanů*. Prague, 1925.
———. *Původ a Počátky Slovanů Východních*. Prague, 1925.
Nikol'sky, N. K., *Materialÿ dlya Povremennogo Spiska Russkikh Pisateley i Ikh Sochineniy (X-XI Veka)*. St. Petersburg, 1906.
———. *Povest' Vremennÿkh Let kak Istochnik Russkoy Pis'mennosti i Kul'turÿ*. Leningrad, 1930, 1940.
Obolensky, K. M., *Lětopisets Pereyaslavlya Suzdal'skago*. Moscow, 1851.
Ostrogorsky, G., "L'expédition du prince Oleg contre Constantinople," *Annales de l'Institut Kondakov*, XI (1940).
———. *Geschichte des byzantinischen Staates* (*Byzantinisches Handbuch*, I, 2). Munich, 1952.
Palmieri, A., "De Orientalium in schismate defendendo peccatis," *Acta Academiae Velehradensis*, I-III. Prague, 1912.
Parkhomenko, V., *U Istochnikov Russkoy Gosudarstvennosti*. Leningrad, 1924.
———. "Kievskaya Rus' i Khazariya," *Slavia*, VI (1927).
———. "Rus' i Pechenegi," *Slavia*, VIII (1929).
Pasternek, F., *Dějiny slovanských Apoštolů Cyrilla a Methoda s Rozborem a Otiskem Hlavních Pramenů*. Prague, 1902.
Patapov, P., "K Voprosu o Literaturnom Sostavě Lětopisi," *Russkiy Filologicheskiy Věstnik*, 1910 and 1911.
Pavlov, A., *Kriticheskie Opÿtÿ Istorii Drveněyshey Grekorusskoy Polemiki protiv Latinyan*. St. Petersburg, 1878.
Pipping, H., "De skandinaviska Dnjeprnammen," *Stud. i Nordisk. Filolgi*, II (Helsingsfors, 1911).
Ponomarev, A. T., *Pamyatniki Drevne-Russkoy Tserkovno-Uchitel'noy Literaturÿ*. St. Petersburg, 1894.
Presnyakov, A., *Knyazhoe Pravo v Drevney Rusi*. St. Petersburg, 1909.
Prisëlkov, M. D., *Ocherki po Tserkovno-Politicheskoy Istorii Kievskoy Rusi X-XII V.* St. Petersburg, 1913.
———. *Nestor Letopisets*. Leningrad, 1923.
———. *Istoriya Russkogo Letopisaniya (XI-XV Vek.)*. Leningrad, 1940.
Rasovsky, D. A., "Pecheněgi, Torki i Berenděi na Rusi i v Ugrii," *Seminarium Kondakovianum*, VI (1933).
Réau, L., *L'art russe dès origines à Pierre le Grand*. Paris, 1921.
Rostovtzeff, M. I., "The Origin of the Russian State on the Dnieper," *American Historical Association: Annual Report*, 1920.

Rozhnetsky, S., "Kak Nazÿvalsya Pervÿy Russkiy Muchenik," *Izv. Otd. Russk. Yaz. i Slov. Akademii Nauk*, XIX (1914).
Runciman, S., *History of the First Bulgarian Empire*. London, 1930.
Rÿdzevskaya, E. A., "Legenda o Knyaze Vladimire v Sage ob Olafe Tryugvassone," *Trudÿ Otd. Drevne-Russkoy Literaturÿ*, II (Moscow, 1935).
Šafařik, P. J., *Slovanské Starožitnosti*. Prague, 1837.
S. Sakač. De dignitate episcopali S. Cyrilli Thessalonicensis," *Orientalia Christiana periodica*, XVI (1950).
Schlumberger, G., *Sigillographie de l'empire byzantin*. Paris, 1884.
——. *Un empereur byzantin au Xe siècle: Nicéphore Phocas*. Paris, 1890.
——. *L'épopée byzantine à la fin du Xe siècle*. Paris, 1895-1905.
Sedelnikov, A., "Drevnyaya Kievskaya Legenda ob Apostole Andree," *Slavia*, III (1924).
Serebryansky, N., *Drevnerusskie Knyazheskie Zhitiya*. Moscow, 1915.
Shakhmatov, A. A., "Iskhodnaya Tochka Lětoschisleniya Pověsti Vremennÿkh Lět,' *Zhurnal Minist. Narodnago Prosv.*, CCCX (1897).
——. "Tolkovaya Paleya i Russkaya Lětopis'," *Stat'i po Slavyanověděniyu*, ed. V. J. Lamansky. St. Petersburg, 1904.
——. "Skazanie o Prizvanii Varyagov," *Izv. Otd. Russk. Yaz. i Slov. Akademii Nauk*, IX (1904).
——. "Korsunskaya Legenda o Kreshchenii Vladimira," *Sbornik Statey v Chest' V. J. Lamanskago*. St. Petersburg, 1906.
——. "Kak Nazÿvalsya Pervÿy Russkiy Khristianskiy Muchenik," *Izvěstiya Akademii Nauk*, 6. Ser. 1907. "Povest' Vremennÿkh Let' i ee Istochniki," *Trudÿ ODRL*, IV (Leningrad, 1940).
Smirnov, V., "Chto takoe Tmutorakan'," *Vizant. Vremennik*, XXIII (1923).
Sobolevsky, A., "Zametki po Slavyanskoy Mifologii," *Slavia*, VII (1928).
Solov'ëv, S., *Istoriya Rossii*, I. 4th ed. Moscow, 1888.
Sreznevsky, I., *Skazaniya o Svyatÿkh Borisě i Glěbě*. St. Petersburg, 1860.
Stender-Petersen, A., "Zur Bedeutungs-Geschichte des Wortes *vaeringi*," *Acta Philol. Scand.*, VI (1931).
——. *Die Varägersage als Quelle der altruss, Chronik*. Leipzig, 1934.
Stepanov, N. V., "Lětopisets Nikifora," *Izv. Otd. Russk. Yaz. i Slov. Akademii Nauk*, XVII (1912).
Sukhomlinov, M. I., "O Drevney Russkoy Lětopisi kak Pamyatnike Literaturnom," *Sbornik Otd. Russk. Yaz. i Slov. Akademii Nauk*, LXXXV (1908).
Sÿchov, N. P., "Drevneyshiy Fragment Russko-Vizantiyskoy Zhivopisi, *Seminarium Kondakovianum*, II (1928).
Syuzyumov, M., "K Voprosu o Proiskhozhdenii Slova 'Ῥῶς, 'Ῥωσία, Rossiya," *Vestnik Drevney Istorii*, II (1940).
Szujski, J., *Dzieje Polski*, I. Cracow, 1895.
Tatischchev, V. N., *Istoriya Rossii*, I. St. Peterburg, 1768.
Taube, M. de, *Rome et la Russie avant l'invasion des Tatars (IX-XIIIe siècles)*. Paris, 1947.
Thomsen, W., *Der Ursprung des russischen Staates*. Halle, 1870.
——. *The Relations between Ancient Russia and Scandinavia and the Origins of the Russian State*. Oxford, 1877.
Tikhomirov, M. N., *Drevne-Russkie Goroda*. Moscow, 1946.

Selected Bibliography

Tolstov, S., *Po Sledam Drevnekhorezmiyskoy Tsivilizatsii*. Moscow-Leningrad, 1948.

Tolstoy, I. and Kondakov, N., *Russkiya Drevnosti*. St. Petersburg, 1891.

Tompkins, S. R., "The Varangians in Russian History," *Mediaeval and Historiographical Studies in Honor of J. W. Thompson*. Chicago, 1937.

Trautmann, R., *Die altrussische Nestor-Chronik*. Leipzig, 1931.

Vasiliev, A. A., "Economic Relations between Byzantium and Old Russia," *Journal of Economic and Business History*, IV (1932).

———. *The Goths in the Crimea*. Cambridge: Mediaeval Academy of America, 1936.

———. *The First Russian Attack on Constantinople in 860-61*. Cambridge: Mediaeval Academy of America, 1946.

———. "The Second Russian Attack on Constantinople," *Dumbarton Oaks Papers*, VI (1951), 161-225.

———. *History of the Byzantine Empire*. Madison: University of Wisconsin Press, 1952.

Vasil'evsky, V. G., "Russko-Vizantiyskie Otrÿvki," *Zhurnal Minist. Narodnago Prosv.*, 1878.

———. "Zhitie Sv. Stefana Surozhskago," *Zhurnal Minist. Narodnago Prosv.*, 1889.

———. *Trudÿ*. St. Petersburg, 1909.

Vernadsky, G., *Opÿt Istorii Evrazii*. Berlin, 1934.

———. *Political and Diplomatic History of Russia*. Boston, 1936.

———. "The Status of the Russian Church during the First Half-Century Following Vladimir's Conversion," *The Slavonic Year-Book*, 1941.

———. *Ancient Russia*. (G. Vernadsky and M. Karpovich, *A History of Russia*, vol. I) New Haven: Yale University Press, 1946.

———. *Kievan Russia*. New Haven: Yale University Press, 1948.

Vogel, W., *Die Normannen und das frankische Reich*. Heidelberg, 1906.

Weingart, M., *Byzantské Kroniky v Literatuře Církevněslovanské*. Bratislava, 1922.

Yakovlev, V., *Pamyatniki Russkoy Literaturÿ XII-XIII Věkov*. St. Petersburg, 1872.

Yushkov, S. V., *Obshchestvenno-Politicheskiy Stroy i Pravo Kievskogo Gosudarstva*. Moscow, 1949.

Zakrevsky, N., *Opisanie Kieva*. Moscow, 1868.

Zabolotsky, P., "K Voprosu ob Inozemnÿkh Pis'mennykh Istochnikakh Nachal'noy Lětopisi," *Russkiy Filologicheskiy Vestnik*, I (1902).

Zelenin, D., *Russische Volkskunde*. Berlin, 1927.

Zernov, N., "Vladimir and the Origin of the Russian Church," *Slavonic and East European Review*, LXX (1949), LXXI (1950).

Zlatarski, V., *Istorijata na bulgarskata dŭržava*. Sofia, 1918.

Table of Princes

Occupants of the Chief Rurikid Thrones During the Period Covered by the Primary Chronicle

A. Kiev (Great Princes)

Oleg I, + 912 (?)
Igor' I, 913-945 (?)
St. Olga, Regent, 945-964
Svyatoslav I, 964-972
Yaropolk I, co-prince 970; 972-978
St. Vladimir I, 978-1015
Svyatopolk I, 1015-1019
Yaroslav I, the Wise, 1019-1054
Izyaslav I, 1054-1068
Vseslav I of Polotsk, usurp., 1068-1069
Izyaslav I, restored, 1069-1073
Svyatoslav II of Chernigov, usurp., 1073-1076
Vsevolod I of Pereyaslavl', usurp., 1076-1077
Izyaslav I, restored again, 1077-1078
Vsevolod I, 1078-1093
Svyatopolk II, 1093-1113
Vladimir II Monomakh, 1113-1125
Mstislav I Harald, 1125-1132

B. Pereyaslavl' and Rostov-Suzdal'

Yaroslav (s. of St. Vladimir I), 988-1010 (to Novgorod, 1010)
St. Boris (s. of St. Vladimir I), 1010-1015
Elias (s. of Yaroslav I), c. 1019 (to Novgorod, 1019)
Vsevolod (s. of Yaroslav I), 1054-1076 (usurps Kiev, 1076)
Vladimir Monomakh (s. of Vsevolod I), 1076-1078 (to Chernigov, 1078)
Rostislav (s. of Vsevolod I), 1078-1093
Vladimir Monomakh (s. of Vsevolod I), again, 1094-1113 (succeeds to Kiev, 1113)

C. Novgorod

Vladimir (s. of Svyatoslav I), 970-978 (succeeds to Kiev, 978)
Vÿsheslav (s. of St. Vladimir I), 988-1010
Yaroslav of Rostov (s. of St. Vladimir I), 1010-1019 (succeeds to Kiev, 1019)
Elias of Rostov (s. of Yaroslav I), 1019-1020
Vladimir (s. of Yaroslav I), 1036-1052
Gleb of Tmutorakan' (s. of Svyatoslav II), c. 1069-1078
Svyatopolk (s. of Izyaslav I), 1078-1088 (to Turov, 1088)
David (s. of Svyatoslav II), 1088-1095 (to Smolensk, 1095)
Mstislav (s. of Vladimir II), 1095-1125 (succeeds to Kiev, 1125)

D. Murom-Ryazan'

St. Gleb (s. of St. Vladimir I), 1010-1015
Izyaslav (s. of Vladimir II), 1096
Yaroslav (s. of Svyatoslav II), 1097-1123 (to Chernigov, 1123)

E. Smolensk

Vyacheslav (s. of Yaroslav I), 1054-1057
Igor' of Vladimir-Volÿnsk (s. of Yaroslav I), 1057-1060
Vladimir Monomakh (s. of Vsevolod I), c. 1077-1095
David (s. of Svyatoslav II), 1095-1097 (to Chernigov, 1097)
Vladimir Monomakh (s. of Vsevolod I), again, 1097-1113 (succeeds to Kiev, 1113)

F. Polotsk

Izyaslav (s. of St. Vladimir I), 988-1001
Vseslav I (s. of Izyaslav), 1001-1003
Bryacheslav (s. of Izyaslav), 1003-1044
Vseslav II (s. of Bryacheslav), 1044-1069 (usurps Kiev, 1068-1069)
Mstislav (s. of Izyaslav I), 1096
Svyatopolk (s. of Izyaslav I), 1069-1071 (to Novgorod, 1078)
Vseslav II (s. of Bryacheslav), again, 1071-1101
David (s. of Vseslav II), 1101-1129

G. Chernigov and Novgorod-Seversk

Mstislav of Tmutorakan' (s. of St. Vladimir I), 1024-1036
Svyatoslav (s. of Yaroslav I), 1054-1076 (usurps Kiev, 1073-1076)
Vsevolod (s. of Yaroslav I), 1076-1077 (usurps Kiev, 1076-1077; succeeds to Kiev, 1078-1093)
Boris (s. of Vyacheslav of Smolensk), 1077-1078
Vladimir Monomakh of Pereyaslavl' (s. of Vsevolod I), 1078-1094 (to Pereyaslavl' 1094)
Oleg of Tmutorakan' (s. of Svyatoslav II), 1094-1096 (to Novgorod-Seversk, 1097)
David of Smolensk (s. of Svyatoslav II), 1097-1123
Yaroslav of Murom (s. of Svyatoslav II), 1123-1129

H. Vladimir-Volÿnsk

Vsevolod (s. of St. Vladimir I), 1010
Igor' (s. of Yaroslav I), 1054-1057 (to Smolensk, 1057)
Oleg (s. of Svyatoslav II), c. 1073-1077 (to Tmutorakan', 1083)
Yaropolk of Vÿshgorod and Turov (s. of Izyaslav I), 1078-1084
{ Volodar' (s. of Rostislav of Tmutorakan'), 1084 (to Peremÿshl', 1092)
{ Vasil'ko (s. of Rostislav of Tmutorakan'), 1084 (to Terebovl', 1092)
Yaropolk of Turov (s. of Izyaslav I), again, 1084-1085
David of Dorogobuzh (s. of Igor' of Vladimir-Volÿnsk), 1085-1086
Yaropolk of Turov (s. of Izyaslav I), 3rd time, 1086
David of Dorogobuzh (s. of Igor' of Vladimir-Volÿnsk), again, 1086-1097
Mstislav (s. of Svyatopolk II), 1097-1099
David of Dorogobuzh (s. of Igor' of Vladimir-Volÿnsk), 3rd time, 1099-1100 (to Dorogobuzh, 1100)
Yaroslav of Brest (s. of Svyatopolk II), 1100-1123

I. Tmutorakan'

Mstislav (s. of St. Vladimir I), 1010-1036
Gleb (s. of Svyatoslav II), 1064
Rostislav (s. of Vladimir of Novgorod), 1064-1065
Gleb (s. of Svyatoslav II), again, 1065 (to Novgorod, c. 1069)
Rostislav (s. of Vladimir of Novgorod), again, 1065-1066
Roman (s. of Svyatoslav II), c. 1069-1077
{ David (s. of Igor' of Vladimir-Volÿnsk), 1081-1083 (to Dorogobuzh, 1084)
{ Volodar' (s. of Rostislav of Tmutorakan'), 1081-1083 (to Peremÿshl', 1092)
Oleg of Vladimir-Volÿnsk (s. of Svyatoslav II), 1083 (to Chernigov, 1094)

Index of Names

Aaron, Moses' brother, 103, 104
Abel, 99, 100, 133
Abimelech, 82, 134
Abraham, 58, 82, 97, 101, 102, 125, 127
Adam, 58, 86, 99, 100, 101, 106, 109, 156, 178
Adonai (Lord Adonai), 125
Adriaca, 51
Adrian of Rome, 115
Adrianople (Adriangrad), 71
Adriatic Sea, 51
Aeolia, 51
Aepa, son of Girgen, 204
Aepa, son of Osen', 204, 214
Agamemnon, 71
Agathon of Rome, 115
Aklan, son of Burch, 214
Albania, 51
Alexander, brother of Emperor Leo (VI), 62, 64, 65, 66
Alexander of Macedon, the Great, 59, 184, 185
Alexandria, 115
Alexius, Byzantine Emperor, 202
Al'ta, a river, 126, 133, 146
Altunopa, a Polovcian, 196, 201
Amazons, 57
Ammon, ancestor of Bulgars, 184
Amos, the prophet, 105, 146, 177
Amphilochius, Bishop of Vladimir, 202
Amund, 73
Anastasius, of Kherson, 112, 116, 119, 121, 132
Anastasius, the great (of the City of God), 70
Anatolius of Constantinople, 115
Andrew, Saint, Apostle, Peter's brother, 53, 54; Church of, 168 (in Kiev), 170 (in Pereyaslavl'); Holy Andrew, 218

Andronicus, Saint, 63
Angantyr, a Rus' envoy of Oleg, 65
Anna, wife of Vladimir I, 112, 124
Antichrist, 152, 163
Antioch, 70, 115
Antiochus, king of the Seleucid dynasty, 144
Antonius, a monk, 139, 140, 141, 161, 162, 163
Antonius, church father, 157
Antonius, prior of St. George's, 169
Apollinaris of Alexandria, 115
Apollonius of Tyana, the Sage, 70
Arabia, 51
Arcadia, 51
Ares, 105
Arfast, 73
Arius, 114, 115
Armenia, 51
Arslanapa, Polovcian prince, 201
Asaduk, Polovcian prince, 212
Asia, 51
Asin', Polovcian prince, 213
Askbrand, merchant, 73
Askold, boyar with Rurik, 60, 61
Asmund, tutor of Svyatoslav I, 78, 80
Asser, son of Jacob, 102
Assur, 52
Assyria, 51, 107, 164
Asup, Polovcian prince, 201
Athanasius of Alexandria, 115
Athos, Mt., see also Holy Mountain, 139
Authulf, merchant, 73
Authun, merchant, 73
Avars, 55, 56
Azguluy, Prince of Tarev, 214

Baal, 105
Babylon, 51, 52, 164
Babylonians, 57

Bactria, 51
Bactrians, 57
Bagubars, Polovcian prince, 213, 214
Balaam, prophet, 70, 71
Bandyuk, servant of Vladimir II, 180
Barlaam, prior of the Crypt Monastery, 140, 141
Baruch, 106
Basil I, Byzantine Emperor, 60
Basil II, Byzantine Emperor, 89, 111, 112
Basil, Saint, 115, 207; Church of, 113 (in Kherson), 94, 117 (in Kiev), 127, 129 (in Vÿshgorod)
Basil (Vasiliy) see Vladimir Monomakh
Bela Vezha, 84, 213
Beldyuz', a Polovcian chief, 201
Belgorod, 94, 119, 122, 149, 169, 190
Belkatgin, Polovcian prince, 212
Belobereg, 76, 90
Beloozero, 55, 59, 60, 151, 185, 186
Bel'z, 136
Berendi, a Tork, 190
Berendiches, 193
Berestovo, 94, 124, 139, 155, 182, 183
Bethel, 104
Bethlehem, 106 (B. Ephrathah), 107
Bithynia, 51, 72
Bjorn, 73
Blachernae, the Church of Our Lady of the, 60
Black Bulgarians, see Bulgarians
Black River, 60
Blud, general of Yaropolk I, 91, 92, 93
Bohemia, 86, 122, 133; Bohemian forest, 211
Boldinÿ hills, 162
Boleslav I, of Poland, 122, 132, 136, 139
Boleslav II, of Poland, 149, 150
Boleslav III, of Poland, 200
Bolush, a Polovcian prince, 143
Bonyak, a Polovcian prince, 182, 183, 196, 197, 203, 213, 214
Borichev, 54, 78, 116
Boris, son of Vladimir I, 94, 119, 124, 126, 127, 128, 129, 131, 133, 154, 155, 169, 177, 199 (Saint B.), St. B. Day, 213

Boris, son of Vyacheslav, grandson of Yaroslav I, 165, 166, 212
Bosporus, 51, 83
Brahmans, 57
Brest, 133, 134, 191, 195, 197, 199, 211
Britain, 51, 57
Brodÿ, 212
Bruni, merchant, 73
Bryachislav, son of Izyaslav, grandson of Vladimir I, 124, 134, 139, 145, 148
Bryachislav, son of Svyatopolk II, 202
Budÿ, general of Yaroslav I, 132
Bug, 55, 56, 132, 195, 213
Bulgaria, 63, 71, 73, 90; Bulgarian lands, 53; Bulgarian country, 63
Bulgarians, 59, 60, 62, 63, 64, 71, 72, 73, 84, 87, 97; Black Bulgarians, 76; Danube Bulgarians, 193; Bulgarian woman, 94
Bulgars, 53, 55, 96, 97, 110, 111, 135, 169, 184
Burch, 214
Buzhians, 55
Buzh'sk, 193, 198, 199
Byzantium, 70

Cadiz, 51
Caesar, 108
Caiaphas, 70
Cain, 99, 100, 126, 128, 133
Camalia, 51
Canaan, 101
Canaanites, 104, 155
Cantors, the palace of the, 78
Cappadocia, 51
Caria, 51
Carinthians, 53
Carpathian Mountains, called Hungarian, 52
Caspian Sea, 53
Caspians, 53, 184
Catherine, daughter of Vsevolod I, 204
Cephallenia, 51
Chalcedon, 114
Chaldeans, 57
Chenegrepa, Polovcian prince, 201
Cheremis', 55

Index

Cheremisians, the, 55
Chern', see Isaac (the monk)
Chernigov, 64, 65, 74, 134, 135, 142, 143, 148, 162, 164, 165, 166, 167, 168, 169, 171, 174, 175, 176, 179, 180, 182, 197, 212, 213, 214, 218
Chertorÿysk, 198
Cherven, 95, 132, 136, 195, 197
Chios, 51
Chiteeviches, 212, 213
Chosroes, King of Persia, 55
Christ (see also 'Jesus' and 'Jesus Christ') 58, 59, 71, 82, 83, 86, 107, 118, 127, 129, 130, 161, 211, 218, 219; Emmanuel, 106
Christian, 66, 67, 76, 77, 154; Christian blood, 165, 186, 202; Christian faith, 83, 95, 113, 119, 137, 153; Christian land, 86; Christian laymen, 138; Christian nations, 117, 130, 138, 172, 178; Christian men, 218; Christian people, 96, 119, 179, 206; Christian souls, 165, 210; Christian subjects, 138, 213
Christians, 58, 60, 66, 68, 77, 97, 112, 113, 121, 125, 126, 127, 143, 147, 180, 183, 184
Christmas, 214
Chronicle (by Georgius Hamartolus), 57, (Greek Chronicle), 58
Chud', 52, 55
Chud' beyond the portages, 52
Chudin, 78, 148, 155, 165
Chuds, 59, 60, 64, 91, 119, 136, 153
Church of Our Lady of the Blachernae, 60
Church of St. Andrew in Kiev, 168
Church of St. Andrew in Pereyaslavl', 170
Church of St. Basil in Kherson, 113
Church of St. Basil in Kiev, 94, 117
Church of St. Basil in Vÿshgorod, 127, 129
Church of St. Demetrius in Suzdal', 186
Church of St. Elias, 77
Church of St. George in Kiev, 144
Church of St. Irene, in Kiev, 61
Church of St. Mamas, 74
Church of St. Michael in Pereyaslavl', 170
Church of St. Michael near Kiev (Vÿdubichi), 150, 169, 175, 188, 204, 205
Church of St. Nicholas in Kiev, 61
Church of the Holy Apostle Peter, in Kiev, 169
Church of St. Sophia in Kiev, 136, 137, 138, 139, 143, 174, 175, 177
Church of St. Sophia in Novgorod, 139, 142, 185
Church of St. Theodore in Pereyaslavl', 170
Church of the Annunciation in Kiev, 137
Church of the Crypts, 156; see also Crypt Church of the Holy Virgin
Church of the Holy Apostles in Berestovo, 139
Church of the Holy Virgin in Kiev, 78, 95, 116, 119, 120, 121, 124, 138, 139, 166, 172, 179; Crypt Church of the Holy Virgin in the Theodosian Monastery, 169; Shrine of the Holy Virgin, 183
Church of the Holy Virgin in Klov, 204
Church of the Holy Virgin in Tmutorakan', 134, 145
Church of the Redeemer in Chernigov, 136, 164, 165
Cilicia, 51
Clement, prior, successor of Stephen, 171
Clement, Saint, 116
Coelestinus of Rome, 115
Coelesyria, 51
Colchis, 51
Commagene, 51
Constantine the Great, 59, 82, 124
Constantine (V), the Iconoclast, Byzantine Emperor, 145
Constantine (Porphyrogenitus), Byzantine Emperor, 66, 71, 73, 74, 82
Constantine (VIII), Byzantine Emperor, 89, 111, 112
Constantine, brother of Methodius, the Slavic apostle, 62, 63

Constantine, general of Izyaslav I, 148
Constantine, the new (i.e. Vladimir), 124
Constantine, son of Dobrÿnya, 132
Constantinople, 114, 115
Corcyra, 51
Cordyna, 51
Cornelius, 125
Crete, 51, 218
Croats, 56, 64, 72, 119
Crypt Church of the Holy Virgin, 169; see also Church of the Crypts
Crypt Monastery, 139, 141, 142, 154, 156, 169, 180, 183, 186, 203, 204
Cumans, Polovcians, 184
Cyprus, 51
Cyrene, 51
Cyril of Alexandria, 115
Cyril of Jerusalem, 115
Cyrus, 115
Cythera, 51
Czechs, 53, 62, 164; Czech woman, 94

Dalmatia, 51
Damasus of Rome, 115
Damian, the presbyter, 159
Dan, 104
Daniel, the prophet, 82, 156
Danube, 52, 55, 56, 62, 71, 73, 84, 86, 138; Danube Bulgarians, 193; Danubian Slavs, 53
David, 58, 82, 87, 92, 104, 106, 107, 118, 121, 128, 129, 156, 183, 205, 217
David, son of Igor', grandson of Yaroslav I, 168, 187, 188, 189, 190, 191, 192, 193, 194, 195, 196, 197, 198, 199, 213
David, son of Svyatoslav II, grandson of Yaroslav I, 181, 182, 185, 187, 191, 196, 197, 198, 199, 200, 203, 204, 214
David, son of Vseslav I, grandson of Bryachislav, 200, 202
Dazh'bog, old Slavic god, 93
Demetrius, Saint, 64, 169; Church of, 186 (Suzdal'); Monastery of, 141 (Kiev)
Dereva, 78, 79, 81, 87, 90, 91, 119

Derevlians, 53, 55, 56, 58, 61, 64, 71, 78, 79, 80, 81
Dervis, 51
Desna, river, 52, 53, 82, 119, 204, 212
Diogenes, Polovcian prince, 180
Dioscorus, 114
Dir, boyar with Rurik, 60, 61
Dmitr, David's squire, 190
Dmitr, son of Ivor, 204
Dnieper, 52, 53, 54, 55, 58, 60, 62, 76, 82, 85, 90, 116, 119, 131, 135, 139, 146, 150, 174, 176, 182, 191, 204, 213
Dniester, 52, 56
Dobrÿnya, uncle of Vladimir I, 87, 94, 96, 132
Dobrÿnya, son of Raguel, 186
Dolobsk, 200
Domitian, Roman Emperor, 69
Domnus of Antioch, 115
Don, 204, 214
Dorogobuzh, 168, 195, 197, 199
Dorogozhich, 92
Dregovichians, 53, 55
Dryutesk, 173, 212
Duben, 198
Dulebians, 55, 56, 64
Dvina, river, 52, 53, 55

Easter, 157, 158, 168, 175, 193, 211, 214
Eber, ancestor of Hebrews, 101
Eden, 99
Efling, 73
Egypt, 51, 58, 102, 103, 104, 107, 108
Egyptians, the, 58, 102, 103, 109
Eistr, envoy, 73
Eleutherius, Saint, 76
Eli, the priest, 104
Elias, Saint, see Church of St. Elias
Elias of Jerusalem, 115
Elijah, the prophet, 156
Elovit, 127
Elymais, 51
English, the, 52, 59
Enoch, the prophet, 134
Ephesus, 114
Ephraim, the Metropolitan, 170, 171
Ephraim of Rostov, 186
Epirus, 51

Esau, 102, 155
Esdras, 107
Ethiopia, 51; Queen of Ethiopia, 83
Euboea, 51
Euphrates, 51
Eupraxia, daughter of Vsevolod I, 203, 204
Eustathius, son of Mstislav, grandson of Vladimir I, 136
Eutyches, 114
Eutychius of Constantinople, 115
Euthymius, church father, 157
Evagrius, 114
Eve, 99, 100, 109
Ezekiel, the prophet, 105, 118, 125
Farulf, a Rus' envoy of Oleg, 64, 65
Fast, a Rus' envoy of Oleg, 66
Flood, the, 58, 101
French, the, 52
Freystein, envoy of Haakon, nephew of Igor', 73
Freystein, merchant, 73
Freystein, envoy, 73
Frothi, envoy, 73
Frithleif, a Rus' envoy of Oleg, 65
Frutan, merchant, 73

Gabriel, angel, 103, 107
Galatia, 51
Galindians, 143
Gamal, merchant, 73
Gelaeans, 57
Genoese, the, 52
George, a Hungarian, Boris' servant, 127
George, Saint, 169; Monastery of, 137 (Kiev); Church of, 144 (Kiev)
George, son of Vladimir II, 204, 214
George, the Metropolitan, 142, 154, 156
Georgius (Hamartolus), 57
Georgius of Constantinople, 115
Germans, 52, 97, 98, 110, 111
Germanus, the prior of St. Saviour's, 154, 183
Germany, 110, 164; German ceremonial, 110
Gideon, 109, 134, 184
Gihon, the river, see Nile
Girgen, Polovcian prince, 204

Gleb, son of Vladimir I, 94, 119, 128, 129, 131, 154, 155, 169, 177, 199 (Saint G.)
Gleb, son of Svyatoslav II, grandson of Yaroslav I, 144, 154, 158, 165, 211, 213
Gleb, son of Vseslav I, 202, 204, 214
Glogau, 211
Golden Gate (Kiev), 137
Golotichesk, 150
Goltav, 213
Gomorrah, 97
Gordyata, 78, 211
Gorodets, 135, 166, 191, 198
Goroshin, 212
Goryaser, 128
Gospel, 121, 208
Gotlanders, 52, 59
Greece, 53, 61, 64, 67, 68, 69, 71, 74, 75, 82, 86, 93, 95, 111, 112, 119, 138, 142, 149, 150, 156, 168, 170, 180; Greek territory, 67, 75; Grecian territory, 180
Greek, ceremonial, 111; city, 111; envoys, 77; faith, 110, 111, 112; fire, 72; generals, 71; law, 76; nation, 74; ship, 76; ships, 138; soldiery, 88; subject, 76; wife, 91; woman, 93, 94
Greeks, 53, 56, 59, 60, 62, 63, 64, 65, 66, 67, 68, 69, 71, 72, 73, 74, 75, 76, 77, 78, 85, 87, 88, 89, 90, 95, 97, 98, 109, 110, 111, 112, 116, 138, 145
Gregory the Theologian, 115
Grim, envoy, 73
Gruden (called November), 190
Gunnar, a Rus' envoy of Oleg, 65, 73
Gunnfast, merchant, 73
Guthi, 73
Gyuryata Rogovich of Novgorod, 184

Haakon the Blind, Varangian prince, 135
Haakon, nephew of Igor', 73
Hadrian, Roman Emperor, 71
Hagar, mother of Ishmael, 102
Halfdan, 73
Halfdan, merchant, 73
Hallvarth, envoy, 73
Ham, 51, 52, 53, 100, 155

Hamartolus, see Georgius (Hamartolus)
Haran, son of Terah, brother of Abraham, 101, 102
Harold, a Rus' envoy of Oleg, 65
Hebrews, the, 63, 101, 155
Hegri, envoy, 73
Helena (see Olga), 82
Heming, merchant, 73
Heraclea, 72
Heraclius, Byzantine Emperor, 55
Herod, 107, 108
Hezekiah, King of the Jews, 164
Hilarion the Metropolitan, 139, 140
Holy Andrew, see also Andrew, Saint, 218
Holy Cross, 68, 77, 128, 188, 189, 218; Lord's Cross, 63, 128; Cross (only), 108, 127, 149, 154, 156, 163, 164, 167, 173, 175, 195, 210
Holy Fathers, 114
Holy Ghost (Holy Spirit), 63, 108, 109, 113, 114, 126, 130, 209, 218, 219
Holy Mount, see also Athos, Mt., 139, 140, 141
Holy Trinity, 58, 68, 118
Holy Week, 157, 174
Holy Writ, 172
Hosea, the prophet, 96, 105, 106
Hroald, merchant, 73
Hroarr, a Rus' envoy of Oleg, 65
Hrollaf, a Rus' envoy of Oleg, 64, 65
Hungarian hill, 61, 62
Hungarians, 196, 198; Hungarian lands, 53; mountains, 130; race, 127; reinforcements, 196
Hungary, 86, 122, 130, 202

Ignatius, monk, 157
Igor, 59, 60, 61, 64, 71, 72, 73, 74, 77, 78, 79, 80
Igor', nephew of Igor', 73
Igor', son of Yaroslav I, grandson of Vladimir I, 142, 143, 168, 187, 188, 191, 197, 200
Illyria, 51
Illyricum, 63
Il'men', the Lake, 53
India, 51
Indians, 57
Ingivald, merchant, 73
Ingjald, a Rus' envoy of Oleg, 65
Ingjald, merchant, 73
Ionia, 51
Irene, Saint, 61 (Church of, in Kiev); 137 (Convent of, in Kiev)
Isaac, 97, 102
Isaac the cook, 163
Isaac the monk, 161, 162, 163, 164
Isaiah, the prophet, 105, 106, 107, 117, 130, 146, 147
Isaiah, Bishop of Rostov, 169
Isgaut, envoy, 73
Ishmael, 102, 178, 183, 184
Iskal, prince of the Polovcians, 143
Iskorosten, 78, 80
Islanders, Bactrians, 57
Israel, 103, 104, 105, 106, 108, 125, 178
Issachar, son of Jacob, 102
Italians, 52
Italy, 115
Ithaca, 51
Itlar', Polovcian prince, 180, 181, 213
Ivan, son of Tvorimir, 138
Ivan, son of Zhiroslav, 165
Ivan the Khazar, son of Zakhariy, 203
Ivar, envoy, 73
Ivor, 204
Izborsk, 59
Izech, a squire of Svyatopolk, 190
Izyaslav, son of Vladimir I, grandson of Svyatoslav I, 94, 119, 124, 134, 139
Izyaslav, son of Vladimir II, grandson of Vsevolod I, 181, 185, 186
Izyaslav, son of Yaroslav I, grandson of Vladimir I, 135, 140, 141, 142, 143, 145, 146, 148, 149, 150, 154, 155, 162, 165, 166, 179, 187, 211, 212

Jacob, 97, 102, 106
Jambres, 154
James, the presbyter, 158
Jannes, 154
Japheth, 51, 52, 55, 100, 185
Jehovah, 83, 87, 105, 107
Jeremiah, the prophet, 105, 106, 107
Jeremy, monk at Crypt Monastery, 159, 160

Jerusalem, 58, 97, 104, 107, 108, 115, 130, 144
Jesus, see also 'Christ' and 'Jesus Christ', 107, 108
Jesus Christ, see also 'Christ' and 'Jesus', 109, 114, 117, 118, 126, 127, 156, 159, 163, 164, 176, 219
Jewish, children, 103; Khazars, 97; people, 102, 109
Jews, the, 58, 98, 102, 103, 104, 105, 106, 107, 108, 109, 110, 164
Job, 178
Joel, the prophet, 146, 147
Johannes surnamed Tzimiskes, 89
John the Apostle, 83, 167, 216
John the Baptist, 108
John, Bishop of Chernigov, 169, 171
John, the Metropolitan, 168, 169, 170
John, the Prior, 164, 169
Jordan, 108
Joseph, 107, 108
Joshua, son of Nun, 104
Jotun, 73
Judah, son of Jacob, 102; judge, 104, 105
Jude, 70
Judgment Day, 110
Justinian, Byzantine Emperor, 144
Juvenal of Jerusalem, 115

Kagan, prince of Khazars, 84
Kanitzar, envoy, 73
Kapich, 92
Kari, envoy, 73
Karl, a Rus' envoy of Oleg, 64, 65
Karlsefni, envoy, 73
Karni, a Rus' envoy of Oleg, 65
Kasogians, 84, 134, 145
Kazimir, Polish prince, 139
Kchi, Polovcian prince, 201
Khalep, 213
Khazars, 55, 58, 59, 60, 61, 77, 84, 97, 134, 168; Jewish Khazars, 97; Ivan the Khazar, 203
Kherson, 53, 76, 90, 111, 112, 113, 116, 145
Khersonians, 72, 113; Khersonian fishermen, 76; Khersonian priests, 119
Khodota, Vyatichian prince, 212

Khorevitsa, 54
Khoriv, 54, 55, 60
Khorol, 203, 212
Khors, old Slavic god, 93
Khortitsa, 201
Kiev, 51, 54, 55, 56, 58, 59, 61, 62, 64, 65, 69, 73, 74, 78, 79, 80, 81, 82, 83, 85, 86, 87, 90, 91, 92, 93, 95, 96, 113, 116, 119, 120, 121, 124, 126, 130, 131, 132, 134, 135, 136, 137, 140, 142, 143, 146, 148, 149, 150, 155, 156, 165, 166, 167, 168, 169, 170, 174, 175, 176, 177, 180, 181, 182, 183, 185, 187, 188, 189, 190, 191, 192, 194, 196, 197, 199, 205, 214
Kievets, 55
Kill, envoy, 73
Kitanopa, Polovcian prince, 201
Kiy, 54, 55, 60
Klakki, 73
Kleshchino, the Lake, 55
Klov, 204
Klyaz'ma, 186
Koksus', 214
Kolchko, servant, 191, 192
Koloman, Hungarian king, 196
Kordna, 212
Kors', 52, 55
Kotsel, prince of Moravian Slavs, 62, 63
Krasno, 213
Krivichians, 55, 57, 59, 60, 61, 64, 72, 91, 119
Ksnyatin, 214
Kulachek, 187
Kul'mey, 193
Kuman, Polovcian prince, 201
Kunop, 154
Kunuy, a Polovcian, 187
Kupan, the Bishop, 196
Kursk, 181, 211
Kurtek, Polovcian prince, 201
Kurya, Prince of the Pechenegs, 90
Kurya, Polovcian prince, 182
Kussi, merchant, 73
Kÿtan, Polovcian prince, 180

Laban, uncle of Jacob, 102
Lamech, the prophet, 133
Land of Rus', see Rus', land of
Land of the Sun, Sea called, 184

Latins, 63, 115
Lazar', 194
Lazarus, Saint, 157
Lazarus, prior of St. Michael's, 169
Lazarus, of Pereyaslavl', 203
Lazarus, of Vÿshgorod, 155
Leah, daughter of Laban, 102
Leif, envoy, 73
Leithulf, a Rus' envoy of Oleg, 66
Leo from Salonika, father of Constantine and Methodius, 62
Leo of Rome, 115
Leo (III), Byzantine Emperor, 145
Leo (VI), Byzantine Emperor, 62, 63, 64, 65, 66, 68, 71, 82
Lesbos, 51
Letets, 158
Let'gola, 52
Lev, see Leo (VI), Byzantine Emperor
Levi, son of Jacob, 102
Libya, 51
Listven', 135
Lithuania, 138
Litva, 52, 55
Liv', 52, 55
Locris, 51
Logozhsk, 212
Lot, 82, 101, 184
Lovat', 53
Lubno, 214
Lubnÿ, 203
Luga, 81
Luke, the Evangelist, 115, 178
Luke, Bishop of Belgorod, 169
Lukoml', 212
Lutichians, 53
Lutsk, 168, 194, 197
Lyakhs, 52, 53, 56, 62, 95, 96, 132, 133
Lyashko, 127
Lÿbed', 54, 55, 86, 94
Lycaonia, 51
Lychnitis, 51
Lycia, 51
Lydia, 51
Lyubech, 61, 64, 87, 131, 139, 187
Lyut, son of Sveinald, 90

Macedon, 184
Macedonia, 51, 71; Macedonian territory, 62

Macedonians, 72
Macedonius, 114
Maeotis, 51
Magyars, 56, 62, 63, 64, 71, 72
Mahomet, 96, 97, 98
Mal, prince of Derevlians, 78, 79
Malachi, prophet, 105, 147
Malfrid, 124
Malk of Lyubech, 87
Malusha, mother of Vladimir I, 87
Mamas, Saint, Church of, 74; Quarter of, 65, 75
Manni, merchant, 73
Marah, 103
Maria, Yan's wife, 172
Marinus, Bishop of Yur'ev, 171, 181
Marmaris, 51
Massyris, 51
Mathew, Evangelist, 118, 121, 125, 216
Matthew, monk, 160
Maurentania, 51
Mauricius, the Emperor, 145
Mazovians, 53, 138, 139
Medes, 52
Media, 51
Medveditsa, 186
Meletius of Antioch, 115
Menander, 71
Menas, Bishop of Polotsk, 203
Merians, 59, 60, 61, 64
Merya, 52, 55
Mesopotamia, 51
Methodius, Slavic apostle, 62, 63
Methodius of Patara, 184
Metrophanes, of Constantinople, 115
Micah, prophet, 106, 118
Michael, Bishop of Yur'ev, 154, 156
Michael (III), Byzantine Emperor, 58, 59, 60, 62
Michael, monk from the Studion Monastery, 142
Michael, Saint, 99, 188; Church of, 150, 154, 169, 170, 175, 204, 205
Michael Tol'bekovich, 160
Midian, the land of, 103
Midianites, 109
Mikulin, 212
Minsk, 145, 202, 212, 214
Moab, ancestor of Caspians, 184

Index

Moesia, 51
Mohammedan faith, 96
Moislav, prince of Mazovians, 139
Mokosh', old Slavic god, 93
Molossia, 51
Monastery of St. Demetrius in Kiev, 141
Monastery of St. George in Kiev, 137
Monastery of St. Irene in Kiev, 137
Monastery of St. Michael, see Church of St. Michael
Monastery of Studion, see Studion, Monastery
Monastery of the Crypts, see Crypt Monastery
Monastery of the Holy Virgin in the Boldinÿ Hills, near Chernigov, 162
Monastery of the Redeemer, 185
Monomakh, Byzantine Emperor (Constantine IX), 138
Morava, 53
Moravia, 63
Moravians, 53, 62, 63
Mordva, 52, 55, 202
Mount of Olives, 108
Mosaic Exodus, 58
Moses, 58, 82, 102, 103, 104, 105, 107, 154, 156, 205
Msta, 81
Mstikha, son of Sveinald, 78
Mstislav, son of Izyaslav I, grandson of Yaroslav I, 150, 179
Mstislav, son of Svyatopolk II, grandson of Izyaslav I, 196, 197, 198
Mstislav, son of Vladimir I, grandson of Svyatoslav I, 94, 119, 134, 135, 136
Mstislav, son of Vladimir II, grandson of Vsevolod I, 165, 181, 186, 187, 199, 200
Mstislav, son of Vsevolod, grandson of Igor', great grandson of Yaroslav I, 198, 200, 203
Munthor, envoy, 73
Murom, 60, 119, 169, 181, 185, 186, 187, 217
Muroma, 52, 55
Muromians, 60
Mysia, 51

Nahor, son of Terah, brother of Abraham, 101
Narva, 55
Nazareth, 107, 108
Nebuchadnezzar, 71
Nemiza, 146
Neradets, 168, 169
Nero, Roman Emperor, 144
Nestorius, 114
Nevo, the Lake, 53
Neyatin, 150
Nezhata, 166
Nicaea, 114, 115
Nicephorus, 78
Nicephorus, the Metropolitan, 202
Nicholas, the Metropolitan, 191
Nicholas, monk at the Crypt Monastery, 157
Nicholas, prior of Pereyaslavl', 154
Nicholas, Saint, 61 (Church in Kiev)
Nicomedia, 72
Nikita, the Bishop, 187
Nikon the prior, 160, 163, 169
Nile, 51
Nimrod, 100
Ninevites, 156
Noah, 51, 100, 109
Noricians, 52
Normans, 52, 59
Novgorod, 53, 54, 55, 59, 60, 61, 81, 87, 91, 94, 119, 122, 124, 130, 131, 132, 134, 135, 136, 139, 142, 143, 144, 145, 153, 154, 165, 169, 181, 184, 185, 186, 187, 199, 211, 212
Novgorodians, 153, 181, 199, 200
Numidia, 51
Nun, father of Joshua, 104
Nura, 199

Obrov, 212
Odresk, 212
Oka, river, 55, 56, 84
Oktoechos, 63
Ol'beg, son of Ratibor, 181
Oleg, successor of Rurik, 56, 59, 60, 61, 64, 65, 66, 69, 71, 73
Oleg, son of Svyatoslav I, grandson of Igor', 85, 87, 90, 91, 139
Oleg, son of Svyatoslav II, grandson of

Yaroslav I, 164, 165, 166, 168, 179, 180, 181, 182, 185, 186, 187, 188, 191, 197, 198, 199, 200, 202, 203, 204, 212, 213, 214, 216
Oleif, merchant, 73
Oleif, 73
Oleshki, 168
Olga, 64, 73, 78, 79, 80, 81, 82, 83, 84, 85, 86, 87, 111
Ol'ma, 61
Ol'zhichi, 82
Orestes, son of Agamemnon, 71
Orient, 51
Origen, 114
Orogost', deputy of Vladimir II, 198
Orontes, 70
Orsha, 146
Osen', Prince of the Polovcians, 168, 204
Oster', 119
Ostromir, father of Vÿshata, 144
Ovchin, Polovcian prince, 214

Palestine, 145
Palm Sunday, 157
Pamphylia, 51
Pannonia, 63
Pantherius, the Domestic, 72
Paphlagonia, 51, 72
Paradise, 99, 108, 109, 110
Pasÿncha square, 77
Paul, the Apostle, 63, 97, 118
Paul, monk, 158
Pechenegs, 56, 71, 72, 73, 85, 86, 89, 90, 93, 119, 120, 121, 122, 123, 124, 126, 131, 132, 136, 137, 184, 193, 202
Pechera, 52, 55, 184
Peleg, 52
Pellene, see Peloponnese
Peloponnese, 51
Peremil', 193
Peremÿshl', 95, 169, 188, 196, 198
Perevolok, 174
Pereyaslavets, 85, 86, 87, 89, 90
Pereyaslavl', 64, 65, 74, 119, 120, 142, 143, 154, 167, 168, 170, 171, 174, 175, 180, 182, 200, 203, 211, 212, 213, 214
Perm', 52, 55

Persia, 51
Perun, old Slavic god, 65, 74, 77, 90, 93, 116, 117
Pesochen, 174
Peter the Stammerer, 115
Peter the Monk of Alexandria, 115
Peter, son of Symeon of Bulgaria, 72
Peter, Saint, Apostle, 53; Church of, 169 (Kiev)
Peter, Bishop of Pereyaslavl', 154
Pharaoh, King of Egypt, 58, 71, 82, 102, 103
Philip, Saint, Day of, 174
Phocas, the patrician, 72
Phoebus, 116
Phoenicia, 51
Photius, Patriarch, 60
Phrygia, 51
Pilate, 63, 108
Pinsk, 188, 191, 195, 197
Pishchan', 96
Pochayna, 83
Pogorina, 191
Poland, 122, 133, 136, 148, 155, 162, 168, 193, 195, 196, 197, 198, 200, 211
Poles, 136, 149, 150, 155, 164, 174, 193, 195, 211; a Pole, 160; Polish aid, 195; Polish escort, 150; Polish support, 165
Politian of Alexandria, 115
Polota, stream, 53, 55
Polotians, 53, 55
Polotsk, 60, 64, 91, 119, 134, 145, 149, 150, 173, 199, 203, 211
Polovcians, 58, 62, 143, 146, 148, 149, 150, 165, 167, 168, 174, 175, 177, 179, 180, 181, 182, 183, 184, 187, 191, 193, 196, 197, 199, 200, 201, 202, 203, 204, 212, 213, 214
Polyanians, 53, 54, 55, 56, 58, 59, 60, 61, 62, 63, 64, 72
Pomorians, 53
Pontus, 52, 53, 72
Pope, the, 63, 97
Porey, 144, 165
Pozvizd, son of Vladimir I, 119
Predslava, daughter of Svyatopolk II, 202

Predslava, daughter of Vladimir I, 73, 128, 131
Predslavino, 94
Pretich, general of Svyatoslav I, 85, 86
Priluk, 174, 212
Pripet', river, 52, 53, 204
Prussians, 52
Psalter, 63, 127, 156, 206
Pskov, 64, 82, 137
Put'sha, 126, 127
Putyata, general of Svyatopolk II, 197, 198, 202, 203

Rachel, 102
Radim, 56
Radimichians, 56, 61, 64, 96
Radko, 169
Raguel, 186
Rakom, 130
Rastovets, 150
Ratibor, lieutenant of Vsevolod I, 168, 180, 181
Ratibor, deputy of Vladimir II, 198
Rededya, Prince of the Kasogians, 134
Redeemer, see Church of the Redeemer, also see Monastery of the Redeemer
Red Palace in Chernigov, 212
Red Sea, the, 103
Rehoboam, 104
Reuben, son of Jacob, 102
Rhinocurura, 51
Rhodes, 51
Rimov, 213
Rodnya, the city of, 92
Rogned, daughter of Rogvolod, wife of Vladimir I, Yaroslav's mother, 91, 94, 124
Rogvolod, of Polotsk, 91
Roman, son of Svyatoslav II, grandson of Yaroslav I, 165, 167, 168
Romans, the, 52, 98, 115, 144
Romanus (I), Byzantine Emperor, 71, 72, 73, 74, 77
Rome, 53, 54, 63, 70, 98, 115, 124
Romnÿ, 214
Ros', 92, 136, 181, 213, 214, 215
Rostislav, prince of Moravian Slavs, 62
Rostislav, son of Mstislav, grandson of Izyaslav I, 179

Rostislav, son of Vladimir, grandson of Yaroslav I, 144, 145, 168, 206
Rostislav, son of Vsevolod I, grandson of Yaroslav I, 150, 169, 174, 175, 176, 187, 188, 213
Rostov, 60, 64, 119, 150, 169, 173, 181, 185, 186, 187, 211, 213, 214, 217; Lake of, 55
Rozhne plain, the, 195
Ruditsa, 188
Rurik, 59, 60, 61
Rurik, son of Rostislav, grandson of Vladimir, great grandson of Yaroslav I, 169, 174
Russes, 52, 58, 59, 60, 61, 62, 63, 64, 65, 66, 67, 68, 69, 72, 73, 74, 75, 76, 77, 87, 88, 89, 90, 96, 97, 111, 112, 119, 120, 124, 131, 132, 138, 165, 181, 201
Russia, 202
Russian cities, 64; delegation, 110; envoy, 68, 73; forces, 201; law, 66, 76; name, 206; nation, 73; princes, 146, 195, 199, 200, 201; prisoner, 68; sea, 53; slave, 68; soldiery, 203; subjects, 76, 77; troops, 201
Russians, 63, 66, 72, 74
Rus', 51, 52, 55, 56, 59, 62, 63, 66, 68, 69, 73, 74, 76, 77, 78, 82, 83, 85, 86, 87, 88 89, 90, 91, 95, 124, 130, 133, 135, 137, 138, 139, 140, 142, 143, 150, 160, 165, 167, 168, 170, 175, 177, 180, 181, 187, 191, 200, 201 202
Rus', land of, 51, 58, 60, 71, 73, 74, 77, 84, 93, 112, 117, 125, 129, 136, 144, 146, 148, 149, 159, 165, 169, 172, 176, 180, 187, 188, 191, 192, 193, 198, 200, 202, 217, 218; Sons of Rus', 118; Rus' nation, 65
Ryazan', 182, 187

Sabbas, church father, 157
Sabbath, the, 97, 99, 105
Sakov, 181, 199
Sakz', Polovcian prince, 213
Salonika, 62
Samaria, 104
Samoyedes, 184

Samuel, the prophet, 104, 105 156
San, 196
Saracens, 145, 184
Sarah, ancestor of Saracens, 184
Sarai, 101, 102
Sarakÿne, 184
Sardinia, 51
Sarmatia, 51
Satan, 99 (also as Sathanael), 100, 127, 151, 188
Sauk, Polovcian prince, 212
Saul, 70, 82, 104
Sbÿslava, daughter of Svyatopolk II, 200
Sceva, 70
Scripture, the, 63, 117, 121, 156, 170
Scythia, 51; Great S., 56, 64
Scythians, 55
Sem', 53
Semtsya, 212
Serbs, 53
Seres, 57
Sergius, 115
Serug, 101
Seth, 100, 155
Setoml', 137, 144
Severians, 53, 55, 56, 59, 61, 64, 135
Sharukan, Polovcian prince, 203, 214
Shchek, 54, 55, 60
Shchekovitsa, 54, 69
Sheksna, 151, 152
Shem, 51, 52, 53, 100
Shepol', 192
Shinar, the plain of, 52
Sicily, 51
Sigbjorn, envoy, 73
Sigfrid, envoy, 73
Silistria, 64, 89
Silvester, Pope, 115
Simar'gl, old Slavic god, 93
Simeon, son of Jacob, 102
Simon, the Magician, 71, 153
Sinai, Mt., 104, 156
Sineus, Varangian prince, 59, 60
Sinope, 53, 54
Slavic, alphabet, 62; books, 63; language, 53, 63; nation, 63; race, 52, 53, 55, 56, 62, 63; writing, 63
Slavs, 51, 52, 53, 54, 55, 56, 59, 60, 61, 62, 63, 64, 65, 72, 91, 119, 132, 136
Slavs, the land of the, 54
Slavlya, river, 214
Slavyata, deputy of Svyatopolk II, 180
Slothi, envoy, 73
Smolensk, 55, 61, 128, 142, 143, 146, 165, 181, 182, 185, 211, 212, 213, 214
Smyadÿn', 128
Snovid, son of Izech, 190
Snov', 149
Snovsk, 148
Sodom, 97
Sodomites, the, 82
Solomon, 58, 83, 84, 87, 94, 104, 121, 125, 126, 137, 167
Sophia, Saint, see Church of St. Sophia
Sophronius, prior of St. Michael's, 154
Sozh, 56
Sozhitsa, 165
Spaniards, the, 52
St. Andrew, see Andrew, Saint
St. Basil, see Basil, Saint
St. Boris, see Boris, son of Vladimir I
St. Clement, see Clement, Saint
St. Demetrius, see Demetrius, Saint
St. Eleutherius, see Eleutherius, Saint
St. Elias, see Church of St. Elias
St. George, see George, Saint
St. Gleb, see Gleb, son of Vladimir I
St. Irene, see Irene, Saint
St. Lazarus, see Lazarus, Saint
St. Mamas, see Mamas, Saint
St. Michael, see Michael, Saint
St. Nicholas, see Nicholas, Saint
St. Peter, see Peter, Saint
St. Philip, see Philip, Saint
St. Saviour, 154
St. Sophia, see Church of St. Sophia
St. Theodore, see Theodore, Saint
Stanislav, son of Vladimir I, 119
Starodub, 182, 212, 213, 218
Stavko, son of Gordyata, 211
Steggi, envoy, 73
Steinvith, a Rus' envoy of Oleg, 64, 66
Stephen the Cantor, prior of the Crypt Monastery, later Bishop of Vladimir, 158, 159, 160, 162, 164, 171, 180, 204

Stephen, prior of the Monastery of Our Lady of Blachernae in Kiev, 183
Stephen, Byzantine Emperor, 73, 74
Stephen of Hungary, 122
Stoething, 73
Stribog, old Slavic god, 93
Strizhen', 166
Studion, Monastery, 142
Stugna, 119, 176
Styr, merchant, 73
Sudislav, son of Vladimir I, 119, 137, 143
Sudomir', river, 134
Sula, 53, 119, 203, 212, 213, 214
Supoy, 212
Sur'bar, Polovcian prince, 201
Suten', 201
Suteysk, 197, 211
Suzdal', 134, 135, 185, 186, 187
Svanhild, wife of Oleif, 73
Svein, merchant, 73
Sveinald, 78, 80, 89, 90, 91
Sveinki Borich, merchant, 73
Sverki, envoy, 73
Svyatopolk, prince of Moravian Slavs, 62
Svyatopolk I, son of Vladimir I, 93, 94, 119, 124, 126, 127, 128, 130, 131, 132, 133, 134
Svyatopolk II, son of Izyaslav, grandson of Yaroslav I, 165, 169, 175, 176, 177, 179, 180, 181, 182, 183, 187, 188, 189, 190, 191, 192, 193, 195, 196, 197, 198, 199, 200, 201, 202, 203, 204, 211, 213, 214
Svyatopolk, son of Yaroslav I, grandson of Vladimir I, 150
Svyatosha, son of David, grandson of Svyatoslav II, 196, 197, 203
Svyatoslav I, 59, 73, 78, 80, 83, 84, 85, 86, 87, 88, 89, 90, 91, 139
Svyatoslav II, son of Yaroslav I, grandson of Vladimir I, 136, 142, 143, 144, 145, 146, 148, 149, 151, 152, 154, 155, 156, 158, 162, 164, 165, 168, 181, 187, 188, 191, 200, 203, 211, 216
Svyatoslav, son of Vladimir I, 94, 119, 130

Svyatoslav, son of Vladimir II, grandson of Vsevolod I, 180, 203
Svyatoslavl', 213
Swedes, 52, 59
Sylvester, Prior of St. Michaels, 205
Symeon of Bulgaria, 63, 64, 71, 72
Syria, 51, 145
Syrtis, 51

Talets, 127
Tarasius of Constantinople, 115
Tarev, 214
Tauria, 51
Taz, Bonyak's brother, 203
Terah, Serug's son, 101
Terebovl', 188, 193, 194
Thebaid, 51
Theoctistus, the Prior, 204
Theodore, the General, 72
Theodore, Saint, 143, 157, 186, 187; Church of, 170 (Pereyaslavl')
Theodoret of Antioch, 115
Theodosius the Great, 173
Theodosius, prior of the Crypt Monastery, 141, 142, 154, 156, 157, 158, 159, 160, 162, 163, 164, 170, 171, 172, 183, 203, 204, 205; Theodosian Monastery, 169
Theopemptos, the Metropolitan, 138
Theophanes, 72
Theophanes of Antioch, 115
Theophilus, secretary of Tzimiskes, 89
Thermuthi, daughter of Pharaoh, 102
Thessaly, 51
Thorbjorn, merchant, 73
Thorfrid, merchant, 73
Thorstein, merchant, 73
Thorth, 73
Thrace, 51, 71, 145; Thracian territory, 62
Thracians, 72
Throand, a Rus' envoy of Oleg, 66
Throand, 73
Tigris, 52
Timotheus of Alexandria, 115
Tirr, merchant, 73
Tivercians, the, 56, 61, 64, 72
Tmutorakan', 119, 134, 144, 165, 166, 168, 179

Torchesk, 175, 176, 177, 179, 213
Torchin, Gleb's cook, 128
Torchin, deputy of David and Oleg, sons of Svyatoslav II, 198
Torkmens, 184
Torks, 96, 143, 168, 180, 184, 190, 193, 202, 213
Toropets, 161
Transfiguration, Sacred, 121
Trepol', 176, 177
Troas, 51
Trubezh, 119, 182
Truvor, 59, 60
Tsar'grad, 53, 55, 58, 60, 64, 65, 71, 72, 82, 89, 93, 110, 138, 168, 202
Tugorkan, Prince of the Polovcians, 179, 182, 183, 213
Tukÿ, brother of Chudin, 148, 165
Turiysk, 194
Turov, 91, 119, 167, 169, 175, 188, 191, 211
Turovians, 91
Turÿ, 91
Turyak, 194
Tvorimir, general of Yaroslav I, 138
Tzimiskes, see Johannes surnamed Tzimiskes

Udalrich, of Bohemia, 122
Ugra, 52
Ugrians, 55
Ulan, servant, 191, 192
Ulichians, 56, 61
Urusoba, Polovcian prince, 201, 214
Ust'e, 182
Ut, 73
Uvetichi, 198

Vakeev palace, the, 191
Varangian, allies, 91; followers, 135; race, 60; reinforcements, 124; Russes, 59; Sea, 52, 53
Varangians, 52, 53, 54, 59, 60, 61, 63, 64, 72, 77, 91, 93, 95, 127, 130, 131, 132, 135, 136
Varin, 213
Varyazhko, 93
Vasil'ev, 113
Vasil'evo, 121
Vasil'ko, son of Rostislav, grandson of Vladimir, great grandson of Yaroslav I, 174, 187, 188, 189, 190, 191, 192, 193, 194, 195, 196, 198, 199
Vasiliy, the Regent, 197
Vasiliy, 194
Vasiliy, monk (scribe), 192
Vefast, envoy, 73
Venetians, 52
Vermund, a Rus' envoy of Oleg, 64, 65
Ves', 52, 55, 59, 60
Vÿdubichi, 183, 188
Vigilius of Rome, 115
Virgin, Mother of God, see also Church of the Holy Virgin, 60, 78, 95, 107, 114, 116, 119, 120, 121, 124, 134, 138, 139, 141, 145, 162, 166, 169, 170, 172, 179, 183, 201, 203, 204, 208, 212, 213, 219
Visleif, merchant, 73
Vistula, 53
Vitichev, 181
Vladimir, the city of (Vladimir-Volÿnsk), 119, 142, 143, 167, 168, 169, 171, 180, 188, 190, 191, 192, 194, 195, 196, 197, 198, 199, 203, 211, 212, 213, 214
Vladimir I, son of Svyatoslav I, 59, 85, 87, 91, 92, 93, 94, 95, 96, 97, 98, 107, 109, 110, 111, 112, 113, 116, 117, 119, 120, 121, 122, 124, 125, 134, 137, 138, 174, 183
Vladimir II, son of Vsevolod I, grandson of Yaroslav I, 142, 164, 165, 166, 167, 168, 169, 174, 175, 176, 180, 181, 182, 183, 185, 186, 187, 188, 189, 191, 192, 193, 197, 198, 199, 200, 201, 202, 203, 204, 205, 206, 216, 218
Vladimir, son of Yaroslav I, grandson of Vladimir I, 134, 136, 138, 139, 142, 144
Vladislav, Duke of Poland, 195
Vladislav, 73
Vlakhs, the, 53, 62
Voik, 73
Voin', 143, 167, 204
Voist, envoy, 73
Volga, 52, 53, 55, 84, 128, 135, 150, 151, 186, 206

Index

Volhynians, the, 55, 56
Volkhov, river, 52, 53, 94, 144, 154
Volodar', son of Rostislav, grandson of Vladimir, great grandson of Yaroslav I, 168, 188, 193, 194, 195, 196, 198, 199, 202
Volos, old Slavic god, 65, 90
Volyn', 132, 165 (Volÿn')
Voronitsa, 213
Vratislav, 78
Vruchiy, 91
Vseslav, son of Izyaslav, grandson of Vladimir I, 124
Vseslav I, son of Bryachislav, grandson of Izyaslav, great grandson of Vladimir I, 139, 144, 145, 146, 148, 149, 150, 155, 162, 199, 200, 203, 212
Vsevolod, son of Vladimir I, 94, 119
Vsevolod I, son of Yaroslav I, grandson of Vladimir I, 136, 142, 143, 145, 146, 148, 149, 150, 154, 155, 164, 165, 166, 167, 168, 169, 170, 173, 174, 175, 176, 185, 187, 188, 191, 192, 199, 203, 204
Vsevolozh', 192, 194
Vyacheslav, son of Vladimir II, grandson of Vsevolod I, 187, 203
Vyacheslav, son of Yaropolk, grandson of Izyaslav I, 200, 202
Vyacheslav, son of Yaroslav I, 136, 142, 143, 166
Vyagro, 196
Vyatichians, the, 56, 57, 59, 84, 95, 119, 211, 212
Vyatko, 56
Vÿgoshev, 197
Vÿnkina, 169
Vÿr', 214
Vÿshata, general of Novgorod, 138, 144, 151, 203
Vÿsheslav, son of Vladimir I, 94, 119
Vÿshgorod, 81, 94, 126, 127, 143, 155, 165, 173, 177

White Croats, the, 53
White Ugrians, the, 55
Wolf's Tail, Vladimir's general, 96

Yam', 52, 55, 138
Yan, son of Vÿshata, 138, 151, 152, 153, 169, 172, 176, 203
Yan, *starets*, 203
Yanka, daughter of Vsevolod I, 168, 170
Yaropolk I, 59, 85, 87, 90, 91, 92, 93, 139
Yaropolk, son of Izyaslav I, 150, 165, 166, 167, 168, 169, 188, 191, 196, 199, 200, 202, 212, 213
Yaropolk, son of Vladimir II, grandson of Vsevolod I, 200, 202, 203
Yaroslav I, son of Vladimir I, 59, 61, 94, 119, 124, 128, 130, 131, 132, 133, 134, 135, 136, 137, 138, 139, 140, 142, 143, 144, 145, 154, 155, 164, 166, 168, 174, 206
Yaroslav, son of Svyatopolk II, grandson of Izyaslav I, 196, 198, 199, 214
Yaroslav, son of Svyatoslav II, grandson of Yaroslav I, 186, 187, 188, 199, 202
Yaroslav, son of Yaropolk, grandson of Izyaslav I, 198, 199, 200
Yaroslavl', 150
Yasians, 84
Yathrib, 184, 185
Yatving, 73
Yatvingians, 95, 138
Yoktan, 52
Yugra, 184
Yur'ev, 136, 154, 171, 181, 202, 213

Zabulon, son of Jacob, 102
Zachariah, the prophet, 106, 107
Zacynthus, 51
Zakhariy, 203
Zarechesk, 203
Zarub, 182
Zavaloch'e, 165
Zbygniew, brother of Boleslav III, 203
Zhelan', 177
Zhidyata, Bishop of Novgorod, 136
Zhiroslav, 165
Zimegola, 52, 55, 203
Zolot'cha, 199
Zvenigorod, 168
Zvizhden', 190